YOSSI KATZ

THE BATTLE FOR THE LAND

YOSSI KATZ

THE BATTLE FOR THE LAND

The History of the Jewish National Fund (KKL)
Before the Establishment of the State of Israel

THE HEBREW UNIVERSITY MAGNES PRESS, JERUSALEM

Published with the assistance of

The Chair for the Study of the History and Activities of the
Jewish National Fund (KKL)
Bar-Ilan University

Keren Kayemeth LeIsrael (JNF) History Research
Institute for Zionism and Settlement

The Schnitzer Foundation for Research
on the Israel Economy and Society,
Bar Ilan University

Translated from Hebrew by
Dr. Amiel Unger

Copy Editing
Shlomo Ketko

ISBN 965–493–222–9

Printed in Israel
Typesetting: Art Plus, Jerusalem

In memory of
GIDEON RIVLIN הי״ד
Murdered by terrorists in Gush Katif
On the Second of Shvat–January 12, 2005
At the age of fifty
Lived in Ganei Tal for twenty-seven years
Married to Simcha
Father of five: Nir, Ya'ara, Omer, Assaf, Gilad

An eighth generation pioneer in our time
He loved, lived and breathed the land of Israel
Loved by all.

"To walk in the paths of your countryside
To feel every stone and clod of earth
To transcend the distances
To breathe the smells
All this in my bare feet."

CONTENTS

LIST OF MAPS

PREFACE

Since renewed Jewish settlement in Palestine began in 1878 and up to the time of the establishment of the World Zionist Organization nineteen years later, a number of Jewish-owned organizations were involved in the purchase of agricultural land for the purpose of the establishment of Moshavot whose members would indulge in agriculture. Among these organizations were the Jewish community associations in Palestine, the Hovevei Zion associations and representatives of Baron Edmond Rothschild. During the final years of the nineteenth century, a new organization came on the scene that began to purchase lands in Palestine for the purpose of agricultural settlement by Jews – this was the Jewish Colonization Association (JCA) founded by Baron Maurice de Hirsch. However, the activities of these organizations did not go beyond the actual purchase and basic preparation of the land required for the initial establishment of the Moshavot.

The Jewish National Fund (JNF) founded in 1901 by the World Zionist Organization, was the first institution established for the distinctly defined purpose of purchasing lands in Palestine, and of registering them as owned by the Jewish People in perpetuity. This was in order to attain goals related to settlement, to fulfill the needs of the community, to meet financial aims and to assist in obtaining political entitlement that would lead to the establishment of a Jewish State in Palestine. The idea of the JNF was first proposed by Prof. Hermann Schapiro to the delegates at the First Zionist Congress held in Basle in 1897, but although the idea was accepted in principle, the Congress delegates decided to postpone the actual foundation until a suitable constitution had been drawn up.

Four years later, at the end of 1901, the Fifth Zionist Congress approved the establishment of the Jewish National Fund. The Sixth Zionist Congress in 1903 stipulated the following basic premises: The Jewish National Fund would serve as the agent of the World Zionist Organization with the purpose of purchasing land in Palestine and registering it in the ownership of the Jewish People to be held as national land in perpetuity; the JNF's finances would be based on contributions; the Fund would not be permitted to sell the land but only to lease it. The Sixth Zionist Congress rejected the ban that the previous Congress had instituted to the effect that the JNF could not begin to function in the purchasing of land until a minimum of 200,000 Palestine Pounds (P£) had been collected. It was also stated that the Fund would be permitted to use up to three quarters of the monies in its treasury at any time for the purpose of purchasing land. Up to 1907, when the JNF's constitution was approved and it was registered in London as the Jewish National Fund Limited, the use of its finances was approved by the Smaller Zionist General Council.[1]

The focus of the JNF's activities, at least from the beginning of the 1920s, was the task of redeeming the land and registering it as owned by the Jewish People, although from its inception and until the establishment of the State of Israel, the JNF was involved not only in purchasing rural and urban lands but also in the financing of the establishment of settlements, afforestation, preparation of the land for settlement, development of water resources, dissemination of information, Zionist education in Palestine and in the Diaspora, and numerous other activities. The majority of the JNF's financial resources were devoted to the implementation of these goals.[2] Throughout this period the JNF gave priority to the redemption of agricultural land, but it purchased urban lands as well. On the eve of the Israel War of Independence the JNF's land resources were estimated as totaling one million dunams.[3]

The JNF's income derived first and foremost from contributions. Over the years, as the JNF's functions expanded – especially in land purchase during the period covered by this book – it diversified the types of contributions and also found other sources for additional income. At first, the JNF's contributions came from the small sums put into the "Blue Box" that was distributed far and wide, from contributions from affluent persons, from payment for registration in the "Golden Book" and amounts paid for the planting of trees in the name of persons designated by the contributor. Later, the type of contributions and the method of collecting them were expanded

---

1 Shilony (1991), pp. 1–37; Doukhan-Landau (1979), pp. 53–57; Kressel (1951), pp. 23–46; Agmon (1951a), pp. 121–153. On the idea of the nationalization of land in the JNF doctrine, see in detail Metzer (1979), pp. 40–53; Katz (2002).

2 See e.g., Granovsky (1944), pp. 161–162. The majority of the deliberations in the Directorate dealt with issues related to the purchase of lands.

3 CZA, KKL5/14070, letter from Weitz to Zuckerman 26.9.1947. See also Appendix 3.

to include wills and legacies of individuals; "life bequests," through which donors endowed capital or property to the JNF and in return were paid a fixed annuity for their maintenance during their entire life; transfer of real estate to the benefit of the JNF; soliciting funds for special projects such as the purchase of lands in the Galilee and the Hula Valley, the purchase of lands for the establishment of settlements such as that which was to bear the name of Ussishkin; appeals in synagogues during Festivals, organization of celebrations and bazaars at which collections were made for the benefit of the JNF; distribution of JNF stamps to be affixed to certificates and documents of World Zionist Organization institutions.

The JNF also had other sources of income such as loans of various types and for various periods, including long-term interest bearing debentures. During 1936–1948, the period covered by this work, the total amount of loans undertaken by the JNF increased considerably in order to meet the costs of land purchases it was to implement. Another source of income was from rentals from leases which expanded over the years with the increase of settlements established on JNF land. Bank deposits to the credit of the JNF also provided income. Cooperation with privately owned capital, which will be discussed in detail in this book, including the plans for the establishment of "Garden Cities"– was a further source of finance. Settlers, especially for urban settlement, were involved in financing the purchase of land registered under the name of the JNF. We will discuss another source of income, even though it was not of great significance, that existed during the 1920s up to mid-1930s – the receipt of commission and revenue from the Phoenix Insurance Company for life insurance organized by the JNF, which thus acted as a sort of insurance agent.[4]

The income of the JNF served first and foremost for the purchase of land, especially for agriculture. Other items of expenditure included information, education, lectures on organization and administration, the preparation and development of land and water projects (including drainage and the battle against malaria), and afforestation. During the period covered by this work, the JNF participated in the financing of one quarter up to one third,

---

4   Eretz Israel (1923), pp. 21–28; Report Exec. (1925), pp. 157–163; idem (1927), pp. 1–9; idem (1931), pp. 98–99; idem (1933), pp. 97–99; idem (1935), pp. 164–167; JNF Report (1937), pp. 57–72, 87; Report Exec. (1937), pp. 181–184, 196–207; idem (1939) pp. 148–152; JNF Report (1947), pp. 68–71, 74–137; Ulitzur (1939), pp. 124–150; Ettinger (1947), pp. 92–98.

and at times even more, of the costs involved in the establishment of new settlements, thus providing support for projects of the Jewish Agency. As will be seen in the final chapter of the book, on the eve of the establishment of the State of Israel the JNF was required to provide a substantial amount of its assets for the finance of security and political projects arising from the urgent needs of the hour.[5]

The purpose of this work is to examine the methods employed by the JNF in purchasing land from 1936 up to the establishment of the State of Israel in 1948, stressing especially the land purchases for agriculture, which was given absolute priority by the JNF. The chapters of the book examine the institution's decision-making process, purchasing methods and policy, and the priority given to purchasing of lands in the various regions of the country and the changes that took place as a result of current events. It also examines the policy of purchasing from Jewish owners and cooperation with private capital, extraordinary tasks in land purchase the JNF was required to undertake as a result of political developments; restrictive factors to the implementation of purchases and implementation of plans, and the methods the JNF used to overcome these restrictions; relations with the various settlement organizations – such as the Jewish Agency, the Palestine Land Development Company (PLDC), the Histadrut Agricultural Center and others – in the work of the JNF; the JNF's contribution to the development of settlement and attaining the Zionist political goals in Palestine.

The major part of this work dealing with the years 1936–1948 covers the decisive period in the history of Zionist settlement in Palestine, designated by Yosef Weitz as the "Stormy Period." Weitz was director of the JNF Lands Department and served as the central person in the advancement of the settlement project of that period. The unique aspect of this period that began with the outbreak of the Arab disturbances in 1936 and ended with the establishment of the State of Israel in 1948, was to a certain extent the frequent security and political events that led to situations whereby strategic-political components were the deciding factors in the purchase of lands and their settlement. The JNF, which during this period was the

---

5 See: CZA, KKL 10, deliberations by the JNF Directorate on the annual budgets were generally held in September; JNF Report (1947), pp. 45–67; Ettinger (1947), pp. 92–98; Ulitzur (1939), pp. 124–150. The data relating to 1945 is from CZA, KKL10, minutes of JNF Directorate meeting, 10.7.1945.

almost sole Jewish purchasing body of agricultural land from Arabs, and in contrast to the past developed during this period its own independent mechanism for land purchase, was the institution that was required to provide the land basis for settlement. These settlements were established to attain political goals, the central one being the fixing of the boundaries of the future Jewish State, while struggling against the severe British restrictions on the purchase of lands as imposed by the 1939 White Paper and the 1940 Lands Law. At the same time, the JNF was required to provide land for the consolidation of existing settlements and the needs that arose after the end of the Second World War and the imminent establishment of the State of Israel. The JNF undertook the responsibility for the lands owned by individual Jews that would otherwise have been lost to Jewish ownership because of the special conditions existing during the period covered by this work. It was also the peak period of the JNF's activities in land purchase, despite the restrictions imposed. In all, during the twelve years of the so-called "Stormy Period" the land expanse purchased by the JNF encompassed over 60 percent of those lands purchased from 1901 to 1948, and at the time of the establishment of the State of Israel over half of the Jewish-owned land was registered in the name of the JNF.[6]

The chapters of this work are based on a developmental approach – each chapter deals with a significant period of the JNF's activities. Chapter One serves as an introduction, and it summarizes the JNF's activities in the purchase of lands from its inception up to 1935. Chapter Two relates to the period of 1936–1939; it begins with the outbreak of Arab disturbances in 1936 and ends just prior to the promulgation of the Lands Law at the beginning of 1940. Chapter Three deals with the JNF's activities from the time of the promulgation of the Lands Law, when it was forced to reevaluate its work in the light of the Law and other obstacles that arose; it ends in 1945. During the course of this year in which Chapter Four begins, significant changes came about in the JNF Directorate with the election of a permanent Chairman – a position that had not been filled since the death of Menachem Ussishkin in 1941. The feeling that political decisions on the Palestine issue were about to be made, and the resultant activities in the areas of land purchase and settlement – these were the characteristic traits

---

6   CZA, KKL5/10514, summary of JNF land capital in urban and rural areas, 1938; CZA, KKL5/15635, summary of lands purchased by JNF, 1947; CZA, KKL5/14070, letter from Weitz to Zuckerman 26.9.1947; appendix 3; Metzer (1998), pp. 86–87.

of the years 1945–1948 during which the JNF was required to participate in important undertakings that were determined by the special requirements of the period. During this period the JNF became involved in new areas resulting from the aftermath of the Holocaust and it was required to examine its purchasing policy in the light of international factors regarding the Palestine issue at the end of the Mandate.

Surprising as it may seem, in contrast to the relatively large amount of general publications produced by the JNF (including a number of books on the occasion of the institution's jubilee) as well as diaries and books written by senior JNF officials, such as Yosef Weitz and Dr. Avraham Granovsky (Granot) – little methodical historic research (geographic–historic and economic–historic) has been carried out that has examined the various aspects of the JNF's activities in the numerous and variegated areas over the century of the institutions existence. Reference has been made to the JNF's activities in relevant research works dealing with the history of Zionist settlement and the upbuilding of the country, but apart from the study by Zvi Shilony on the JNF's work in the period up to the First World War, almost no comprehensive and methodic research has been published on any one of the areas in which the JNF has been active, nor on its unique organization and its role within the institutions of the World Zionist Organization. Shilony's study deals with the period during which the JNF's activities were less significant in comparison to its work in Palestine in later times and in comparison to the activities of other Jewish organizations such as PICA which overshadowed that of the JNF during the period from the beginning of the century up to the First World War.

The scarcity of historic research on the JNF could possibly be explained against the background of the following factors: Firstly, the predilection of the research on the history of Zionism to deal mainly with its political and social aspects, and less, if at all, with issues relating to everyday matters of settlement. These issues were examined relatively late in the development of the historic research that dealt with the modern history of Zionism and Palestine, the period that in the 1970s began to arouse interest in the geographic-historic fields. Secondly, the image of the JNF that developed over the years as an institution whose main function was collecting donations (the "Blue Box") and in technical functions (afforestation, preparation of the land for settlement) and as existing under the shadow of the Jewish Agency. It would appear that with the establishment in 1960 of the Israel Lands Administration and the transfer of the JNF lands to that body only served to strengthen that image. Over the years, access to the tens of thousands, or more, documents in the various sections of the JNF archives was not convenient. There were times, when as a result of technical limitations, part of the archives were placed in the custody of the Central Zionist Archives, and the conditions there made the study of them rather difficult. It was only during the past decade that the situation changed radically when the main sections of the JNF archives were recatalogued by the Central Zionist Archives. Furthermore, the archives of Yosef Weitz were only recently organized within the Central Zionist Archives.

The present work is designed to fill these lacunae to a certain extent and to describe the policy of the JNF in the purchase of lands during one of the most crucial periods in the history of the JNF, of Zionist settlement and of the history of the Jewish community in Palestine – the period in which the JNF became the leading and decisive factor in dealing with land along with the Jewish Agency and the settlement movements in the establishment of settlements throughout the country.

The consolidation of the results of the research presented in this work has been made possible first and foremost through the use of the considerable archival material in the archives of the JNF (including the archives of the JNF Office in Tiberias) stored in the Central Zionist Archives in Jerusalem. This documentation includes the minutes of the meetings of the JNF Directorate; the reports to the annual general meetings of the Jewish National Fund Company; the vast amount of correspondence within the JNF, between the institution and other organizations; a variety of reports and memoranda. It should be pointed out that the extent of the documentation existing within the JNF is vast, and presents the researcher no small challenge in sifting, sorting and discerning material of significance. Use has also been made of the archives of various organizations connected to the JNF and its activities, such as the Jewish Agency Executive; the Settlement, Political and other Departments of the Jewish Agency; the Enlarged Zionist General Council and the Smaller Zionist General Council; the Palestine Land Development Company; the Geulah Company; the Central Office for the Settlement of German Jews in Palestine; PICA; the Anglo-Palestine Bank, and many others. Also the archives of many prominent personalities involved in the activities of the JNF have been examined, such as those of Yosef Weitz, Avraham Granovsky, David Ben-Gurion, Eliezer Kaplan, Zalman Lifschitz, and others. Use was made of the reports submitted by the JNF to the Zionist Congresses, JNF publications that appeared in a variety of formats and within different frameworks, the diaries and works of Yosef Weitz, the writings of Avraham Granovsky, background literature and research works. Personal interviews were conducted with persons who were employed by the JNF during the period covered by this book.

This work and the research that preceded it was the result of the initiative of Shimon Ben-Shemesh and Dr. Gabriel Alexander who at the end of the 1980s established the Research Institute for the History of the Jewish National Fund. They made an important contribution to the advancement of the study of the history of Zionism, of Jewish settlement in Palestine and of the JNF. I wish to express my thanks to the JNF and the Chairman of the Directorate, Yehiel Leket, who also serves as Chairman of the Research Institute, for their generous assistance in the carrying out of my research and in funding the publication of this work. Thanks also are due to Dr. Alexander who encouraged me throughout the various phases of the research and assisted me greatly with his advice and support.

I wish to acknowledge the devoted assistance of the personnel of the Central Zionist Archives, of the Israel State Archives and the librarians in the National and University Library, the Ben-Zvi Institute library and the Map Library of the Geography Department of The Hebrew University of Jerusalem, which houses the JNF map archives. The photographs in this work are from the JNF's computerized photograph collection, and I wish to acknowledge especially the assistance given me by Ms. Sima Zelig in locating the photographs.

Thanks are due to the anonymous referees of the manuscript of the Hebrew version of this book, whose comments assisted me in improving the quality of the work, to Dan Benovici, the former director of The Magnes Press who personally supervised each phase of the production, his dedicated staff especially Ram Goldberg and Hanna Levy. Also, heartfelt thanks go to Dr. Amiel Unger who translated this book, and Mr. Shlomo Ketko who edited it.

Last but not least, I wish to express my deep appreciation to my wife Ruth, our children David and his wife Sarit, Yonatan and his wife Mira, Michal and her husband Gilad, Meirav, Avihai and Dan, and our grandchildren Roni, Nou'a and Yishai whose devotion, patience and encouragement enabled me to devote so much time to this research.

Yossi Katz

Efrat June 1, 2005

CHAPTER ONE

Shaping the Policy and Purchases in the Valleys, 1901–1935

From 1901, when the Fifth Zionist Congress ratified the establishment of the Jewish National Fund (hereafter JNF), up to the First World War, no comprehensive lands purchase policy had crystallized. The isolated purchases that will be discussed below also attest to the absence of a general policy. This situation belied the fact that central personages within the Zionist Movement leadership had expressed their positions about the policy to be followed with regard to land purchases and the role of the JNF in this scheme.[1] In general, the JNF was apprehensive about investing its capital in land purchases because under Turkish law it could not make the purchase in its own name. The purchase of lands in the name of foreign nationals also encountered difficulties, and the risk of expropriation by the authorities should the land remain uncultivated in the course of three consecutive years (Mahlul) was likewise daunting. Indeed, although the Sixth Zionist Congress in 1903 stipulated that under certain conditions the JNF could begin implementing land purchases in Palestine, arguments against such land purchases were voiced at the Seventh Congress which convened in 1905. The thrust of the objections was that "there is no possibility to implement purchases on a secure legal basis." Therefore, the Eighth Zionist Congress in 1907 decided that for the time being no land purchases would be made in Palestine employing JNF monies. Nonetheless, during 1906–1907 the JNF decided to examine each land purchase proposal on its merits and to determine if there were sufficient guarantees that would allow it to undertake the heavy responsibility for the purchase.[2] In any event, the JNF did not occupy a central position amongst the Jewish and Zionist bodies engaged in land purchases during this period.

1   Katz (1982), pp. 47–51; Ussishkin (1934), pp. 107–109; Ruppin (1937), pp. 1–8.
2   Katz (1986b), p. 101 – quotation from there; Doukhan-Landau (1979), p. 87.

Up to the First World War, the JNF purchased lands at Deleika and Um Junni (subsequently Kinneret and Degania), and at Hittin and also parts of Beit Arif. These purchases had not been planned in advance and all were bought from Jewish owners. The purchases were connected with the Zionist General Council's efforts to establish a school and farm for the orphans brought to the country after a pogrom against the Jews in the Russian town of Kishinev in 1903. The JNF found it difficult to resist the requests to use the monies it had collected to make the purchase of lands on which to settle the Kishinev orphans.[3] In addition, the JNF purchased from the Anglo–Palestine Company Bank (APC, which later became the Bank Leumi) land in Hulda in the Judean foothills, which the JNF intended to develop into olive plantation projects. Likewise, a number of additional purchases were made in the Jezreel Valley. All in all, the agricultural land capital of the JNF at the close of the second decade of the twentieth century and on the eve of the opening of the Land Registration Offices (Tabu) in October 1920 totaled 22,000 dunams (4 dunams = 1 acre). This represented less than 6% of the total Jewish–owned agricultural land area in Palestine at the time (see Map 1 and Appendices 3, 4, 7).[4]

The JNF's concerns over problems that were liable to arise should it purchase lands, were counterbalanced by criticism over its inaction. The land purchases described above, apparently induced the JNF at the beginning of 1908, to adopt Arthur Ruppin's proposal regarding the nature of its work in the future. The JNF would only purchase lands for which operative plans existed for the immediate settlement of these lands. JNF funds would be utilized solely for purchases of lands to be used for the benefit of the public, for example, for the establishment of an agricultural training farm, an experimental station, public buildings, land of historical value and expanding the land already under JNF ownership. The JNF would only purchase lands in which private enterprise was not interested. JNF funds would furnish loans to enable others to purchase lands. Indeed

---

3   Shilony (1990), pp. 161–164; Shilony (1998), pp. 125–164; Katz (1983), I, p. 66; II, pp. 174–175.

4   Shilony (1998), pp. 161–164; Kressel (1951), p. 80; CZA, KKL5/10514, summary of JNF land purchases in towns and villages, 1938. Cf. also CZA, A246/397, report of Zalman Lifschitz on the purchase of Jewish-owned lands in Palestine, 1.4.1936. The urban lands owned by the JNF at that time amounted to only 19 dunams, see Weitz (1952), p. 12.

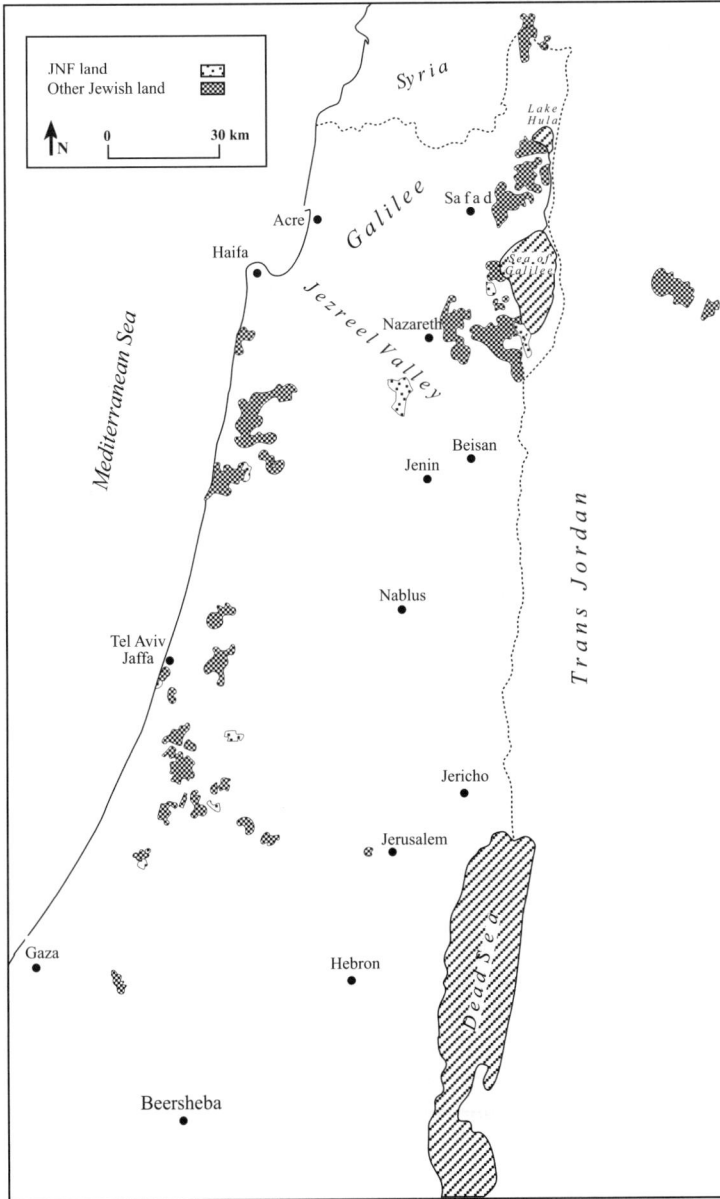

Map 1: Jewish land property and JNF land property in Palestine
at the end of 1919
Source: JNF map archives, Map 4086

until the First World War, JNF funds were used to finance World Zionist Organization–sponsored projects that were totally unconnected with land purchases. These projects included the large loan extended to the founders of the Ahuzat Bayit Company which facilitated the beginning of construction of the neighborhood which would subsequently become the city of Tel Aviv. It was the JNF as well which put up half of the capital for founding shares in the formation of the Palestine Land Development Company (hereafter the PLDC) that was established in 1908 and which served for many years as the instrument for purchasing lands on behalf of the JNF and on behalf of private capital.[5] In July 1920, the annual Zionist Conference which took place in London adopted cardinal decisions which molded the future direction of the JNF. One of these decisions constituted a compromise between the demands of representatives of the Jewish workers parties in Palestine who sought to award the JNF the exclusive right to purchase lands in Palestine, and the position of other participants at the conference (such as American Zionists) who were not prepared to forfeit the role of private capital in land purchases. The conference stipulated that the JNF would be entrusted with the principal task of purchasing lands in Palestine, transferring them to public ownership and allowing them to serve as the infrastructure for the national settlement project. Nonetheless, in order "to purchase quickly extensive land areas in Palestine," the JNF would have to identify methods which would also allow private capital to take an active part in land purchases, while simultaneously imposing limitations to counteract any adverse influence of such capital and to ensure that these lands would pass to public ownership in the future.

The conference also decided that firstly "the JNF's goals are: to purchase lands in Palestine with national contributions and make them public property; to transfer them through inheritable lease for both cultivation and for construction; to permit those workers who had no capital to settle on the land; to guarantee Jewish labor; to ensure that the land would not remain uncultivated, and to preclude land speculation." Secondly, henceforward JNF resources would be devoted exclusively to purchasing lands in urban and rural areas, to upgrade them and perform the necessary initial site

5   Shilo (1985), p. 120; Doukhan-Landau (1979), p. 107; For details of the various projects
     in which the JNF was involved up to the First World War, see Shilony (1990b); Katz
     (1986b). On the fact and consequences of the JNF holding half the founding shares of
     the PLDC see CZA, J85/396, letter from Ussishkin to Gluskin, 7.12.1936.

preparation in order to bring them to a condition suitable for settlement.[6] These resolutions were contrary to the pre-War period when the JNF's monies were expended also on settlement, educational, public and other projects. From now on, the use of JNF funds was prohibited for these purposes (Keren Hayesod was to finance settlement expenses). To meet the needs of financing land purchases in Palestine, the JNF could invest all its funds without limitation, as well as obtain loans for these purposes. Thirdly, as settlement would no longer be permitted in isolated and dispersed outposts, the JNF was to purchase extensive and contiguous areas.[7] In 1922, the JNF's Head Office moved to Jerusalem, and Menachem Ussishkin was chosen to head the JNF's Directorate. Nechemiah De Lieme had headed the Directorate previously from the end of the War until 1921.[8]

Although the London Conference had resolved that the JNF was to purchase land in urban and rural areas, during the early 1920s the JNF concentrated almost all its efforts in the purchase of agricultural land areas. The reasons behind this clear preference for agricultural land over urban lands, is revealed in detail by the JNF Report for the years 1921–1923:

> For various reasons the JNF must expand the land areas first of all in the rural and subsequently in the urban areas. The primary purpose is to restore our people to working the land and in this manner create an agricultural toiling people. Our people are in their vast majority estranged from working the soil and lack the spiritual forces for the vast revolution which must take place in the traits and habits of the urban immigrant and if it does not encounter conditions facilitating settlement, then it will be inevitably drawn to the town.... The World Zionist Organization, which embodies the idea of the Jewish people's return to the soil, in its broader sense and prophetic vision,

6   Report (1921), p. 74, the quotation from there; Report WZO (1921), pp. 31–36; Bein (1976), pp. 206–212; Granovsky (1929), pp. 198–210; Kressel (1951), pp. 78–85; Bistritsky (1950), pp. 199–211. The JNF's activities also included afforestation and the provision of drinking water to the settlers. In 1929, the JNF was no longer required to provide water to new settlements, cf. Weitz (1952), pp. 25–26. See also Granovsky (1938), p. 161, which stresses that as a result the JNF concentrated its activities and devoted most of its finances to land purchase.

7   Granovsky (1938), p. 161. See especially the main points of the London Conference in *Karnenu* (Sept. 1945), p. 1.

8   Kressel (1951), pp. 77, 87–88.

cannot be dragged along by a transient viewpoint, but must pave
the way for attaining the national goal: the settlement of a laboring
agricultural people whose creation is primarily and most essentially
predicated on agricultural land. Urban land is expensive and even if
the JNF wished to satisfy the momentary demand for urban lands,
its paltry resources would not suffice. Therefore, in practice, the
JNF could not follow a land policy for purchases in urban and rural
areas but the follower of a policy of land purchases *in the village and
adjacent to the town* [emphasis in the original] in a location where
suburbs and garden cities can be created and which will also carry
the imprint of agriculture.... The JNF's land policy must be in the van
of agricultural settlement, in advance of it, to prepare the lands for it,
so that no interruption in settlement work should occur as the result
of the lack of land.[9]

Indeed, the large purchases carried out by the JNF in the Jezreel Valley
during 1921–1923 which increased the JNF's land holdings in the area
to 73,600 dunams, and facilitated the establishment of the Moshavim and
Kibbutzim in the Jezreel Valley, was a clear expression of this policy.[10]

The implementation of this policy was preceded by a controversy between
the members of the JNF's Palestine Office (Arthur Ruppin, Akiva Ettinger
and Menachem Ussishkin) and Nechemiah De Lieme, Chairman of the
Directorate. The Palestine Office pressed for making the initial purchases
in the Valley, after Yehoshua Hankin had already received an option,
but De Lieme opposed purchasing the Valley lands and contended that
preference should be given to purchasing the Greek Patriarchate's holdings
in Jerusalem and areas in the Negev. He felt that purchases in Jerusalem
would not only lead to the creation of an appreciable land reserve for the
JNF that would allow the organization to influence urban development, but
by leasing them the JNF could generate appreciable income which it could
possibly exploit for new purchases.

There were those who spoke of the need to exploit the JNF's funds to
purchase plantation lands in the Coastal Plain from which the JNF could
also have profited. However, the concept that the JNF would give preference
to the purchase of areas intended for the creation of dense settlement of

---

9   Eretz Israel (1923), pp. 75–76. See also, Zionist Activity (1922), p. 70.
10 Eretz Israel (1923), pp. 68–69.

Akiva Ettinger

Nechemiah De Lieme

High Commissioner Arthur Wauchope and Menachem Ussishkin, 1928

Arthur Ruppin

agricultural labor triumphed, especially as this was the need of the hour. Hundreds of workers awaited settlement which was delayed due to a dearth of land. The JNF therefore clearly preferred to obtain a "social return" to an "economic return." De Lieme who opposed the purchase of lands in the Jezreel Valley was forced to resign.[11] In its report for summer 1922, the WZO Executive noted the polemic connected to the purchase of the lands in the Jezreel Valley, and summed up this issue by observing:

> To our great joy, we must say that there is not a single person who had visited Palestine recently, and took stock of the new national property and the pioneers cultivating this land and preparing to build many settlements who would not recite the traditional "Shehehiyanu"[12] blessing, over this growth of national property in Palestine.[13]

---

11   Kressel (1951), pp. 86–88; Bein (1976), pp. 215–221; Granovsky (1929), pp. 201–203.

12   Shehehiyanu, "Blessed are You…who has kept us alive." Benediction that expresses gratitude to God for having enabled one to experience a particularly joyous occasion.

13   Zionist Activity (1922), p. 69.

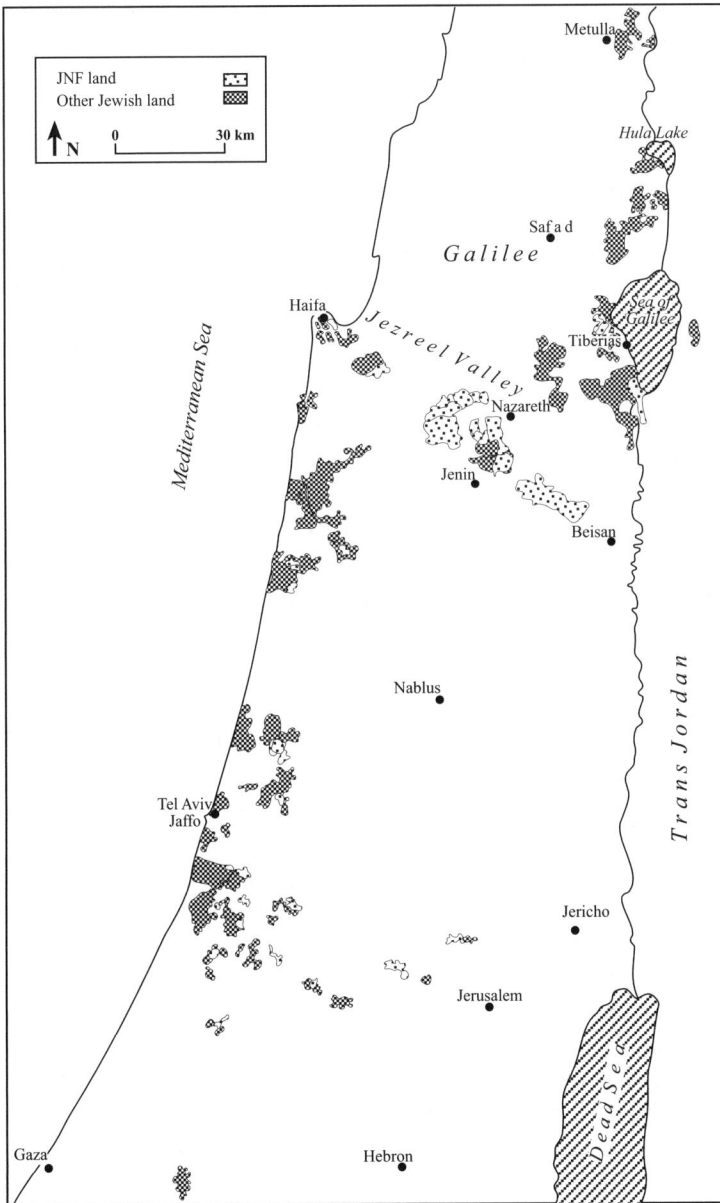

Map 2: Jewish land property and JNF land property in Palestine
at the end of 1924
Source: JNF map archives, Map 1579

JNF policy during the early 1920s and the preference it extended to the Jezreel Valley produced a situation whereby it neglected the plantation areas on the Coastal Plain (see Map 2 and Appendix 5). Despite demands from both the workers and the Jewish Agency's Settlement Department to purchase lands for establishing auxiliary farms, and workers settlements adjacent to the established Moshavot (villages), the JNF refused and advanced the following explanations: First of all, at the quoted price one could continue expanding agricultural property in the grain growing regions. Secondly, Jewish private enterprise had already displayed an inclination to purchase land in the plantation areas and it was therefore preferable to turn to locations where no purchase activity was being carried out by other Jewish bodies. Thirdly, purchases in the plantation areas involved buying Jewish-owned land – something that contradicted the JNF's principle of ensuring first of all a maximal transfer of extensive areas to Jewish ownership. However, in the middle of the 1920s a turnabout occurred in the JNF's attitude to the plantation areas. This was due not only to increasing pressure by workers to establish worker settlements, given the expansion of the citrus growing Jewish villages and the demand for labor by companies and private individuals who had invested in the citrus groves, but was also a result of the rapid and successful development of the plantation branch, the influx of private capital, unforeseen difficulties in the development of the Jezreel Valley, and the development of the city as a market for agricultural produce. There were also the ideas propounded by the agronomist Zelig Sosskin to establish small farms for intensive cultivation, proposals which were well received within the World Zionist Organization. At that time, there was an increased interest in areas for growing intensive agricultural species that were less dependent on climactic changes and small land areas with good prospects of successful development. All this prompted the JNF in the course of the 1920s, to begin making purchases along the coast plain, in Judea and the Sharon.[14]

The JNF's entry process into the Coastal Plain reached its peak with the completion of the purchase of 33,500 dunams in Wadi el Hawarith (the Hefer Valley). Yehoshua Hankin had signed a contract for these lands in 1927 and the completion of the purchase was facilitated in 1929 by a

---

14   Bein (1976), pp. 315–316; Kressel (1951), pp. 102–103; Weitz (1952), pp. 36–37; Amit (1998), p. 158.

contribution from Canadian Jewry. The quality and importance of this purchase is stressed in a JNF Report as follows: "The area represents the choicest lands in the plantation area, vast plains, large percentage of citrus lands, irrigated lands, lands for fodder and rain water plantations; abundant water, the waters of the Alexander River, flowing along the land from east to west, and shallow subterranean waters." The Hefer Valley was also intended to serve as a bridge between the Sharon area north of Tel Aviv and the Samaria area south of Haifa, and thus establish Jewish contiguity along the Coastal Plain. Estimates spoke of the possibility of settling about 1,500 to 2,000 families there – five times the number settled on the same area of land in the Jezreel Valley. Indeed this land purchase laid the foundation for the establishment of new Jewish settlements which would reinforce the position of Jewish labor and fortify the political status of this region. The final transfer of these lands was completed only in 1934 due to protracted negotiations with the authorities and complicated legal proceedings (see Map 3).[15] The JNF also implemented agricultural purchases in the Jordan Valley, expanding its holdings in the vicinity of the Sea of Galilee and Um Junni as well as in the vicinity of Zemach (see Map 4).[16]

As mentioned above, the JNF's activity in the urban areas was minimal, but purchases there were not totally neglected.[17] By virtue of the London Conference and especially due to the influence of De Lieme, a number of purchases in the Jerusalem, Tel Aviv and Haifa areas were implemented up to 1922.[18] However, from 1923, land purchases were cut back to a minimum. The JNF did not take the initiative in purchasing lands in the cities except in matters of emergency situations such as saving Jewish lands which could revert to Arab ownership. In the towns, land purchases were made only to accommodate national institutions while the lands that were purchased in urban vicinity were outside the towns and were intended for semi-urban farms.[19] This condition persisted in the first half of the 1920s but an increasing number of voices were heard within and without the JNF,

15 JNF Report (1939), pp. 14–15, 33–38, quotation from p. 14; Weitz (1952), pp. 36–37; Bein (1976), pp. 316, 339; Kressel (1951), p. 33. See also Kark (1990), pp. 345–362; Orni (1990), pp. 363–371.
16 Report Exec. (1927), pp. 9–11; JNF Report (1937), p. 17.
17 Bein (1976), pp. 313–314; Report Exec. (1931), pp. 31–36.
18 Zionist Activity (1922), p. 70; Greizer (1994), pp. 70–74.
19 Greizer (1994), p. 74; Report Exec. (1925), p. 174.

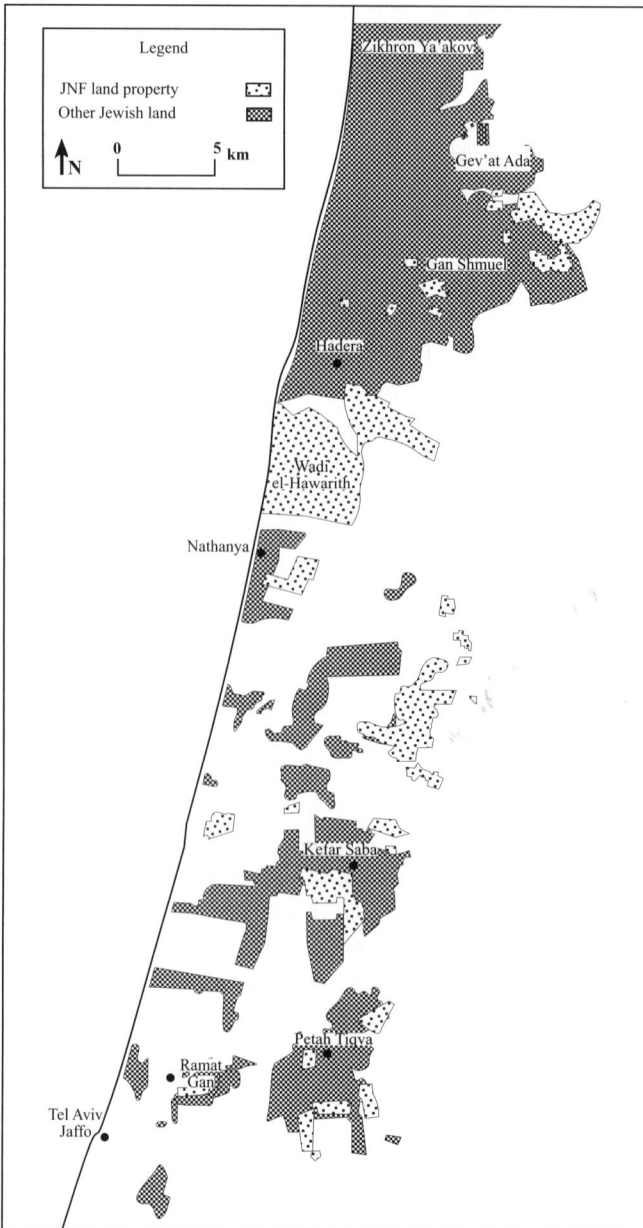

Map 3: Jewish land property and JNF land property in the Sharon Area in 1929
Source: JNF archive, Map 3013A

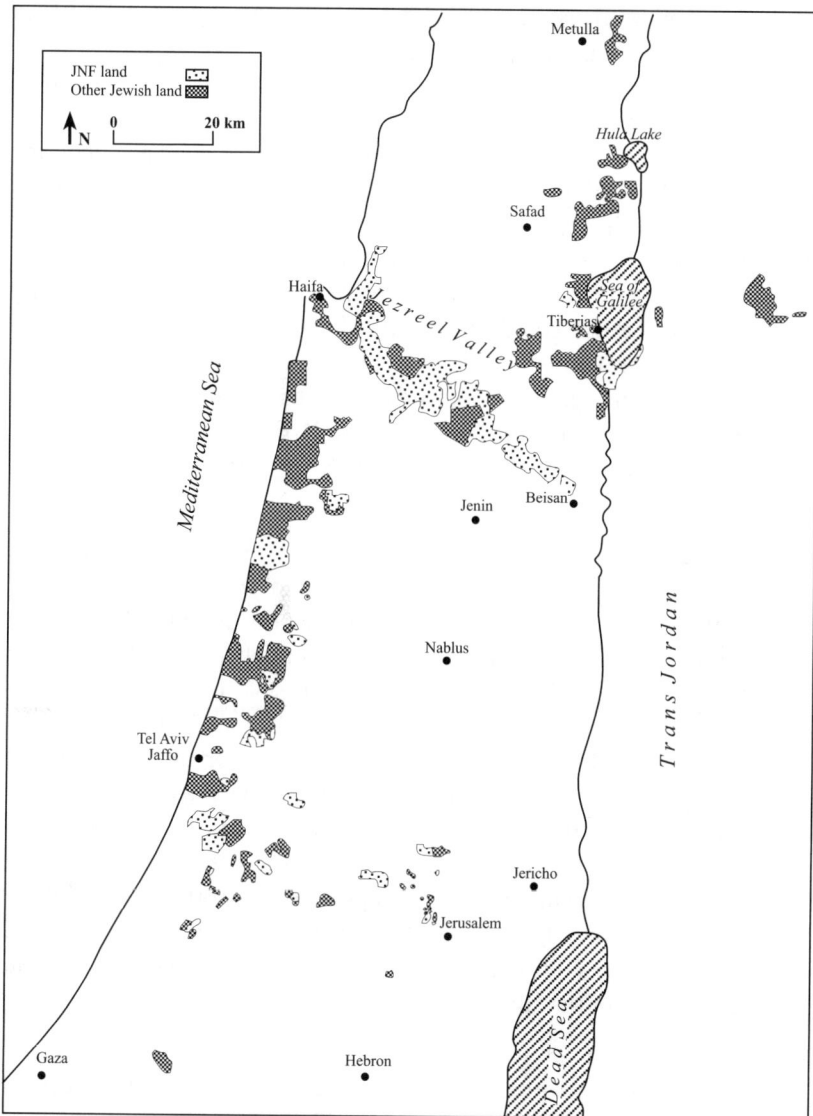

JNF land

Other Jewish land

0   20 km

N

Metulla

Hula Lake

Safad

Haifa

Jezreel Valley

Sea of Galilee

Tiberias

Mediterranean Sea

Jenin

Beisan

Nablus

Trans Jordan

Tel Aviv
Jaffo

Jericho

Jerusalem

Dead Sea

Gaza

Hebron

Map 4: JNF land in Palestine at the end of 1929
Source: JNF map archives, Map 4051

primarily from workers, regarding the necessity of expanded JNF land purchases in the towns and their vicinity.

The experience of Tel Aviv's development during the boom period of the Fourth Aliyah (1924–1931) and later the immigration wave that flowed largely to Tel Aviv and other cities accounted for the demands upon the JNF to expand its activity in the towns. The vast appreciation of land prices and rent with the increased demand for apartments led to a realization of the importance of creating sufficient land reserves in advance to meet the expansion needs of the city. Furthermore, there was an ever-increasing awareness that the JNF could not limit its work only to the most immediate needs of agricultural settlement, but it was obligated to conduct a land policy that anticipated the future of both urban and agricultural settlement.[20] It was Avraham Granovsky, the Director of the JNF's Financial Department, who unflaggingly pleaded the case for the JNF's entry into urban activity. He emphasized inter alia that:

> It is a sad fact that an institution which is obligated to conduct a national land policy did not know how to purchase and maintain important land areas for itself surrounding the city [Tel Aviv] at the proper juncture, i.e., when Tel Aviv was initially founded, during the first years of its existence or at least in the first years following the First World War when Tel Aviv had not yet undergone its transformation from a suburb of the city of Jaffa to an important self-sufficient urban center. At that time it was possible to purchase these lands at a cheap price, those very same lands whose prices, with the rapid flourishing of Tel Aviv, inordinately sky-rocketed…. A Jewish city provides new immigrants with employment opportunities and these could be optimally exploited by creating settlement opportunities. But the pre-condition for this is the preparation of land reserves in the vicinity of the city.[21]

Indeed the JNF Report to the 14th Zionist Congress in 1925 already revealed a turnabout in urban policy.[22] After deliberations, the JNF decided in that year to purchase part of the lands of Jedera (the Zebulun Valley – Haifa Bay) which were offered to it, and these lands were intended for the

---

20 Bein (1976), p. 314; Banker (1977), pp. 116, 122–124.
21 Granovsky (1929), pp. 60–61; Granovsky (1938), pp. 105–219.
22 Report Exec. (1925), p. 167.

future urban development of Haifa. In 1928, the JNF consummated a huge additional purchase at the site, and thus had at its disposal 32,000 dunams for the urban development of Haifa (see Map 4). These areas constituted two-thirds of the entire area (additional areas in the vicinity were purchased by private companies). In 1929, Granovsky summed up: "By making this area of lands in the Haifa vicinity national property, the Jewish character of this district was guaranteed. Herzl's prophecy will come to pass and Haifa will not only be a major city, but a Jewish city."[23]

The JNF report to the 1929 Congress added that "from now on, one can supervise the land utilization of most of the Haifa–Acre Valley based on sound national economic foundations, not only in its agricultural sense but also in the sense of industry which is slated to occupy a very important place in the future."[24] This reserve facilitated the establishment of the industrial area in the region as well as of the adjoining townships. Nonetheless, the JNF maintained its fundamental position pursuant to which its major objective was "primarily to implement the purchase of large land blocs in rural areas which would allow the World Zionist Organization to realize its settlement and economic plans on a grand scale." In the vicinity of the towns, only such purchases would be implemented, "while it was still possible to purchase them at prices that are not in excess of the prices of agricultural lands, for the purpose of founding suburban neighborhoods and accommodating important national institutions."[25]

In 1929 Arab mobs rioted and massacred Jews in Hebron and Safed. From then on until the year 1936, a downturn occurred in the pace of JNF land purchases as well as in the activity of the PLDC in comparison to the years 1920–1929. A number of factors accounted for this: the global economic depression which erupted in 1929 led to a decrease in JNF income from contributions[26]; the 1929 riots and in their wake the reports of the Shaw and Hope-Simpson Investigation Commissions as well as the White Paper of 1930[27] produced a difficult and pessimistic atmosphere and

---

23   Report Exec. (1927), p. 9; Reichman (1979), pp. 175–177; Granovsky (1929), pp. 207–208, quotation from there; Bein (1976), pp. 312–313; Giladi (1973), p. 95.
24   JNF Report (1937), p. 15.
25   Weitz (1952), p. 32.
26   Report Exec. (1931), pp. 100, 106–107.
27   White Paper – Statement of British policy recommending for security and economic reasons the prohibition of Jewish immigration and settlement in Palestine.

demoralized those who financed and promoted the Jewish settlement project in Palestine[28]; the prohibition on the export of capital which a number of countries imposed[29]; disputes between the various political parties within the Zionist Movement and the proliferation of appeals which competed with one another[30]; and the general rise in land prices. The latter was caused by increaséd demand for land and a decrease in supply connected with the recovery from the economic crisis in the latter half of the 1920s; but especially in the wake of the Fifth Aliyah (1932–1939) and the economic boom;[31] land disputes and trespassing which were on the rise since the 1929 riots produced a situation where the JNF and the PLDC had to invest large amounts of money in maintaining and safeguarding their land capital inter alia by intensively cultivating the lands. These expenditures came at the expense of capital available for implementing new purchases. A new law in 1928 imposed the burden of the land tax on the owner of land even if he derived no benefit from it. For reasons of convenience, the Government preferred to collect this tax from the JNF and not from the settlers, whereas the JNF found it difficult to collect the reimbursement from the settlers.[32] Other laws, such as the law for the protection of tenant farmers and laws for resolving long-standing disputes, encumbered land purchases and dragged the JNF into numerous court battles with their attendant expenses.[33]

This is the place to expand on the role of the British Mandatory Government as a factor that did not facilitate but actually encumbered JNF land purchases from Arabs, a policy which applied to other Jewish bodies as well. Nevertheless, let it be emphasized that the Government did not prevent purchases by Jews from Arabs even during the 1940s when the Lands Law (see below in detail) came into effect, prohibiting in principle purchases by Jews from Arabs in most areas of Palestine. The underlying intention of the Government policy in land transfers till the middle 1930s was primarily to protect tenant farmers. These subsisted from the cultivation of most of the land that their owners offered for sale to the JNF, to the

---

28   Report Exec. (1931), pp. 100, 106–107.
29   Idem (1933), p. 90.
30   Ibid., p. 97
31   Banker (1977), pp. 126, 159–164; Horowitz (1944), pp. 15–21; Halevi (1979), pp. 10–30.
32   Report Exec. (1933), pp. 90–91.
33   Idem (1935), p. 162.

PLDC and to other Jewish bodies. The British believed that if they would not act to prevent the eviction of tenant farmers from the land following upon their sale, a class of brigands, robbers and landless peasants would be created, who would constitute an economic burden on the administration in Palestine. The British sought to avoid this at all cost, given their policy of preserving a strategic presence in Palestine and the Middle East at a minimal expense to the British Exchequer and the taxpayer. Thus the protection of the tenant farmer imposed the burden for compensation on the seller and the purchaser and not on the British Government in London or in Palestine.

Already in 1918 the Mandatory Government adopted measures to preserve the rights of those subsisting on agriculture when it ordered the closure of the Land Registration Offices (Tabu) and thus sought to prevent the sale of land. During the Ottoman period, no special protection was extended to the tenant farmer and the Arab land-owners could evict tenant farmers without paying them compensation and this is what they did in practice. When land was sold, the new owners could evict tenant farmers and indeed Jewish purchasers inserted a condition at the time of purchase that the land would be free of tenant farmers. Since many peasants mortgaged their lands and at the end of the War they did not have the means of repaying their debts, the British were forced to help them and this was one of the reasons why the British Military Government announced in November 1918, that all land transactions were null and void and the Land Registration Offices were closed. Only at the end of 1920 were these offices opened again after the Land Transfer Ordinance was promulgated – an ordinance which inter alia sought to guarantee the rights of the owners of small plots and tenant farmers to cultivate the lands in their possession. This ordinance was the first legal measure of the Mandatory Government that was intended to tie the landowner and the tenant farmer to their land. Paragraph 6 of the ordinance declared that the District Governor would not give his assent to the land transfer until it was guaranteed to his satisfaction that in the case of agricultural land the owners or the tenant farmer preserved for themselves sufficient land in the district or in any other place to maintain themselves and their families. However, in 1921 the ordinance was amended and government intervention in land transfers was limited. It likewise emerged during the 1920s that the legal protection extended to tenant farmers was circumvented systematically by Arab landowners and by Jewish purchasers. The British officials responsible for protecting the tenant farmers found it difficult to supervise the implementation of ordinances pertaining to land plots intended for providing a livelihood since they possessed no information on landownership in Palestine, the condition of the tenant farmers and land utilization. It also emerged that the vast majority of the tenant farmers preferred monetary compensation for land than earning a living.

At the end of 1926, the Government recognized the inefficiency of protecting the tenant farmers within the existing legal framework and the need to cut down the circumvention of the 1929 Land Transfer Ordinance regarding the protection of tenant farmers. This was the background to the legislation of the ordinance of June 1929 protecting the tenant farmer. The ordinance decreed that a tenant farmer who cultivated his land for at least one year could not be removed from it unless he received an alternative area for his livelihood. The ordinance also enjoined the landowner to pay appropriate compensation for improvements in the land that had been made by the tenant farmer and that the latter could not receive it unless the landowner had given his written agreement in advance to such improvements. It should be noted that the ordinance applied not only to tenant farmers who actually cultivated the land but also to those with rights to the land, including rights for pasture and drinking water for animals. However, the buyers and sellers could also circumvent this ordinance in various measures, amongst others, by leasing the land for a period of less than a year, and through monetary compensation arrangements to the tenant farmers.

Indeed in the beginning of 1930, the High Commissioner, John Herbert Chancellor, recognized the fact that the ordinance for protecting the tenant farmer could not provide effective defense to all the peasants. In the meantime, the Shaw Commission Report was published. The Shaw Commission was dispatched to the country in the wake of the 1929 disturbances, and its findings blamed the World Zionist Organization for its failure to scrupulously regulate Jewish immigration in terms of the country's absorption capacity and that a class of Arabs deprived of their land had been created. The report bitterly assailed Jewish settlement which caused the removal of Arabs from their land. Following the report, Chancellor sought to prohibit the sale of lands from Arabs to Jews, but he was compelled to defer all legislation until he heard the findings of the expert, John Hope-Simpson who at Shaw's request was sent out to examine all aspects connected to immigration and settlement on land.

The Hope-Simpson Report found that given the volume of lands suitable for cultivation, there was no room for further Jewish immigration to Palestine, and led to the promulgation of the Passfield White Paper in October 1930 which blamed Jewish settlement for creating a class of landless Arabs and alluded to legislation which would prohibit land ownership transfers. In this manner, the British sought to assuage the Arabs. However in response to pressure from the Jewish Agency, a letter from Ramsey MacDonald to Weizmann in February 1931 rescinded the idea of such provisions, but spoke of temporary supervision over the sale and transfer of Arab lands. In any case, this was a far cry from Chancellor's original intention to restrict Jewish settlement, but he vigorously insisted that protection of the rights of farmers of all types should be expanded. The British Government also sought an appearance before the League of Nations to declare that measures for protecting the Arab tenant farmer had been taken. Hence, in May 1931 an amendment to the Ordinance for the Protection of the Tenant Farmer was approved, and for the first time protection was extended to the rights of shepherds who had uninterruptedly resided in a specific area for five years. This amendment was exploited frequently by peasants who demanded compensation from the landowner on the pretext that they had previously been shepherds. Another amendment to the ordinance stipulated that the High Commissioner could oppose mandatory compensation as a substitute for land requisite for the support of the tenant farmer. Thus, in practice, the High Commissioner was awarded de facto supervision of the land transfers, but the Colonial Secretary clarified to Weizmann that the option of mandatory compensation was not totally foreclosed.

However, loopholes were found in the 1929 ordinance and its amendments as well. In response to massive Jewish purchases during the early 1930s from small-scale landowners, a new law for protecting the tenant farmer was promulgated in 1933. This ordinance rescinded the previous one and sought to be more stringent and provide effective protection to the tenant farmers. The central principle of the new ordinance stipulated that no tenant farmer (including a person, a family, a tribe) who cultivated the land for a year would be ousted by the landowner unless provision was made for his subsistence with a plot of land which would suffice for his livelihood, as would be determined by a Government committee. In addition, the tenant farmer was provided with protection against any arbitrary increase of rental fees. Furthermore, he was entitled to compensation for improvements which he had carried out on the land if he were evicted from it. It should be noted that the Government did not obligate itself to extend protection to the landowner who cultivated the land independently or to an agricultural worker, similar to that it had granted the tenant farmer or the landless person under the ordinance.

Ways were found to circumvent this ordinance as well such as informal agreements between the landowner and his tenant farmers under which the landowner who was interested in removing the tenant farmers, waived the share of the harvest which he was entitled to as an annual rental and paid the tenant farmer's tithe, and in recompense the tenant farmer would vacate the land. However, the immediate result derived from the application of the ordinance was an appreciable increase in the number of disputes regarding the rights to use the land and its sale, as well the initiation of numerous suits by the tenant farmers to assert their rights of tenancy. Thus, the Jewish purchasers had to pay the tenant farmers appreciable sums in order to induce them to withdraw their lawsuits. Most of the lawsuits that were initiated in the beginning of 1934 concerned lands in the Coastal Plain where the main land purchase efforts from Arabs were concentrated. In the period between the beginning of 1934 to January 1937, 271 lawsuits were presented in the Tulkarm District, of which 167 were upheld and 104 were denied. The lawsuits were presented to the committees appointed specifically for this purpose and were dealt with immediately. There were tenant farmers who viewed the new ordinance as an opportunity to improve their material condition, either by extorting monetary compensation from the owner who was interested in selling his land when it was free of tenant farmers or by establishing control over the land and cultivating it until the time that their suit was adjudicated. One result of the new situation which the ordinance created, was that the sellers demanded that Jewish purchasers including the JNF, should transfer appreciable sums to them for compensating the tenant farmers as a preparatory step toward the sale of the land. In this manner, the landowner could directly negotiate with his tenant farmers while the Jewish purchasers provided the money for compensation.

The new ordinance for the protection of the tenant farmer therefore created severe problems for Jewish land purchases. In addition to the above, since the ordinance recognized the tenant farmers' rights vis-à-vis the landowners and did not impair these rights even following the transfer of land ownership, the purchaser just like the seller could expect to be sued by the tenant farmer. Even if the seller drew up a contract to sell his lands when they were clear of lawsuits by tenant farmers, the purchaser had no assurance that he would not liable to tenancy lawsuits or that tiresome and costly legal proceedings which originated with the sellers would not be shunted upon him. Arrangements with those who sued for tenant farmer rights generally mandated agreements for out of court monetary compensation and thus the purchaser had to pay double compensation – once prior to the ownership transfer and again subsequent to the purchase. In addition, under the ordinance, from the moment that the tenant farmer obtained legal recognition of his tenancy from the administration, he became a liability to the landowner for his entire life. Since no limitations were placed on the size of the tenant farmer's farm, there were tenant farmers who demanded lands in excess of those they needed for their livelihood or which they could cultivate. They would then lease parts of it to others in return for leasing fees.

In an attempt to expand and intensify the protection of tenant farmers' rights still further and as part of the policy of balances adopted by High Commissioner Arthur Wauchope who sought to create in Palestine a quasi bi-national state where an equilibrium between the two peoples would exist, an amendment to the protection of the tenant farmer ordinance was ratified in June 1936. The definition of "tenant farmer under law" was expanded and included a person who was hired by the landowner for agricultural labor for monetary remuneration. The Mandatory Government sought to provide further protection and included also protection for the landowner who cultivated the land independently. This legislation did not eventuate; given the Arab disturbances and the recommendation of the Royal Commission to re-examine all land legislation. Furthermore, until February 1940, when the Lands Law was promulgated, which we will explore in detail in Chapter Three, no new laws restricting Jewish purchases were legislated.

In sum, it can be said that from 1920 onwards, the Government did not prevent the sale of land to Jews. However, the legislation it initiated for the protection of the tenant farmers made the purchase of lands difficult and the implementation of the various ordinances gave rise to litigation. This also led to substantial increases in the price of land which the JNF and other land purchasing institutions were required to pay.[34]

---

34   Stein (1980), pp. 66–68; Katzburg (1993), pp. 339–342; Katz (in press); Reichman et al. (1991), pp. 206–215; Kano (1980), pp.17–21; Stein (1984), pp. 35–59, 80–141, 187–192.

On the eve of outbreak of the 1929 Arab riots, the JNF formulated principles to govern its work in the future. First of all, the need to create a land reserve in the area of the plantations was discussed, because this was the only region suitable for the settlement of affluent people. It was assumed on the basis of experience accumulated over the preceding years, that a demand for land by people of substance could be anticipated. Therefore, the JNF would be required to purchase all lands available in that area. Secondly, the JNF had to create a land reserve within the veteran Moshavot and in their immediate vicinity for houses and auxiliary farms for the workers. In this manner one could help guarantee Jewish labor in the villages. Thirdly, the JNF had to complete purchases in the Jezreel Valley and earmark them for the expansion of existing farms. Likewise, it had to purchase lands in the areas of the concessions in Naharaim and the Dead Sea. In the cities as well, and especially in Tel Aviv, the JNF planned the creation of land reserves on the model of its activity in Haifa Bay. The intention was to establish neighborhoods for workers in these areas. The JNF planned to expend efforts to purchase government-owned lands.[35]

However, in practice most of the agricultural purchases the JNF concluded in the period 1929–1935 were in the Beisan and Jezreel Valleys.[36] The high price of lands in the Coastal Plain caused the JNF to invest significantly less in this region than it had planned and channel resources for the first time to the Beisan Valley and the border area. In this region land prices were still low but Jewish settlement activity had not yet penetrated there. The JNF intended to open a new settlement region which would create land and settlement contiguity between the Jezreel Valley and the Beisan Valley. The nature of the soil and the abundance of water assured the possibility of establishing intensive communities and therefore a dense population could be settled there. The JNF began purchasing lands in the Beisan Valley through the PLDC in 1931, but until 1934 this land reserve did not exceed a few thousand dunams. In 1934, the JNF decided to step up its purchase efforts and in 1935 it was already engaged in clustering the purchases in the Beisan Valley into an area of 26,000 dunams. Many options remained open for continued future purchases in the region.[37]

35   JNF Report (1937), pp. 33–38.
36   Report Exec. (1931), p. 94; idem (1933), p. 169; idem (1937), p. 190.
37   See for example Report Exec. (1935), p. 169; Katz (1999)), pp. 20–21, 45, 59–60; idem (1994c), pp. 81–100; CZA, S25/6530, memorandum of Granovsky, "The Land

The Hula Valley, 1940

Nearly half of the JNF purchases in the Jezreel Valley represented purchases from the Kehiliath Tzion Company after the latter encountered a severe financial crisis and could not meet its obligations. An appreciable portion of the land purchased by the JNF in the Jezreel Valley was intended for the expansion of existing communities. The purchases in the East Jezreel Valley dovetailed with the JNF's current objective of putting down roots in the Beisan Valley (see Map 5).[38]

The purchases along the Coastal Plain took second place during the years 1929–1936 from the standpoint of their volume. During 1929–1931, the volume of purchases in this area exceeded those in any other region. However, the high prices there prevented the continued preference of this region during the balance of the period. Generally, the lands located adjacent to the large plantation Moshavot were suitable for citrus and were

---

Problem and the Political Consideration," 1938; Weitz (1947), pp. 76–77; Granovsky (1938), pp. 23, 110–111.

38   Report Exec. (1933), p. 93; idem (1935), p. 170; Weitz (1947), pp. 76–77; idem (1951), p. 27; Katz (1999), p. 45.

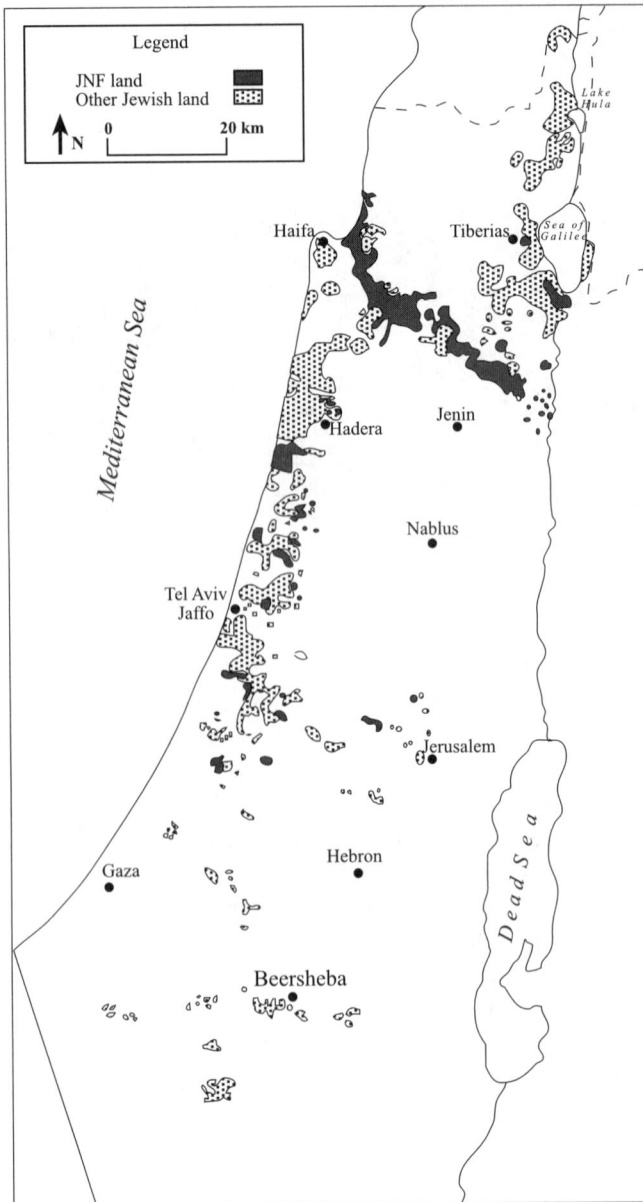

Map 5: Jewish land property in Palestine and JNF land property
at the end of 1935
Source: JNF map archives, Map 4021

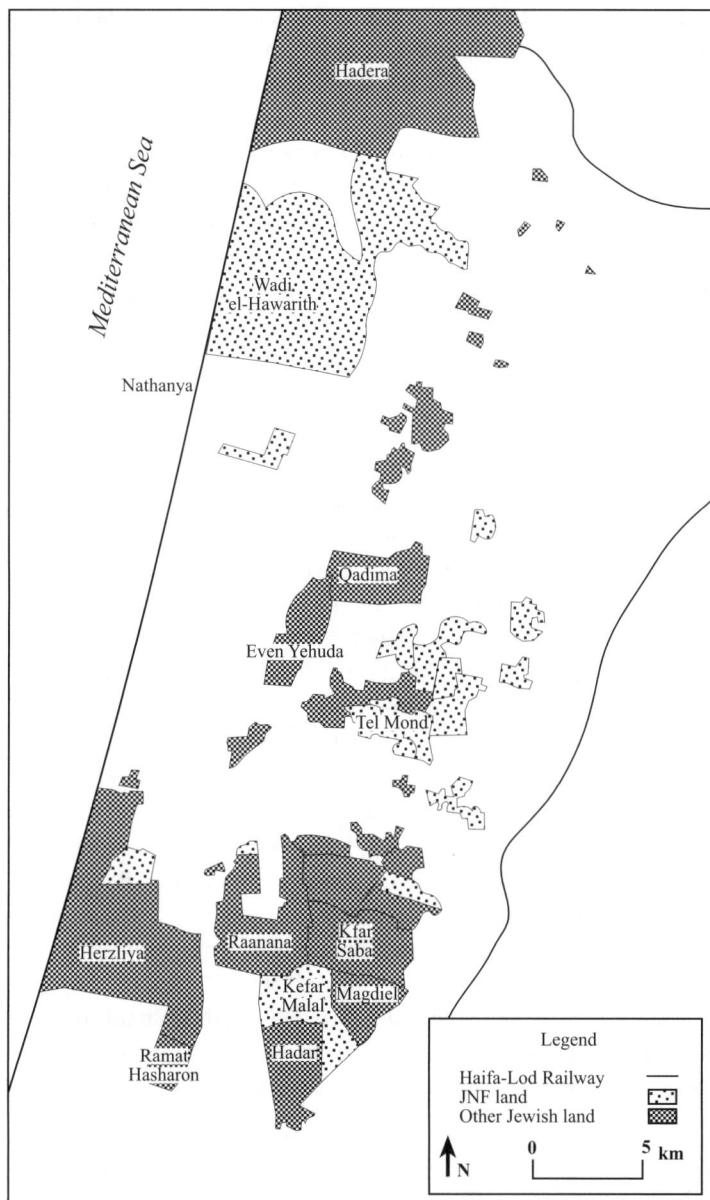

Map 6: Jewish land property and JNF land property in the Sharon Area
at the end of 1934
Source: JNF archive, Map 9663A

intended for the expansion of existing settlements, the establishment of new Moshavim and Kibbutzim, auxiliary farms for workers in the villages and in worker camps.[39] Particularly striking in the period under discussion was the conclusion of development works in the Hefer Valley by the JNF and the beginning of settlement by Kibbutzim and Moshavim, as well as by middle class settlers. Part of the lands in the Hefer Valley earmarked for the settlement of the middle class was leased by the JNF to the Yakhin Company which engaged in site preparation and preparing the plantations until the stage when the trees bore fruit and the owners could settle. The JNF leased 3,000 dunams in the Hefer Valley to the Mandatory Government for a limited period in order to settle the Bedouins who were moved from the site until the Government could find alternative areas for their settlement (see Map 6).[40]

Following the PLDC purchase of the Hula Concession in 1934, the JNF began to display an interest in making purchases in the Northern Hula region. This derived from a need to create an appreciable concentration of lands in the Hula Valley, north of the concession area before their value would rise due to the implementation of the swamp drainage project and the development of the area. It was clear that the economic feasibility of the drainage project was dependent on the allocation of as large as possible land areas for Jewish settlement not only in the swamp areas, but also in the vast valley to their north and up to the headwaters of the Jordan River. In this way the water resources located in the north of the valley could be retained. Nonetheless until the end of 1935 the JNF did not carry out any purchases there.[41] At the end of 1935 the JNF affiliated with the Jewish Colonial Association (JCA) with a view to jointly purchasing the Hula Concession from the PLDC in the future.[42]

The main urban land purchases of the JNF were concentrated during this period in Tel Aviv and they totaled 400,000 square meters. They were intended first and foremost for the establishment of workers' neighborhoods, a neighborhood for teachers and municipal officials, the expansion of existing workers' neighborhoods and the establishment of a

---

39   Report Exec. (1931), pp. 94–95; idem (1933), pp. 91–92; idem (1935), p. 170.
40   Idem (1933), p. 94; idem (1935), p. 170.
41   Weitz (1947), pp. 31–32; Katz (1999), p. 116, n. 20.
42   CZA, KKL5/4746/1, information report No. 7/96, 23.3.1936; CZA, information report No. 6/1937, 20.1.1937.

farm for female workers in the north of the city. In most cases, the workers themselves financed an appreciable portion of the cost of building plots or transferred loans to the JNF to implement the purchases. However, in any case, it was the JNF that retained the ownership and it leased the land to the workers. In Jerusalem, the volume of urban purchases was limited to only 93,000 square meters. In the main, it was earmarked for the needs of public institutions such as the Hebrew University, the Teachers' Seminary in Beit Hakerem, the Teachers' Seminary of the Mizrachi Movement and a school for the blind. Lands were also purchased for expansion of the female workers farm in Talpiot and the expansion of Kibbutz Ramat Rachel. In the city of Haifa, the JNF purchased only a few thousand square meters but during those years it carried out extensive preparation of the land in the Zebulun Valley for urban settlement, including industrial centers and establishing the first small townships there – Kiryat Hayim, Kiryat Motzkin and Kiryat Bialik.[43]

In the beginning of 1936, the JNF's land capital totaled 360,000 dunams, constituting 30 percent of the total area under Jewish ownership in Palestine in town and village (see Map 5 and Appendices 3, 4).[44]

---

43   Report Exec. (1931), pp. 95–96; idem (1933), pp. 94–95; idem (1935), pp. 170–172; Greizer (1994), pp. 70–74; Ulitzur (1939), pp. 144–146.

44   CZA, A246/397, report by Zalman Lifschitz on Jewish landholdings in Eretz Israel up to 1.4.1936; CZA, KKL5/10514, Summary of land purchased by JNF in urban and rural areas in 1938; CZA, S44/60b, Address by Weitz to JNF Directorate, 23.1.1936.

CHAPTER TWO

Policy and Practice in Light of New Political Needs, 1936–1939

The JNF's Organizational and Administrative Structure, Prerogatives and Decision Makers

In 1907, the JNF was registered in London as a limited corporation and its by-laws were approved. The supreme body was the General Assembly of the JNF Company Ltd. composed of members of the Expanded Zionist General Council of the World Zionist Organization (WZO) who held voting shares in the Jewish Colonial Trust (the World Zionist Organization bank established in 1898). The General Assembly was authorized to elect a Directorate whose number would be determined by the General Assembly. Some of the directors, but no more than three, would be appointed directly by the WZO Executive. These directors were called governors and they had a veto power over the decisions of the directors if they unanimously expressed their opposition to them. The WZO Executive also had the power of veto on activities the Directorate intended to carry out. Decision-making powers were entrusted to the Directorate for managing all JNF affairs, which elected a chairman from among its members and appointed executives for day-to-day operations. A third of the Directorate was required to resign every year and be replaced by others, however those resigning had the right to reelection.[1]

---

1   CZA, KKL5/13892, memorandum of the incorporation and articles of incorporation of the Jewish National Fund Ltd., incorporated on 8 April 1907; Eretz Israel (1923), pp. 41–42. It is of interest to note that the by-laws did not mention the fact that has been a slogan of the JNF for over a century, that land bought by the JNF was the property of the Jewish People in perpetuity. It did however state that lands could not be sold but leased. On this matter see CZA, KKL5/8828, letter from Mohilewer to S. Ussishkin 23 March 1939.

Meeting Room of the Board of Directors at the Head Office of JNF

Over the years, the General Assembly of the JNF Company became a formal body. The number of its members who participated in its meetings was very small and during 1936–1947 no more than 4–5 members attended. The by-laws did not require the participation of more than four members to ensure that the meeting had a legal quorum. The business of the Assembly, when it convened once a year at a time and place determined by the Directorate, was to approve the financial reports of the JNF, ratify land purchases concluded during the year and approve the election of the directors whose candidacy had been previously determined by the Directorate and ratified by the WZO Executive. During 1937–1938 the General Assembly did not deviate from these activities, although under the by-laws it could guide or restrict in advance the Directorate's activities. Decision making powers, responsibility and policy making in all spheres of JNF activity were concentrated in the hands of the Directorate, and under the by-laws the General Assembly could not in any case annul or intervene in activities which had already been carried out by the Directorate.

The composition of the Directorate did not have to be identical to the membership of the General Assembly, not even partially. Aside from the governors, the by-laws stipulated that the members of the Directorate would be experts in "political economy or the laws of a particular country, or in technical matters that could be of utility regarding any of the goals of the association." It was customary for the Directorate to present every year for ratification before the Zionist General Council of the World Zionist Organization those members who had withdrawn (as obligated by the by-laws) and had been requested by the Directorate to stand for reelection or alternatively to authorize new candidates to replace those who had either withdrawn or were now deceased. Similarly, approval was sought from the Zionist General Council when the Directorate sought to expand its number of members. The General Assembly of the JNF Ltd. formally and conclusively ratified these appointments.[2]

---

2   CZA, KKL5/13892, memorandum of incorporation and articles of incorporation of
     the Jewish National Fund Ltd. –quotation from there; CZA, KKL5/7347, invitation to
     members of JNF Company Ltd., to General Assembly, 16.12.1936; CZA, KKL5/8826,
     invitation, as above, to General Assembly, 11.11.1936; CZA, KKL5/7347, proceedings
     of General Assembly, 30.5.1939; CZA, KKL5/10565, members of JNF Company
     Ltd., to General Assembly, 4.4.1937; CZA, KKL5/8826, includes, among others,
     following documents: letter from JNF Head Office to Neiditch 12.4.1938, invitation
     to members of JNF Company Ltd. to General Assembly, 30.5.1939, proceedings of
     General Assembly, 30.5.1939; CZA, KKL5/10565, invitation to members of JNF
     Company Ltd. to General Assembly, 25.6.1940; CZA, S53/437f., includes, among
     others, the following documents: proceedings of General Assembly, 25.6.1940, report
     of Directorate to General Assembly, 25.6.1940, report of Directorate to General
     Assembly, 24.12.1941; CZA, KKL5/11860, proceedings of General Assembly,
     28.12.1941; CZA, S53/437f., report of the Directorate to General Assembly, 17.9.1942;
     CZA, KKL5/11860, invitation to members of JNF Company Ltd. to General Assembly,
     17.9.1942; ibid., proceedings of General Assembly, 4.10.1942; CZA, S53/43j., report
     of the Directorate to General Assembly, 23.12.1943; CZA, KKL/12754, proceedings
     of General Assembly, 26.12.1943, 11.3.1945; CZA, KKL5/13979, proceedings of
     General Assembly, 21.10.1945; CZA, KKL5/22307, report of Directorate to General
     Assembly, 3.11.1946; CZA, KKL5/13979, proceedings of General Assembly,
     3.11.1946; CZA, KKL5/15905, proceedings of General Assembly, 30.12.1947; CZA,
     S8/92, letter from Organization Department to Jewish Agency Executive 19.11.1941;
     Eretz Israel (1923), pp. 12, 41–42. E.g., in 1939 the JNF Company Ltd. numbered
     11 members: Ussishkin, Bodenheimer, Gruenbaum, Halperin, Hantke, Weizmann,
     Neiditch, Soloveichick, Simon, Klee, Kenan. Cf. CZA, KKL5/8826, invitation to
     members of JNF Company Ltd., to General Assembly, 8.5.1939. For example, the

From 1923 until his death in 1941, Menachem Ussishkin headed the JNF Directorate. He also served from 1935 as the Chairman of the Zionist General Council and by token of this post was also a member of the Executive of the World Zionist Organization, which was identical with the Jewish Agency Executive. Likewise, Ussishkin served as the JNF representative on the Jewish Agency's Board of Directors. Serving alongside Ussishkin in 1936, as directors of the JNF were Dr. Avraham Granovsky (who served as the JNF treasurer and the head of its Financial Department from 1921), Rabbi Meyer Berlin (Bar-Ilan), the agronomist Professor Yitzhak Vilkansky, Shmuel Zuchovitzky, Berl Katznelson, Herman Stroock, who also served as a representative of the JNF on the Zionist General Council, Zalman Schocken and David Ben-Gurion. The latter served as the Chairman of the Jewish Agency Executive. Both Ben-Gurion and Schocken served as governors representing the Zionist Executive on the JNF Directorate. Until the death of Ussishkin, this composition of Directorate members did not alter. Three members of the Directorate who resigned at the end of the year as obligated under the by-laws were re-elected by the Directorate as candidates for an additional term and their candidacy was approved in accordance with the procedure described above by the Zionist General Council and the General Assembly of the JNF Company.[3]

The WZO Executive did not intervene during 1936–1939 in the election of members of the Directorate, although the JNF by-laws allowed it do so. It also did not insist that the number of governors should be three as allowed by the by-laws, but contented itself with two. Furthermore, apart from a single instance, the possibility that the WZO Executive would intervene to annul a decision by the Directorate, a right reserved to it under

---

General Assembly, 4.10.1942 was attended by only four members. Cf. CZA, KKL5/ 11860, proceedings of General Assembly, 4.10.1942.

3   Granot (1951a), p. 17; CZA, KKL5/13979, list of members of JNF Directorate during 1940–1946. For details about the members of the Directorate see Appendix 1. See also CZA, KKL10, minutes of JNF Directorate meetings in 1936–1941; ibid., proceedings of Smaller Zionist General Council session, 26.8.1941; CZA, S8/92, the following letters: Lauterbach to the Executive 24.11.1941, 3.12.1941, WZO Organization Department to Executive 19.11.1941, JNF to WZO Executive 4.8.1942; CZA, S5/333, proceedings and resolutions of Enlarged Zionist General Council session, 27.8.1936; CZA, S5/333, proceedings of Smaller Zionist General Council session, 10.5.1939, 7.12.1939; ibid., minutes of Jewish Agency Executive meeting, 18.6.1939; CZA, KKL10, letter from Epstein to Ussishkin 28.5.1941.

Menachem Ussishkin at the Head Office of JNF, 1921

the JNF by-laws, did not arise for discussion in the WZO Executive.[4] The
sole instance when the possibility of intervention by the Executive arose
was in mid-1939 when Ben-Gurion demanded that the WZO Executive
convene a special meeting of the JNF Directorate when the latter decided
not to implement specific land purchases in the Upper Galilee as demanded
by Ben-Gurion and the Jewish Agency Executive in general. Ben-Gurion
made it clear that if the Directorate would not change its position, he would
have to bring the issue for a decision before the Smaller Zionist General
Council. Ben-Gurion was certain that his demand would be endorsed.
Ussishkin, who feared for the independence of the Directorate, expressed
vigorous opposition to intervention by the Smaller Zionist General Council
in the decisions of the Directorate, but Ben-Gurion vigorously insisted that
"he does not see that the Directorate of the JNF should be above everything
else. The Executive as well [the Executive of the Jewish Agency] brings

4   CZA, S8/92, letters referred to in n. 3 above.

Rabbi Meyer Berlin (Bar-Ilan)

Avraham Granovsky (Granot)

Berl Katznelson

Prof. Yitzhak Vilkansky

Zalman Schocken

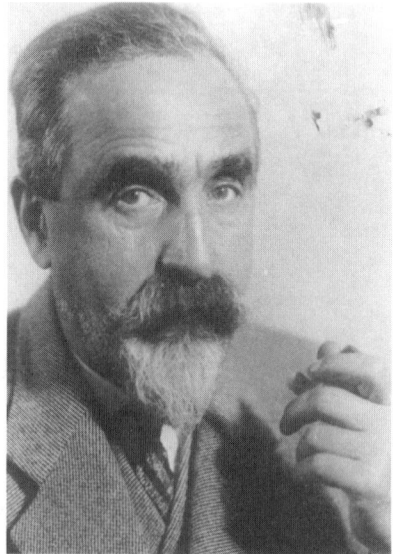

Herman Stroock

matters before the Zionist General Council and takes instructions from it. There is no question that it is exempt from the Zionist General Council's powers of decision-making." In the end, the Directorate altered its decision without the need to test the legal power of the Jewish Agency Executive vis-à-vis decisions that were taken by the JNF Directorate which were not acceptable to the former. Nonetheless, as will be demonstrated below, this affair is instructive regarding the role of the Jewish Agency Executive in certain decisions taken by the JNF Directorate.[5]

5   Ibid., minutes of Jewish Agency Executive meeting on 18.6.1939. Six months prior to this a violent argument arose at a meeting of the Directorate between the two Governors (Ben-Gurion and Schocken). The matter concerned the purchase of additional lands for Ein Gev from the Jewish Company Kidmat Kinneret. Schocken threatened to impose a veto if the Directorate took a decision that differed with his opinion, and Ben-Gurion threatened to appeal to the Jewish Agency Executive against Schocken's use of the veto if it were imposed. In the end, a compromise solution was found that was acceptable to both. It would appear that neither Schocken nor Ben-Gurion was aware that according to the JNF's by-laws a veto could be imposed on the JNF Directorate's decision only when all the Governors objected to the decisions taken by the Directorate. A single Governor did not have the right of veto. Cf. article 3 of the Jewish National Fund Ltd. Company's by-laws, CZA, KKL5/13892.

Building of the Head Office of JNF upon its transfer to Palestine

The body that was intended to implement the Directorate's decisions and oversee the JNF's day-to-day operations in Palestine and throughout the world, from the time that Head Office transferred to Jerusalem in 1922, was the JNF's Executive. During 1936–1939, this Executive was comprised of Menachem Ussishkin as Chairman of the Directorate and the directors of the four main departments in the Head Office: The Lands and Forestry Department, headed from 1932 by Yosef Weitz; the Financial Department, headed by Granovsky; the Propaganda Department and the Organization and Fund Raising Department. In practice, the Executive was divided into two: the Executive for Land and Settlement Affairs (hereafter the JNF Executive or the Executive) whose members were Ussishkin, Granovsky and Weitz; the Executive for Propaganda and Organization whose members were Ussishkin, Granovsky and the heads of the departments for Propaganda and Organization.[6] The Lands Department, through Weitz, was to submit purchase proposals for discussion in the Executive. After it had

---

6   Weitz (1951), pp. 14–15; Guide (1937), pp. 1–2; CZA, KKL10, minutes of JNF
    Directorate meetings during 1936–1939.

deliberated on the proposals and thrashed out the details these proposals were to be transferred to the Directorate for discussion and decision. Weitz was constantly present at the deliberations of the Directorate and took an active part in the discussions. The decisions of the Directorate, which included general guidelines for its activities, were returned to the Executive and to the Lands Department for implementation. The deliberations of the Directorate were issue-oriented and detailed in general, and they reflected differences of opinion on both practical and ideological issues. On many occasions the decisions were taken by a majority vote. In any case, this body was not a rubber stamp of the Executive or a formal body for authorizing its recommendations. The converse is true. Concentration on minor details was not generally the business of the Directorate, but on the other hand it was the sole authority for the ratification of exchanges of land between the JNF and other bodies, even if this referred to the minutest plot.[7]

Head Officers of the JNF and Workers of the Head Office in Jerusalem, 1940

7   Ibid., see also Granot (1952), pp. 196–198, 204; also, e.g., CZA, KKL10, minutes of JNF Directorate meetings, 30.3.1936, 6.7.1936, 2.12.1936, 19.12.1938; personal interview with Hiram Danin, Jerusalem 8.10.1997.

The Economic Background of the Period and Tendencies
of Land Sale Offers by Arab Sellers

During the first half of the 1930s, Palestine enjoyed a situation of economic prosperity. Four factors contributed to this: First, this period witnessed Jewish immigration and the import of capital and especially Jewish capital to Palestine. This capital flowed to the country as a result of both push and pull forces. On the one hand, there was the feeling of insecurity, the rise of anti-Semitism and the unfavorable economic conditions prevailing in Europe. On the other hand, there were factors attracting capital investment in Palestine. Indeed, during the first half of the 1930s, the import of capital and Jewish investments reached their peak. Secondly, there were advantages stemming from the devaluation of the Pound Sterling to which the Palestine currency was linked. The process of the local currency's devaluation that began in 1931, increased the importance of capital imports on the economy and encouraged its investment in real estate. Thirdly, the decline in prices throughout the world, resulting from the great economic depression of 1929, enabled Palestine to obtain imported merchandise at bargain prices and thus the attractiveness of investment in Palestine increased. Fourthly, these were boom years for citrus groves. At the time, thanks to new theories on vitamins and general changes in taste and custom, the consumption of fruits, vegetables and dairy products grew and the consumption of cereals declined somewhat. Citrus fruit became most popular and thus Palestine, where citrus comprised three quarters of total exports, benefited. Citrus was in great demand and its export rose rapidly. In addition to all these factors, a huge increase occurred in the purchasing power accompanying the flow of immigration and capital to Palestine. Thus capital flow served not only to finance investments made in all branches of the economy, especially in building and citrus groves, but also to finance consumption.

As opposed to the years 1932–1935, defined as a period of economic comfort, the years 1936–1939 were defined as a period of crisis. From autumn 1936, the factors stimulating the Palestine economy in previous years began to weaken. Since the value of other currencies began to depreciate, the devaluation of the Pound Sterling no longer exerted a positive influence, especially as the price structure adjusted at a rapid rate to the new situation of the currency. The positive influence exerted by the other factors operating during 1932–1935 was also canceled out over time. In the years 1936–1938, prices began rising in the world market and imports, which occupied such an important place in the Palestine economy, became more expensive. The easy terms for marketing citrus declined, due to the expansion of citrus groves throughout the world as well as in Palestine, leading to the depreciation of citrus prices. The two principal factors in the economic development of Palestine, capital imports and immigration diminished since 1936, given the limitations imposed by many countries on exporting capital and the Arab disturbances and their repercussions during 1936–1939. Thus the imports of capital and immigration declined to half the 1935 level and the branches that were linked to investments, such as the building industry, manufacturing and agriculture (supplying commodities to workers engaged in the investment economy) were severely impaired. All these factors produced a situation where after a period of inflation lasting till 1936, a period of deflation set in which typified the years 1936–1939. Deflation brought all its attendant repercussions such as reduced credit, price declines, unemployment and symptoms of economic arrest.

In the wake of the crisis, the Palestine economy did not actually collapse, but faced the twin negative influences of the period of Arab riots on the one hand, and the sharp drop and severe economic conditions after two bad years for the citrus crop, on the other hand. The economy, which was geared to rapid expansion, had to adjust to conditions where the pace of the development was far slower. The sharpest drop occurred in building, which had previously generated a large part of purchasing power in Palestine. The decline in wages and the cutbacks in the employment of building workers, led to a general drop in the standard of living. Per capita consumption in the Jewish community declined appreciably and unemployment increased. On the other hand, the Arab disturbances led to the creation of an economic situation which closely resembled a war economy. The security forces took in many people who under other circumstances would have remained without work. For security reasons the dimensions of public works were also expanded and special institutions to finance them were established. All these factors enabled the country to overcome the difficulties of the period. Due to the disruption of links with Arab sources of manpower, a larger number of Jewish workers was absorbed by agriculture. A transfer of manpower from highly paid professions to professions where wages were lower was discernible; the percentage of building workers decreased and movement from village to town was arrested. In general, Jewish capital investment declined from 10 million Pounds Sterling (hereafter P£) in

1935 to P£5.5 million in 1936, P£5.3 million in 1937 and P£4.7 million in 1938. Investment in citrus groves ceased, while investments in the mixed agricultural economy increased. Capital invested in construction declined by an appreciable measure and at a rapid pace.[8]

The period covering the years 1936–1939 was characterized by contradictory trends from the standpoint of land sale offers by Arab sellers.[9] On the one hand, the waves of terror during this period, intimidated the landowners who refrained from selling land to the Jews, even if they so desired. Thus, "from the time of the disturbances until the end of 1936, we purchased only minute areas of territory. The Arabs are terror-stricken and a certain amount of time elapsed until we found our way back to them.... In the months of July–September [1938] purchases came to a halt, not because there were no lands for sale or the Arabs did not want to sell but because the terror wave took a really terrible turn and imposed fear on all property owners."[10] However, Arab property owners had a major interest to sell their property during the years of the disturbances and this expressed itself in the lands being offered for sale. The possibilities for land purchases multiplied to such an extent that Granovsky saw fit to emphasize in 1938: "[It] would not be an exaggeration if we were to say that in all the years that the Zionist project has progressed since the World War of 1914–1918, there was no more opportune time than this for enhancing Jewish land capital in Palestine. There were never such manifold and varied offers as in the recent period."[11] Weitz explained in 1937 that: "such a situation of possibilities for land purchases in various areas of the country has not existed since the war. Offers are coming in from various directions – from Arab owners who themselves do not reside on the land and who are living in Palestine or abroad; and from Arab villagers who themselves reside on the land and who each possess more than 100 dunams."[12]

8 Horowitz (1944), pp. 36–51, 134; Gross & Greenberg (1944), p. 37; Banker (1977), pp. 159–166.

9 Granot (1952), p. 72; Granovsky (1940), pp. 34–37.

10 Granovsky (1940), pp. 34–35; CZA, A246/699, letter from Weitz to Ben-Shemesh 28.10.1938.

11 Granovsky (1940), p. 36; CZA, KKL10, minutes of JNF Directorate meetings, 6.12.1937, 25.4.1938.

12 CZA, KKL10, minutes of JNF Directorate meeting, 6.12.1937.

The increase in the supply of lands offered by Arab sellers was due to a number of factors. First, there was the general economic distress of the years 1936–1939 which was further exacerbated as a result of the Arab riots. This reality brought the Arabs to a state where "they saw no other way to improve their situation save by selling their lands in order to survive and provide themselves with the essential needs for their existence. Two years of riots impoverished the Arab economy, both the large estate owners and the peasants. There are no other resources in the Arab monetary cycle, there is no market for their products, there is no livelihood to be found in the town and gangs extorted their remaining resources. Estate owners fled abroad, their expenses multiplied and they could not collect tenancy payments."[13] The need for cash arising from the sore distress to which the property owners and perforce all those tied and dependent upon them in the Arab economy were exposed, in the final result overcame their fear of the terror. Therefore the terror could not, over the long term, stanch the outburst of land offers. Secondly, the decline in land purchases by Jewish private capital during the period of the Arab riots, and the fact that the JNF remained almost the only Jewish land purchaser at that time, induced a decline in the general demand for land and a drop in land prices (in comparison with the 1932–1935 boom period). For this reason as well, and on top of the destitute economic situation and the Arab disturbances, the property owners' need for cash increased greatly during this period, leaving them no option but to increase the supply. It should, however, be noted that the decline in property prices was not catastrophic. In the opinion of JNF leaders this stemmed from expectations on the part of those property owners whose situation had not yet reached bottom that the demands for land would intensify with the expansion of the Jewish national home.[14] Thirdly, political uncertainty prevailed following the publication of the Royal Commission's Report in mid-1937. The Arab landowners felt that their situation would be aggravated when a Jewish State would be established. Their apprehension was fed by rumors "that the future Jewish State will impose heavy taxes on its citizens which would compel the landowners to sell their property."[15] Therefore, they sought to intensify their sales at

---

13   Granovsky (1940), p. 36.
14   Ibid., pp. 30–37; CZA, KKL10, minutes of JNF Directorate meeting, 6.12.1937.
15   Granot (1952), p. 72.

present and receive returns which they highly doubted could be obtained after partition. Later, as clouds gathered in Europe, the landowners feared that a World War would erupt, and they would be unable to sell their land, and thus sought to speed up sales in the present.[16] Fourthly, at a number of locations tenant farmers had left the lands to join the rioting gangs and the landowners sought to exploit this opportunity to sell their holdings.[17]

The JNF's Method of Operation and General Preferences in Land Purchases

The dominant figure in the Jewish National Fund's Lands Department in the period covered by this book was Joseph Weitz. By the nature of things, he was also dominant in the JNF Executive in matters connected with purchasing, and in shaping the Executive's policy. He likewise played a central role in the deliberations of the Directorate. His centrality in all matters pertaining to JNF land purchases is indisputable, and we would not be far from the truth if we would contend that Weitz was in fact the Lands Department. Since 1937 when the JNF began its re-involvement in settlement matters, Weitz was the dominant figure in the JNF in this sphere as well. He immigrated to Palestine from Poland in 1908, was one of the Second Aliyah laborers and joined the Hapoel Hatzair movement. In 1919, he worked in the JNF and in the Settlement Department of the World Zionist Organization, specializing in plantations and forestry, and became the JNF's expert on forestry. In June 1929, Weitz was appointed to be the deputy for Akiva Ettinger in managing the JNF Lands and Forestry Department and he left the Settlement Department. In 1932, upon Ettinger's resignation, Weitz was appointed to head the Department.[18]

Weitz, like other members of the Directorate, Granovsky and Ussishkin, was involved in the JNF's activities from the time that the JNF began the second phase of its work in Palestine following the First World War. He identified totally with the tasks and goals of the JNF in furthering Zionist

---

16   CZA, S25/9838, letter from Fein to Shertok, summer 1938 (no exact date).
17   Ibid.
18   Granot (1940), pp. 318–322; Weitz (1951), p. 9; idem (1995); Goldman (1950), pp. 475–483; Meerovitch (1975), II, pp. 97–100; CZA, A246/891, Weitz's autobiography.

Yosef Weitz

objectives. Prior to the outbreak of the 1936 Arab riots, he defined the fundamental role of the JNF as creating widespread agricultural land reserves upon which a Jewish community earning its livelihood from agricultural labor could develop. In his opinion, the percentage of residents engaged in agriculture should never drop below 40 percent. He did not believe that private initiative could be depended upon to fulfill this goal because private initiative "was dependent on transient circumstances. The burden of this task is imposed first and foremost on the Jewish National Fund."[19] He also maintained at that time in the context of the war between Italy and Ethiopia and the efforts of private enterprise to unload its land reserves that "one cannot rely upon the private individual and one should not entrust him with the responsibility for purchasing the most vital need for our settlement. This responsibility can be shouldered only by the JNF. This is the institution prepared to fulfill this role in normal and abnormal years, in good times and bad times. Only through this institution can we obtain and guarantee the territorial foundation in Palestine."[20] He therefore believed that the JNF

19   *Karnenu* 13, no. 3 (January 1936), p. 36.
20   JNF: Palestine National Committee news bulletin (January 1936), p. 10; see also Land (1937), p. 5.

should be interested in purchasing all the land in Palestine "and the purchase of parts of it is a problem of what comes first and what comes later, a question of price and the like."[21] All the purchase offers which reached the JNF accumulated on Weitz's desk. He was the person responsible for sifting through the proposals and reaching a decision on which proposals merited being brought to the Executive and the Directorate. A perusal of the many files containing the various proposals for 1936–1939, reveals that Weitz employed a series of guidelines in handling them. Some of these were also operative guidelines set down by the Directorate. First of all, he demanded an exact description of the proposed land, a basic requirement for further process.[22] Secondly, the proposals were rejected for areas which were not large enough for the establishment of a complete settlement, save for those cases where the intended purpose was to supplement existing settlements. In contradistinction, Weitz evinced a preference for offers of land which abutted those already owned by the JNF, or bordering on lands owned by the Palestine Land Development Company (PLDC). Lands in complete and large blocs were preferred, whereas divided and scattered plots, which could not be formed into a single unit, were generally turned down. Thus for example, Weitz rejected a detailed plan from the Tsur Company to purchase for the JNF "everything that becomes available in the Sharon region.... The entire Sharon region should be considered as land located in the vicinity of Jewish villages and every parcel offered for sale should be purchased under optimal conditions."[23] Weitz explained his categorical objection in brief: "Our viewpoint does not coincide with this [that of the Tsur Company] and we have no possibility of purchasing scattered plots without knowing in advance that these plots can be united into a suitable unit and that somebody is definitely responsible for clustering and uniting them."[24]

The nature of the soil in terms of its economic potential was also an important criterion in the selection of the proposals. The same applied to

---

21   CZA/KKL5/10517, letter from Weitz to Ben-Shemesh 9.10.1938.

22   See, e.g., CZA, KKL5/8777, the following letters: From Weitz to Hankin 25.2.1936, Weitz to Eliach 6.3.1936, Aricha to Weinberg 26.4.1936; CZA, KKL5/10517, letter from Weitz to Ben-Shemesh 9.10.1938.

23   CZA, KKL5/8916, letter from Tsur – a Company for Settlement Development and Building Ltd. to JNF Head Office 15.11.1937.

24   CZA, KKL5/10516, letter from Weitz to the Tsur Company 19.11.1937.

price, payment terms and the time that would elapse till the land would be received. In cases that Weitz believed the price exorbitant or agreement on payment schedules was not reached, the bid was rejected. If the land on offer was occupied by tenant farmers, this constituted a serious drawback. In cases where such purchases were considered, Weitz sought an advance guarantee in the purchase contract that the lands would be turned over to the JNF when they became vacant. In this context, he strenuously opposed arrangements whereby the JNF would receive lands and carry out settlement preparations before the body selling to the JNF had secured the removal of the tenant farmers. Mafruz lands (single ownership) were also preferable to Musha lands (cooperative ownership), save for cases where a guarantee would be given that all the owners would agree to the sale. It should be emphasized that the Directorate was especially sensitive about such matters as the lowering of prices, spreading out payments, guaranteeing the removal of the tenant farmers by the sellers and the purchase of Mafruz lands. The Directorate's decisions on the purchases were accompanied by directives to the Executive on these matters. Nonetheless, in isolated cases the Directorate authorized purchases where the removal of tenant farmers was the JNF's responsibility.[25]

25 For examples of this policy see CZA, KKL5/8777, the following letters: Weitz to Histadrut Agricultural Center 23.2.1936, Weitz to PLDC 15.3.1936, Aricha to Weinberg 26.4.1936, Weitz to Manfeld 25.11.1936; CZA, S55/201, letter from Weitz to Ruppin 23.2.1936; CZA, S44/60c, report on Ju'ara lands by Weitz 29.3.1936; CZA, KKL9/ 399, letter from Weitz to Hankin 4.12.1936; CZA, KKL5/8777, letter from Weitz to Hankin 5.4.1937; CZA, S44/60b, report by Weitz about Abu Gosh lands 3.3.1937; CZA, S7/404, letter from Weitz to the Central Office for the Settlement of German Jews in Palestine, regarding Nokiv lands; CZA, KKL9/339, letter from Nahmani to Hankin 9.5.1937; CZA, S7/404, letters from Granovsky to Landauer 19.8.1937 and 20.8.1937; CZA, KKL5/8777, letter from Weitz to Hankin 17.9.1937; CZA, KKL5/ 10516, letter from Weitz to Lobman-Haviv 26.11.1937; CZA, KKL5/10516, letter from Tsur Co. to JNF 15.11.1937, letter from Weitz to Tsur Co. 19.11.1937; CZA, KKL9/374, letter from Weitz to Brontman 24.12.1937; CZA, KKL5/10516, letter from Weitz to Blomberg 6.1.1938; CZA, S7/535, letter from Harzfeld to Landauer 31.3.1938; CZA, KKL5/10517, letter from Weitz to Tsur Co. 23.6.1938; CZA, KKL5/ 8905, letter from Weitz to Rassco 29.6.1938; CZA, KKL5/10517, letter from Weitz to Tsur Co. 1.7.1938, letter Weitz to Zuckerman 20.1.1939; CZA, S53/437j, information bulletin of JNF and Keren Hayesod Head Offices 13.7.1939; CZA, KKL10, minutes of JNF Directorate meetings, 6.7.1936, 2.12.1936, 4.1.1937, 25.4.1938, 6.7.1938, 8.8.1938, 28.12.1938, 26.4.1939, 29.6.1939,19.12.1939; CZA, minutes of Jewish Agency Executive meeting, 9.4.1939.

In general Weitz tended to turn down purchase proposals on lands that belonged to Jews. During the period of 1936–1939 he believed that the JNF should invest its limited resources in redeeming lands from non-Jews and not in purchasing lands from Jews.[26] Thus, for example, one of his reasons for opposing in early 1936 the acquisition of lands from the Jewish Company Hamakabim Hakadmonim Association in Gezer was "that the JNF does not see any justification for the purchase of lands from the Hamakabim Hakadmonim Company, especially at this juncture when financial resources are limited and the need for redeeming **new land** is greater."[27] He did not accept the explanation of Avraham Hartzfeld, Chairman of the Agricultural Center of the Histadrut (the General Confederation of Labor founded in 1920), who was interested in purchasing the land for one of the Kibbutzim and contended that even if the land was formally under Jewish ownership "in practice, if they will not extricate the land from the Arab tenant farmers the land will slip totally out of the hands of its Jewish owners."[28] Another purchase proposal, this time from the Gan Shlomo Jewish Company for the settlement of Ruhama in the Northern Negev, was rejected by Weitz "since the JNF is not interested in purchasing land from Jews."[29] The request by Kibbutz Hulata that the JNF purchase on its behalf land from one of the farmers in Yesud Hama'ala (a Moshava in Upper Galilee) was turned down because "it is not one of its tasks [of the JNF] to purchase lands from a Jew in general and especially in a place such as Yesud Hama'ala which is rich in land and poor in people."[30] Weitz also turned down proposals to purchase lands that had been purchased by Jewish companies and individuals or

---

26   See, e.g., CZA, S44/161, letter from Harzfeld to Ben-Gurion 2.1.1936; CZA, S55/201, letter from Weitz to Ruppin 23.2.1936; CZA, KKL/58777, letter from Weitz to Hankin 8.8.1937, letter from Hankin to Weitz 10.8.1937; CZA, S7/404, letter from Landauer to Harzfeld 17.8.1937; CZA, KKL/510516, letter from Weitz to Ettinger 7.12.1938; letter from Weitz to Histadrut Agricultural Center 12.12.1937; CZA, KKL/9/374, letter from Weitz to Brontman 24.12. 1937; CZA, KKL5/10516, letter from Weitz to Salor 29.3.1938; CZA, KKL5/8905, letter from Weitz to Rassco 29.6.1938; CZA, KKL5/8344, letter Weitz to Landauer 22.12.1936; CZA, KKL5/8376, letter from Weitz to Jewish Agency Labor Department 25.6.1937.
27   CZA, S55/201, letter from Weitz to Ruppin 23.2.1936.
28   CZA, S44/161, letter from Harzfeld to Ben-Gurion 2.1.1936.
29   CZA, KKL5/10516, letter from Weitz to Ettinger 7.12.1937.
30   CZA, KKL5/10065, letter from Kvutzat Hulata to JNF 2812.1938, letter from Weitz to Kvutzat Hulata 9.1.1939 –quotation from there.

negotiations had been carried out and agreements reached prior to the Arab riots and because of the ensuing situation sought to sell the lands. Weitz was particularly opposed to purchasing these lands if they were located at a distance from a Jewish area or contiguous to an Arab area.[31] Thus, for example, he turned down the proposal to purchase Kefar Etzion (in the Hebron Hills) from the creditors of the El Ha-Har Jewish Company and those who had purchased from it.[32] He turned down the proposal to purchase Dehaishe near Bethlehem[33] and rejected a proposal to purchase plots from Jews in the abandoned Kefar Uriah estate (in the Judean Hills).[34] In certain cases, not only did he turn down proposals to purchase from Jews, but did not hesitate to add that he expected to receive Jewish-owned lands as a contribution from owners who had abandoned the land and were presently offering it to him for sale.[35] Neither Weitz nor Granovsky displayed great enthusiasm in mid-1939 for Moshe Smilansky's proposal to complete the purchase of lands in the Northern Negev, where Smilansky was involved on behalf of private individuals.[36]

31   CZA, KKL5/10516, letter from Weitz to Salor 29.3.1938; CZA, KKL5/10519, letter
     from Yavneh Company for Settlement in Palestine to Ussishkin 29.5.1939.
32   CZA, KKL5/10519, letter from Halevy-Horowitz, Receiver of the Geula Vebinyan
     Bank, Ltd. 29.6.1939, letter from Weitz to Geula Vebinyan Bank Ltd.13.7.1939. For a
     detailed description see Katz (1992), pp. 19, 40–42.
33   CZA, KKL5/11822, letter from Abulafia to JNF Executive 10.11.1939, letter from
     Weitz to Abulafia 14.11.1939.
34   CZA, KKL5/10519, letter from Weitz to Leizerowitch 26.6.1939.
35   CZA, S55/201, letter from Weitz to Ruppin 23.2.1936; CZA, KKL9/374, letter from
     Weitz to Brontman 24.12.1937; CZA, KKL5/11387, letter from Doshoff to JNF
     3.6.1938, letter from JNF to Rodensky 4.7.1938.
36   CZA, KKL5/8777, letter from Weitz to Smilansky 17.5.1937; CZA, Smilansky's
     memorandum on land he had bought in the vicinity of Gaza, no date, but apparently
     from April 1939; CZA, KKL5/10465, letter from Weitz to Smilanksy 14.7.1939,
     letter from Smilansky to Weitz 6.8.1939; CZA, KKL10, minutes of JNF Directorate
     meeting, 26.4.1939 – especially the address by Granovsky on p. 14. It should be noted
     that during the period dealt with in this chapter, the JNF Directorate did not have
     a clear-cut policy about not purchasing Jewish-owned lands. Granovsky stated in
     connection with the purchase of Nokiv lands from the Kidmat Kinneret Company
     (through PLDC) that: "he was not one of those who objected in principle to the
     purchase of land from Jews," cf. minutes of JNF Directorate, meeting, 6.7.1936 in
     CZA, KKL10. There were also cases of proposals for purchase of land from Jews that
     came up for deliberation and were approved, among which some were not even for
     political or strategic requirements. Cf., CZA, minutes of JNF Directorate meetings,

It should be noted that the principles of the aforementioned policy were generally preserved, even after the end of 1938, when given the political conditions which will be explained in detail below, the JNF's policy was to make as many purchases as possible.[37] It is possible that this policy, derived from the necessity to set priorities dictated by limited financial resources which influenced the extent of purchases in certain regions and locations, motivated Moshe Smilansky's rebuke to Weitz in August 1939. Smilansky, who was apparently not aware of the particulars of the JNF Executive's policy and was disappointed with the way the JNF handled his proposal to purchase Jewish land in the Northern Negev, wrote inter alia:

> Till when will you spiritually perjure yourselves by saying that you made efforts to transfer **all land** that could be transferred **immediately** in order not to miss the opportunity. Indeed...the JNF made every effort, but these efforts thanks to the efforts of the Jewish nation, amount almost to nothing...was there no possibility to **immediately** transfer to Jewish ownership almost 3,000 dunams of Arab citrus groves and 6,000 dunams **near the large Moshavot** at a time when

---

    7.5.1939, 6.7.1936, 25.4.1938, 8.8.1938, 14.12.1938, 26.4.1939, 19.12.1939; CZA, minutes of Jewish Agency Executive meeting, 13.6.1937.

37 See, e.g.: CZA, KKL5/10517, the following letters: Weitz to PLDC 29.12.1938; Weitz to Noteah Co. 29.12.1938, Weitz to Kroll 2.1.1939, Weitz to Zuckerman 20.1.1939, Ben-Shemesh to JNF Head Office 10.2.1939, Weitz to Ben-Shemesh 17.2.1939, Weitz to Ussishkin 20.2.1939, PICA, to JNF 28.3.1939, Weitz to PICA 2.4.1939; CZA, KKL9/238, letter from Sokolowitz to Nahmani 21.4.1939; CZA, S25/6559, memorandum from Smilansky on lands he had purchased near Gaza, no date but apparently from April 1939. CZA, KKL5/10519, letter from Weitz to Ben-Shemesh 28.5.1939, CZA, KKL5/10517, memorandum of Hari of JNF 16.6.1939, regarding Abu Shosha (Gezer) lands; CZA, KKL5/10519, including among other documents, the following letters: Weitz to Tsur Co. 14.6.1939, Weitz to A. Leizerowitz 26.6.1939, Weitz to Tsur Co. 29.6.1939, JNF to I. L. Toibman 30.6.1939; CZA, S53/437j, information bulletin from Head Offices of JNF and Keren Hayesod 13.7.1939, Weitz to Geula and Binyan Bank Ltd. 13.7.1939; CZA, KKL5/10465, letter from Weitz to Smilansky 14.7.1939, letter from Smilansky to Weitz 6.8.1939; CZA, S53/1689, letter from PLDC to Ben-Gurion 3.8.1939; CZA, KKL5/10517, letter from Weitz to Benkser 13.9.1939; CZA, KKL5/11821, memorandum prepared by JNF Lands Department (apparently by Ben-Shemesh) 23.10.1939; CZA, KKL5/10624, letter from Eliyahu & Hayim Romano Co. to Nahmani 13.11.1939; CZA, KKL5/11822, the following letters: Weitz to S. Bitschkow 26.11.1939, Weitz to Glanz 11.12.1939, Weitz to Nahmani 22.12.1939, Weitz to Glanz 25.12.1939, Weitz to Schecter 26.12.1939.

the JNF does not have a solitary dunam to build a worker's dwelling in the village. Was there no possibility at least until **yesterday** to **immediately** transfer in the Lands Registration office, the 5,000 dunams near Gaza which I brought to your attention – was it for lack of will or for the lack of money that you did not accept this land? Are these two isolated cases? I believe that there were tens of similar cases.[38]

On the Way to Centralizing the Purchases of the JNF Lands Department: Replacing the Exclusivity of the Palestine Development Company

From the London Conference in 1920 up to 1936 the vast majority of JNF purchases were implemented via the PLDC. This company was established in 1908, at the initiative of the World Zionist Organization, and the majority of its founding shares were held by the JNF and Keren Hayesod (the financial instrument of the WZO for financing agricultural settlement). It was entrusted by the London Conference to implement purchases on behalf of both the JNF and private Jewish capital. The intention was to bestow "market power" upon a single purchaser which would provide it with an advantage over the many sellers who were in competition with each other.[39] It was stipulated in the agreement between the JNF and the PLDC, signed in the early 1920s, that the PLDC would inform the JNF about all lands it intended to purchase, and the JNF would have first right of refusal in any purchase where the PLDC was involved (except in cases where the PLDC was acting on behalf of a third party). Likewise, the PLDC was obligated to implement all purchases which the JNF should request it to make on its behalf. It appears that this agreement was also linked to an increase in JNF held founding shares in the PLDC, which was part of a liquidation of the PLDC's debt to the JNF which took place in the early twenties. The increase

---

38 CZA, KKL5/10465, letter from Smilansky to Weitz 6.8.1939, letter from Weitz to Smilansky 14.7.1939.
39 Ashbel (1969), p. 78; Report Exec. (1921), p. 74; Merhavia, p. 226; CZA, J85/396, letter from Ussishkin to Gluskin 7.12.1936; Congress (1925), pp. 43–44.

in founding shares also guaranteed the JNF a majority of the votes in the
PLDC General Assembly which "could influence the conduct of PLDC
land purchases and JNF land purchase policy."[40] The PLDC was therefore
an implementing body (but possessing a degree of policy independence)
while the JNF and private capital were the financial backers both in terms
of placing advance orders and by subsequently purchasing lands from the
PLDC. Thus a division of labor was created in land redemption, as the
PLDC by its own testimony served

> as a necessary instrument for the JNF.... Under the difficult
> circumstances from a political and legal standpoint besetting lands
> purchased in Palestine, which involved protracted negotiations,
> frequent lawsuits and the ever present danger of a serious loss, the
> JNF could not assume direct negotiations with the sellers. For this
> purpose it needs a company like the PLDC that would assume all this
> complicated business. By dealing with the PLDC the JNF's expenses
> in purchases are reduced to 1.5% on lands which it had ordered and
> to 3% on lands that had been purchased previously by the PLDC at its
> own risk. These expenses are incomparably lower than the expenses
> that would be incurred in maintaining a separate and permanent JNF
> purchase department.[41]

Yehoshua Hankin was the person who managed and plotted the course of
PLDC activity. His experience in land purchases dating from the 1890s
was incomparable. He worked for the company from 1910, and from 1926
until his death in 1945 (at the age of 80) he was also one of its directors.[42]

During 1936–1939, the JNF ceased implementing its purchases
exclusively via the PLDC. The PLDC through Hankin and his assistants,

---

40   The agreement related to both urban and rural land. It also stipulated that the PLDC
    could not make purchases for a third party without the prior agreement of the JNF,
    in cases where such land bordered on JNF held land or "within those areas that came
    under JNF land policy." Cf., CZA, KKL10, minutes of meeting of JNF Executive in
    Palestine, 3.4.1922; Reichman (1979), pp. 39–40; Ashbel (1929), pp. 44, 78; Report
    Exec. (1929) – the quotation from there.
41   Report Exec. (1925), pp. 171–172. See also CZA, KKL10, minutes of JNF Directorate
    meeting, 1.5.1922.
42   For further details see, e.g., Ashbel (1929); Agmon (1951b), pp. 147–154; Meerovitch
    (1975), I, pp. 77–105.

continued to make an appreciable part of JNF purchases,[43] but the JNF
ever increasingly linked up with other bodies – private individuals and
companies alike – in implementing purchases. Furthermore, direct contacts
were made between land sellers and the JNF Land Department.[44]

Yosef Nahmani was one of those private individuals with whom the
JNF established contact at a relatively early stage. During 1922–1935, he
specialized in purchasing lands in the Galilee for PICA (Palestine Jewish
Colonial Association), and at the end of 1936 he began operating in the

---

43   From 1936 till August 1940, the JNF carried out 60% of its purchases through the
     PLDC. Cf. CZA, S25/6546, letter from Weitz to Hankin, 18.8.1940; also CZA, KKL5/
     11820, list of lands purchased through PLDC during 1935–1940. Cf., CZA, KKL5/
     10514, the land reserves of the JNF in town and country, 1938; CZA, KKL5/15635,
     JNF land purchases during 1940–1947.

44   See, e.g., CZA, KKL5/8777, letter from the Arab landowner Katit to JNF 19.10.1936,
     letter from Weitz to Manfeld 25.12.1936; CZA, KKL5/10516, the following letters:
     Tsur Co. to JNF Head Office 15.11.1937, Weitz to Tsur Co. 19.11.1937, Weitz to
     Lobman-Haviv 26.11.1937; CZA, A107/816, letter from Winschall to Hankin
     5.12.1937, Hankin to Winschall 6.12.1937; CZA, S53/1675b, letter from Thon to
     Kaplan 8.12.1937; CZA, KKL5/10516, letter from Weitz to Danin 12.1.1938, letter
     from Weitz to Nahmani 2.2.1938; CZA, KKL5/8905, letter from Weitz to Rassco
     29.6.1938; CZA, A246/699, letter from Weitz to Ben-Shemen 28.10.1938; CZA,
     KKL5/10517, letter from Hankin to JNF Head Office 19.12.1938, letter from Ben
     Shemesh to JNF Head Office 10.2.1929; CZA, KKL5/10519, the following letters:
     Yavneh Co. to Ussishkin 29.5.1939, Weitz to Yavneh Co. 9.6.1939, memorandum
     from Huri re Abu-Shisha lands 16.6.1939; CZA, KKL5/11822, letter from Weitz to
     Tsur Co. 28.1.1940, letter from Weitz to PLDC 8.12.1940; CZA, microfilm CM428/2,
     minutes of PLDC Executive meeting, 8.12.1939; CZA, KKL10, minutes of JNF
     Directorate meetings, 2.1.1936, 6.7.1936, 3.3.1937, 25.4.1938. In fact already in 1924,
     the JNF Directorate had decided not to limit its land purchases to those made through
     the agency of the PLDC but would also buy through other companies and through
     private buyers and would "also try to make land purchases through its own means." To
     this end, it was also decided to gather information about possible sales, and to set up
     archives in which information would be registered systematically and where maps and
     other documentation regarding the purchase of lands would be concentrated. Cf. CZA,
     KKL10, minutes of JNF Directorate meeting 29.1.1924. The reason for these decisions
     was probably a certain dissatisfaction with the functioning of the PLDC and annoyance
     regarding the debts it had incurred and disagreement with the rate of commission it was
     paying – issues that were intimated during JNF Directorate meetings and the decisions
     taken. Cf. ibid., minutes of meetings, 23.2.1923, 17.5.1923, 29.9.1925, 30.9.1925;
     Amit (1998), pp. 158–163, 175–178. However, in fact, up to the mid 1930s the PLDC
     continued to serve as the main land-purchasing agent for the JNF.

same capacity for the JNF. At first his purchases were coordinated by Hankin and in agreement with the JNF he also functioned on behalf of the PLDC. However, in the course of time, Nahmani worked exclusively on behalf of the JNF, but disputes with Hankin also arose.[45] As we shall see in the following chapter, Nahmani subsequently became a JNF employee in the post of Director of the JNF's Galilee office in Tiberias.

Among other private individuals who served as purchase agents for the JNF during 1936–1939 was Yoav Zuckerman of Gedera who specialized in making purchases mainly in the Judean Plains and the South,[46] Gad Machnes of Petah Tiqva,[47] Attorney Dr. Avraham Weinshal,[48] and Attorney Aharon Ben-Shemesh, who worked for the JNF, both in an independent capacity and also within the framework of the Tsur Company.[49] In the early 1920s Avraham Ben-Shemesh was employed by the PLDC but left as a result of tensions with Yehoshua Hankin.[50] It should be emphasized that these persons, even if they worked for the JNF, were not considered as employees in the full sense of the term and this was not their exclusive occupation.

45   See, e.g., CZA, KKL9/339, letter from Nahmani to JNF Head Office 6.11.1936; CZA, KKL9/22, letter from Weizmann to Nahmani 23.12.1936; CZA, KKL5/10516, letter from Nahmani to JNF Head Office 8.2.1938; CZA, A246/747, letter from Weitz to Nahmani 24.11.1938; CZA, KKL5/10517, letter from Weitz to Luzia in Damascus 7.11.1939; CZA, KKL9/446, letter from Nahmani to the Lands Department in the JNF Head Office 7.11.1939; CZA, KKL5/10624, letter from the Eliyahu & Hayim Romano Land Purchasing Agency to Nahmani 13.11.1939; CZA, KKL9/339, letter from Weitz to Nahmani 24.11.1939, and letter from Weitz to E. Romano 24.11.1939; CZA, KKL5/10624, letter from Hankin to Nahmani 17.12.1939; Weitz (1951), p. 557.

46   CZA, KKL5/10517, the following letters: Zuckerman to Weitz 3.5.1938, 10.11.1938, Weitz to Tsur Co. 23.6.1938, Zuckerman to Weitz 8.12.1938.

47   See, e.g., Weitz (1951), pp. 17, 559; CZA, A238/8, letter from Hankin to Ussishkin 27.11.1939.

48   See, e.g., CZA, A107/816, letters from Weinshal to Hankin 5.12.1937, 6.12.1937; CZA, S53/1675d, letter from Thon to Kaplan 8.12.1937; CZA, KKL5/10517, letter from Weinshal to Hankin 7.12.1938.

49   See, e.g., CZA, A246/699, letter from Weitz to Ben-Shemesh 28.10.1938; CZA, KKL5/10517, letter from Ben-Shemesh to JNF Head Office 10.2.1939; CZA, KKL5/10519, letter from Weitz to Ben-Shemesh 28.5.1939; Shimon Ben-Shemesh, personal interview, Jerusalem 27.11.1996; Hiram Danin, personal interview, Jerusalem 8.10.1997.

50   Shimon Ben-Shemesh, ibid., Hiram Danin, ibid.

Among the private companies with implemented purchases together with the JNF, were Tsur, the Development and Construction Company, which also engaged in land purchases throughout the country. It was owned by a number of partners including Yisrael Teiber, M. Palai, Y. Schreier and Aharon Ben-Shemesh. The latter served as the company's legal adviser and also carried out purchases on its behalf.[51] In certain cases, the JNF also employed the services of the Geulah,[52] Hanoteah[53] and Yavneh Companies.[54] Weitz also had no qualms about maintaining direct links with PLDC workers in the Haifa office without Hankin's knowledge.[55]

Lawyer Aharon Ben-Shemesh

51 CZA, KKL5/10516, letter from Tsur Co. to JNF Head Office 15.11.1937; CZA, A246/699, letter from Weitz to Ben-Shemesh 28.10.1938; CZA, KKL5/10517, letter from Tsur Co. to JNF Head Office 6.5.1938; CZA, KKL5/11822, letter from JNF to Tsur Co. 28.1.1940; CZA, KKL5/10475, letter from Tsur Co. to JNF 6.9.1938; S. Ben-Shemesh, personal interview (see n. 49); CZA, KKL5/9946, letter from Tsur Co. to JNF Head Office 27.12.1937, letter from Weitz to Tsur Co. 5.1.1938.

52 The JNF cooperated extensively with the Geula Co. in the purchase of lands of Hanita. Cf. e.g., CZA, KKL5/10026, letter from Weinshal to JNF 5.1.1938; CZA, J85/1396, letter from Granovsky and Weitz to Geula Co. 10.1.1938.

53 See, e.g., CZA, KKL5/8905, letter from Weitz to Rassco 29.6.1938.

54 CZA, KKL5/10519, letter from Yavneh Co. to Ussishkin 29.5.1939, letter from Weitz to Yavneh Co. 9.6.1939.

55 See, e.g., CZA, A246/747, letters from Weitz to PLDC employees in Haifa: Stromeza, Wolf and the Danin brothers (whom Weitz called "colleagues") 28.10.1938, 24.11.1938.

During 1936–1939, no coordinating framework existed for the demarcation of the areas of activity for the various bodies engaged in purchases and upon whom the JNF Land Department relied. Since they were privately owned, the various bodies worked independently.[56] Therefore, it is not surprising that situations developed where a number of these bodies were involved in transactions for the acquisition of the same plots – a reality that often hampered the purchase. Weitz generally sought to prevent dual or triple involvements in the same proposal in which the JNF was interested. In those cases where a particular agent commenced work on a purchase proposal, where another JNF affiliated body, including the PLDC, had a previous involvement, Weitz insisted that the second agent should remove itself from the purchase. Likewise, Weitz demanded that various middlemen refrain from intervening in purchases where the JNF was already involved with another agent, or referred the intermediary to those bodies which were already involved on behalf of the JNF. Since by 1936, the JNF had increasingly become almost the sole Jewish body engaged in purchasing agricultural lands, it was difficult to spurn such requests/demands from Weitz.[57] At the close of the period discussed in this

56   Tsur Co., for example, did not restrict its activity to a particular area, cf. CZA, KKL5/ 10516, letter from Tsur Co. to JNF Head Office 15.11.1937; CZA, KKL5/10517, letter from Tsur Co. to JNF Head Office 6.5.1938; CZA, KKL5/11822, letters from Weitz to Tsur Co. 15.12.1939, 17.12.1939. It should be pointed out that in 1936–1937 various proposals were examined for the creation of a body that would coordinate the activities of the main purchasing bodies of land from Arabs, but none of these plans was carried out. Cf. CZA, KKL5/8745, letter to Horin from Yakhin Co. 23.11.1936 with the attached proposal to create means for control and organization of lands in Palestine and their sale overseas; CZA, S55/201, memorandum by K. Ruppin on the establishment of a Lands Office in the Jewish Agency; CZA, KKL5/8745, letter to the members of the committee for the examination of the possibility of creating means for the organization and control of land matters 31.12.1936; ibid., letter to Weitz concerning the council for the organization of the purchase of lands and control of sales to Jews in Palestine and in the Diaspora 24.1.1937; CZA, S25/6542, letter from Weitz to Kaplan 17.5.1937 concerning the conclusions of the committee that had deliberated on the establishment of an organization for the purchase of lands in Palestine (also in files KKL5/8745, S53/1686a).

57   CZA, KKL5/8777, letter from Weitz to Eliach 6.3.1936, letter from Weitz to Tsur Co. 30.9.1937; CZA, J85/396, letter from Ussishkin to Gluskin 7.12.1936; CZA, KKL9/22, summary of minutes of meeting between A. Granovsky and Hankin 25.3.1937; CZA, KKL5/10516, the following letters: letter from Weitz to the Histadrut Agricultural

chapter, we can distinguish Weitz's tendency to finalize a list of agencies with which his department collaborated and assign each of them distinct areas of activity.[58]

Despite the aforesaid, Weitz's failure to coordinate (deliberate or otherwise) in certain cases with Hankin, and the direct contacts Weitz had with PLDC employees behind the back of Hankin, produced a situation whereby both Hankin and his personnel, as well as the private individuals with whom the JNF was affiliated, worked on the very same land purchase proposal earmarked for the JNF. This situation not only exacerbated relations between Hankin and Weitz, and between Hankin and agents working for the JNF, but it also hampered the purchase itself. It thus occurred, to the dismay of all those involved, that on certain Galilee purchases Hankin and Attorney Avraham Weinshal or Weinshal and employees in the PLDC Haifa office were simultaneously and uncoordinatedly functioning. In the beginning of December 1938, Weinshal wrote, for example, to Hankin:

> I have been told that officials of the Haifa bureau of the PLDC not only dealt with the matter of Hirbat El Masood, but also entered into negotiations regarding the lands of Arbin, Geordia and Admit. I have no possibility of verifying whether this information is correct, but it is undoubtedly most important that I should know what is going on in this matter because I have been dealing with it for some time. It is inadmissible that I should be told to carry out the purchase of the land while I am in the process of dealing with it; other people will enter into negotiations with the owners or with middlemen regarding purchase of the land for that very same purchaser – the JNF. Such a situation only leads to price increases and various complications which have caused delay in finalizing the purchase.

Center 17.12.1937, letter from Weitz to Lani 28.12.1937, letter from Granovsky to Z. Cohen 2812.1937; CZA, KKL5/10517, letter from Weitz to Tsur Co. 23.6.1938, letter from Weitz to Teichmann 1.7.1938; CZA, KKL5/11822, letters from Weitz to Glanz & Riefen Land Agency 11.12.1939, 20.12.1939, letters from Weitz to Tsur Co. 15.12.1939, 17.12.1939, 25.12.1939, 31.12.1939.

58   CZA, KKL5/10517, letter from Weitz to Luzia 9.7.1939; CZA, KKL9/448, letter from Nahmani to JNF Head Office 7.11.1939; CZA, KKL9/339, letter from Weitz to Nahmani 24.11.1939, letter from Weitz to E. Romano 24.11.1939; CZA, KKL5/10624, letter from Hankin to Nahmani 17.12.1939; CZA, KKL5/11822, letter from Weitz to Tsur Co. 15.12.1939; letter from Weitz to Glanz and Reifen 31.12.1939.

After posing a series of demands, Weinshal sums up as follows:

> Only in such a manner will it be possible to guarantee undivided activity and prevent irrational competition over the purchase of land for the very same purchaser.[59]

Why did the JNF cease from 1936, as opposed to its previous practice, to view the PLDC as the exclusive or nearly exclusive body which would make purchases on its behalf, and why did the JNF change this policy and work with a variety of agents? It would seem that this can be explained as a consequence of a number of factors. Firstly, the JNF expanded its sphere of activity in land purchases at the time that constraints induced the PLDC to cutback its own sphere of activity. Secondly, the JNF was disappointed that the PLDC and Hankin had rejected the JNF's proposals for changes and the introduction of efficiencies in their method of operation and especially regarding greater coordination between Hankin and the JNF Executive. Thirdly, the difficulty occasioned when "two monarchs" – Weitz and Hankin – sought to rule "under one crown." Fourthly, the PLDC's failure to meet its obligations aroused major dissatisfaction in the JNF Executive. Fifthly, differences of opinion emerged between JNF leaders and Hankin regarding the nature and scope of lands purchase work to be effected by national capital in the years 1936–1939. Below we will examine these factors in detail.

The expansion in the JNF's sphere of activity as the consequence of the PLDC's difficulties
Time-related factors produced a situation where the JNF had to significantly expand its work in land purchases over and beyond that prior to 1936. It was no longer a matter of dealing with purchases of extensive areas owned by effendis and isolated estate owners, but rather the purchase of more limited areas belonging to hundreds of owners which required a concerted effort to locate both the sellers and the plots. The PLDC found it difficult

---

59   CZA, KKL5/10517, letter from Weinshal to Hankin – quotation from there. See also CZA, KKL5/10517, letter from Hankin to the PLDC Haifa Office 7.12.1938; CZA, A107/816, letter from Weinshal to Hankin 5.12.1937, letter from Hankin to Weinshal 6.12.1937; CZA, S53/1675d, letter from Thon to Kaplan 8.12.1937; CZA, A246/747, letter from Weitz to employees of the PLDC Haifa office – Stromeza, Wolf and Danin 24.11.1938; CZA, KKL5/10517, letter from Hankin to JNF Head Office 19.12.1938.

to simultaneously consummate extensive and complex transactions. As a result of the "Hula Concession" purchase in 1935, the company's resources dwindled significantly. The expectations that it would be able to sell the concession to the JNF and to the Amica Company, did not materialize. Furthermore, from 1936, the investment by private capital in land purchases dwindled significantly and thus the PLDC was left with an inventory of lands and liquidity difficulties. Trespassing by Arabs on Jewish-owned lands increased considerably during the period of the Arab disturbances, numerous difficulties in finding a solution to the problem of tenant farmers on lands which the company had purchased and the diminution of the special credit conditions the company had enjoyed – all these also combined to encumber the company's ability to function on a scale that could satisfy the JNF's demands. As explained below, the JNF itself began to cooperate with private capital for agricultural purchases which therefore reduced still further its need to rely on the PLDC in this sphere. Under these conditions, the JNF Executive could no longer continue its almost exclusive reliance on the PLDC.[60]

Disappointment in the JNF over the rejection of its demands by the PLDC and the Weitz–Hankin dispute

Differences of opinion between the two bodies had emerged already in the 1920s, due to conflicting interests whereby the PLDC and Hankin did not completely fulfill their part of the agreement with the JNF made in the early 1920s. In the 1930s, by virtue of its position as the principal buyer from the PLDC, the JNF Executive insisted on greater coordination and participation in the process of land purchases. In the JNF's opinion, these could prevent various mishaps, the cost of which the JNF would have to shoulder in the end, although it was not at fault. Likewise, the JNF recommended to the PLDC that it expand its staff involved in land purchase activities by adding experienced personnel and take steps to establish coordination between them and the JNF. These proposals and demands raised by the JNF already prior to 1936, were reiterated with

---

60   Katz (in press); CZA, S25/6546, joint letter from Weitz and Granovsky to Hankin 18.8.1940, letter from Hankin to JNF Head Office 11.8.1940; Weitz (1951), p. 16; Goldstein (1990), pp. 254–259.

greater insistence after 1936.[61] Irrespective of whether the demands were based on practical considerations or whether they revealed deep frustration over the fact that the PLDC, which to a large extent owed its very existence to the JNF,[62] was excluding the JNF also from matters directly related to it, the import was the same. By accepting these proposals, Hankin and the PLDC would be agreeing to reduced centralization in land purchase work which had hitherto been controlled by Hankin, and employing the work methods in which he believed and had utilized for decades, as well as to a derogation of his undisputed status in the area.[63] It is not surprising that the proposals were rejected by the PLDC, and especially by Hankin. "Therefore the JNF Executive had no recourse but to work according to its method – that is, to control its own affairs. Even if for such purpose you will have to use other agents outside your company."[64]

There is no doubt that Weitz, with his dominant personality, and enjoying the confidence of Ussishkin, could no longer agree to a contradictory situation. The JNF was on the verge of becoming the exclusive Jewish body engaged in agricultural land purchases, but the direction of purchase activity and control over everything connected with it, were still entrusted to Hankin, while Weitz, the JNF's Lands Department head remained, as before, outside the picture. It is conceivable that Hankin's advanced age (in the latter half of the 1930s he was already over 70), as opposed to the relatively younger Weitz (who had not reached 50), with all that this signified, also stoked Weitz' aspirations to succeed Hankin as the director of the national land redemption project. The pushing aside of Hankin by expanding the JNF's affiliation with additional purchasing bodies was therefore unavoidable.[65] It is obvious that the period in which the PLDC's

---

61 CZA, S25/6546, joint letter from Weitz and Granovsky to Hankin 18.8.1940. For further information about the relations between the two bodies see Amit (1998), pp. 151–178.

62 See, e.g., CZA, J85/396, letter from Ussishkin to Gluskin 7.12.1936.

63 For the methods Hankin used in the purchase of lands and the centralization he insisted upon, see, e.g., Granovsky (1952), pp. 167–173; Agmon (1951b), pp. 147–154; Meerovitch (1975), I, pp. 77–105; Agricultural Center Bulletin (Dec. 1945), pp. 2–7.

64 See n. 52 above – the quotation from there. See also CZA, KKL5/3273, letter from Weitz to Ussishkin 18.7.1929.

65 Shimon Ben-Shemesh, personal interview in Jerusalem 27.11.1996; Hiram Danin, personal interview in Jerusalem 8.10.1997. It should be noted that already in 1929, Weitz complained to Ussishkin about Hankin's lack of cooperation on land matters

prestige was on the decline because of the difficulties described above, and on the other hand when the JNF was in the spotlight, constituted a convenient moment for Weitz to snatch the leadership in land purchases which had been fulfilled by Hankin for decades. On the way to "seizing leadership" Weitz did not hesitate to "join up" with PLDC field workers while they were still working for the PLDC, and all this was done behind the back of Hankin.[66] Subsequently, these employees would transfer to the JNF and work under Weitz's supervision.[67]

Hankin, who was already displeased by Weitz's assumption of the post of JNF Lands Department director,[68] had few options left. He sent off letters to the leaders of Zionist institutions including Weizmann,[69] in which he attacked the JNF for the new technique it had adopted in expanding its affiliations with bodies other than the PLDC, and outlined the damage this technique would cause the land redemption project. Nonetheless, he could not turn the clock back and return the JNF to the bosom of the PLDC. Following are a number of passages from his bitter letters on the subject:

> I find it difficult to comprehend your entire method regarding lands purchases. You are abandoning the official office – the PLDC – and are going off with pimps. You are paying exorbitant prices and these

---

in general and especially about the possibilities of land purchases. Weitz stressed the absurdity arising from the PLDC's plans to take command of all matters relating to land purchase and determining the Zionist land policy. Weitz complained that "our land institution [JNF], which was given the most important task of controlling the land policy of the Jewish people, was in a situation of lack of information, and not knowing in which direction it was going," and he therefore demanded that "the time has come that the Jewish National Fund should truly direct the land policy, not passively but actively." Cf. CZA, KKL5/3273, letter from Weitz to Ussishkin 18.7.1929.

66 CZA, A246/747, letters from Weitz to PLDC Haifa employees – Stromeza, Wolf and the Danin brothers, 28.10.1938, 24.11.1938; CZA, KKL5/10517, the following letters: Hankin to the PLDC Haifa office 7.12.1938, Weinshal to Hankin 7.12.1938, Weitz to Hankin 12.12.1938.

67 See below, Chap. Three, p. 151.

68 According to Hiram Danin (in a personal interview in Jerusalem 8.10.1997), who worked closely with Hankin, when Weitz assumed the post he demanded that Hankin provide him with detailed reports on purchases being made on behalf of the JNF. Hankin's reaction was to protest to Ussishkin: "Is this youngster going to give me orders?!"

69 CZA, KKL5/10468, letter from Hankin to Weizmann 2.11.1938.

activities are harming our entire land policy....[70] Your aforementioned letter purports that Mr. Machnes presumably handled this matter, when you know full well how much time, effort and expenses our company has invested in the purchase of land of Samara. We were just about to finalize with the sellers...when Machnes appeared and he only had to raise his hand to pluck the ripe fruit, the fruit of our tiresome and prolonged labor. Was it not your obligation to refrain from abetting Mr. Machnes in this matter and to inform him explicitly from the very first moment that he should not intrude upon this matter in order not to compete with us when there was only one purchaser [the JNF].... It is worthwhile noting at this opportunity, that if Mr. Machnes had not intruded in the matter of the aforementioned purchase, our company, in the absence of any competitor, would have definitely managed to bring down the price and purchase the land for you on the best of terms and with the minimum of expenses.... Land redemption is the JNF's *raison d'etre* and it is also the purpose of the PLDC activity. It is difficult to understand why we shouldn't work shoulder to shoulder in mutual understanding and in cognizance of the historical responsibility which rests upon us regarding our destitute people.... It is difficult to understand why in this tragic moment, when we need to unite all our paltry forces in order to stand in the breach, why particularly now rifts are emerging in our relationship in which the PLDC is not at fault – rifts which are increasing and widening until they will become one deep abyss.... It is superfluous to add that under the terms of unfair competition at our expense, when acting on behalf of the same purchaser – the JNF – Mr. Machnes will enjoy the upper hand. Again he will pluck the fruit of our prodigious labor.... By all these activities the list of which grows longer, day-by-day, they are undermining the existence of the PLDC. You are effacing its value, limiting and totally paralyzing its activity. It would be worth reminding you, among other things, the difficulties caused us on your account until we receive our money from you, while you always hasten to pay up in cash for all land that is not purchased via us. However, at the very same time, you should not forget that you are besmirching by this behavior the good

70   CZA, A238/8, letter from Hankin to JNF Head Office 7.2.1937.

name of the JNF by directly associating with these unconscionable pimps who purchase lands for you without any scruples about the means used. In such a manner, you are allowing them to cast a heavy shadow over the national institution that is so dear to us and you are handing our sworn external enemies a most dangerous tool. I am very sorry, My dear Mr. Ussishkin...but it would be best in all respects, if you became aware of the bitter truth in all its nakedness, while time still remains, and take the necessary vigorous measures in order to uproot the evil that has become so rooted in that department of yours which is handling land purchases.[71]

Yehoshua Hankin on the bank of Nahal Hadera in Heftziba, 1935

71   CZA, A238/8, letter from Hankin to Ussishkin 27.11.1939. See also CZA, KKL5/8895, letter from Hankin to Ussishkin 6.2.1938; CZA, KKL5/10468, letter from Hankin to Weizmann 2.11.1938; CZA, KKL5/10517, letter from Hankin to JNF 19.12.1938. See also CZA, A238/8 letter from Hankin to JNF 7.2.1937; CZA, KKL5/8346, letter from Hankin to JNF 27.4.1937, letter from Hankin to JNF 21.5. 1937.

Hankin unsuccessfully demanded that the JNF employees abandon their deals with the Arabs.[72] However, he was unable to do anything but to come to terms with the situation that had developed and concede that the PLDC could no longer determine "a land policy without the JNF, because if the JNF affiliates with various pimps, no policy which it sets will prevail."[73]

The PLDC's failure to fulfill obligations
Within the JNF there were feelings of disappointment and even stronger sentiments against the PLDC's failure to meet previous obligations, a failure which inflicted damage upon the JNF and the entire settlement project. Additionally there was a sense that the JNF monies entrusted to the PLDC were not fulfilling the purposes for which they had been allocated. These sentiments also fueled the process as a result of which the PLDC lost its role as the exclusive land purchaser on behalf of the JNF. The JNF was most irate when the PLDC did not meet its obligations to evict tenant farmers from the lands of Yoqne'am (in Lower Galilee), which the JNF had purchased from the PLDC by the end of 1934. Criticism was leveled over the specific failure to meet the obligation which severely damaged the process of settlement of Kibbutz Hazorea, impaired the commitments the JNF had tendered, breached the trust which various parties who intended to assist the settlement of Kibbutz Hazorea had placed in the JNF and adversely effected the JNF's income. The JNF was greatly angered over the entire way in which the PLDC handled the issue and the fact that for a long time the PLDC "had deceived both the JNF and the Kibbutz [Hazorea]." This aggravated the suspicion that the PLDC preferred the interests of

---

72   CZA, S53/1675d, letter from Thon to Kaplan 8.12.1937. CZA, A107/816, letter from Hankin to Weinshal 6.12.1937 – in this letter to Weinshal, who, as mentioned above, acted on behalf of the JNF in the purchase of lands in Upper Galilee, Hankin wrote: "You are certainly aware that the Palestine Land Development Company, Ltd., centralizes all activities relating to the purchase of land in Palestine and you have no right to interfere in these activities. You are an attorney and you should deal with matters concerning your profession, and if you wish to assist to your utmost ability, we hereby wish to thank you for your help but this assistance should be restricted to your role as attorney and for the fee of an attorney."

73   CZA, microfilm no. CM428/2, minutes of PLDC Directorate meeting, 8.12.1939. See also CZA, KKL5/10624, letter from Hankin to Nahmani 17.12.1939; CZA, KKL9/446, letter from Nahmani to Lands Department of the JNF Head Office 7.11.1939, and cf. letter from Hankin to JNF Head Office 7.2.1937.

private settlers in the Moshava of Yoqne'am over those of the JNF and Hazorea. Although it is not our task to decide the question of whether the JNF was justified in its severe criticism of the PLDC, it is pertinent for the purpose of this study to recognize the degree of tension which existed between the two bodies, the lack of trust and suspicion which undoubtedly contributed to the process of separation between the two. In the course of a special meeting the Directorate convened in October 1937 on this issue, Weitz suggested that the JNF vigorously denounce the PLDC's conduct and demand the return of JNF monies invested in Yoqne'am, together with interest as well as the monies invested by Hazorea. Rabbi Berlin demanded that severe measures be taken against the PLDC, whereas Ussishkin emphasized, "the fact under discussion was just another link in a chain of many facts all adducing to non-fulfillment of obligations by the PLDC toward the JNF. The JNF Executive had not divulged this information to the Directorate because of the feelings toward Yehoshua Hankin. However, this time, the PLDC has perpetrated an exceptional inequity toward the JNF which cannot be ignored in any way without a fitting response and vigorous action." Granovsky, who was the most extreme spokesman in the discussion, called for issuing an ultimatum to evict the tenant farmers and if the PLDC would not meet it, then "the JNF would cease its work relations with it."

Nonetheless, the Directorate decided to content itself with dispatching a sharply worded letter to the PLDC rather than presenting an ultimatum. It was not realistic to totally sever contacts with the PLDC, in view of the fact that the JNF was affiliated with the PLDC in the consummation of a number of purchases in various locations "and the JNF has no possibility to drop these purchases in the middle."[74] It should be noted that the issue

---

74   See in detail CZA, KKL10, minutes JNF Directorate meeting, 18.10.1937 – all the
     quotations from there. See also CZA S7/404, letter from Weitz to Central Office for the
     Settlement of German Jewry in Palestine 18.4.1937 – in this letter Weitz stresses: "The
     JNF will not agree to and will not allow any settlement activities on Nokiv lands before
     it will be transferred to the JNF by the PLDC, unenclosed and free of tenant farmers up
     to all its boundaries. We are certain that you will agree with us not to make the same
     mistake as was made regarding the Yoqne'am lands and that the act of Mafruz had not
     been carried out although it had been undertaken by the PLDC, prevents still today
     the activities of the settlements to whom they had been designated." In a personal
     interview on 22.10.1997, Hiram Danin pointed out the extreme difficulties the PLDC
     faced in evicting the tenant farmers because of the legal issues involved. He stated

of the eviction did not reach its conclusion even a year later. At a meeting of the Directorate in July 1938, sharp and bitter words were again uttered against the PLDC, but no decision was taken to sever working relations with it.[75]

Differences between Hankin and the JNF regarding the general land policy of the Zionist Organization

Beyond the issue of the PLDC's failure to fulfill its obligation to evict the tenant farmers in Yoqne'am and the ensuing complications to the JNF as a result, during the years 1936–1939 substantial differences of opinion emerged between Hankin and the JNF regarding the general land policy that the World Zionist Organization should adopt during that period. The first dispute erupted already in 1936, immediately after the outbreak of the Arab disturbances. Hankin demanded a total cessation of land purchases from the Arabs as an act of retribution against the Arabs which would be maintained "until they would express their regret over their actions and would conclude a peace treaty in accordance with the local customs – a treaty which noted and publicized that they expressed regrets, pledged future cooperation with us, while recognizing our rights."[76]

Ussishkin, who was one of the recipients of Hankin's letter, was astounded by the very proposal, especially since it emanated from Hankin, who had always favored the continuation of practical measures in Palestine under all circumstances. Ussishkin also rejected the rationale behind the proposal and in this fashion he expressed the general attitude within the

---

that the JNF Directorate did not understand this because it was influenced by Weitz's reports claiming that the blame should be placed squarely on the PLDC.

75   CZA, KKL10, minutes of JNF Directorate meeting, 6.7.1938. See also CZA, KKL5/ 10468, letter from Weitz to Hankin 24.2.1939, complaining about the non-eviction of tenant farmers from the lands of Rehaniya as had been undertaken by the PLDC. It should be pointed out that at the beginning of 1939 the PLDC accused Granovsky that during his visit to Europe he had made derogative statements regarding the lands at Heftziba that the PLDC had proposed for sale and thus had caused it harm. See CZA, KKL5/4495, letter from Thon to Granovsky 21.3.1939. See also additional complaints by the PLDC against the JNF, ibid., letter from Thon to Ussishkin 5.8.1938.

76   CZA, KKL5/7421, letter from Hankin to Zionist General Council in Zurich 19.8.1936. Six months prior to this, at the beginning of 1936, Hankin had submitted a plan for the purchase of 4 million dunams of land throughout the country. Cf. CZA, S25/6546, Hankin's plan for the redemption of lands during the next decade, 7.1.1936.

JNF. He summed up his reply to Hankin: "No my friend. We are not going to follow you on this path."[77]

A short time later, further disputes emerged. Hankin, as opposed to Ussishkin, expressed vigorous support for the idea of the Partition Plan as published by the Royal Commission in December 1937.[78] In total contradistinction to the position taken by the Jewish Agency and the JNF,[79] at the close of 1937 Hankin did not attach any importance to the urgency of land purchases in the Galilee, to guarantee the area's inclusion within the boundaries of the Jewish State when partition would be implemented in practice. On the basis of the Royal Commission's recommendations, which did not include the vicinity of Beersheba within the boundaries of the Jewish State, despite the existing Jewish land holdings there, he drew a corollary for the Galilee: "The English won't take into account whether we have a few thousand dunams and they will do what they think right for their own benefit."[80] Hankin continued to believe in the idea of partition as the sole method for solving the Arab–Jewish dispute even a year later after the Partition Commission had published its findings, claiming that it was impossible to implement the Royal Commission's plan. Due to his adherence to the partition idea, Hankin argued that land should be purchased only within the boundaries of the alternative partition plan formulated by the Jewish Agency in 1938 and submitted to the Partition Commission.[81] This position was also rejected by the JNF as will be described in detail below.

77 CZA, KKL5/7421, letter from Ussishkin to Hankin 19.2.1937 (also in KKL5/8741). See also on relations between Ussishkin and Hankin, "Relations that were not at all cordial," and Ussishkin's indignation at the fact that Hankin, on more than one occasion had presented the JNF with a fait accompli that was not at all acceptable to it and had used its monies in ways that had caused it considerable losses – Meerovitch (1975) I, pp. 94–95 – the quotation is from there, p. 103.

78 CZA, A107/816, letter from Hankin to Weinshal 6.12.1937. He stressed that he did not believe that immediate settlement on lands that had been purchased would determine the partition boundaries.

79 See, e.g., CZA, KKL10, minutes of JNF Directorate meeting, 6.12.1937; CZA, S5/10250, memorandum written on 6.12.1937, presumably by Ben-Gurion – following meeting of the Directorate on that day. See also CZA, A107/816, letter from Weinshal to Hankin 5.12.1937.

80 Ibid., letter from Hankin to Weinshal 6.12.1937. He stressed that he did not believe that immediate settlement on the lands that had been purchased would be of assistance in determining the partition boundaries.

81 CZA, KKL5/10468, letter from Hankin to Weizmann 2.11.1938. For details of the

Until the report of the Partition Commission was published, the tendency within the JNF was to give priority to consummating purchases that would guarantee the boundaries as proposed in the Jewish Agency's partition plan. However, after the publication of the Partition Commission's report, Weitz recommended implementing wide-scale purchases precisely in those areas that were not included within the boundaries of the Jewish State by the Royal Commission and mainly in the Judean Hills, Samaria and the Galilee. "With the purchase of these aforementioned areas we will expand our boundaries in one shot. This would constitute the conquest of the land in a true fashion and create a bulwark against all sorts of plans regarding partition in any form whatsoever that can reemerge."[82]

With the publication of the White Paper in mid-1939, Hankin proposed to the World Zionist Organization that it almost totally cease land purchases. This proposal was primarily predicated on the assumption that the economic pressures to which the Arabs would be subjected as a result would impel them to lobby the government against these decrees. Furthermore, a cessation in purchase activity would yield a general depreciation of land prices.[83] This time as well, both the rationale and the conclusions were vigorously rejected by Ussishkin who found it difficult to believe that such proposals were actually penned by Hankin. He summed up his attack on Hankin:

> I am most grieved by your views and what scares me even more is that if the person expressing this viewpoint is Hankin, the person who for fifty years symbolized, in idea and practice, the redemption of the land, this will exert a catastrophic influence on others. Before we will obtain something from the Arabs, I am sure we will obtain from the Jews what we never imagined – an attitude of apathy and frailty toward all our hopes for redemption and the JNF.[84]

Jewish Agency's partition plan, including the plans for the boundaries, see Katz (1998b), pp. 401–439.

82 CZA, KKL5/10715, letter from Weitz to Ussishkin in his capacity as Chairman of Zionist General Council 31.10.1938.

83 CZA, KKL5/10468, letter from Hankin to Jewish Agency Executive 1.6.1939, letter from Ussishkin to Hankin 6.6.1939 (also in file S25/9837).

84 CZA, KKL5/10468, letter from Ussishkin to Hankin 6.6.1939 (this letter is to be found as well in file S25/9837).

It would appear that these substantial differences also contributed to the change in relations between the JNF and the PLDC and the former's decision to work with other agencies which engaged on its behalf in land purchases. It should be noted that the expanded JNF ties with agencies other than the PLDC laid, as stated above, the basis for establishing an independent JNF apparatus for land purchases. This apparatus operated on a regional basis under the management and supervision of the JNF Lands Department which began operations in the beginning of the 1940s and will be examined in detail in the following chapter of this work.

The Establishment of the "Auxiliary Companies" of the JNF: Meheiman and Himnuta

Two auxiliary companies were established by the JNF in the course of 1936–1939 to fulfill the functions whose need arose during this period and which the JNF could not fill due to its by-laws. The Meheiman Company was established in Autumn 1936 and the Himnuta Company was established in Summer 1938. It should be pointed out that the two companies were under the full control of the JNF and had no independent powers or land policy of their own. It would not be an exaggeration if we would call them in fact fictitious companies, although their importance over the years, and especially that of Himnuta, was immense.[85]

The background to the establishment of the Meheiman Company is connected to the opportunity the JNF received in the latter half of 1936

---

85   A pioneering study on the establishment of these two companies is to be found in Alexander (1988), pp. 164–184; idem (1993), pp. 80–97. On the issue of the two companies being an integral part of the JNF with no independent powers, proof can be found, for example, in the fact that at the beginning of 1942 the JNF applied to the Director of the Income Tax Department of the Palestine Government to exempt the companies from payment of tax as in the case of the JNF itself. In explaining this request it was stated: "These companies were established for the specific purpose of dealing on behalf of our company [the JNF] with certain transactions, such as the purchase of real estate, etc. These auxiliary companies do not carry out independent transactions nor do they have any independent income of their own. Their activities are solely on behalf of the JNF and all their expenses are covered by the JNF Ltd." See CZA, L51/597, letter from Granovsky to the Commisioner for Taxes 16.1.1942.

to purchase lands in the German Colony in Haifa from the Templars who wished to return to Germany, and this was to be in return for monies which had accumulated to the JNF's credit in Germany. The funds had accumulated in Germany primarily from "life bequests," one of the JNF fund-raising tools through which donors endowed capital or property to the JNF and in return were paid a fixed annuity for their maintenance during their entire life. This combination for the purchase of land in Haifa, made it possible for the JNF to easily transfer monies from Germany to its treasury in Palestine. The Meheiman Company under the full control of the JNF, and in whose name the lands in Haifa were registered, served as a trustee, retaining the purchased lands for the owners of the living bequests until they waived their share in them and transferred the lands to the JNF. From the very outset, the JNF had no interest in these lands but only in the capital transferred via them, and it considered selling them at a later stage in order to purchase agricultural lands. However, under its by-laws the JNF was not permitted to sell lands but only to lease them. The by-laws of the Meheiman Company, in contradistinction, deliberately included the possibility of engaging also in the sale of land, and thus the option for the JNF to sell the Meheiman lands in the future was preserved.

Through the Meheiman Company, the JNF was able to conceal the identity of real purchaser from the Arab Land Registry officials in Haifa who would undoubtedly have attempted to thwart the deal. Subsequently, in October 1939, Granovsky proposed selling the land that had been purchased in Haifa with the money of the life bequests in order to enable the purchase of extensive agricultural lands which the JNF had decided upon at the time.[86]

It should be emphasized that beyond these goals, the JNF had no intention of using the Meheiman Company (nor Himnuta) as a systematic tool for the sale of urban lands it had acquired by regular purchases. In response to a proposal broached at the beginning of 1938 by Colonel Kisch[87] to sell the urban lands of the JNF in Haifa, and with the proceeds purchase agricultural lands, Granovsky categorically stated:

86　Alexander (1988), pp. 164–184; CZA, KKL10, minutes of JNF Directorate meetings, 6.12.1937, 18.10.1939; CZA, L51/596, letter from JNF to Bart 9.4.1940, letter from Granovsky to Bart 5.6.1940.

87　Frederick Hermann Kisch, member of World Zionist Organization Executive.

We must point out that similar proposals have been put forward from time to time and have been deliberated upon by members of the JNF's Directorate. However, the position which the JNF has adopted on this matter has until now been negative. The negative position stemmed from reasons of principle, namely that the sale of lands purchased for the nation, even if it could bring about a decent monetary profit that could be utilized to expand the land area of the JNF, contravenes the founders' intention and the purpose of the institution. Proposals similar to that which you are bringing before us, were raised during the period of economic boom, but even then the JNF did not find it appropriate to avail itself of the sale of its lands. These lands must remain in accordance with the fundamental idea which underpins the basis of the JNF – the perpetual property of the Jewish people.[88]

The fact that the Meheiman Company was established exclusively for commercial needs for the Haifa area, and this was stipulated in its by-laws, necessitated when the requirement arose the establishment of a company for similar purposes which would not be restricted to a specific location. This was the immediate reason behind the formation of the Himnuta Company through which the JNF intended in 1938 to purchase the German-owned land in the Beisan Valley with the money of the life bequests that had accumulated on its behalf in Germany and thus enable the transfer of its funds from Germany through land transactions. However, Himnuta as a company engaged in the purchase and sale of lands, was intended to serve also as a broad legal tool intended to bypass the JNF by-laws prohibiting the sale of lands and thus aid the JNF in raising capital, be it by cooperation with private capital or by selling certain pieces of real estate. Raising capital from various sources in addition to contributions and loans, constituted a vital need for the JNF, once it had decided in 1937 to expand its agricultural purchases most substantially, as will be discussed below.

The cooperation of the JNF with private capital in purchasing lands as had been decided a short time prior to the establishment of Himnuta, involved the sale of lands that had been purchased on behalf of private capital – a function prohibited to the JNF. Therefore, in circumstances

---

88   CZA, KKL5/10468, the following letters: Kisch to Granovsky 30.12.1937, Granovsky to Kisch 4.1.1938 – quotation from there, Kisch to the JNF 9.1.1938, Granovsky to Kisch 16.1.1938, Kisch to the JNF 25.1.1938.

where the purchase was tied to collaboration with private capital,[89] it was registered in advance in the name of the Himnuta Company until the lands were transferred to the real owners. Likewise, real estate that had reached the JNF as a result of a contribution, a life bequest or even purchases which the JNF had no intention of retaining but intended to sell at a suitable opportunity in order to use the receipts "as a financial means for redeeming the land," were also registered under the name of Himnuta. It is possible that the JNF could have used the PLDC for those very same purposes for which the Himnuta Company was established, but as has been explained above, since 1936 the JNF sought to concentrate and manage its affairs by itself and was in the process of severance from the PLDC.[90]

At the beginning of July 1938, a detailed contract was signed between the JNF and the Himnuta Company defining relations between the two, and which resembled the contract signed between the JNF and the Meheiman Company. From the various clauses, one can discern the degree to which Himnuta constituted an integral part of the JNF. This was beyond the fact that 16 out of the 20 shares issued by the Himnuta Company were already registered in the JNF's name and three others in the name of senior JNF officials who also managed the company. Granovsky himself represented the JNF at the annual general meetings of Himnuta.[91] The contract contained the following clauses, among others:

> The Himnuta Company receives transfers of property under its name from any person whom the JNF will inform Himnuta in writing that it should receive these transfers; the JNF obligates itself to assume all expenses involved in the receipt of these transfers and absolves Himnuta from such expenses.... The JNF obligates itself to manage all the aforesaid property matters. Himnuta agrees and obligates itself to deal with the property as instructed by the JNF, as if the JNF was the real owner of the property and Himnuta was only an agent

---

89 On JNF cooperation with private capital see below.

90 Alexander (1993), pp. 80–97 and the sources quoted – quotation is from p. 86, from a review of the Himnuta Company, 9.12.1940; CZA, KKL10, minutes of JNF Directorate meeting, 6.12.1937, 18.10.1939; CZA, L51/597, report of the Himnuta Company, 11.5.1941.

91 Alexander (1993), p. 93; CZA, L51/597, minutes of Himnuta Company Annual General Meeting, 30.12.1941.

or representative. Himnuta obligates itself to the JNF not to enter into any obligations toward a third party without receiving written authorization from the JNF.... Himnuta agrees and obligates itself to transfer to the JNF or to persons designated by the JNF the aforesaid properties, all or in part, without any delay, and the JNF undertakes that Himnuta will not be required to meet any expenses in connection with these transfers.[92]

Given the reality that the Himnuta Company (like Meheiman) was in fact the JNF, one of the JNF's senior officials subsequently raised the legal ethical question "if there is no distinction between the property of the auxiliary companies and the other property of the JNF but merely a technicality, perhaps the sale of this property (registered in the names of the auxiliary companies) is prohibited, as in the case of other JNF property (something which runs contrary to both our intentions and our practice)."[93] But it appears that the matter did not excessively trouble either the JNF Executive or its Directorate.

The Security and Political Events that Constituted the Background to the Shaping of Policy Regarding the Volume of Purchases and Regional Preference During the Years 1936–1939

From the time of the establishment of the JNF, different variables exercised an influence both on the scope of its land purchase activity and the regions in which the organization operated. The supply of lands for sale and the means at the JNF's disposal were central factors amongst these variables. Indeed, regarding the variable of supply, Weitz declared in October 1942: "Throughout my twenty years of activity I do not recall an instance where we were able to purchase the land that we wanted and chose. We always purchased what others wanted to sell. We purchased what it was possible to

92 See the contract in ibid. A similar contract was signed between the JNF and the Meheiman Company and is also in the same file.
93 The quotation and the legal ethical question are from a letter from Mohilewer to S. Ussishkin, 18.8.1941, in Alexander (1993), p. 29.

buy at that time."[94] Nevertheless, within the given framework of supply and demand during 1936–1939, what influenced JNF policy on purchase volume and areas of preference should be examined. Although Weitz declared in 1939, that "experience has taught us that regarding...the purchase of land in Palestine, boundaries should not be defined a priori nor should a plan be elaborated in advance regarding time and place," in the very same breath he added that "we are not absolved from defining the intention and purpose to which we are aspiring, and to demarcate accordingly the principal lines of our activity."[95]

It transpires that the frequent and unique security and political events during 1936–1939 exerted a great influence on the "demarcation of intent and purpose" in terms of territorial purchase preferences and the volume of purchases,[96] although the policy was not necessarily implemented in full. These events also influenced JNF efforts to raise resources that would permit it to carry out purchases within the scope upon which it had decided, as will be pointed out below.

At the beginning of 1936, and even before the Arab riots broke out, the British Mandatory Government had planned to introduce a law that would prohibit the sale of lands by Arabs to the Jews beyond a certain limit requisite for maintaining the livelihood of the peasant sellers. The proposed legislation came in response to the demands of Arab leaders at the end of 1935, but did not include the Beersheba district, the cities and the areas with citrus plantations. This was a continuation to ordinances decreed in the past, such as the law protecting the tenant farmers, and which made land purchases by Jews most difficult. This law was never put into effect but obligated the Jewish national institutions to consider the possibility that it would be implemented.[97] This threat had not yet passed,

---

94　*Agricultural Center Bulletin* (Oct. 1942) p. 11, from the address by Weitz at the 39th Agricultural Council meeting held on 14.10.1942.

95　CZA, KKL5/11781, memorandum by Weitz, "The main lines for the continuation of our activities for land purchase," 6.9.1939.

96　Granovsky (1940), pp. 69–77.

97　CZA, proceedings of Smaller Zionist General Council sessions, 10.11.1936; Political Report (1937), pp. 14–16, 53–55; CZA S44/60c, circular letter 31/36 sent by the JNF Propaganda Department to the JNF National Office on 6.2.1936 in connection with "The New Lands Law to be made public by the Palestine Mandatory Government" (also in CZA, KKL5/8741); see also CZA, minutes of joint meeting of Jewish Agency

and Arab disturbances erupted in April of that year which surpassed in their extent, duration and severity all the previous waves of disturbances the Jewish community had endured. A report of the Jewish Agency Executive to the Zionist Congress in 1937 explained that "first and foremost they confronted the entire Jewish community with the immediate danger of death and destruction." From April to March 1937 ninety-three Jews were killed in ambushes and over four hundred were wounded. Property damage totaled P£250,000, whereas the general strike was intended to paralyze the economic life of the country and destroy the Jewish community. The disturbances continued for three and a half years. More than ever, the institutions had to take into account the security component in their settlement decisions and this definitely had repercussions on the land issue. In addition, the Arabs listed the Jewish lands purchase project as one of the reasons for the disturbances, for in their contention it endangered their political status in the country. They demanded the prohibition of Jewish land purchases. The fear that the British would respond to these demands and especially under the pressure of the disturbances, obligated the institutions and the JNF in particular to address the question of the extent and future direction of purchase activity.[98]

Faced with these worrisome occurrences in Palestine, the British announced their intention already in May 1936, to appoint a special investigating commission, whose task was to examine the fundamental causes of the disturbances, ascertain if the Arabs and Jews had justified grievances regarding the implementation of the Mandate. If it would be ascertained that there was a tangible basis to these complaints, the commission was requested to provide recommendations to effect the removal of these grievances and the prevention of their recurrence. In August 1936 a Royal Investigation Commission headed by Lord Peel was appointed.[99] Precisely at that time, news reached the heads of the Jewish Agency that the British policy makers were planning to solve the Palestine problem through cantonization.[100] At the beginning of 1937, the Jewish Agency

---

Executive, JNF and PLDC, 19.2.1936, "to deal with the issue of lands in Palestine" (also in KKL5/8764, S25/9844, S25/6538).

98   Political Report (1937), pp. 17–21 – quotation is from p. 17; Granovsky (1940), pp. 69–71; Cohen, M. (1978), pp. 10–31; Klieman (1983), pp. 4–5.

99   Palestine Royal (1937), p. iv.

100   Sharett (1971), I, pp. 227–230.

Executive learned that the Royal Commission was planning to recommend cantonization or partition as a solution to the Palestine problem. As weeks passed, the information available to the Zionist leadership, that the Royal Commission intended a partition solution, was corroborated. The details of the proposed partition, and first and foremost the proposed boundaries, were not clear to the Zionist leadership until very close to the publication of the Commission's report in July 1937. The British Government's support for the recommendations of the Royal Commission was also not clear. The majority in the WZO Executive supported the idea of partition and also did its utmost to exert influence to ensure that the Commission's report including the partition map would accord with Zionist interests.[101]

In July 1937, the Royal Commission published its recommendation for the solution of the Arab–Jewish problem. The main points referred to the ending of the Mandate and the partition of Palestine into two states: a Jewish State that would include the entire Galilee, the Jezreel Valley and the Coastal Plain; the Arab State would include the Judean and Samarian hills, the Negev and Transjordan. It also recommended imposing the British Mandate permanently on Jerusalem and Bethlehem, as well as a corridor that would include these cities to the Mediterranean coast. The Commission also appended to its report a partition plan (see Map 7) as well as a recommendation that in the process of the partition and setting the borders, an exchange of population and lands would be carried out between the two states being established in order to reach a maximum division between the two entities. The Royal Commission also recommended the prohibition of purchase of land by Jews in the areas of the proposed Arab State.[102]

The British Government decided to adopt the Royal Commission's recommendations. However, a few months later, fissures began to appear in this government policy because the Arab world opposed the partition solution and apprehension was expressed that the Arabs would adopt an anti-British stance in the event of a future conflagration in Europe. Government circles expressed criticism over the details of the Royal Commission's

---

101   CZA, S25/277, resolutions of Zionist General Council sessions, 20.4.1937–27.4.1937; Katz (2000a), pp. 18–20 and sources quoted in nn. 2–10; Ben-Gurion (1982), pp. 110, 123, 125, 162, 167, 173, 176, 192, 197, 199, 203, 228, 249, 256–269, 272; Katz (1991), pp. 402–407.

102   Palestine Royal (1937), pp. 380–393.

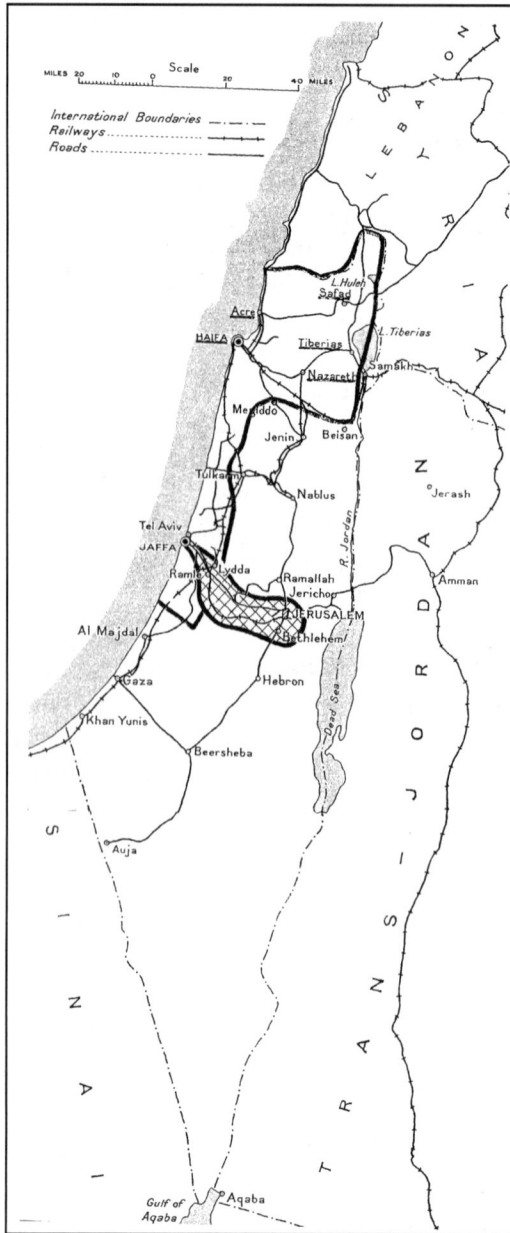

Map 7: Partition plan of Palestine proposed by Royal Commission, 1937
Source: Royal Commission Report, Map 8

proposal, such as the inclusion of the entire Galilee within the boundaries of the Jewish State, despite the appreciable Arab concentrations there. The British Parliament and the institutions of the League of Nations also criticized the Royal Commission's partition plan (but not the principle itself) and they requested that the Government elaborate, following additional investigation, a final partition plan worked out in detail. In December 1937, the British Government decided to issue the clarification that it was not obligated in any manner to ratify the Royal Commission plan. It rejected the recommendation regarding a forced transfer of populations, and announced its intention to conduct additional investigations, such as verifying the possibility of implementing the partition plan and determining a detailed and precise plan. For this purpose the Government appointed in March 1938 an additional investigation commission – the Partition Commission – headed by John Woodhead. The Commission stayed in Palestine until the month of August, and in October of that year it published its findings.[103]

The World Zionist Organization Executive supported the idea of partition in principle and was authorized by the 20th Zionist Congress, which took place in summer 1937, to conduct negotiations with the British on partition. However, it was also opposed to certain aspects of the Royal Commission's plan. Primarily it opposed the boundaries assigned the Jewish State in certain areas, as expressed in the partition map of the Royal Commission. With the assistance of a committee of experts (that relied on an opinion paper prepared by Weitz), the Jewish Agency Executive formulated an alternative map, which it officially submitted to the Partition Commission in May 1938. The plan which took into consideration security, economic (including control over the water sources), political and transport considerations, demanded the expansion of the Jewish State beyond the boundaries allotted by the Royal Commission and a contraction of the area occupied by the British corridor (including west Jerusalem) in favor of the Jewish State. The expansions were demanded along the Coastal Plain, and in the South. Likewise the Jewish Agency demanded the retention of the entire Beisan Valley (including parts of the eastern bank of the Jordan River), the southeast Jezreel Valley and the Gilboa Mountains within the boundaries of the Jewish State. With regard to the Galilee, the Zionist plan

---

103   Katz (2000a), pp. 12–14 and the sources quoted in nn. 40–46.

demanded the total adoption of the Royal Commission's recommendations, which included the entire Galilee within the boundaries of the Jewish State (see Map 8).[104]

The Woodhead Commission publicized its findings in October 1938, turning down the Zionist partition plan. In general it arrived at the unanimous conclusion that within the framework of its purview the Commission was unable to recommend partition boundaries that would offer a fair chance to establish a Jewish State and an Arab State, where each state would be viable. The various alternatives to the partition boundaries as raised during the Commission's deliberations, and which were also published, were from the standpoint of the Zionist interests inferior to the Royal Commission's recommendations. The alternative preferred by the Woodhead Commission (Plan C) "which while imperfect...is the best plan that the majority can craft" (see Map 9), left but a minuscule State along part of the Coastal Plain in Jewish hands. Another alternative left the bulk of the Galilee outside the boundaries of the Jewish State and impaired the position of the frontier areas. In any case, the findings of the Partition Commission were in keeping with a policy the British Government had already agreed upon, namely the abandonment of the partition idea.[105]

In February 1939, the British Government convoked a round table conference (the St. James Conference in London) with the participation of Jewish and Arab representatives to discuss ideas for finding a solution. In anticipation of the meeting, the Government adopted a political line that was based on two principles: freezing the growth of the Jewish national home and extending limited autonomy to the residents of Palestine. The deliberations continued in London for a month. In the course of these discussions the British Government was subjected to Arab pressure and its position was dictated to a large extent by the political conditions in Europe on the eve of the Second World War, as the Government felt that it was vital to attain an arrangement which would be acceptable to the Arabs. The conference broke up without reaching agreement, and two months later, in mid-May 1939, the Government published a White Paper. This document, which expressed a policy declaration, was a unilateral measure adopted by

104 Katz (1991), pp. 407–439.
105 Palestine Partition (1938), pp. 238–281 – quotation is from p. 99; Katzburg (1974), pp. 45–57; Hour (1940), pp. 12–13; Dothan (1983), pp. 161–165.

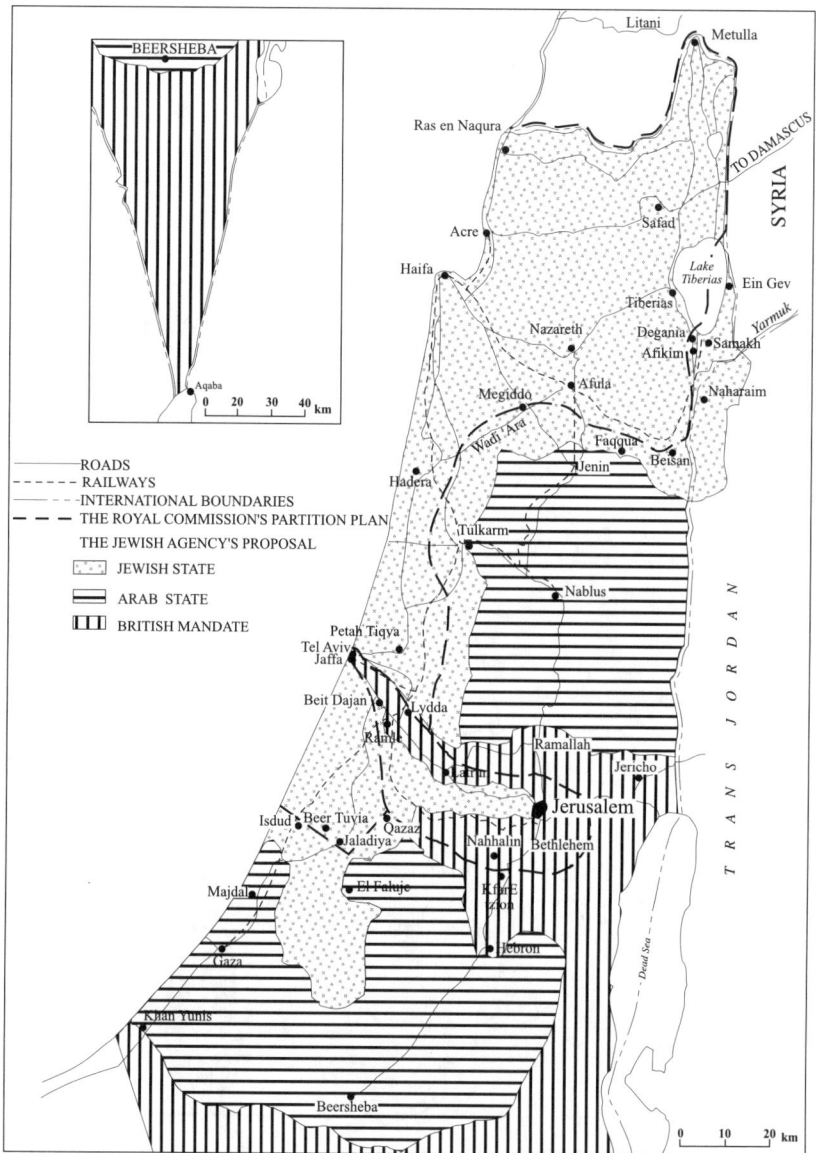

Map 8: Proposal of Jewish Agency Executive for the partition of Palestine, 1938
Source: Partition Commission Report, Map 7

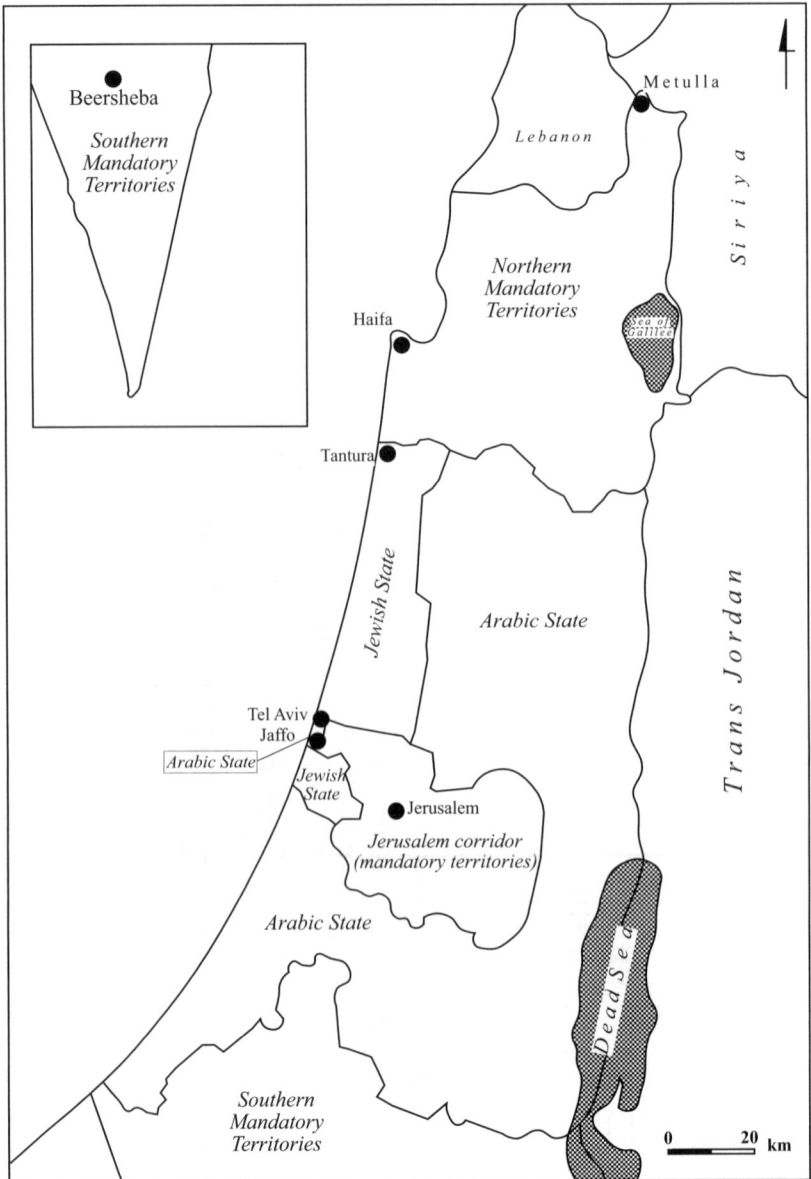

Map 9: The "C" Plan of the Partition Commission (Woodhead Commission)
Source: Partition Commission Report, Map 10

the British Government – a course of action which the Government had threatened to take several times during the course of the conference.[106]

The background to the publication of the White Paper and the accompanying announcement regarding restrictions on land purchases by Jews, was the British Government's retreat from the partition plan – a plan it had adopted immediately upon the publication of the Royal Commission's Report in summer 1937. It emerges that the British pull back from the partition plan had already begun at the close of 1937. First of all, the Arabs expressed vigorous opposition toward the idea – an opposition that reinforced the position of the British Foreign Office which opposed the partition idea from the outset. The Foreign Office believed that partition would not solve the Palestine problem due to the minimal area allotted to the Jewish State. When the Jewish State would arise it would not be able to absorb many immigrants; the Jews would aspire to expand to adjacent Arab territory, and thus new dangers would be created. Therefore, the Foreign Office believed that the Government's obligation to the partition policy was contingent first and foremost upon the assent of the parties to the issue. The Foreign Office sought to appoint a new commission (the Woodhead Commission) that would examine the feasibility of implementing the Royal Commission's plan and would also propose alternatives. The Foreign Office therefore sought to challenge the partition policy and allow for a different arrangement in Palestine that would dovetail with what it considered to be Britain's vital interests in the Middle East.

Concomitantly, in November 1937, the international situation in Europe began to deteriorate; Italy drew closer to Germany and these turnabouts aroused trepidation among Britain's military leadership. The chiefs of staff warned the Government of the grave dangers threatening Britain and the Empire and pressured it to adopt diplomatic measures to mitigate the danger. Apprehension was expressed that persistence in the partition policy would provoke the Arab and Moslem world, which vigorously opposed this policy and the possibility of establishing any form of Jewish sovereignty in Palestine, to join Britain's enemies in the event of a conflagration. A Foreign Office memorandum stated inter alia: "to address the Palestine problem as an isolated issue is not only useless but also most dangerous. All the evidence demonstrates that this question is more important than any

---

106   Ibid., pp. 165–168; Katzburg (1974), pp. 59–81.

other problem in the Middle East, and all our future relations with Middle Eastern countries are dependent almost totally on the manner in which we handle this issue. Our opponents in Europe have not ignored this fact. It is difficult to evaluate the dangers of a European conflagration, but they are altogether too real for our potential enemies that they should be prepared to ignore this field of activity where they can cause us problems." It was therefore essential to reach an arrangement with the leaders of the Arab world and thus cut back Britain's military obligations.

In a Cabinet discussion that took place in December 1937, the majority already believed that Britain should withdraw from the partition policy, but in doing so, should adopt delaying tactics in order to afford the Government an honorable retreat. The method which was devised was to appoint a Partition Commission headed by John Woodhead whose prerogatives were defined in a manner that would enable it to reach the conclusion that it could find no way to delineate a practical manner for implementing a partition plan. Already in September 1938, the Government could surmise that the conclusions of the Partition Commission would establish that the Commission would meet its expectations in finding that a solution to the Palestine problem through partition and the establishment of two independent states was not practical. Formally, the findings of the Commission were published only in November 1938, and thus the Commission fulfilled the hopes the government had placed in it.

With the publication of the Partition Commission's Report, a Government announcement was also published stating that the Government had reached the conclusion that the partition plan, as proposed by the Royal Commission, was not practical. The Government would continue to exercise control over Palestine in its entirety and intended to work for a new solution based on understanding between Jews and Arabs. In declaring that it would continue its mandate over all of Palestine, the Government sought, on the one hand, to assure the Arabs that it would not hand over part of Palestine to Jewish rule. On the other hand, it sought to assure the Jews that it had no intention of accepting the Arab demand to establish an Arab State in Palestine where the Jews would always be a minority. In February 1939, representatives of both sides were invited to a conference in London in order to discuss future policy with the government with a view to solving the Palestine problem by an arrangement that would be agreed upon by Jews and Arabs.

The international situation and Britain's assessment of the possibility for a global conflict and the necessity on Britain's part to reinforce her political and strategic position in anticipation of such a possibility, is what obligated the Government to reach an agreement that would prove acceptable to Arabs and guarantee continued British control over Palestine. For this reason it saw a need to freeze the process of consolidating the Jewish national home by imposing restrictions on Jewish immigration and the sale of land to Jews. Likewise, Britain attempted to satisfy the Arab desire for self-rule in a manner that would be consonant with continued British rule. These were the underlying principles behind the new British plan that had begun to crystallize from October 1938 until the London Conference.

Already in October, the initial conclusions began to be formulated, namely to restrict Jewish immigration and the sale of lands to Jews in order to circumscribe the territorial area of the national home or a canton which could develop into a Jewish State, which would in turn be part of the Arab Federation that would arise in the Middle East. In November–December, the basis of the political plan for Palestine was elaborated and it was presented to the Cabinet at the beginning of January 1939. The new plan dealt with three issues: the legal status of Palestine, immigration and the sale of lands. Regarding the legal status, two alternatives for the regime were proposed: the first would establish a bi-national state where both peoples would enjoy equal status as expressed in equal representation within the institutions of the central government; the second called for partition within the framework of an Arab federation. But the bulk of the memorandum in which the plan was presented was devoted to immigration. It was made clear that the problem should not be addressed from an economic standpoint, as the Jews demanded, because there were weighty political considerations regarding the immigration issue which were related to the Arab States' stance vis-à-vis Britain – considerations which obligated Britain to agree to far-reaching concessions in favor of the Arabs. Furthermore, the plan proposed the imposition of restrictions on the sale of lands to Jews, but beyond setting forth the principle, it provided no details on how this was to be implemented.

The deliberations in London took place over the course of five weeks, but the conference broke up without reaching agreement. Two days before the conference closed on March 15th, the government presented its final proposals. An independent state in Palestine would be established following a transition period of ten years; total Jewish immigration over five years would be 75,000 and at the end of the five years, its continuation would be contingent upon Arab assent; the sale of lands to Jews would be restricted. Both sides rejected the proposals and thus on May 17, 1939 the British Government announced its new policy for Palestine known as the 1939 White Paper. The White Paper addressed three components: constitution, immigration and lands. The chapter on the constitution noted that the Government's goal was to establish within ten years an independent state in Palestine where both the Arabs and Jews would participate in government in a manner that would guarantee the vital interests of each of the two peoples. The chapter on immigration dealt with permitting Jewish immigration to an extent which would not exceed 75,000 during a period of five years, while emphasizing that at the end of the five year period, the Government would be freed of its obligation to facilitate the continued development of a national home through immigration. The chapter on land stipulated that the High Commissioner would receive prerogatives to restrict the sale of land to Jews.[107] It was decreed in both the White Paper and in an additional official British declaration from early June 1939, that prohibited and restricted zones for Jewish land purchases would soon be defined in a law to be promulgated by the High Commissioner, and the restrictions would go into effect retroactively to the publication date of the White Paper.[108] The WZO responded with a decision that it would not comply with the decrees of the White Paper "intended to arrest or retard our growth in Palestine (immigration, land, settlement, etc.)."[109] Subsequently, in February 1940, the Lands Law was promulgated, half a year after the Second World War had erupted in Europe. On the basis of the precedent furnished by the previous war, the JNF leaders put forward the theory already at the start of the War, that changes would ensue in the global map with the War's conclusion which would also include changes in attitudes towards the Palestine problem. Zionism renewed its expectations for determining the political future of Palestine. Therefore "everything which we manage to create until the end of the War can augment our position and guarantee us better conditions when the time for reshaping the country's fate will arrive."[110]

---

107   Katzburg (1974), pp. 35–81; idem (1993), pp. 399–432; Cohen (1978) pp. 66–78; Katz (2000a), pp. 1–16, 177–179.
108   Palestine Policy (1939); Dothan (1983), pp. 167–168; Weitz (1951), pp. 213, 217; Granovsky (1940), pp. 74–75.
109   CZA, proceedings of Smaller Zionist General Council session, 26.6.1939.
110   Granovsky (1940), p. 77. This statement was made in 1939.

The period commencing with 1936 and lasting until the publication of the Lands Law four years later abounded in security and political developments, recommendations and political decisions. From the Zionist standpoint the period was also marked by uncertainty regarding the Government's intention to adopt these or other recommendations as well as the time frame that would be required for implementing these decisions and concluding the relevant processes. In any event, all this uncertainty was directly linked to the territorial issue. Therefore, the problematic situation would have a direct bearing in shaping the JNF's course of activity regarding the volume of purchases and regional preferences, as will be described in detail in Chapter Three.

The Formulation of Policy Regarding the Volume of Purchases and Regional Preference

At the beginning of 1936, the JNF Directorate deliberated on various proposals submitted to it by the Executive on how it could best employ its limited resources. Should it concentrate on purchasing land north of Lake Hula (see Map 10) where the JNF had already in 1935 begun to display a major interest after the PLDC had purchased the concession on the Lake?[111] Or perhaps it would be preferable to consummate all feasible purchases in accordance with the proposals that had been submitted to the Directorate. The logic of those favoring focused activity was that it "was desirable to concentrate on the Hula Valley, given the financial situation which does not permit dispersion." Ussishkin and other members of the Directorate voiced a different opinion: "It is essential to purchase what we can concretely obtain immediately." The JNF should make efforts to obtain a substantial loan of P£200,000–300,000 in order to purchase lands. Ussishkin decided on his position in light of a new British law which was then in the drafting stage. Under this law, the Jews would not be permitted unlimited land purchases but they could purchase only up to the minimum required for maintaining the livelihood of the Arab sellers. Ussishkin believed that it was necessary to consummate purchases on a vast scale before this law came into force. Other members of the Directorate expressed their disappointment with

111   See above p. 22.

private capital which had begun to dispose of its land holdings following
the war between Italy and Ethiopia and its repercussions on economic
trends in Palestine. Those Directorate members believed that this situation
obligated the JNF to enter into purchase agreements in those areas which
had formerly been the domain of private capital. In any event, during the
year 1936, the Directorate found it difficult to adopt a clear decision in the
dilemma counterposing "concentration" to "expansion."[112] Nonetheless,
given the apprehension surrounding the enforcement of the "Minimum
Law," Ussishkin and Ben-Gurion proposed pressing the Government to
allow Jewish land purchases on the East Bank of the Jordan River. Such
purchases would make it possible to compensate Arab farmers who sold
lands on the West Bank of the Jordan River and thus provide a solution
acceptable to the Government, should the law prohibiting purchases beyond
the required minimum necessary for the upkeep of the present sellers go
into effect.[113]

The Arab disturbances which erupted in April 1936, brought about a
drastic drop in the supply of lands offered for sale, although the supply
never ceased totally. The few purchases which the Directorate discussed
and approved up to the middle of 1936, on the one hand, reflected the
JNF's failure to make a clear choice in the dilemma pitting concentration
against expansion. On the other hand, there was continuity in the direction
of land purchases which had characterized the pre-1936 period when
the established policy was intended to respond to the needs of settlers
and settlement bodies. This was carried out by the creation of territorial

---

112   CZA, KKL10, minutes of JNF Directorate meeting, 2.1.1936, 23.1.1936 – the
       quotation from the latter. For the deliberations on the JNF's financial situation see
       also ibid., minutes of JNF Directorate meeting, 12.2.1936. See also CZA, S44/60b,
       Weitz's address at JNF Directorate meeting, 6.2.1936 to "All JNF workers wherever
       they may be," in which he stated, inter alia: "The Law has not yet come into effect
       and it is not clear when it will, in one month or six months, the details have not yet
       been worked out…yet the consequences of the law are clear: A certain sector of the
       lands will be beyond the possibility of purchase…our reaction, the reaction of the
       entire Jewish People, to this new edict can only be the increase of our purchasing
       power at the highest possible degree in order to seize what we can before the law
       comes into effect." See also CZA, S25/9844, minutes of joint meeting of Jewish
       Agency, JNF, and PLDC Executives, 19.2.1936 to deliberate on the issue of lands in
       Palestine.
113   Ibid., minutes Jewish Agency Executive meeting, 29.10.1936, 1.11.1936.

reserves in new areas where Jewish settlement had not penetrated (or had penetrated only on a limited scale) and where land prices were still cheap in comparison with those in the Coastal Plain. This was one of the main reasons for the beginning of JNF activity in land purchases in the Beisan Valley.[114]

In anticipation of the appointment of the Royal Commission in summer 1936, and given the political precedents that occurred following the 1929 Arab disturbances, both the JNF and the Jewish Agency sensed that the dispatch of the Royal Commission presaged imminent restrictions on land purchases. The restrictions would be imposed by force of a law, prohibiting sales beyond a minimum required for the subsistence of the peasant farmer – a measure broached already at the beginning of 1936. Furthermore, the heads of the Jewish Agency discovered during the summer of 1936, that members of the British Government were weighing the possibility of solving the Palestine problem through cantonization: "defining districts where Jews could expand and defining districts where Jews could not settle." The Jewish Agency and JNF leaders expressed their vigorous opposition to both the restrictions on purchases and the cantonization scheme. However, this anxiety required them to adopt a lands purchase and settlement policy that would thwart the possibility of implementing the very things they dreaded.[115] On the other hand, the disturbances obligated a lands purchase and settlement policy that would give major priority to security needs. It was difficult to formulate a land purchase policy that would take into account both security and political needs simultaneously, especially as the purchases themselves were contingent first and foremost on the supply inventory. It was in this context, that Ussishkin, at a meeting of the WZO Executive which took place in August 1936, expressed the dilemmas and appropriate conclusions as follows:

114 CZA, KKL10, minutes of JNF Directorate meeting, 6.7.1936; CZA, S44/60b, lecture by Granovsky on "The land problem and political gains," 5 December 1938; CZA, KKL5/10475, JNF Information Bulletin 1938/4, 18.2.1938; Granovsky (1944), pp. 169ff; idem (1952), pp. 58–59.

115 Sharett (1971), I, pp. 227–230; CZA, S5/333, proceedings of Expanded Zionist General Council session, 27.8.1936, the address by Ussishkin; ibid., proceedings of Smaller Zionist General Council session, 10.11.1936 – quotation is from the address by Shertok; ibid., minutes of Jewish Agency Executive meeting, 29.10.1936.

What is our purchase strategy for the future? Before the War, we had a major debate on this question. What strategy is preferable in land purchases? Dispersion or unification? One opinion stated that all purchases should follow the tendency that one Jewish plot should adjoin the second Jewish plot which in turn would be contiguous with a third plot. Another opinion believed that it was actually better to create both larger and smaller settlement points throughout the entire country to enmesh the country in a net of Jewish settlement points. I, too, participated in this debate, and I must say that from a current strategic perspective, from a security standpoint, the first position is the correct one. If concentrated Jewish settlement and a more preponderant Jewish area will exist, then security will be enhanced, but from the perspective of the broader future of the Jewish people in Palestine, dispersion is more important. For if we concentrate on scattered locations, we would put an end to this terrible idea of cantonizing Palestine. Palestine is so tiny, especially since they took Transjordan from us, and if they intend to create another Pale of Settlement, they won't leave anything for the Jews. However, if in all places there will be Jewish settlement points, this will serve as a brake against these strange ideas of cantonization. But these are theoretical perspectives and anybody can think what he would like to think. However, in practice, the purchases in the coming days cannot be made in line with a program – whether we adopt this program or the alternative program. We, less than anybody else, can decide where to purchase. The master of the situation, in the final analysis, is the Arab who decides to sell and thus we cannot make any program specifying that this we want to purchase and this we don't. We must desire what we can obtain today, when I don't know what tomorrow will bring. These actions will bring into being the method of dispersion rather than concentration. Dispersion, however, will in the end produce concentration. This does not mean that if it would prove possible to purchase lands in the vicinity of Jewish settlements, then we won't make the purchase. Even at a time when we are drawing up contracts for lands in non-concentrated areas, we will try to concentrate them at a later stage. We don't know when we will be able to purchase, but now already we must prepare massive resources.[116]

116   CZA, S5/333, proceedings of Expanded Zionist General Council session, 27.8.1936.

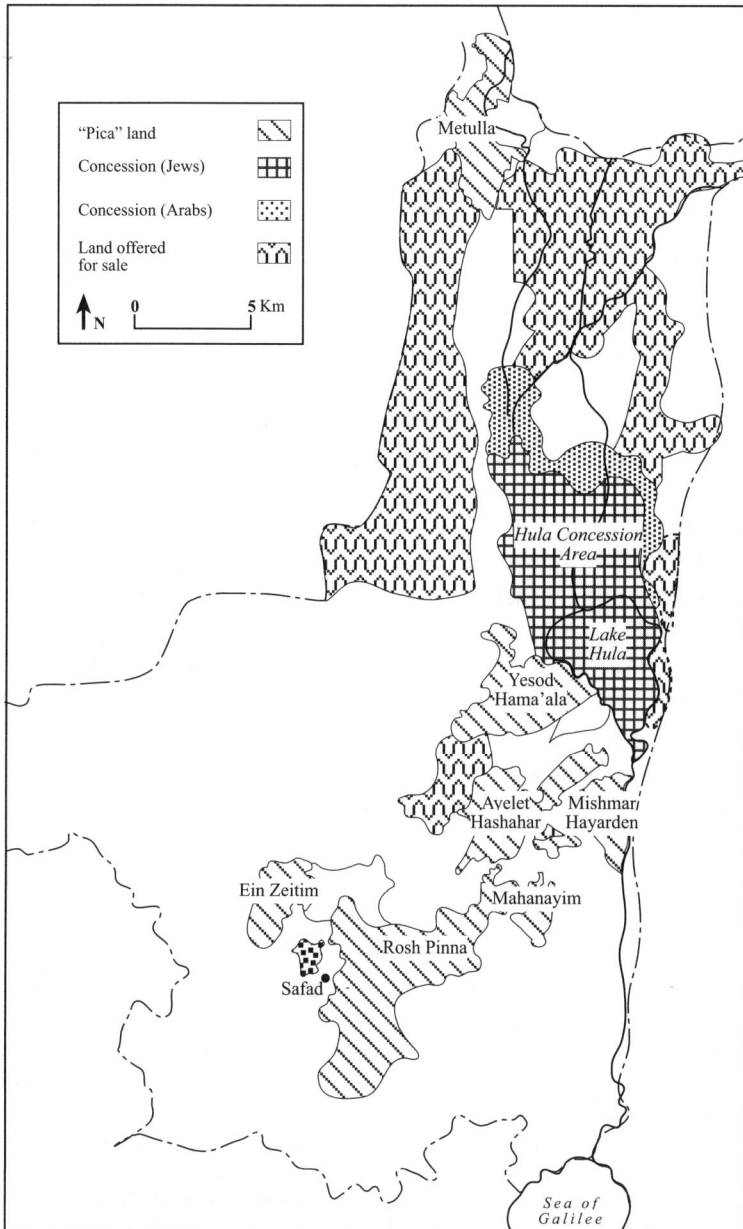

Map 10: Lands proposed for sale in the Upper Galilee in 1936
Source: JNF map archives, Map 1578

At this stage of events, Ussishkin recommended first and foremost adopting a policy which would generally expand purchases, a policy he had recommended already at the beginning of 1936. Secondly, he believed that proposal for implementing purchases should be considered either for their political contribution or for their security contribution. His inclination was to award priority to the political aspect – that is to disperse purchases, "but a dispersion that will in the end result bring about concentration."[117] Indeed, the deepening involvement of the JNF from the second half of 1936 in the purchases of the Beisan Valley (which had begun prior to 1936 in order to create new settlement reserves),[118] and in the Northern Hula (an interest dating back to 1935 following the PLDC purchase of the concession, and until the time of the outbreak of the Arab disturbances a few hundred solitary dunams were purchased there). A further outgrowth of this policy was the Directorate's decision in December 1936, to embark upon the purchase of the Kadesh Naftali ridge in the Eastern Upper Galilee "in order to create a concentration of lands in the vicinity of the Upper Galilee in Jewish hands."[119] (Regarding the sale of lands in the Upper Galilee at that time see Map 10.) That same policy also accounted for the JNF initiative in purchasing the lands of Nukeib (subsequently Ein Gev) in July of that year. Amongst the various reasons for this purchase, Ussishkin emphasized: "It is desirable that there should be Jewish settlement points in the northern boundary of Palestine" and that "it is desirable that the entire vicinity of the Sea of Galilee will be located within areas of Jewish-owned land."[120] Toward the close of the year 1936, it became ever more evident to the Jewish

---

117   Ibid.
118   For the beginning of the JNF's involvement in land purchases in the Beisan Valley; see also Katz (1999), pp. 45ff.
119   CZA, KKL10, minutes of JNF Directorate meeting, 2.12.1936 – quotation is from the statement of Ussishkin. See also ibid., minutes of JNF Directorate meetings, 6.7.1936, 3.3.1937; CZA, KKL5/8777, letter from Elitzur to Granovsky and to Weitz 13.7.1936; CZA, S44/60b, memorandum from Weitz dated 28.2.1937 regarding lands in the Beisan Valley.
120   CZA, KKL10, minutes of JNF Directorate meeting, 6.7.1936. See also address by Ussishkin at Expanded Zionist General Council meeting, 23.4.1973, CZA, S52/141 where he reported on the political direction of the functioning of the JNF during the past year: "At the time the plans for land development the predominating trend was to go to these distant areas. Apart from the issue of the quality of the soil there was also the desire to expand the borders to be on the safe side."

Agency Executive that the continuing Arab disturbances mandated a multi-directional settlement policy and by the nature of things this decision had a territorial component which the JNF was asked to assume. First of all, there were discussions regarding the need to save the isolated settlements through purchase of lands in the surrounding vicinity that would facilitate their expansion and the establishment of additional adjacent settlements. Amongst the isolated settlements mention was made of reinforcing Atarot, north of Jerusalem, Kefar Yavetz in the Eastern Sharon and Kefar Hahoresh near Nazareth. Secondly, the discussions pointed to the urgency of making purchases in strategic locations in the mountain regions to allow the establishment of special settlements that would protect against Arab gangs from establishing complete control in the mountain areas. These were not purely agricultural settlements, but those whose primary mission was to improve the security situation. It was equally clear that there was no reason to establish such settlements in distant locations in the heart of the Samarian Hills or in the center of Galilee but first and foremost along the corridor from Sha'ar Hagai to Jerusalem and to the north and south of Jerusalem. The priority accorded to the establishment of "protective settlements" in the vicinity of Jerusalem coincided with an additional objective which David Ben-Gurion proposed at the time. Ben-Gurion, who was chairman of the Jewish Agency Executive and served as a Governor-Director in the JNF, emphasized the need to strengthen the Jewish control over Jerusalem and its environs. Indeed, from Map 11 we can discern the contemporary paucity of Jewish-owned land in general and JNF-owned land in particular in the Jerusalem area. In any case, if prior to the disturbances the Jewish Agency had spoken exclusively about settlement in the valley and plains area, in the wake of the disturbances it began advocating gaining control over the mountain regions.[121] An additional objective imposed on the JNF following the Arab disturbances, was to make limited land purchases in the vicinity of the Jewish settlements in Judea to resettle refugees from Jaffa.[122]

---

121 CZA, S44/161, letter from Ussishkin to Ben-Gurion 3.11.1936 (also in S25/9839); CZA, S25/9839, letter from Shertok to Ben-Gurion 5.11.1936; CZA, minutes of Jewish Agency Executive meeting, 3.1.1937.
122 CZA, KKL10, minutes of JNF Directorate meeting, 4.1.1937.

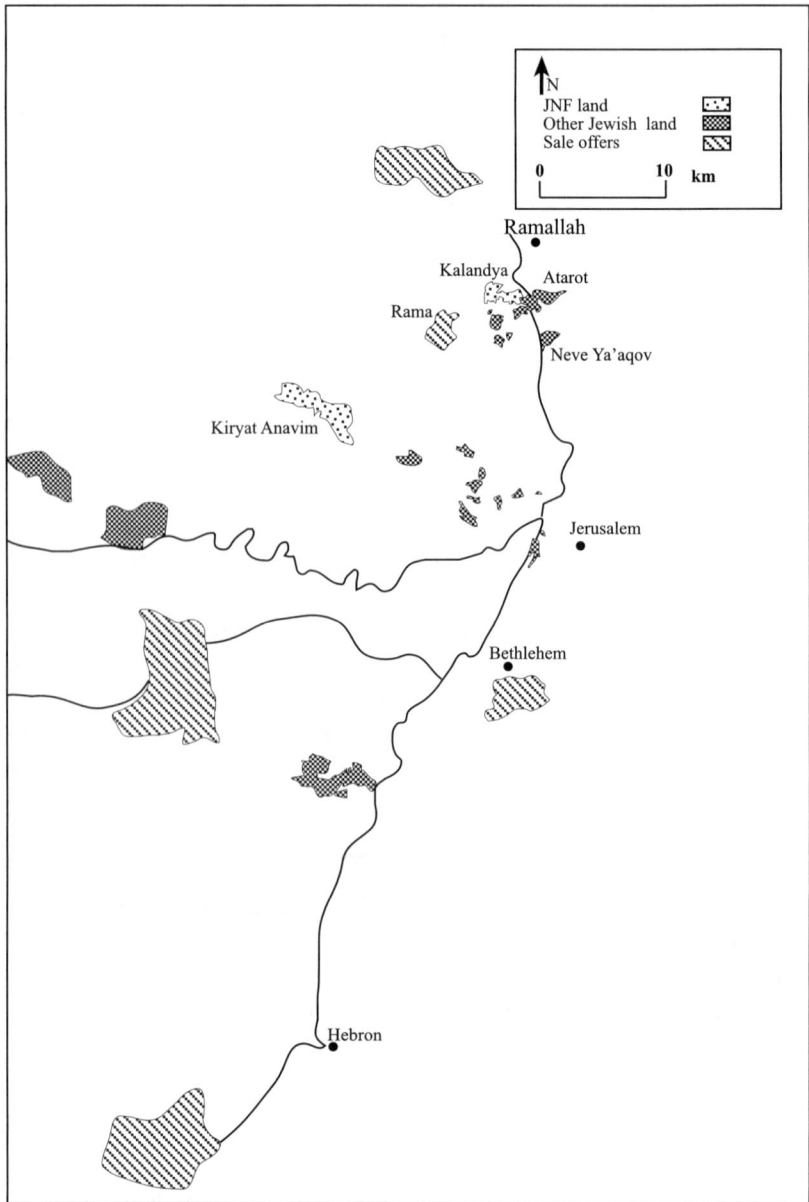

Map 11: Jewish land property and JNF land property in the Jerusalem area
in 1936
Source: JNF map archives, Map 1570

An important share of the purchases ratified by the JNF Directorate at the close of 1936 and at the beginning of 1937 was guided by the security-strategic objectives discussed above. As Granovsky emphasized in the beginning of 1937, "The JNF's finances must assist the purchase of land which has either strategic or settlement importance."[123] Hence the Directorate unanimously decided to purchase lands near Atarot for the establishment of Kefar Hotzvim and in their explanations, the members emphasized that the purchase would help strengthen isolated Atarot and would fortify and expand Jerusalem.[124] Similar strategic considerations accounted for the Directorate's decision to purchase about 4,000 dunams near Abu Ghosh. Weitz explained this as follows:

> From numerous perspectives, it is important that this area of land should be under JNF control, not only from an economic standpoint but also from the point of view of Jewish settlement and the national strategic aspect. This area of land includes hills which overlook the Jerusalem–Jaffa road.... Here is an opportunity of purchasing in one shot 4,000 dunams in a single territorial unit. Any failure to exploit this opportunity would be a major error. This area lies adjacent to the Jerusalem–Jaffa road and the water pipeline to Jerusalem that will supply drinking water to settlements in its vicinity and will create the possibility of safeguarding the water pipeline.[125]

For 120 refugee families from Jaffa, the JNF purchased small plots near Kefar Saba, Petah Tiqva and Nes Tziyona. The refugees were expected to work in the adjacent Jewish settlements.[126]

During the first months of 1937, the Jewish Agency Executive received reports which indicated that the Royal Commission intended to recommend

123   Ibid., minutes of JNF Directorate meeting, 3.3.1937.
124   Ibid., minutes of JNF Directorate meeting, 2.12.1936.
125   Ibid., minutes of JNF Directorate meeting, 3.3.1937. From the minutes it transpires that Granovsky objected to this purchase arguing the fact that the area stretches over an area of only 600–800 meters distance from the Jerusalem–Jaffa road and the lack of possibility to establish a settlement there immediately, negates the advantages of the purchase. See also CZA, KKL10, proceedings of Smaller Zionist General Council session, 21.3.1937. CZA S44/60, memorandum from Weitz on the Abu Ghosh lands, 28.2.1937.
126   CZA, KKL10, minutes of JNF Directorate meeting, 4.1.1937.

either cantonization or the partition of Palestine into two states. It was clear to the Executive that in either case regional limitations on land purchases by Jews would be forthcoming. With this in mind, the Expanded Zionist General Council, which devoted a large portion of its deliberations in April 1937 to the issue of the Royal Commission, adopted a resolution which clarified that the World Zionist Movement would vigorously oppose any restriction on land purchases. It was clear to the Zionist General Council, as well as to the Zionist leadership in general, that resolutions would not suffice. The assumption was that limitations would be imposed on those areas where the Jewish presence was sparse or non-existent, because the Royal Commission might recommend Arab control over these areas. Therefore, Ussishkin contended during the deliberations of the Expanded Zionist General Council: "It is necessary in my opinion to seize places as remote as possible in order to guarantee the boundaries of our country to the fullest." In practice, he recommended the continuation and broadening of the same land purchase policy which he had recommended in mid-1936 under which the JNF worked to broaden its activity in the Eastern Upper Galilee and in the Beisan Valley. This policy was indeed put into practice by the JNF.[127] During those deliberations of the Expanded Zionist General Council, Weitz recommended that the JNF lands ringing the Beisan Valley be settled immediately and in this manner determine the Jewish future of the valley, which had up to now been nearly devoid of Jewish settlements. This recommendation supplemented Ussishkin's and contributed to the decisions taken by the Jewish Agency and JNF to immediately accelerate settlement on the lands of the Beisan Valley (Tirat Tzvi and Ma'oz) even prior to the publication of the Royal Commission's recommendations. For that same reason, the lands of Nukeib (Ein Gev) and Ideniba (Kefar Menachem) were settled.[128]

---

127   CZA, S5/2141, proceedings of Extended Zionist General Council session, 23.4.1937
      – reference is from Ussishkin's address; CZA, S5/277, resolutions of Extended
      Zionist Council session, Jerusalem 20.4.1937–27.4.1937; Congress (1937), p. 364;
      Land (1937), pp. 15–16.
128   Ibid., pp. 27–32; CZA, minutes of Jewish Agency Executive meeting, 6.6.1937. See
      in detail Katz (1999)), pp. 64–72; idem (1994c), pp. 1–20; idem (1994b), pp. 7–28;
      Weitz (1951), pp. 93–101; CZA, minutes of Jewish Agency Executive meetings,
      13.6.1937, 20.6.1937, 4.7.1937.

Ma'oz Hayim, 1946

Ein Gev, 1942

Beisan Valley

Kefar Menachem, 1937

The Directorate did not conduct a fundamental discussion on the JNF's future work to assess the repercussions of the partition recommendation prior to the publication of the Royal Commission's Report, nor in the initial months following its publication. A discussion in connection with the report took place only in December 1937. It is not clear why such a fundamental discussion was not held at an earlier juncture, and it is possible that the cause was Ussishkin's adamant opposition to the very idea of partition. Nonetheless, from the deliberations on specific purchase proposals submitted by the Executive to the Directorate and from the comments of JNF Executive members, it emerges that the uncertainty regarding the eventual implementation of partition together with the ambiguity surrounding the partition boundaries produced a decision to go ahead with purchases to the extent which the confines imposed by the JNF's available resources made possible. The 20th Zionist Congress' exhortation to the JNF in August 1937 regarding "a speedy and vigorous redemption of new land areas to form a solid foundation for the establishment of a Jewish homeland,"[129] as well as the impact of the current Arab disturbances, also influenced this decision. Thus in regard to a proposal for purchasing a 4,000 dunams area near Even Yehuda, Ussishkin contended in mid-1937 that "if there will not be a partition of the country, the land capital of the JNF will be augmented as a result of purchasing this land area and if heaven forbid a partition of the country would occur, the price of this area of land would double and it would be difficult to purchase it later."[130] Regarding another proposal, this time in Migdal Tzedek near Rosh Ha'ayin, Granovsky contended that "in these difficult times, we should not fix hard and fast rules: 'This land should be purchased, and that land not.' One should 'seize' the moment, hasten and purchase every area of land whose purchase is feasible." As Rabbi Berlin explained, "at a time like this one should purchase every plot of land that becomes available, and not only agricultural land."[131]

In December 1937, the Directorate held a basic discussion on the issue of the future direction of JNF activity. The deliberations took place under the influence of three factors: First, a copious number of sales proposals

---

129   Congress (1937), p. 364 – resolutions relating to the national institutions.
130   CZA, KKL10, minutes of JNF Directorate meeting, 18.10.1937; Weitz (1951), pp. 109–110.
131   CZA, KKL10, minutes of JNF Directorate meeting, 18.10.1937.

had accumulated during the past few months on the desk of the JNF Executive (see Map 12). This was a result of the economic distress which seized the country inducing the Arabs, who did not see any other way to ameliorate their condition, to sell their lands. The Arab disturbances which continued over an appreciable time, caused economic damage to both the estate owners and the peasants. Many estate owners fled the country and could not collect the rents from the tenant farmers. On the other hand, since the outbreak of the Arab disturbances, the JNF remained the lone Jewish factor that was prepared to consummate tangible purchases – a total of some 250,000 dunams. "Such a situation laden with possibilities for purchasing land in various areas of the country has not existed since the War."[132] Secondly, no government restriction had yet been issued with regards to purchases in areas earmarked for the Arab State as proposed by the Royal Commission, and it was not clear how long such a situation would obtain. Thirdly, considering its current obligations, the JNF's resources would not suffice to finance the purchase of all that was offered for sale or even part of it, and this situation made the setting of priorities mandatory.

However, the setting of priorities was necessitated first and foremost by the partition recommendations and the prevailing uncertainty over whether partition would actually be implemented. If it were implemented, would the boundaries of the Jewish and Arab States correspond to the recommendations of the Royal Commission or not, and what were to be the permanent boundaries set by the British Mandate? Apprehension was voiced in particular with regard to the Central and Western Upper Galilee. The Royal Commission had included the entire Galilee within the boundaries of the Jewish State, but given the appreciable Arab settlement concentrations in the Central and Western Upper Galilee and the absence of a Jewish ownership there (save for Nahariya), quite a few individuals in the British Government disputed the recommendation of the Royal

---

132 Ibid., minutes of JNF Directorate meeting, 6.12.1937 – quotation is from the address
      by Weitz. For details of the lands proposed for sale and Weitz's memorandum "Land
      Proposed for Sale," 21.10.1937, see CZA, KKL5/10516. See also CZA, S5/10250,
      memorandum 6.12.1937, written by Ben-Gurion regarding the JNF Directorate
      meeting that day; CZA, S25/7630, lecture by Granovsky "The land issue and its
      political implications" delivered on 5.12.1938; Granovsky (1940), pp. 33–36.

Commission to include these areas within the boundaries of the Jewish State.[133]

In fact, the Directorate was required to provide responses to two principles questions: The first, given the lands available could the JNF undertake a long-term plan of purchases that would require finances beyond its current resources, or in other words, where would it find the resources required for purchases on a large scale? The second question was how would its priorities be determined under a plan for limited land purchases that had been developed by the JNF Executive? This included the possibility of buying 43,000 dunams and for the first time a proposal for purchases in Western Upper Galilee was made. This proposal had been submitted by the JNF Executive for immediate implementation and it was the first time since 1936 that the Directorate had been required to take a decision on purchases on such a large scale.

The issue of "setting priorities" comprised a number of secondary issues: whether, where and with what urgency purchases should be carried out within the boundaries of the proposed Jewish State, within the proposed Arab State and within the area of the British controlled corridor as recommended by the Royal Commission? The members of the Directorate all agreed that the situation and the complete obscurity regarding future political decisions that were about to be made required extensive purchases. As Ussishkin put it: "From the point of view of our political situation in Palestine, the JNF is of course obligated to urgently carry out purchases of new lands as far as possible."[134] Ben-Gurion stated emphatically: "Since we do not know what the future holds, the purchase of land in certain areas is a decisive historical matter, and we must first of all find the large amounts that will enable us to carry out all the purchase of all the lands being offered for sale and desirable from a political viewpoint...purchase of lands at this time is in a sense the salvation of our homeland."[135]

---

133   CZA, KKL10, minutes of JNF Directorate meeting, 6.12.1937 – from the statement by Ben-Gurion; ibid., minutes of Jewish Agency Executive meeting, 15.11.1937; CZA, S25/6530, lecture by Granovsky, ibid.; CZA, KKL5/10575, JNF Information Bulletin 1938/4, 18.2.1938; Granovsky (1940), p. 42.
134   CZA, KKL10, minutes of JNF Directorate meeting, 6.12.1937.
135   CZA, S25/10250, memorandum written by Ben-Gurion regarding the JNF Directorate meeting held that day. See also CZA, KKL10, minutes of JNF Directorate meeting, 6.12.1937.

Various proposals were raised within the Directorate to find the finances required, since it was clear that current income sources would not suffice to cover extensive purchases and meet previous obligations.[136] Amongst the proposals tabled was a special contribution project or obtaining a loan from affluent Jews throughout the world in the sum of one million Palestine Pounds – a project that would be headed by Chaim Weizmann, President of the WZO. Due to the importance of the entire fiscal issue, Ben-Gurion proposed convening a joint session of the Directorate with the Jewish Agency Executive and with Weizmann's participation to find a solution to the question of resources.[137] The Directorate and the Executive decided to take immediate action in issuing long-term bonds in Palestine, obtaining loans from institutions and private individuals in Palestine and collaboration with private capital in land purchases.[138]

However, although the Directorate was united behind a policy of implementing extensive purchases, differences of opinion arose regarding

136   Granovsky described to the Directorate the current sources of income (donations, testaments in cash and in property, living bequests, rents from leases, emission of bonds overseas and loans) and stressed the difficulties that had arisen from the fact that more and more countries had introduced currency restrictions. Obtaining a loan in England six months earlier for the amount of P£100,000, encountered difficulties because of the sensitivity of the creditors to the JNF by-laws restricting the use of the land to Jewish lessees to be toiled by Jews only. See CZA, minutes of JNF Directorate meetings, 6.7.1936, 6.12.1937.

137   CZA, minutes of JNF Directorate meeting, 6.12.1937. See also CZA, minutes of JNF Directorate meeting held on 8.2.1928 regarding the convening of a special committee consisting of members of the Directorate, the purpose of which was to decide on how to obtain finances from affluent persons – whether through loans or large one-time donations to the JNF "for the redemption of extensive areas of land as a national possession, that has become the historic–national necessity of the hour" – quotation from the resolutions of JNF Directorate meeting, 8.2.1938, ibid.

138   See CZA, minutes of JNF Directorate meetings, 8.2.1938, 6.12.1938. See also CZA, KKL5/10475, JNF Information Bulletin 1938/4, 18.12.1938. An emission of bonds in the amount of P£100,000 in Czechoslovakia was approved and the accruing funds would be sent to Palestine in the form of goods within the "Ha'avara" agreement between the WZO and the German Government in 1933 allowing the transfer of capital in the form of goods. See CZA, KKL10, minutes of JNF Directorate meetings, 8.2.1938, 25.4.1938 in which the sources and amounts of loans to the JNF are detailed. It should be stressed that the JNF objected in principle that its lands should be used as surety for loans but agreed to grant mortgages on its general funds. See CZA, minutes of JNF Directorate meeting, 28.12.1938.

the question of priorities. Ben-Gurion believed that purchases in the Upper Central and Western Galilee should top the list of priorities, because "if a State will be established, we are not yet certain of the Upper Galilee (the Safad and Acre District) despite the decision of the [Royal] Commission. The area north of Acre and west of Safad is in danger because no Jewish settlement exists there (aside from Nahariya) and there is a dense Arab population there.... We must do everything in order to hinder the extraction of the Galilee from our possession."[139] Next in importance, he placed purchases in the Wadi Ara and South Beisan Valley regions – two regions that were incorporated within the boundaries of the Arab State as proposed by the Royal Commission but were of immense importance to the Jewish State. The Beisan Valley was critical because of its settlement potential, its location astride the eastern border of Palestine, and as an area linking the Jezreel Valley to the Jordan Valley. Wadi Ara was critical because of its immense importance as a link between the Coastal Plain, the Jezreel Valley and the Lower Galilee. Ben-Gurion identified as a third priority, purchases beyond the Jewish State's southern boundary set by the Royal Commission's proposal. Ben-Gurion considered purchases in the area of the British-controlled corridor to be of less importance as he assumed that no special restrictions would be imposed in this region and settlement possibilities would be determined according to the economic absorption potential.[140]

Shmuel Zuchovitzky also ranked purchases in the Western Upper Galilee at the top of his list of priorities. However, as opposed to Ben-Gurion, Zuchovitzky attached special importance to purchases in the corridor because he assumed that land prices in that region would appreciate markedly in the future, both due to the special status of the corridor area as well as its proximity to Jerusalem, which would have an influence in the event that instead of the corridor a British enclave surrounding Jerusalem alone would be proclaimed. The agronomist Professor Yitzhak Vilkansky and Avraham Granovsky also ascribed particular importance to purchases in the corridor, because in any event "it is important that Jewish settlement points will exist on the road between Jerusalem and Tel Aviv." In third place, Zuchovitzky identified the Beisan Valley region. Zuchovitzky could

139   CZA, S25/10250, memorandum dated 6.12.1937 written by Ben-Gurion following upon the JNF Directorate meeting held that day.
140   Ibid. See CZA, minutes of JNF Directorate meeting, 6.12.1937.

see no logic in purchases within the heart of the "Arab State." This opinion was shared by Vilkansky: "In such a case we will be the subjects of the Emir and we will strengthen his hands and power. Not a solitary dunam should be purchased in the Arab State. We should purchase three million dunams in the area of the Jewish State and it would be a pity if we diverted even a penny to another purpose."[141]

Granovsky, in contradistinction to the above members of the Executive, as well as Ben-Gurion, placed purchases within the boundaries of the Arab State as proposed by the Royal Commission, at the head of the list of priorities, both with respect to territories bordering on the Jewish State as well as territories in the heart of the Arab State.[142] In the presentation of his argument, he emphasized:

> It is extremely important that we develop the positions which we have obtained and especially around the proposed borders. The fact that we had land in our possession and settled that land, is what influenced the demarcation of the boundaries by the Royal Commission. The Commission attempted, to the extent that it was possible, to incorporate within the areas of the Jewish State all the territorial capital in Jewish hands. The expansion of Jewish capital can therefore acquire signal importance at the time of the final demarcation of the borders and therefore it is most important that we should purchase tracts in as many areas of land as possible even in those portions of the country which will be situated in the future within the areas of the Arab State. Future developments cannot be seen in advance, and who knows, maybe it will be precisely our positions in those areas of the country that will serve as a vantage point for Jewish development in the Arab area of Palestine as well. The size of our areas in this section of the country will prove to be of special importance, once we enter negotiations regarding the transfer of the Arab population, since we will then be able to propose to them these areas as alternative properties in recompense for their lands within the Jewish State.

141   Ibid.
142   Ibid.

Granovsky placed purchases in the Jerusalem corridor in second place, and his third priority was the Beisan Valley.[143]

The Directorate's decision, adopted unanimously, expressed the majority opinion regarding the order of priorities and sought to direct the work of the Directorate and Lands Department with regards to land purchases as follows: Gaining a foothold in the Upper Western Galilee to prevent its severance from the Jewish State; reinforcing Jewish control over the Jerusalem corridor; reinforcing Jewish hold in the Beisan Valley which would lead to the inclusion of the entire valley within the boundaries of the Jewish State; expansion of the foothold in the strategic area of Wadi Ara (connecting the Coastal Plain and the Lower Galilee) in order to expand the boundaries of the Jewish State in this important area. On the other hand, purchase proposals for lands located both within the areas of the proposed Jewish State as well as in the heart of the Arab State were not authorized. Thus it was decided to go ahead with purchases in the Western Upper Galilee on the border with Lebanon (East of Bessa, i.e., Hanuta, to the extent of 10,000 dunams), in the Jerusalem corridor (the vicinity of Kiryat Anavim – 4,000 dunams), outside the boundaries of the Jewish State (Butimat, north of Wadi Ara – 6,000 dunams) and in the southeast of the Beisan Valley (the land of Hamra – 4,000 dunams). The total cost of the purchases that were ratified was P£300,000 and the purchases in the Galilee were made conditional upon the assent of the Settlement Department of the Jewish Agency to settle the location forthwith in order to safeguard the purchase.[144] Guaranteeing the entire Galilee and expanding the boundaries

---

143   CZA, S25/6530, lecture by Granovsky "The land issue and its political implications" delivered on 16.11.1937 – quotation from there. See also Granovsky's comments, CZA, KKL10, minutes of JNF Directorate meeting, 6.12.1937. See also Granovsky, "Even in the Jewish State, we will not Receive Land Free of Charge," *Davar*, 19.11.1937, p. 4.

144   CZA, KKL10, minutes of JNF Directorate meetings, 6.12.1937, 8.12.1936. See also ibid., minutes of Jewish Agency Executive meeting, 6.12.1938 which reported the completion of the purchase of the lands of Hanita and the continuation of negotiations for extensive areas to the extent of 20,000 dunams. Apparently at the joint meeting of the Jewish Agency Executive and the JNF Directorate held on 12.12.1937 at which the Jewish Agency Executive expressed the desire that the JNF make extensive purchases in Western Galilee and the Jewish Agency Executive undertook to arrange immediate settlement of such lands. See CZA, minutes of Jewish Agency meeting, 6.2.1938; also CZA, KKL5/10475, JNF Information Bulletin 1938/4, 18.2.1938

in other areas therefore represented the goals of the JNF in the wake of the Royal Commission partition plan. These goals dovetailed with the goal of promoting an alternative Partition Plan in which the Political Department of the Jewish Agency was busily engaged at the time and which was submitted in May 1938 by the Jewish Agency Executive to the Partition Commission (see Map 8).[145]

Although by December 1937 the Directorate had established clear purchase priorities that excluded the Sharon as well as other areas of the Jewish State as proposed by the Royal Commission, during the course of 1938 the Directorate was requested to discuss purchase proposals submitted by the JNF Executive for lands in the Sharon and in the Coastal Plain. This digression came as a result of the vast supply of lands offered for sale throughout the entire country, the existing settlements' critical need for land, the possibility of quickly obtaining and settling the land and finally

---

which summarizes "JNF activities in Upper Galilee and the Hula region." See also Mossad Harav Kook Archives, Central Archives of the World Mizrachi, minutes of Smaller Council of World Mizrachi Movement, 8.12.1937, the comments of Rabbi Berlin. For political reasons, there was no intention to carry out purchases beyond the international boundary with Lebanon. See CZA, S25/9838, letter from Shertok to D. Schwartz 18.4.1938; CZA, S25/1892, letter from Shertok to JNF Executive 28.4.1938, letter from Weitz to Shertok 6.5.1938.

145 Katz (1991), pp. 401–439, see especially on pp. 416–417 Weitz's comments when asked to express his opinion on whether to include the entire Galilee region in the Jewish State or to relinquish certain parts in exchange for the inclusion of the Negev within the Jewish State. Weitz stressed that "to demand the Negev as an appendix to the Jewish State or to reserve it for Jewish settlement under the British Mandate – yes, oh yes – but to pay for it with a large section of Upper Galilee which would constitute a quarter of the area within the boundaries of the Jewish State as recommended by the Royal Commission – no, oh no –.... The exchange of Upper Galilee for the Negev is of doubtful value, even if they were both of equal political worth. Upper Galilee, with its mountains and valleys is certainly of agricultural worth. It is certain that wherever we will plant a tree or sow seeds they will bear fruit, whether sparse or abundant, where stones and rocks abound we have to break them up or remove them, build terraces and ensure that the soil will not erode. The rest is provided by nature: good climate, sufficient water...from the point of view of agricultural settlement and absorption, Galilee is more important than the Negev, even though the former seems to be populated while the latter has no settlers. It should also be stressed that Galilee has many tens of thousands of dunams of land belonging to non-resident owners and thus it will be easier to make purchases there" (CZA, S25/7673, letter from Weitz to D. Yosef 5.12.1937).

the argument that many middle class Jewish families in Europe could be rescued if it would prove possible to arrange their settlement on lands which the JNF would purchase in the Coastal Plain. In the deliberations of both the Executive and the Directorate, opinions were expressed in favor of a flexible policy that would enable such purchases. It was clear that their implementation would come at the expense of purchases deemed politically important, and especially in the North. Additionally, land prices in the coastal area were much higher than those in the frontier areas (about P£15 as opposed to P£3 per dunam). Weitz, who advocated flexibility, contended that one should no longer speak about "what was preferable," but resources must be found to implement all possible purchases, because this hour of opportunity with such an abundant supply could pass. Ben-Gurion, and to a large extent Ussishkin, did not share this opinion but sought to continue in giving total priority to purchases which fulfilled a political goal, especially in the Galilee, while nonetheless allowing only necessary purchases in the Coastal Plain. Ben-Gurion emphasized that

> The following must be take into account: (a) Land in the Sharon Valley – if it would not be redeemed by the JNF it would be purchased by private Jewish individuals, which has not been the case with the north of the country. (b) Partition may not be implemented and then there will be land decrees and a stiffening of the laws of the land in areas populated by an Arab majority. In his opinion, land purchases should be made in Judea and in the Sharon Plain when a vital necessity arose such as in the economic factor as in Na'ana, or a strategic economic factor such as in Kefar Yavetz. However, not 'willy-nilly' in the Sharon Plain. He proposed, therefore, to adopt a general decision that the JNF should purchase at the present time lands in Judea or the Sharon Valley only when an overriding necessity occurs.

Indeed, in making its decision, the Directorate upheld the total priority of purchases in the North. The second priority was for large areas of land whose price was very cheap, and the third priority, purchases in various locations for the settlement of new immigrants. The decision of the Directorate therefore, reiterated that purchases necessary from a political standpoint topped the scale of priorities.[146] However, a possibility was left

146   See, e.g., JNF Directorate reports on intensified activities by the JNF in purchasing

for the JNF Directorate to implement additional purchases in certain cases for strategic and settlement purposes along the Coastal Plain.[147] Indeed, in the course of 1938, the JNF did implement such purchases along the Coastal Plain.[148]

A stubborn concentration on purchases with political importance characterized the Directorate's policy until mid-1938,[149] which was halted for a short time in the summer and autumn of that year in anticipation of the publication of the Partition Commission's findings. Ussishkin and others in the Directorate expressed their anxiety about implementing purchases in areas where it was highly doubtful that they would be included in the Partition Commission's recommendations within the boundaries of the Jewish State. They assumed that purchases made so soon after the publication of the report, would not be able to change it. Furthermore, the JNF could lose its appreciable investment in the event that these areas where the purchases were to be implemented would be included in regions prohibited to Jewish settlement. They therefore proposed waiting until the Partition Commission's report was published and the political situation clarified. This was the case, for example, regarding the proposals for the purchase of areas in Irak-Menashia located south of the boundaries of the Jewish State according to the Royal Commission proposals. However, Ben-Gurion and Berl Katznelson believed that no opportunity should be forfeited where there was a possibility for Jewish settlement and precisely by purchasing the site and settling it could lead to its incorporation within the Jewish State. In response to their pressure the JNF Directorate decided to implement the purchase in the event that the Political Department of the Jewish Agency would propose it and that the Settlement Department would obligate itself to settle the site immediately.[150] A similar situation occurred in relation to a purchase of land near Hanita (Hirbat Samach the future Eilon in the Western Galilee) which the JNF was about to consummate

---

lands in Galilee and the Beisan Valley, CZA, KKL10, minutes of JNF Directorate meetings, 6.7.1938, 8.8.1938 – quotation from the latter, minutes of Jewish Agency Executive meetings, 7.10.1938, 14.12.1938.

147   Ibid., 25.4.1938.
148   Ibid., 25.4.1938, 6.7.1938, 8.8.1938, 14.12.1938.
149   See also CZA, KKL5/10514, JNF memorandum "Manifold activities in land purchases during 1938."
150   CZA, KKL10, minutes of JNF Directorate meeting, 8.8.1938.

in the beginning of October. For the very same reasons mentioned above, Ussishkin was hesitant about concluding the purchase which totaled P£35,000. Nonetheless, he decided authoritatively that "on these matters the Political Department decides and he considers its opinion." Moshe Shertok, the Director of the Jewish Agency Political Department, as well as the other members of the Jewish Agency Executive, vigorously supported the purchase. He stated:

> It is possible for us to purchase today 10,400 dunams on the northern boundary in the vicinity of Hanita. It is true that the fate of this portion of land is not clear. There are four possibilities before us and these are: (1) that partition of the country will be implemented and concomitantly a Jewish State including the Galilee will arise. If this were to be the case, we would not be in a hurry at all about this purchase. (2) Partition will occur together with the establishment of a Jewish State without the Galilee. (3) In such an event, it is possible that the Galilee would remain under the British Mandate and our rights there would be limited. (4) There would be no partition and in conjunction with this, limitations would be imposed on purchasing lands, and the Galilee would definitely be an area where this limitation would be applied. From the standpoint of the latter two assumptions, it is very important to us to purchase the land now. Hanita exists, and we could in no way imagine that we would reach a pass where we would be forced to evacuate Hanita. Hanita has only 4,000 dunams and therefore it is of inestimable importance, that in this vicinity, a bloc of Jewish agricultural settlements would be created. What we are able to purchase now, no person will be able to extricate from our hands. If the land will be ours, we can settle on it under any regime. This situation thus favors the purchase of the land even if we will not be able to cultivate it immediately with a specific settlement group. We will have to ask the members of Hanita to cultivate the land and there are also other options for conquering the place.[151]

With these words and the demands of the Jewish Agency Executive in mind, the JNF went ahead with consummating the purchase, but not before

---

151   Ibid., minutes of Jewish Agency Executive meeting, 7.10.1938. See also Weitz (1950b), pp. 157–159.

Ascent to Hanita, 1938

Menachem Ussishkin's visit to Hanita, 1938

it had received the undertaking that there would be effective settlement in the area.[152]

In mid-December 1938 the Directorate made decisions regarding a renewed momentum in land purchases and reexamined its priorities policy, and this influenced the JNF's land purchase work during the course of the year 1939. Deliberations and decisions in December took place against a background of three factors: First, the publication of the Partition Commission's report in Autumn 1938 together with the British Government's announcement that it was abandoning the partition idea. Secondly, the political picture had clarified, and it was evident that the British were embracing a policy hostile to the creation of a national home for the Jews and their objective was to mollify the Arabs by measures that would impose severe limitations on Jewish land purchases. In December 1938, Granovsky emphasized: "In the recent period the political situation has become aggravated...in an appreciable manner and to our chagrin there are now not only substantiated apprehensions regarding unusual encumbrances with regards to land purchases that can be expected in the immediate future, but also there is clear information which portends evil. We have decisive information regarding plans to prohibit purchases to an extent that would deprive the Jews of any possibility to purchase agricultural land."[153] Thirdly, given the assumption that the Arabs were suffering from the economic pressure during the years of the disturbances, one could anticipate that a bountiful supply of lands would be up for sale.[154]

The point of departure which Ben-Gurion presented to JNF Directorate regarding the anticipated limitations on land purchases, was that British

---

152 Ibid.
153 CZA, S53/437f, letter from Granovsky to Siegfried Eliezer Hoofien, Manager of APC 10.12.1938 (also in CZA, KKL5/10468).
154 CZA, KKL10, minutes of JNF Directorate meeting, 14.12.1938; CZA, A246/699, letter from Weitz to A. Ben-Shemesh 28.10.1938; CZA, A246/747, letter from Weitz to Nahmani 28.10.1938; CZA, KKL5/10517, letter from Zuckerman to Weitz 10.11.1938; CZA, A246/747, letters from Weitz to Nahmani 24.11.1938, Weitz to Stromeza, Wolff and the Danin brothers 24.11.1938; ibid., letter from Zuckerman to Weitz 8.12.1938, details of purchase proposals that would be under consideration and implementation during the following three months, December 1938; CZA, S53/437f, letter from Granovsky to Hoofien 10.12.1938; CZA, KKL5/10517, letter from Weitz to Hankin 16.12.1938, letter from Weitz to Ussishkin in his capacity of President of the Extended Zionist General Council 31.10.1938.

policy would be determined by the partition program preferred by the Partition Commission, i.e., limitations would be imposed in all areas of Palestine, save for the narrow strip from the vicinity of Tel Aviv to Zikhron Ya'akov which the Partition Commission had suggested as the area of the Jewish State.[155] The fact that the Partition Commission found it necessary to emphasize the appreciable Arab population concentration in the Galilee and disagreed with the recommendations of the Royal Commission regarding the Galilee, made it abundantly clear to the JNF Directorate that with regards to the Upper Galilee, a "total prohibition" on land purchases would be imposed, and the same applied to the country's mountain regions. Regarding the other areas, it was assumed that there would be "severe impositions." The importance of purchasing land before the restrictions set in was therefore appropriate to all land that was offered for sale (outside of the boundaries of the Jewish State according to Plan C of the Partition Commission) and especially to those purchases that could be completed and settled rapidly. However, it was of cardinal importance to implement purchases in the entire Upper Galilee.[156] The assumption that a total prohibition on purchases in the Galilee could be expected was also based on the fact that Britain, now that it had backtracked from a partition policy and was maintaining the Mandate, would strenuously attempt to safeguard her strategic interests along the seacoast, and especially in Haifa, whereas "the settlement in Galilee [by Jews] meant taking control of the sea coast from Haifa to Sidon." This was also the reason why Ben-Gurion emphasized to the JNF Directorate the importance of purchasing lands on Mount Carmel and the necessity of settling Haifa with a Jewish population and factories. It was clear that because of the oil pipeline that originated in Iraq, Britain had a special interest in Haifa "and whoever held the key to Haifa would be given primary consideration by England.... We can 'take control' over Haifa from the Carmel and from Haifa, over the whole of Palestine." Therefore, Ben-Gurion placed purchases on the Carmel at the head of his list of priorities, followed by purchases in the Galilee. But the purchase proposals on the desk of the JNF at that time, did not include lands on the Carmel, and thus the importance of purchases in the Western

155   Palestine Partition (1938), p. 99, Partition Plan C. See Map 9.
156   CZA, KKL10, minutes of JNF Directorate meeting, 14.12.1938 – quotation from
        statement of Ben-Gurion; Congress (1939), p. 426, statement of Shertok.

Galilee, to fortify the Jewish foothold on the seacoast and in the vicinity commanding Haifa, was confirmed from an additional direction.[157]

For all the above reasons, as well as the necessity to reinforce the new settlements in the Galilee, it was clear to the JNF Directorate that priority should be given to purchases in the Upper Galilee. Purchases should be considered where the JNF itself would be called upon to evict the tenant farmers, especially as there were an abundance of proposals along the breadth of the areas spanning from northeast of the Hula up to the seacoast, and there were good prospects for winding up sales quickly. But there were proposals also in the South that gave rise to a fundamental dispute between Ben-Gurion and Katznelson. The former felt that importance should not be attached to this purchase, for "the Negev would apparently be the consolation prize which England would propose to the Jewish people." He recommended instead reinforcing the hold on the Jerusalem–Tel Aviv highway. Katznelson, however, felt that the southern areas had an important settlement potential "and if a prohibition would be imposed on the purchase of lands by Jews in the Galilee, then there is no doubt that a similar prohibition would be imposed on the purchase of lands by Jews in the South. Even if England will award the Jews the Negev, it would prohibit the purchase of lands from Be'er Tuvia to Gaza" (an area where the purchase proposals were located, which were before the Directorate for decision).[158]

The feeling of the members of the Directorate was that in view of the foreseeable prohibitions ("faced with terrible danger") – it would be necessary to ratify all the purchase proposals submitted to them by the JNF Executive and not solely those in the Galilee.[159] Granovsky best expressed this feeling. For various reasons he had previously rejected one of the purchase proposals in the Galilee. However, "faced with the aforesaid danger he could not assume the responsibility of opposing the

---

157   CZA, KKL10, minutes of JNF Directorate meeting, 4.12.1938 – quotation from the statement of Ben-Gurion; Congress (1939), p. 171, statement of Shertok.

158   CZA,KKL10, minutes of JNF Directorate meeting, 14.12.1938 – quotation from there. Cf. ibid., 26.4.1939, at which Ben-Gurion demanded the purchase of lands in the Northern Negev because of the apprehension of prohibition that might be introduced in the future on land purchase in this area. Perhaps information he had received made him change his mind.

159   Ibid., 14.12.1938 – quotation from the statement by Ben-Gurion.

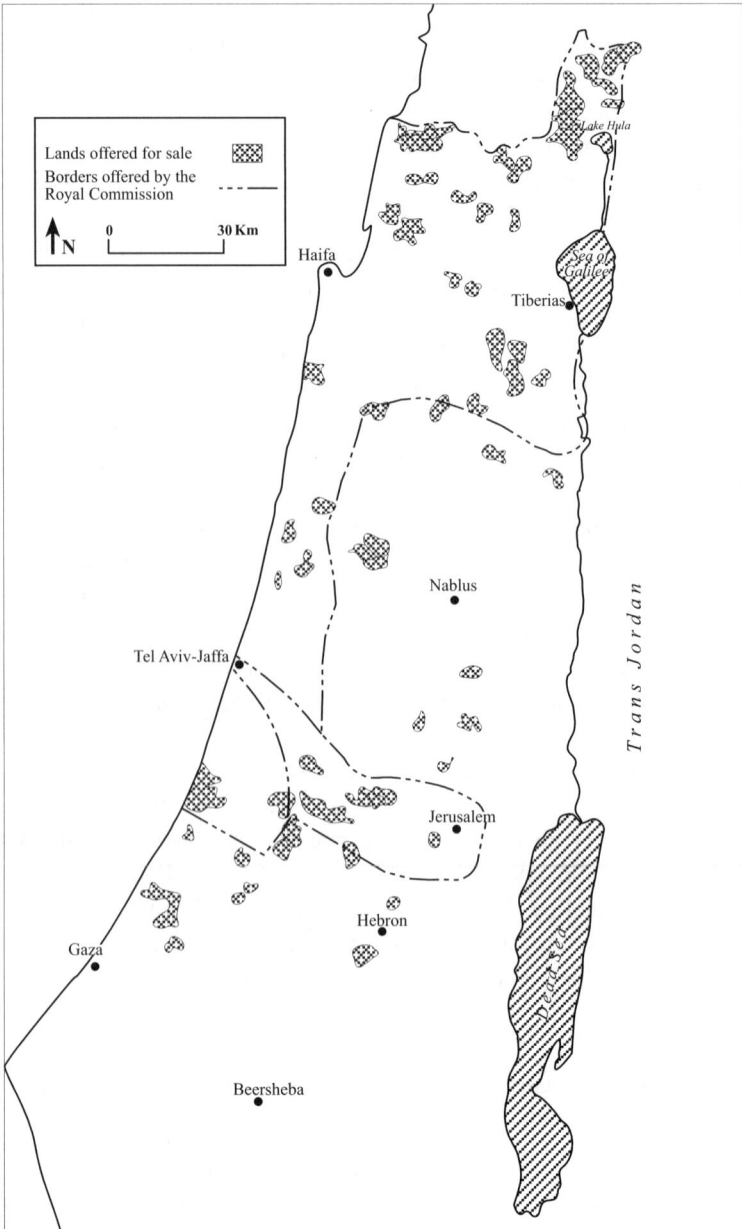

Map 12: Lands offered for sale in the years 1937−1938
Source: JNF map archives, General, 6

purchase and he must assent to it."[160] It fell to Ussishkin and Granovsky, who were responsible for the fiscal stability of the JNF, to raise the problem of the resources for implementing purchases in all its severity. The problem focused on whether the JNF could continue on the same path it had pursued in recent years, and undertake purchases without securing advance assurance of financial coverage. Ussishkin feared that if the restrictive decrees were proclaimed, there would be a drastic decline in contributions, and as a result the JNF would verge on bankruptcy. Whereas Granovsky asked "to what limit can the JNF go in assuming additional financial obligations.... What is the ultimate limit?" At that time JNF obligations totaled more than P£1,100,000 (!), (whereas JNF income in 1939 stood at only P£560,000) and there was no source apparent for defraying these massive obligations. Gravely disappointed, Granovsky observed that the Jewish Agency had approached the Jewish people to assist Keren Hayesod. But "it did not issue a similar summons to the people on behalf of the JNF." Despite the worrisome financial data, the Directorate decided to implement all the purchases on the agenda. It hoped to meet its obligations through a loan from the Anglo-Palestine Company Bank in the maximum sum of P£500,000 for five years (which would be obtained with the assistance of the Jewish Agency), the sale of bonds, and joint purchases with private capital.[161]

Indeed, preference for purchases in the Upper Galilee and purchases beyond the "Partition Commission lines" (including the decision to put down roots in the Northern Negev), and which could be speedily concluded, typified Directorate authorizations and the JNF's purchase activity during the course of 1939 and until the promulgation of the Lands Law in the

---

160 Ibid.
161 Ibid., 14.12.1938 – quotation from there. See also CZA, S53/437f, letter from Granovsky to Hoofien 10.12.1938. For JNF income in 1939 see Appendix 9. The JNF hoped that the APC would approve a loan of P£100,000–200,000, but to the disappointment of the JNF only the amount of P£50,000 was approved. There were among the Bank's Directors those who did not approve the granting of a loan prior to the JNF repaying its previous debt. This caused some of the JNF Directors to propose waiving the loan as a protest, but in light of the political situation which required purchase of lands, they agreed to accept the reduced amount. For details of the receipt of the loan and the disappointment at the behavior of the APC Directors who considered the JNF's loan request by purely commercial principles without relating to the current difficulties, see CZA, KKL10, minutes of JNF Directorate meeting, 28.12.1938.

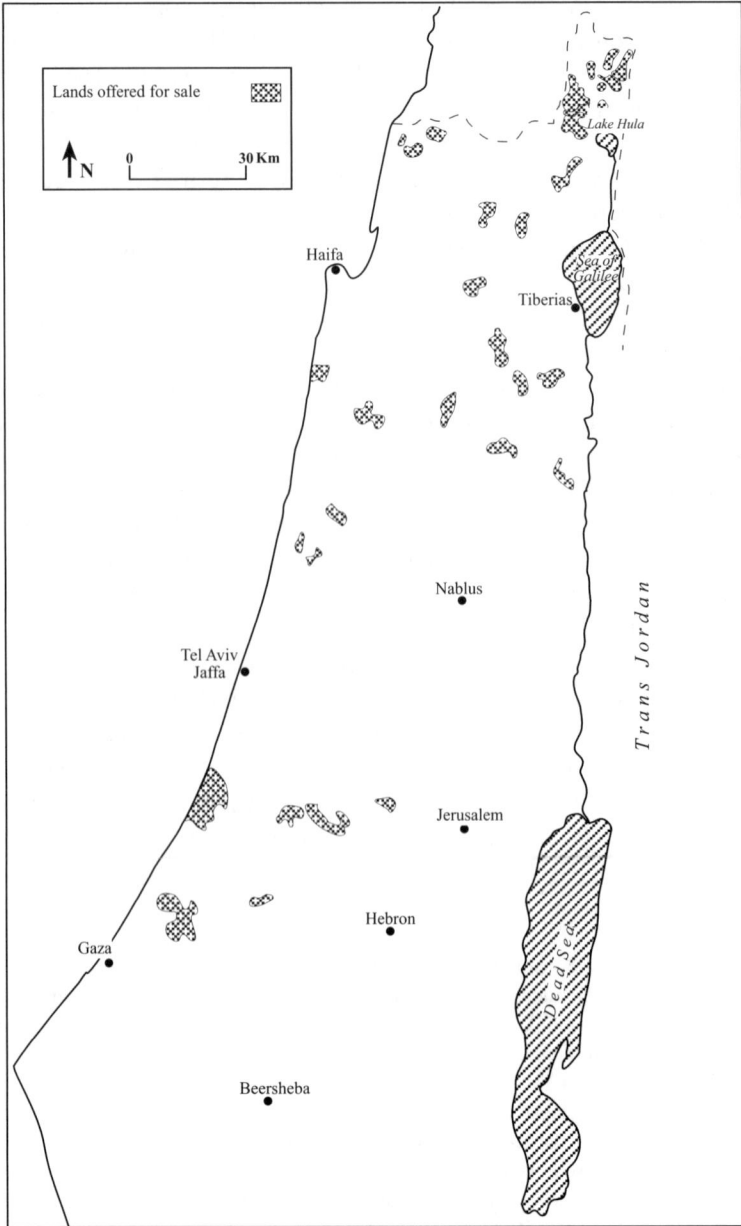

Map 13: Lands offered for sale, summer of 1939
Source: JNF map archives, Map 1553B

beginning of 1940. The sense that harsh decrees were imminent and the availability of a far from negligible supply of land (as can be discerned from Map 13) galvanized activity as long as possible and impelled the JNF "to stretch its fiscal possibilities to the very limit." The Jewish Agency Executive also provided encouragement and perhaps even pressure for maximal purchase activity. The Directorate also emphasized the strategic importance of a number of purchase decisions in the Upper Galilee (such as Azzazit, in the Northern Hula), or the availability of water resources (such as the lands of Dan-Laish–Banias which were the head waters of the Dan). A strategic rationale also accompanied the decision to go ahead with a purchase near Tulkarm, "the 'gateway' to the Sharon Valley, the presence of 2–3 Jewish settlements on the surrounding hills can guard against gangs breaking through the 'gateway' to the Sharon Plain and block them."[162] Nonetheless, the publication of the White Paper in May 1939 and outbreak of the Second World War in autumn of that year, generated a number of further searching deliberations in the JNF Directorate and the Jewish Agency Executive.

A prominent exception to the Directorate's policy during the latter half of 1939 and until the promulgation of the Lands Law, was the decision to purchase Wadi Kabani and Wadi Samara in the Sharon, areas where the PLDC had previously conducted negotiations with the owners.[163] The JNF

---

162 Congress (1939), p. 167, Shertok's statement – the first quotation is from there; CZA, KKL10, minutes of JNF Directorate meetings, 28.12.1938, 26.4.1939 – second quotation is from there, 15.6.1939, 29.6.1939, 18.10.1939, 19.12.1939; CZA, KKL5/ 10517, the following letters: Weitz to Hankin 16.12.1938, Weitz to Zuckerman 20.1.1939, Weitz to Ussishkin 20.2.1939, PICA to JNF 28.3.1939, Weitz to PICA 2.4.1939; CZA, KKL9/238, letter from Sokolowitz to Nahmani 21.4.1939; CZA, KKL5/10465, letter from Nahmani to JNF Lands Department at JNF Head Office 7.11.1939; CZA, KKL5/10617, memorandum "List of lands for which negotiations have been carried out," 1939; CZA, S5/11781, memorandum "Summary of land activities," 1939; CZA, KKL5/11781, memorandum "The main lines for the continuation of our lands purchasing activities," 6.9.1939. See also minutes of Jewish Agency Executive meeting, 5.3.1939, from which it transpires that the availability of lands was also the outcome of the Arabs' apprehension of restrictions. This also transpires from the minutes of Jewish Agency Executive meetings on 18.3.1939, 9.4.1939, 3.12.1939 and from minutes of JNF Directorate meeting, 19.12.1939, CZA, KKL10, see also "From the Partition Commission up to the Land Decrees," at this time; Congress (1939), p. 147.

163 CZA, KKL10, minutes of JNF Directorate meetings, 29.6.1939, 18.10.1939.

Eilon, 1943

Executive justified its purchase recommendation by fears that the Lands Law would apply also to this region and hence the need to increase Jewish control over the Sharon. It is a likely assumption that the fact that this was an especially large area which constituted a continuation to Wadi el-Hawarith with all its inherent settlement potential, together with the fact that the JNF was planning to implement part of the purchase in conjunction with private capital, contributed to the favorable decision.[164] Nevertheless, Katznelson opposed the purchase contending that no restrictions would apply to this region and therefore one could not assent to such a substantial investment of P£95,000 at this time and place. Zalman Schocken as well tended to agree with Katznelson and sought to sound out the Jewish Agency Political Department as to whether restrictions would apply to this area as well.

A letter from Weitz to the PLDC in February 1940 attests to the exceptional nature of the Directorate's decision to acquire Wadi Kabani and Wadi Samara. Weitz, in response to PLDC proposals to implement various purchases in the Sharon, emphasized: "In light of the danger posed by the Lands Law hovering over us, and particularly at this time, we do not see any possibility to channel our financial resources to the purchase

---

164   For further information about JNF cooperation with private capital, see below.

of land in this region, where apparently the law will not be applicable. The difficulty from a fiscal standpoint we are encountering to implement those purchases in the Sharon which we have already undertaken, is sufficient, but to enter into new obligations, is out of the question today." Under certain circumstances, Weitz was prepared to implement the purchase of a plot in the Sharon which supplemented "Tsur Moshe."[165] Another exception during those same years, was the JNF's involvement in purchasing the Yavne lands, an involvement which had commenced already in the 1920s. In the beginning of 1940 it completed the creation of the land infrastructure that facilitated the settlement of Kvutzat Yavne. The JNF engaged in purchasing the land of Yavne in order to realize Ussishkin's idea he had broached in the 1920s to establish a yeshiva in Kerem Deyavne while locating a religious settlement point alongside. In this manner it would be possible to "revive this location" of immensely important historic value.[166] The White Paper published in May 1939 and the clarifications issued by the Mandatory Government, determined that land purchases by Jews would be restricted and even prohibited in various regions, and these prohibitions and restrictions came into effect from the date of the White Paper's publication. The Report of the Partition Commission chaired by John Woodhead was to guide the Government and in other words, the only region where the restrictions and prohibitions on land purchases would not apply, was part of the Coastal Plain (where in any case Jewish settlement was already concentrated). The Lands Law would define the restrictions and prohibited areas, but its date of publication was yet unknown.

Upon the publication of the White Paper, the Zionist Organization, including the JNF, decided that it would not be bound by its prohibitions and what it had portended in the areas of immigration, acquisition of lands and settlement.[167] Nonetheless, in June 1939, the JNF Directorate (apart from

165 CZA, KKL5/1182, letter from Weitz to PLDC 18.2.1940.
166 Katz (1999), pp. 125–130 and the references on these pages. The quotation is from Ussishkin's statement made to the Mizrahi Organization's Steering Committee, CZA, KKL5/11434. In this connection, see also the JNF Directorate's decision to participate in the financing of renovating the area of the graves of Rabbi Yehuda Hanassi and of his family in KKL10, minutes of JNF Directorate meeting, 7.5.1936.
167 Congress (1939), p. 171 – from Shertok's address; CZA, proceedings of Smaller Zionist General Council sessions, 10.5.1939, 26.6.1939; CZA, KKL10, minutes of JNF Directorate meeting, 29.6.1939; CZA, minutes of Jewish Agency Executive

Bernard (Dov) Joseph, 1948

meeting, 12.11.1939; CZA, KKL5/11807, Ben-Gurion's Diaries 31.5.1939; CZA, KKL5/10468, letter from Ussishkin to Hankin 6.6.1939; CZA, KKL5/10465, letter from Weitz to Smilansky 14.7.1939; Political Struggle (1939), p. 1. See also the Congress declaration in Congress (1939), p. 207 which states: "At this moment when the treacherous 'Paper' of the Mandatory Government threatens us with decrees regarding the purchase of land in Palestine, decrees which are liable to uproot the very basis of the building of the homeland of the Jewish People in its land, the Zionist Congress declares that more than ever the redemption of the land is now of political importance of the highest degree and therefore the entire Movement demands that the concern for the land must be its greatest aspiration and efforts…even under conditions of restrictions and decrees with which the treacherous 'Paper' threatens us, the JNF in keeping with its mission in the Zionist upbuilding of the land is obligated to continue its activities despite everything and in every way and means, on condition that it will have at its disposal the extensive means necessary to carry out the numerous commitments it has taken upon itself up till now and the new purchases it is to make under emergency conditions."

Ben-Gurion and Vilkansky) opposed the purchase of Hirbat Masuv which was intended to reinforce the Kibbutzim of Hanita and Eilon in the Western Upper Galilee. The triple risk inherent in the purchase accounted for the opposition: First of all, they were dealing with the purchase of Musha where the Arab partners could block settlement of the land, and therefore the land could be lost to JNF ownership. Secondly, there was serious apprehension that the Lands Law would also encompass the western Upper Galilee in the context of the prohibited zones and by force of the White Paper the prohibition would apply retroactively from the time the White Paper was promulgated. Thus the JNF would forfeit its investments. Thirdly, no solution had yet been found for the problem of tenant farmers. Ben-Gurion, on the other hand, demanded that the purchase be consummated, irrespective of the dangers because this was "the redemption of a large politically strategic area of land in the Upper Galilee, the establishment of a new settlement point in this area and as a result the reinforcement of the two already existing settlement points in that region."[168]

Furthermore, as the WZO Executive's representative in the Directorate, Ben-Gurion raised his demand three days later at the meeting of the WZO Executive and asked for authority to convene the JNF's Directorate for reconsideration. He added that in the event that the Directorate would prove steadfast in its opposition, he would demand the convening of the Smaller Zionist General Council. His position, which was shared by all the other members of the Executive, was that the purchase should be carried out under any conditions without heeding Government warnings and the White Paper. "By not purchasing land, at this time of need, there is a greater danger to the JNF than in its purchase.... If we were to pass up this opportunity, who knows whether we will have a second opportunity to purchase the land." Dov Yosef added that now it was still possible to transfer the land in the Land Registration Office (Tabu) – which would prove impossible after the Lands Law was published.[169]

Aware of the JNF's overall responsibility, Ussishkin clarified to the Jewish Agency Executive that despite the White Paper and the existing apprehension that the High Commissioner would nullify the purchases, he did not in principle oppose land purchases by the JNF. On the contrary,

---

168   CZA, minutes of JNF Directorate meeting, 15.6.1939.
169   CZA, minutes of Jewish Agency Executive meeting, 18.6.1939, and ibid.,
      12.11.1939.

that the JNF had consummated after the White Paper's publication. His opposition, as well as the opposition of the majority of the Directorate's members, was limited to the specific purchase of Hirbat Masuv "where the danger of losing money is substantial." Due to his solicitude for the JNF's independence, Ussishkin was against allowing the Smaller Zionist General Council to deal with this issue and thus he found himself in open confrontation with Ben-Gurion.[170] It is possible that he was also apprehensive of a confrontation regarding the legal interpretation of the status of the Jewish Agency Executive regarding JNF resolutions.[171] It appears that Ussishkin himself was aware of this, and at his own initiative he brought up the issue for reconsideration by the Directorate at the end of June 1939, ten days after the matter had first been discussed. This time the members of the Directorate took a position contrary to that they had expressed two weeks previously. Ussishkin as well, although he did not voice enthusiastic support, was no longer adamantly opposed. There is no doubt that the pressure applied by Ben-Gurion and the Jewish Agency Executive had its effect, especially as the WZO had decided in its entirety upon the publication of the White Paper "that we are working under all conditions." From this standpoint, this purchase was no different than other purchases the Directorate had ratified since the publication of the White Paper.[172] Factors which helped the Directorate adopt a positive decision included a Jewish Agency pledge to arrange for an immediate "settlement conquest" following the consummation of the purchase as well as a legal opinion that should the High Commissioner annul the lands transfer to JNF ownership, the latter could demand the restitution of its investment from the sellers. It appears that by virtue of applying pressures, the Jewish Agency had de facto assumed a shared responsibility for the risks with the JNF, and this also had its effect.[173]

---

170   Ibid., 18.6.1939 – the quotation from there. See also CZA, KKL5/10468, letter from
       Ussishkin to Hankin 6.6.1939.
171   See above, p. 28 regarding the special status of the Jewish Agency Executive relating
       to resolutions of the JNF Directorate.
172   CZA, KKL10, minutes of JNF Directorate meeting, 29.6.1939 – quotation from
       Granovsky's statement. See also CZA, proceedings of the Smaller Zionist General
       Council session, 26.6.1939.
173   CZA, KKL10, minutes of JNF Directorate meeting, 29.6.1939, and see also CZA,
       minutes of Jewish Agency Executive meetings, 7.9.1939 (esp. pp. 6744–6746), and
       12.11.1939 (esp. pp. 6890–6891).

The outbreak of the Second World War in Autumn 1939 posed a severe dilemma for the JNF. The supply of lands for sale expanded still further (amongst other things, as a result of Arab apprehension over the approaching Lands Law, the Arabs'economic plight and the wane of terror) including the possibility of purchasing land from Germans in the German villages. The price of land was also in decline. New proposals now totaled 120,000 dunams at a cost of a million Palestine Pounds. The general feeling in both the Jewish Agency and the JNF was that purchase efforts should be intensified not only because of the impending Lands Law but also because it was of the utmost importance, precisely in a period of war, to fortify Jewish Zionist positions in Palestine in anticipation of the political decisions that would come about at the close of the War. The plight of the Jewish Diaspora was a further reason for buttressing Zionist positions in Palestine, and the JNF would have condemned itself to annihilation if it had announced to its donor reservoir that it had ceased its land purchase activity.[174]

Weitz, for example, emphasized:

> The Zionist Movement must make every effort to operate in this direction so that precisely during the war period it should enhance and strengthen our land capital and not repeat the mistake that was made during the previous war when it refrained from purchasing land.

174 CZA, minutes of Jewish Agency Executive meeting, 7.9.1939, the statements of Ben-Gurion, Shertok, and Gruenbaum. See also CZA, KKL10, minutes of JNF Directorate meetings, 12.10.1939, 19.12.1939. See CZA, KKL5/11821, for Weitz's statement at the internal meeting of personnel of the Information Department held on 24.1.1940, regarding the expansion of land proposals by Arabs, where he stated: "During the past few weeks there has been an increase in the land being offered for sale. There is a feeling as if sluice gates have been opened and the flow that had been stemmed for several years has burst forth and burst its banks. Arab owners of land who previously had not dared to offer their land for sale, are now breathing freely and they come every day to the institutions dealing with the purchase of lands with new offers." At the outbreak of the War, the JNF had hoped that because of the situation England would refrain from implementing the "White Paper" and promulgating the "Lands Law" and thus the possibility of purchasing land would increase. Furthermore, it was assumed that the War situation would not bring about the closure of the Land Registation Offices (see the memorandum "The main points for the continuation of our land buying activities," 6.9.1939, CZA, KKL5/11781). This assumption in fact was confirmed but the previous two hopes were dashed.

The Zionist movement and the JNF in particular should not spend the present war period in idleness or in activity that is insufficient and unsuitable to meet the needs of the great historic hour we are confronting, especially in view of the lesson we learned from the time of the Balfour Declaration until now. We will not be saved by declarations unless we shall direct and intensify the territorial foundation which also constitutes the political basis.[175]

Ussishkin added:

It is essential for the sake of the Jewish people's hopes and its future in Palestine and for the sake of the existence of the Jewish National Fund to decide at this time on purchasing new lands and not to cease the redemption of the land for even a single day.[176]

Katznelson and Ben-Gurion summed up:

He [Katznelson] does not hope for a new declaration by England favoring the land of Israel and the Jewish people. Hope rests entirely on the Palestinian Jewish Community's ability to seize new positions during the War and fortify existing ones. The fate of Palestine, the fate of the Jewish people, is contingent on our success in altering in our favor the practical situation in Palestine during the War, in a real and perceptible manner. He [Katznelson] does not attach hope for the possibility of political conquests. "Conquest" could only take a practical form here in Palestine, and this task is the responsibility of the Jewish community in Palestine.[177]

The present period will determine the situation of Palestine and the Jewish people in their land and their people for generations. Such a situation cannot be accepted passively and with resignation, but vigorous action must be taken to direct it to our advantage.[178]

However, alongside these arguments, the question of the JNF's fiscal capability resurfaced in all its asperity. To what extent, in light of the war situation, was it entitled to assume additional obligations? From Poland

---

175   CZA, KKL10, minutes of JNF Directorate meeting, 12.10.1939.
176   Ibid.
177   Ibid.
178   Ibid., from Ben-Gurion's statement.

with its 3,000,000 Jews, contributions had ceased. The prospects for contributions from Western Europe had come to a standstill as a result of the War. The JNF could not continue to juggle funds as it had in normal years. The banks had stopped extending credit, whereas private lenders were likewise not inclined to grant loans or extend payment dates as they had done in the past. An attempt to obtain a loan in the amount of a million dollars in the United States did not succeed; only half the amount was raised.This new situation not only did not allow the JNF to continue to make new purchases, but also did not permit it to meet its previous financial obligations. "And this conclusion is a 'double-ended stick.' On the one hand, the continuation of land purchases is necessary for the JNF's continued organizational and propaganda work, and on the other hand, if the JNF does not meet the financial obligations it has assumed to this date, it will not be able to survive."[179]

Nonetheless, the Directorate decided to continue purchases and by a majority (with Granovsky and Vilkansky dissenting) it accepted Ussishkin's proposal to adopt a "golden mean" and for the time being ratify new purchases in the ratio of a quarter of the amount offered as submitted to the Directorate by the JNF Executive (30,000 dunams out of 120,000) which called for an investment of P£250,000. Seventy-five percent of the purchases would be concluded in the Upper Galilee (the Hula region, central and western Upper Galilee).[180] The JNF hoped to obtain the funding primarily from the following sources: contributions from the United States following intensified public relations work there, the issuing of dollar bonds, selling off real estate registered under the names of the Meheiman and Himnuta companies, which derived from the living bequest projects in Germany and in Palestine, and collaboration with wealthy individuals who would purchase land jointly with the JNF.[181]

---

179 CZA, minutes of JNF Directorate meeting, 18.10.1939 – quotation from Granovsky's statement; CZA, minutes of Jewish Agency Executive meeting, 7.9.1939; CZA, S53/437, joint Information Bulletin published by Jewish Agency Executive, JNF and Keren Hayesod 1940/4, 23.11.1939; CZA, KKL5/11821, Weitz's statement at the internal meeting of the Information Department personnel, 23.1.1940.

180 CZA, KKL10, minutes of JNF Directorate meeting, 18.10.1939; CZA, KKL9/446, letter from Nahmani to Lands Department at JNF Head Office 7.11.1939.

181 CZA, KKL10, minutes of JNF Directorate meeting, 18.10.1939. Granovsky raised the main issues. See also CZA, S53/437, Information Bulletin issued jointly by Jewish Agency Executive, JNF and Keren Hayesod 1940/4, 23.11.1939.

At the end of 1939, in its last session before the promulgation of the Lands Law, the JNF Directorate authorized the completion of some additional purchases because the terms of these purchase offers did not require immediate payment.[182] The Jewish Agency Executive's position unreservedly favored continued purchases and even applied pressure in this direction. This not only constituted a source of encouragement for Ussishkin to continue to advocate purchases, despite the unbearably difficult problems of finance, but he viewed this as an assumption of shared responsibility by the Jewish Agency for any financial embarrassment the JNF might face as a result of the risks it had undertaken.[183]

Details of the JNF's total purchases during 1936–1939 can be found in maps 14, 15 and appendices 3, 4, 5.

Collaboration on Land Purchases with Private Companies and Private Capital

The widespread land purchase activity which the JNF entered during 1937–1939, as well as its original intentions to purchase the Hula Concession from the PLDC, obligated the JNF to find sources for financing over and beyond contributions and loans. One of the important methods for obtaining finance was the creation of collaborative frameworks in land purchases with the Amica Company, with Africa–Palestine Investments Ltd. Company, and with private capital. The Amica Company was founded in 1933 by the Jewish Colonization Association and the Ha-Ezra Fund (a fund operated jointly by a number of bodies and which was founded in the wake of the 1929 disturbances as a company for agricultural settlement) and it represented the JCA in Palestine.[184] The Africa–Palestine Company

---

182   CZA, KKL10, minutes of JNF Directorate meeting, 19.12.1939.
183   CZA, minutes of Jewish Agency Executive meeting, 7.9.1939, pp. 6744–6746. See also CZA, minutes of Jewish Agency Executive meeting, 12.11.1939, pp. 6890–6891, in which Ussishkin considered the Jewish Agency Executive as a guarantor in the event that the Government would invalidate purchases the JNF had undertaken as a consequence of the "White Paper."
184   On the Amica Company and the Ezra Fund see Merhavia, pp. 324–328; Bein (1976), pp. 332–334, 356, 380. On the difference between the JCA and PICA see in detail: Schama (1978); CZA, KKL5/15620, letter from Granovsky to Gronman 8.10.1946.

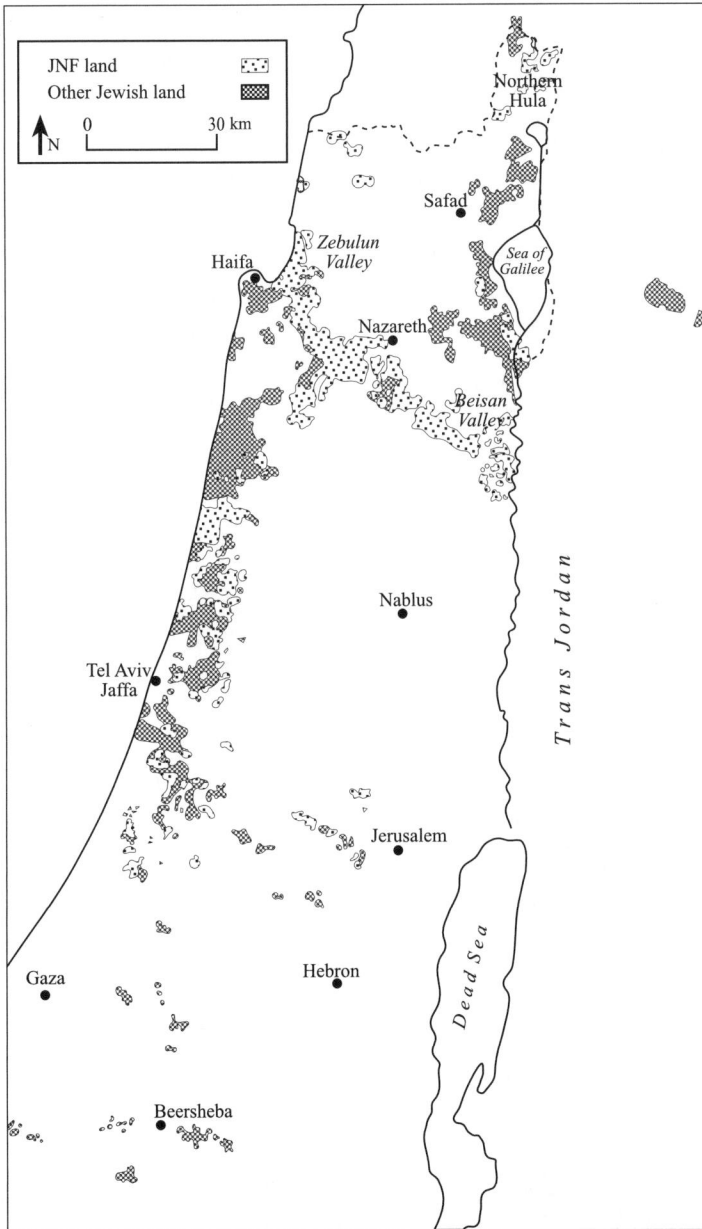

Map 14: Jewish land property and JNF land property in the beginning of 1939
Source: JNF map archives, Map 4095

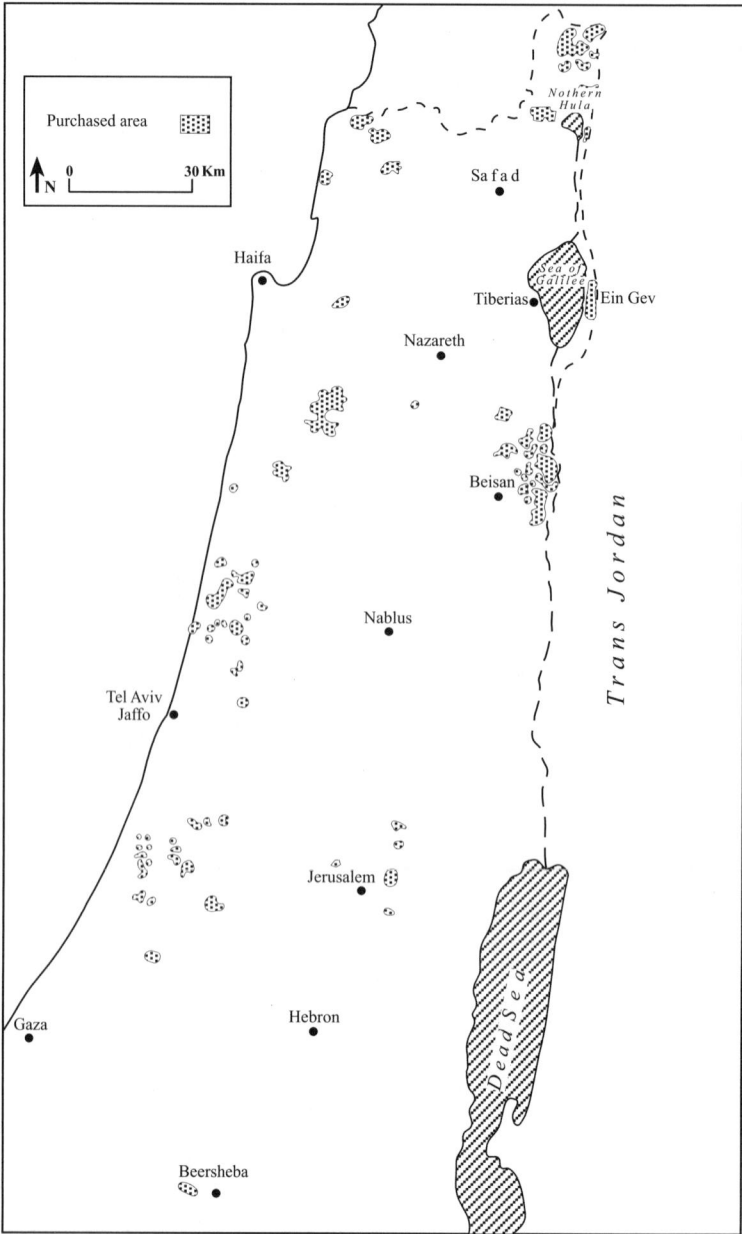

Map 15: Lands purchased by JNF during the events of 1936–1939
Source: KKL archive, Map 4111

was a private investment company founded by the Zionist Federation of South Africa.[185] The JNF was affiliated with these two companies from the beginning of 1936 in purchasing the lands of the Northern Hula and the vicinity, and this was in addition to the JNF's own purchases in this region. As stated above, the JNF's interest in the Northern Hula began following the purchase of the concession by the PLDC in 1934 as it endeavored "to guarantee a Jewish milieu for the Hula Concession by purchasing lands in the north of this valley."[186] However, since the outbreak of the disturbances, there were added strategic and political motivations. An agreement between the Amica Co. and the JNF at the end of 1935 created a consortium for purchasing lands in the north of the Hula with a capital of P£100,000, with each party contributing half the amount. All purchase proposals would be submitted for deliberation to both institutions and completion of the joint purchase would required the prior agreement of both parties. The deeds of sale on joint purchases would be registered jointly under the names of the two parties, similar to the joint purchases the JNF had previously made in Haifa Bay with the Palestine Economic Company.[187] In practice, the JNF's purchase amounts within the framework of this consortium were limited because the conditions of the consortium "constrained our freedom of activity [of the JNF]. Every transfer of land requires the authorization of both companies and the JCA predicates its activity on a conservative financial commercial basis. It is frequently deterred from purchases involving special difficulties, such as Musha lands registered in joint ownership with Arabs, land which has tenant farmers, etc."[188]

185   On the Africa–Palestine Company see: Merhavia, p. 328; Granovsky (1938), p. 218.
186   The quotation is from CZA, KKL5/4746/1, JNF Information Bulletin 1937/f 20.1.1937 concerning "the involvement of the JNF in the Hula."
187   CZA, KKL5/4746, JNF Information Bulletin 1936/g 23.3.1936 concerning "cooperation between the JCA and the JNF in the Hula region." CZA, KKL5/7410, JNF report for the first half of 1936; CZA, KKL10, minutes of JNF Directorate meetings, 2.1.1936, 30.3.1936; Buying Land (1938), pp. 8–9.
188   CZA, KKL5/10475, JNF Information Bulletin 1938/4, 18.2.1938 concerning "JNF Activities in Upper Galilee and the Hula region" – quotation from there; Granovsky (1938), p. 219. Cf. Weitz (1947), p. 32. Regarding the decision in principle of the Amica Company not to enter into purchases in the Hula (except in certain cases) where there are no obligations on the part of the owners to evacuate the peasant farmers see: CZA, KKL5/10010, the following letters: Amica Co. to Granovsky 8.11.1938, Weitz to Passman of Amica Co. 14.11.1938, Amica Co. to JNF Head Office 18.11.1938. Following upon the publication of the Partition Commission Report, Amica Co.

Much more successful from the JNF's standpoint was a consortium which it established with the Africa–Palestine Company. The agreement was signed at the beginning of 1936, but its conditions were different from those established between the JNF and the Amica Company. This agreement was for the joint purchase of 10,000 dunams in the Hula area (with an option for expansion) of which the Africa–Palestine Company would receive from the JNF within three years 3,000 dunams (in one bloc or a number of contiguous blocs), which would be registered exclusively in its name, and free of tenant farmers, or any other lien. The company undertook to transfer to the JNF its share of the investments in the partnership whenever the JNF should request it to do so. In the event that the JNF would not be able to meet its obligations, Africa–Palestine's investment in this project would be transformed into a loan at an interest rate of 5% per annum. On the other hand, Africa–Palestine agreed to turn over to the JNF total and exclusive responsibility for implementing the purchases so that the purchase "would be expedited without any encumbrances or protracted deliberation."[189] Nonetheless, in the beginning of 1939, Africa–Palestine sought to withdraw from the partnership, as it was entitled to under the 1936 agreement. The reason for this was that on the appointed date the JNF failed to turn over to it the Hula lands in the total of 3,000 dunams, free of tenant farmers and all other liens. Given the special priority the JNF attached to the Hula region during those years, the JNF invested major

---

requested the delay of the purchase of Hula lands on which there was a problem of tenant farmers. Concerning litigation and disputes between the JNF and the Amica Co. on the division of expenses, see CZA, KKL5/10009, letter from Amica Co. to Granovsky 20.4.1937; CZA, KKL/10006, minutes of meeting concerning the Hula lands 18.10.1937 with the participation of Hexter, Passman, Granovsky, Weitz and Nahmani; CZA, KKL5/10005, letter from Klee of JNF to Amica Co. 8.4.1938, letter from Weitz to Amica 16.5.1938; CZA, KKL5/10008, letter from Amica Co. to JNF 20.5.1938; CZA, KKL5/10005, letter from Weitz to Amica Co. 7.6.1938. Regarding cooperation between the JNF and Amica Co. concerning the purchase of lands of Kefar Warburg which the Amica Co. had established, see CZA, KKL10, minutes of JNF Directorate meeting, 19.12.1939.

189 CZA, KKL5/10475, JNF Information Bulletin 1938/4, 18.2.1938 concerning JNF activities in the Upper Galilee and Hula area; CZA, KKL5/10469, letter from Weitz to Africa-Palestine Co. Ltd. 16.4.1939; CZA, KKL5/8393, letter from Africa–Palestine to JNF, no date, with details of the agreement between them; CZA, KKL5/10010, letter from Africa–Palestine to JNF 14.7.1936; CZA, KKL10, minutes of JNF Directorate meetings, 23.1.1936, 8.2.1938; Granovsky (1938), p. 218.

efforts to persuade Africa–Palestine not to withdraw from the partnership but to continue joint purchases with the JNF in the Hula area beyond the original 3,000 dunams. It would appear that these efforts were successful[190] and in any event, until the end of 1939, the total purchases in the Hula area within the framework of the consortia, amounted to 25,300 dunams.[191]

On the basis of its partnership with the Amica Co. and the Africa–Palestine Company, from the first half of 1938 the JNF began formulating plans for land purchase partnership with private capital. The intention was to raise through these partnerships significant amounts of capital within a short time, which would assist the JNF in its financial plight. Cooperation would extend to lands in regions attractive to private capital, and first and foremost the Sharon. In this manner, the JNF sought to accumulate resources to be used in regions where private capital did not tend to venture, especially the Upper Galilee. The JNF made these plans public in various locations throughout the world. The JNF Finance Department headed by Granovsky was entrusted with formulating the plans and reaching actual agreement with owners of private capital.

The main plans included the following components: (1) The capital owner (or group of capital owners) would invest between one-third to half the total cost of the land purchase which the JNF intended to effect. The capital owner's minimum investment was for a plot of 1,000 dunams, and the required sum ranged between P£7,000 to P£15,000. Where the investors constituted a group, the share of each participant would be at least P£500. (2) In return for his share in the partnership, the capital owner was obligated to pay the JNF a one-time cash payment via a deposit in the JNF's account in the APC. He was not entitled to demand reimbursement for this payment before a period of twelve months had elapsed. (3) Responsibility for decisions, purchase and registration were totally to be made by the JNF. (4) In cases of the purchase of "Mafruz" land, the purchaser's plot would be immediately transferred to the capital owner. But when dealing with the purchase of "Musha," the land would be registered jointly (in accordance with the shares in the partnership) in the names of the JNF and of the capital owner and at the time it became Mafruz, the appropriate plot would

---

190   CZA, KKL5/10469, letter from Weitz to Africa–Palestine 16.4.1939; CZA, KKL5/10010, letter from Africa-Palestine to JNF 23.4.1939.

191   CZA, KKL10, minutes of JNF Directorate meeting, 18.10.1939.

be registered in the capital owner's name. (5) The capital owner reserved the option to withdraw from the purchase within three years and transfer his plot to the JNF, on condition that it abutted the JNF's lands. In such an event, the JNF had to restore all investments made by the capital owner in installment payments at an interest of 4% over five years. (6) When a capital owner wished to sell his purchase, the JNF enjoyed a first option to make the purchase. In the event that the JNF chose not to exercise its option, the capital owner could sell his plot to a third party, but in order to prevent speculation, the JNF could set a price limit on the sale to a third party.[192] After the outbreak of the Second World War, the plan stipulated that the investor would receive his land or his money after the War.[193]

In order to increase collaboration with private capital as far as possible, it can be ascertained from these plans that there was little risk on the part of the investors. On the other hand, these plans were limited only to capital owners in countries where the export of capital was not prohibited (or in those countries where such prohibition could be circumvented). In practice, these plans placed the JNF in a form of competition with the

---

192 CZA, KKL5/10473, letter from Mohilewer of the JNF to JNF presidium in Bessarabia 2.5.1938; CZA, KKL5/10475, the following letters: Mohilewer to JNF Bureau in Kovno 31.5.1938, Granovsky to JNF Executive in Romania 17.2.1938, Granovsky to JNF Executive in Austria 15.2.1938, Granovsky to the JNF National Committee 8.5.1938; CZA, KKL5/10473, memorandum from de Shalit to Granovsky and Weitz 13.5.1938 regarding cooperation of private capital with the JNF for land purchase in Palestine; CZA, KKL5/10475, Granovsky to Kurtzi 1.7.1938, JNF to Tenenbaum 7.7.1938; CZA, KKL5/10473, Granovsky to de Shalit in Romania 17.7.1938; CZA, KKL5/11786, sample agreement between the JNF and private investor within the framework of cooperation of private capital for land purhase; CZA, L51/1007, Granovsky to Zalheimer 17.10.1939; CZA, KKL5/11786, letter from Mohilewer to Gutloewer 21.11.1939; CZA, KKL5/10475, JNF Information Bulletin 1938/4, 18.2.1938 concerning JNF activities in Upper Galilee and the Hula region; Alexander (1993), p. 96; Granovsky (1938), pp. 139–140, 216–219 sets out further reasons (other than raising capital) to put into operation the plan for collaboration with private capital. However, we have not found archival documentation for this. Cf. CZA, S53/16753d, letter from Landauer to Ben-Gurion, Shertok, Kaplan and Vilkansky 7.1.1938 (also in S7/535); CZA, S25/6559, letter from Harzfeld to Shertok – from which it appears that it was Landauer, of the Central Bureau for the Settlement of German Jews, who first proposed the outline for the plan for collaboration between the JNF and private capital.
193 CZA, KKL5/11736, letter from JNF National Committee in Palestine to JNF Head Office 24.11.1939.

PLDC, the official Zionist body for the purchase of lands through private capital. Although the JNF took pains to emphasize that in establishing the maximum of 1,000 dunams for a party interested in subscribing to the plan it was motivated by a desire that "the JNF does not want to appear on the land trading market as a competitor with the PLDC which engaged in the sale of small plots." An additional reason for setting a maximum of 1,000 dunams was to provide for cases "where a private purchaser or a group of private purchasers would exercise their right and forego the land and it would pass to the JNF, the area has to be of a size which would enable it to be used for settlement purposes. Therefore, a small isolated plot does not enter into consideration in this respect."[194]

Although the essential goal of the plans for collaboration with private capital was to raise substantial capital immediately for consummating widespread purchases which the JNF had to implement due to the pressing needs of the hour, these plans can be viewed as a "deviation" from the JNF's traditional path of engaging exclusively in leasing lands rather than in their sale, as defined in its constitution. Furthermore, it emerges that a proposal calling for the JNF to establish a company that would engage in land sales to private individuals – a proposal which arose at the time when the aforementioned collaboration schemes with private capital went into effect, was rejected by the JNF not on grounds of principle but because "we cannot create a company whose tasks would be similar to those of the PLDC. This would arouse the justified resentment of the PLDC. It is better for us to forego the idea of selling lands to private individuals if only to spare ourselves such entanglements."[195]

Indeed the lands which were the object of collaboration schemes with private capital were registered in the name of the Himnuta Company in order to avoid a situation where the JNF would flout its by-laws prohibiting sale. Yet it remains surprising that the plans for collaboration with private capital did not require deliberations in the Directorate as they touched on a matter of principle.[196] Perhaps this is evidence of how little the JNF was

---

194   CZA, KKL5/10475, letter from Mohilewer to JNF Bureau in Kovno 31.5.1938 concerning collaboration with owners of private capital in land purchases by the JNF.

195   CZA, KKL5/10473, letter from Granovsky to de Shalit in Bucharest 26.6.1938.

196   KKL10, minutes of JNF Directorate meetings, 14.12.1938, 18.10.1938; CZA, KKL5/10475, JNF Information Bulletin 1938/4, 18.2.1938, concerning JNF activities in Upper Galilee and the Hula region.

perturbed by the fact that the organization was almost directly involved in the lands sale business and, moreover, to private capital to which the JNF had stated its opposition on more than one occasion. On the other hand, it would appear that the necessity for obtaining the financial resources to fulfill the special missions which the JNF confronted in redeeming land during that period, and which has been discussed in detail above (pp. 83–122), compelled it to adopt this method as well, and thus justified the deviation, especially as the partnership with private capital was a long way from becoming the JNF's primary business. In this vein, a JNF circular that dealt with the program of collaboration with private capital summed up the issue: "These transactions are invaluable for the JNF which is interested in redeeming the lands in any form whatsoever. By involving private capital, it attracts the private investor to the land market, receives money in cash for activities in this direction and guarantees the redemption of areas that otherwise would not have been purchased due to lack of resources and would have slipped out of Jewish hands."[197] Granovsky, on the other hand, admitted that collaboration with private capital was indeed in contradiction to the JNF's position regarding the priority of national ownership over the lands of Palestine but "we are not blind zealots in defending our principles and in this hour of emergency, one goal awaits us: to redeem the land speedily and ceaselessly."[198]

The first country where the JNF sought to implement plans for cooperation with private capital was Romania where the JNF estimated that it could raise the equivalent of P£100,000. In the wake of preliminary discussions with the chairman of the local Zionist organization, the JNF dispatched Moshe de Shalit in May 1938 to Romania in order to put the plan into operation. After half a year of vigorous work, which proved highly instructive regarding the considerations of private owners of capital, and their suspicions and skepticism, de Shalit managed to sign up capitalists on collaboration contracts totaling over 3,000 dunams in the Sharon (see

197   CZA, KKL5/11786, JNF Head Office circular 14.1.1941. See also CZA, KKL5/
       10473, letter from JNF to Rabbi Namirover 19.5.1938.
198   Buying Land (1939), pp. 13–14. It would seem that it was no coincidence that
       Granovsky who promoted the plan for collaboration with private capital, stated in a
       Directorate meeting in another connection that "he was not among those who opposed
       in principle the purchase of land by Jews." See KKL10, minutes of JNF Directorate
       meeting, 6.7.1936.

Map 16) in the amount of P£40,000 – far less than expected.[199] In Romania a prohibition against the export of capital outside the country's boundaries existed, but "individuals overcame the prohibition on exporting capital by stratagems involving informal transfer."[200] In Romania an interest was evinced in purchasing areas cheaper than the Sharon. Especially cheaper were the lands in the Upper Galilee, "but this can't be offered to private capital because immediately upon purchase of the land possession must be taken and a settlement built there. The land requires massive site preparation and is not suitable for the middle class."[201]

The outbreak of the Second World War encumbered the expansion of collaboration plans with private capital abroad, although JNF activity did not cease there. Thus, a few weeks prior to the German conquest of Belgium, an attempt was made to organize capitalists there and negotiations with them were on the verge of conclusion, but the German invasion thwarted all these efforts. Among the locations that the JNF targeted for partnership with private capital was Wadi Kabani which the JNF was involved in purchasing at that time.[202] In any event, because of the outbreak of the War, the efforts and plans for collaboration with private capital focused on Palestine. In addition to the plans drawn up in 1938, two additional plans were formulated: Issuing interest-bearing bonds, capitalized at P£100,000 (the price of every bond was P£10), and the investor had the option of converting the financial return into the receipt of urban land of appropriate value. This plan was to be jointly operated by the JNF and the Anglo–Palestine Company Bank. But since in effect this was the sale of lands

---

199   CZA, KKL5/10473, letter from Y. Granovsky to de Shalit 17.7.1938, letter from JNF to Rabbi Namirover 19.5.1938; CZA, KKL5/10474, detailed report from de Shalit 9.10.1938 on his mission to Romania and his attempts to find investors for the JNF plan for collaboration with private capital; CZA, KKL5/10473, the following letters: Weitz to de Shalit 14.6.1938, Granovsky to de Shalit in Romania 26.6.1938, Granovsky to de Shalit in Romania 21.7.1938, Granovsky to de Shalit in Romania 22.7.1938; CZA, KKL5/10475, letter from Granovsky to Rabbi Berlin 1.8.1938; CZA, KKL5/10474, letter from Granovsky to de Shalit in Romania 24.8.1938.

200   CZA, KKL5/10475, letter from Granovsky to Rabbi Berlin 1.8.1938. See also CZA, KKL5/11786, JNF Head Office circular 14.1.1941; Alexander (1993), pp. 93–95.

201   CZA, KKL5/10573, letter from Weitz to de Shalit in Romania 14.6.1938.

202   CZA, KKL10, minutes of JNF Directorate meeting, 18.10.1939; CZA, KKL5/11786, JNF Head Office circular 14.1.1941.

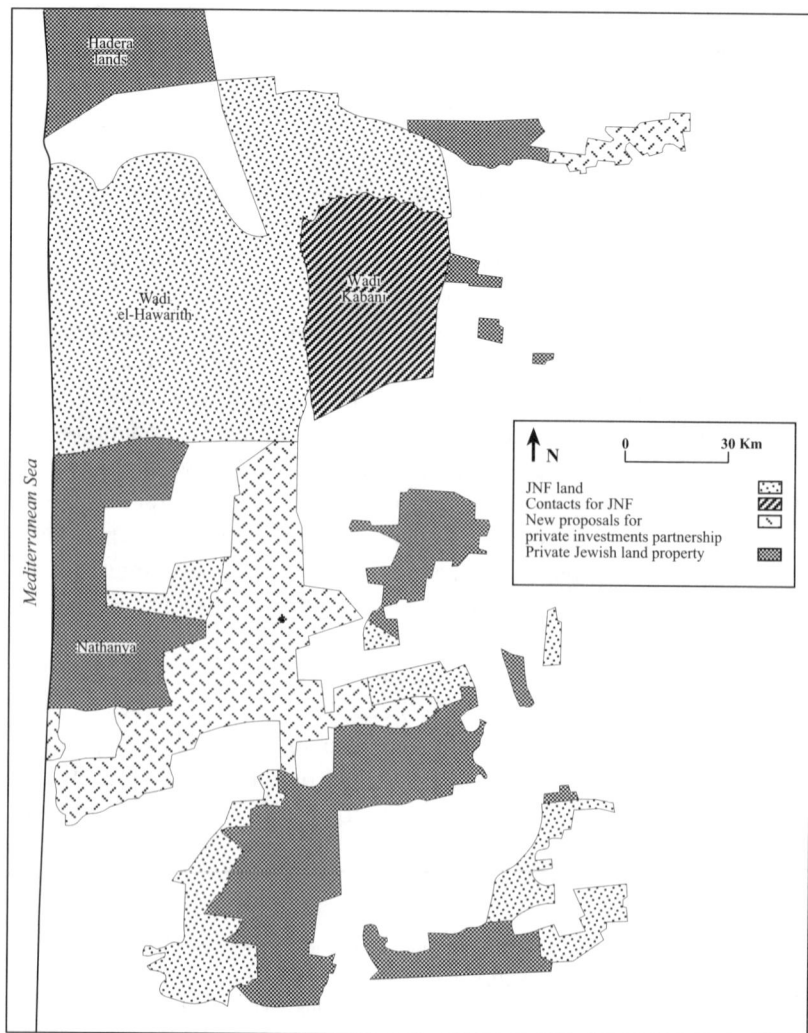

Map 16: JNF land property in the Sharon area and purchase proposals in the
framework of cooperation with private investors, 1938
Source: JNF map archives, Map 1538

by the JNF, the PLDC or the Meheiman Company were registered in the contract as the sellers.[203]

The second plan, similar in principle to the partnership the JNF had with the Africa–Palestine Company, proposed the JNF's affiliation with a group of local investors amassing private capital in the amount of at least P£30,000. The JNF was to confer exclusivity to this company and refer to it all private capital interested in making purchases jointly with the JNF. The latter would purchase lands for the company and register them in the names of the company's trustees. The company reserved an option for four years to withdraw from its intention to purchase and in such case its money would be refunded in annual payments, in addition to profits determined in advance between the JNF and the company, as well as an annual interest of 4.5%. No limitations were imposed by the JNF on the company regarding the manner in which the purchased land would be utilized. On the basis of these principles, a memorandum was signed at the beginning of 1940 between the JNF and Joseph Sinigalia on behalf of a group of investors (subsequently the Matmon Company), but it would appear that the entire venture never got off the ground.[204] It should be mentioned that during the 1940s the JNF continued its plans of collaboration with private capital as will be explained in the following chapter.[205]

---

203   CZA, KKL5/11786, letter from Granovsky to the JNF National Committee in Palestine 12.12.1939; CZA, L51/1007, the following letters: Granovsky to the Executive of the APC 17.12.1939, APC to Granovsky 24.12.1939, memorandum of a meeting on 15.1.1940 with the participation of representatives of JNF and APC.

204   CZA, KKL5/11793, letter from Granovsky to Sinigalia in Ramat Gan 29.1.1940; CZA, KKL5/11786, memorandum dated 29.2.1940 "Concerning the Main Points of the Arrangement between the JNF and Sinigalia on behalf of a Group of Investors"; CZA, KKL5/11793 the following documents: draft agreement dated 4.4.1940 "concerning the main points," of the arrangement between JNF and Sinigalia on behalf of a group of investors," draft of an agreement dated 7.6.1940 between JNF and Matmon Company, Yesodot (no date), letter from Sinigalia to Granovsky 29.7.1940, letter from Granovsky to Sinigalia 3.4.1940, letter from Granovsky to Sinigalia 16.7.1940.

205   See below p. 239.

Organizations Influencing the Jewish National Fund's Purchasing Activities

As outlined above, the Jewish Agency was an important interested party that exerted influence both in determining the extent of the JNF's agricultural land purchases, as well as their location. It was motivated by political–strategic calculations as well as by a desire to reinforce settlements.[206] It emerges that additional parties had a sizable interest in the manner in which the JNF implemented purchases and they worked to steer the JNF purchase activity in a direction consonant with this interest. The JNF had to examine the degree to which the objectives of these organizations, which sought to influence its purchase activity, corresponded to its own policy and priorities. However, it would appear that it could not exclude from its considerations the "power of the organization which sought to exert an influence."

It would appear that the most prominent of these interested parties was the Histadrut's Agricultural Center, headed by Avraham Hartzfeld. The special interest which the Agricultural Center took in JNF purchases began a long time before the period covered by this book, because the Center in practice functioned as the representative of the vast majority of bodies which had set up settlements on JNF land or who were about to settle either within the Kibbutz or the Moshav framework. Therefore, during the period under discussion as well, the Agricultural Center sought to steer the JNF in a direction corresponding to the needs of its constituent bodies, both in terms of the size or site of the purchases. These needs primarily centered on the creation of a territorial base for the establishment of new Kibbutzim and Moshavim and accommodating the expansion needs of the existing ones. Furthermore, the Agricultural Center, which conducted a form of territorial policy of its own in pursuit of its interests, occasionally established direct contact with the land sellers and intermediaries and presented the JNF with

---

206   CZA, KKL5/7421, letter from Ussishkin to Hankin 19.2.1937 (also in KKL5/8741); CZA, S25/7061, letter from Stern to Ben-Gurion and Shertok 6.7.1938; CZA, KKL10, minutes of JNF Directorate meeting, 6.12.1937, 6.7.1938, 15.6.1939; Katz (1999)), p. 84. See also CZA, KKL10, minutes of JNF Directorate meeting, 26.4.1939 concerning the JNF Directorate's approval of the Jewish Agency's request to purchase an area of land on the coast near Herzliya in order to gain control of the boat anchorage there.

the results of those contacts and a list of purchases which it requested the JNF to implement. This form of activity was displeasing to Weitz because it led to price increases and impaired the JNF's centralization of purchase activity. In a letter to the Agricultural Center at the end of December 1937 Weitz emphasized:

> In our opinion it is improper for you to be negotiating with various people and receiving land sale offers from them, because this leads the intermediaries to consider you an additional land purchase body separate from existing institutions and this drives up prices and obfuscates the path to land buying. In our opinion it would be more suitable that in any case when someone approaches you with such offers you should refer him directly to the PLDC or to us.

In a further letter he complains:

> We acknowledge receipt of your letter in which you propose that we purchase an area of 1300 dunams…in the Sharon. Since you are not the intermediaries in the purchase and sale of lands, but 'someone' brought you this proposal, would you therefore be kind enough to refer this 'someone' directly to us in this case and also in similar cases. The undersigned believes that it does not serve the good of the cause that the Agricultural Center should also function as an office for land bargaining.[207]

---

207   CZA, KKL5/10516, letters from Weitz to Agricultural Center 12.12.1937, Weitz to Agricultural Center 17.12.1937 – first quotation from there; CZA, KKL5/10516, letter from Weitz to Agricultural Center 11.1.1938 – the second quotation from there; CZA, S55/201, letter from Hartzfeld to PLDC Executive 31.10.1933; CZA, S44/161, letter from Hartzfeld to Ben-Gurion 2.1.1936; CZA, KKL5/8777, letter from Weitz to Agricultural Center 23.2.1936; CZA, S55/201, letters from Hartzfeld to Ruppin 29.1.1936, Ruppin to Hartzfeld 2.2.1936; CZA, S44/60c, letter from Hartzfeld to JNF 18.3.1936; CZA, KKL5/8777, the following documents: Agricultural Center's memorandum dated 22.12.1938 "Summary of proposals for purchase of lands by the JNF," letters from Weitz to Agricultural Center 4.3.1937, Weitz to Agricultural Center 19.3.1937, Hartzfeld to JNF Head Office 13.6.1937; CZA, S7/404, letter from Landauer to Hartzfeld 17.8.1937; CZA, S7/535, letters from the Habehorot group of Hakibbutz Hameuhad to Agricultural Center 22.3.1938, Hartzfeld to JNF Head Office 2.1.1938; CZA, KKL5/8904, letter from Weitz to Kollar of Agricultural Center 22.7.1938. A typical example of approach made by the Agricultural Center to the JNF is the following: "We hereby propose the purchase of 750–800 dunams of

Avraham Hartzfeld on the Day of the Ascent to Hanita, 1938

It is not clear to what extent the Agricultural Center brought pressure to bear on Directorate members who were its "intimates," such as Ben-Gurion and Katznelson, to further their interest in the JNF. But there is testimony from which it emerges that Ben-Gurion was requested "to stand by us" with regards to one of the disputes between the Agricultural Center and the JNF Executive.[208]

PLDC land called 'Maretz land' on the following conditions…we attach a map of the proposed area and we request that you place this proposal on the agenda of the next JNF Directorate meeting…. This proposal is directed toward the settlement of the Hashomer Hatza'ir kibbutz Bemesilla which is at Giv'at Michael near Nes Tziyona…. The kibbutz undertakes to contribute to part of the investment in this area…and will reach agreement with the PLDC on terms of payment." Cf. CZA, KKL5/8777, letter from Hartzfeld to JNF Head Office 2.5.1937. See also CZA, KKL5/11387, letter from Hartzfeld to JNF Head Office 2.1.1938 concerning the Agricultural Center's request to the JNF to purchase land near Herzliya: "The proposed area costs P£20 per dunam. It is free of any liens by tenants and the transfer at the Land Registration Office can be effected immediately."

208   CZA, S44/161, letter from Hartzfeld to Ben-Gurion 2.1.1936.

Tel Amal – Nir David, 1936

Although one of the JNF's central objectives was to create the territorial foundation for settlement predicated on agricultural labor,[209] there was no unanimity between the Agricultural Center and the JNF on this matter. Thus, while the Agricultural Center had an interest in expanding its settlements which were yearning for land, even if the land to be purchased for this objective was already Jewish owned, the policy of the JNF's Lands Department in the period covered by this chapter, was to refrain from purchasing from Jews, and it turned down the Agricultural Center on such requests. The JNF gave negative replies also in cases where it felt that the price of the land was too high.[210] Nonetheless, the JNF had to consider the Agricultural Center's demands to a great extent, because of the fact that the Histadrut and its settlement bodies assisted the JNF in making purchases via loans, financial participation in purchases, and soliciting contributions which were transferred to the JNF for implementing purchases registered in the JNF's name.

209 See, e.g., Kressel (1951), pp. 79–80.
210 CZA, S44/161, letter from Hartzfeld to Ben-Gurion 2.1.1936; CZA, KKL5/8777, letter from Weitz to the Agricultural Center 23.2.1936; CZA, S55/201, letter from Weitz to Ruppin 23.2.1936; CZA, S7/404, letter from Landauer to Hartzfeld 7.8.1937; CZA, KKL5/10515, letter from Weitz to Agricultural Center 12.12.1937; CZA, KKL5/11387, letter from Weitz to Agricultural Center 27.2.1938.

Already in 1933, an agreement was signed between the JNF and Nir
– one of the Histadrut's financial institutions – according to which the JNF
would purchase areas of land with Nir's resources and with funds supplied
by the Adama B'Hisachon [land savings] project that Nir organized on
behalf of Histadrut members. The territorial areas would be selected with
the agreement of Nir, and those who joined the Adama B'Hisachon project
would be settled on these lands. The monies which Nir would pass on
to the JNF would be considered a multi-year loan to the JNF but 10%
would be deducted from the repayment which would serve as an advance
on leasing payments for the areas of land purchased. Amongst the JNF
purchases implemented through loans from Nir were about 5,000 dunams
that were included in the JNF's original purchases in the Beisan Valley.
Under the terms of the loan, the JNF reserved the area for the Agricultural
Center of the Histadrut which subsequently the Hasadeh group elected as
its choice for settling the location. Regarding that particular loan from Nir,
Weitz relates: "This was a loan on excellent and easy terms which the JNF
was always ready to assume, especially at a time when our fiscal resources
for land purchases were limited and this loan served as the principal factor
enabling our continued activities in the Beisan Valley. We agreed with Nir
upon a proviso that the land purchased was earmarked for the settlement of
Histadrut members."

In a similar fashion the Agricultural Center was involved in fund-raising
in South Africa on the JNF's behalf, which assisted the settlement of the
Tel Amal Kvutza which was the first to settle in the Beisan Valley (at the
end of 1936).[211] Ussishkin as well declared "whoever gives money to the
JNF even in the form of a loan, can determine who will settle on the land
that was purchased with this money."[212]

During the first half of the 1930s the JNF reached agreements with a
number of additional organizations and institutions. The JNF agreed to
purchase lands specifically to meet their needs for settlement purposes. An
example is furnished by the JNF Directorate's decision, at the beginning of
1936, to purchase 4,500 dunams near Mishmar Ha'emek. For this purchase
the JNF obtained a loan from an external body on the condition that the

---

211   Katz (1999), pp. 49–52 and nn. 16–31. The quotation is from CZA, S53/892b, letter
      from Weitz to the General Council of Hapoel Hamizrahi 27.7.1936.
212   Tirat Zevi Archives, Kevutzatenu (Our Group), 15.1.1937.

purchased area would be used for settling a group of Hashomer Hatza'ir. This condition was ratified by the JNF Directorate.[213] On another occasion, the Directorate agreed to purchase 200 dunams in the Sharon from Jewish owners, with funding from Belgian Zionists to establish a Moshav that would bear the name of the president of the Belgian Zionist Federation.[214] The JNF's agreements with various organizations which guaranteed settlement in return for financial resources in one form or another, caused displeasure in the Jewish Agency and at the end of 1936, the Jewish Agency demanded that the JNF "totally desist from such agreements that were concluded without the prior consent of the Jewish Agency's Settlement Department."[215] Prospective settlement groups which wanted the JNF to purchase land for settlement on their behalf also made approaches directly to the JNF.[216]

Another important organization with an interest in implementing purchases through the JNF during 1936–1939, was the Central Office for the Settlement of German Jews in Palestine headed by Gustav Landauer. This office was established as a separate department of the Jewish Agency in 1933, and one of its duties was to assist the settlement on the land of German immigrants. Its budget was based on contributions transferred to it by Jewish organizations overseas which sought to aid the settlement of German immigrants. One of the more important Jewish organizations was the Center for German Jews in London. Within the framework of an agreement with the Central Office, the JNF would make land purchases on behalf of the Office employing the Office's resources to facilitate the agricultural settlement of German Jews on the lands purchased. In summer 1936, commitments from donors of an amount of P£100,000 were made to the JNF to be transferred from the Center for German Jews in London for purchasing lands. By virtue of this agreement with the JNF, the Central

213   CZA, KKL10, minutes of JNF Directorate meeting, 30.3.1936.

214   Ibid., 7.5.1936.

215   Katz (1999), pp. 49–52 and nn. 16–18. See also CZA, minutes of Jewish Agency Executive meetings, 21.12.1936, 6.6.1937.

216   See, e.g., CZA, KKL5/10065, letters from the Hulata group to JNF Executive 28.12.1938, Weitz to Hulata group 9.1.1939. For details of the attempts by the Agriculture Center of Hapoel Hamizrachi to influence the JNF's land purchasing activities see Katz (1999).

Office for the Settlement of German Jews was involved in determining the lands to be purchased and in choosing the settlers.[217]

Thus, for example, in June 1947 the Central Office requested that the JNF purchase about 700 dunams being offered for sale south of Nahariya, for the purpose of establishing a Moshav settlement predicated on small farms (the future Shavei Tziyon),[218] and also requested the lands of Taibe for establishing a Moshav (subsequently Bnei Brith Moledeth).[219] In the previous year, the Central Office was involved in a series of important purchase decisions which the Directorate adopted for the settlement of German immigrants, including Nukeib (subsequently Ein Gev for the Batelem group), in Reihaniya near Yoqne'am and in the south of the Beisan Valley (subsequently Tirat Zvi). All the purchases were to be consummated using the monies of the Center for German Jews in London channeled via the Central Office for the Settlement of German Jews. The Central Office also interceded with the JNF to secure the territorial expansion of existing settlements whose inhabitants were connected with the work of the Central Office.[220]

Similar to the framework of relations between the JNF and the Agricultural Center, agreement did not always prevail between the JNF and the Central Office for the Settlement of German Jews. For example, the JNF refused to implement a purchase for the Central Office employing its resources in the vicinity of Tivon, which was owned by Kehilat Tzion Company, on the grounds that it involved purchase from Jews, and particularly because the price was exorbitant. Although the Office contended against the JNF that its refusal contravened the mutual agreement "under which the JNF would purchase land upon our request, and within the framework of means earmarked for purchasing lands on behalf of immigrants from Germany,"

217   CZA, KKL10, minutes of JNF Directorate meetings, 6.7.1936, 14.6.1937; CZA, S7/404, letter from Landauer to Granovsky 17.8.1937; CZA, S5/333, proceedings of Zionist General Council session, 27.8.1936 – address by Ussishkin; ibid., minutes of Jewish Agency Executive meeting 13.6.1937; CZA, KKL5/11387, letter from Weitz to Landauer 14.4.1938; Katz (1999), pp. 57, 60 and nn. 44, 56–57; Gvati (1981), I, p. 280.

218   CZA, KKL10, minutes of JNF Directorate meeting, 14.6.1937.

219   Ibid., 13.6.1937.

220   Ibid., 6.7.1936. See also CZA, S7/404, letter from Kibbutz Giv'at Brenner to the Central Office 3.12.1936; Katz (1999).

the JNF Executive persisted in its refusal. In his explanations to Landauer, Granovsky emphasized: "Is there justification that the national bodies such as your department and the JNF should purchase land from Kehiliath Tzion at such a high price? Can you justify this from a settlement perspective and from the standpoint of the farmer's ability to pay such a high price?"[221]

Rassco (the Rural and Suburban Settlement Company), which was established in 1934 by the Central Office for the Settlement of German Jews in order to assist the settlement of members of the middle class in a moshav and urban framework, also pressured the JNF during 1936–1939 to implement purchases that would meet the company's needs. Rassco's requests focused particularly on purchases that would assist the expansion of settlements which had been established in the Sharon – Kefar Shmaryahu, Gan Hayim, and Sdeh Warburg; Shavei Tziyon in the Western Galilee, as well as on the purchase of lands in the Sharon for the purpose of establishing new settlements for the middle class. The need for expanding existing settlements stemmed from the economic difficulties of these settlements that required additional land and people. New settlements were needed in response to the intensified demand for suitable agricultural settlement for middle class immigrants, especially from Germany, but also from Austria, Czechoslovakia and Romania: "Precisely at this hour a number of parties interested in settlement are applying to us, when we are unable to offer them suitable proposals...we request that you allow us to continue our work immediately. It is of the utmost importance at this hour to purchase on behalf of immigrants with capital who are prepared in these circumstances to invest their money in productive agricultural settlement."

Rassco indicated specific lands to the JNF which Arabs or Jews were offering to sell and which were relevant to its needs. It was also prepared to participate through various means in financing the purchases and the purchase was in any event to be registered in the JNF's name.[222] However,

---

221   CZA, S7/404, letter from Landauer to Granovsky 17.8.1937 – first quotation from there, letter from Granovsky to Landauer 20.8.1937 – second quotation from there. See also other disputes between Granovsky and Landauer in connection with the purchase of land which the JNF refused to implement or to transfer lands to settlements that were connected to the Central Office for the Settlement of German Jews; CZA, S7/404, letter from Granovsky to Landauer 19.8.1937; CZA, S7/755, letter from Weitz to Landauer 21.10.1938.
222   Merhavia, p. 227; Gvati (1981), I, p. 291; CZA, KKL5/8905, letter from Foeder of Rassco to JNF 18.4.1938 together with additional documents – quotation from there;

the JNF assented only to some of the purchase proposals made by Rassco. It opposed the other proposals either because of their high price or because it involved purchasing from Jews. With regards to Rassco's proposals that the JNF should lease land near Shavei Tziyon, the JNF responded that the "lease proposal...cannot be considered since the JNF can only be the owner of land and not the leaser of land."[223] The JNF also opposed the purchase of 1,000 dunams south of Nathanya, given its current policy to prefer purchases of political–strategic importance.[224]

The Moshavot also approached the JNF to purchase specific lands. Thus, for example, the Rehovot Local Council asked the JNF to purchase from Arabs an area of 60 dunams near Kefar Bilu. Among the reasons put forward by the Local Council was that Kefar Bilu would suffer if this area were not purchased, and that the purchase would help solve the housing problems of workers in Rehovot. The Council emphasized in its request that "We are aware that the JNF has at this time a most important task in redeeming the land in certain parts of the country, but despite our awareness of this we dare propose that the JNF should make a special effort and redeem this area."[225] Another approach to the JNF came from the Nahariya Council requesting the purchase of a tract of land from Arabs near Nahariya which it required to extricate itself from its economic plight.[226] The JNF's considerations in deciding on a reply to these approaches were related to the JNF's general lands purchase preference policy at the time. Decisions were formulated from the standpoint of favoring preferred areas, while shying away from expensive proposals and purchases from Jews, etc., which were explained

---

CZA, S53/1675f, letter from Feiner to Kaplan 13.2.1939. On Weitz's complaints against Rassco because it conducted negotiations directly with Arabs and Rassco's denial see: CZA, KKL5/10653, letters from Weitz to Rassco 30.1.1940, Rassco to JNF 16.2.1940.

223 CZA, KKL5/8905, letter from Weitz to Rassco 29.6.1938.

224 CZA, S53/1675f, letter from Feiner to Kaplan 13.2.1939. It transpires from this letter that Feiner, on behalf of Rassco, had requested the Jewish Agency to put pressure on the JNF to purchase these 1,000 dunams immediately. See n. 227 below.

225 CZA, KKL5/10517, letter from Yehuda Gorodisky, Chairman of Rehovot Local Council, to JNF Head Office 2.6.1938.

226 CZA, KKL5/10303, the following letters: Nahariya Council to Ussishkin 28.12.1938, Schocken to Granovsky 3.1.1939, Granovsky to Schocken 23.1.1939, Nahariya Council to Ussishkin 14.2.1939.

Nahariya, 1939

above.[227] However, each case was evaluated on its merits, and Nahariya received a favorable answer "despite the fact that the land was expensive" because the JNF sought to extricate the Moshava from its financial plight and preserve the stability of Nahariya which was a strategic point on the border of the Western Galilee and functioned as a commercial center to the Kibbutzim Hanita and Eilon.[228]

---

227 CZA, KKL5/8376, letter from Weitz to Jewish Agency Labor Department 25.6.1937; CZA, KKL5/11387, Weitz to Agricultural Center 27.2.1938; ibid., Weitz to Landauer 14.4.1938; CZA, KKL5/8344, letter from Weitz to Landauer 22.12.1936; CZA, KKL5/10406, letter from Weitz to Reiner stressing the JNF's objection to the purchase of lands from Jews because "we are to redeem the land especially in Beisan and the Galilee, etc., for in this manner we are expanding the borders of our homeland"; CZA, KKL5/10065, letter from Weitz to Hulata group 9.1.1939.

228 CZA, KKL5/10203, letter from Granovsky to Schocken 23.1.1939 – quotation from there; ibid., letters from the Nahariya Council to Ussishkin 26.12.1938, 14.2.1939.

CHAPTER THREE

In the Shadow of Restrictions on Land Purchases, 1940–1945

Changes in the Structure and Composition of the JNF Directorate and the Executive

The JNF's supreme body was the Annual General Meeting of the Jewish National Fund Company Ltd.[1] Over the course of years the role of this strictly formal body was constricted to an annual meeting in order to ratify the budget, authorize land purchases, and confirm the members of the Directorate who had been nominated by the Directorate and the Zionist General Council.[2] The Directorate was appointed to determine policy in all spheres of JNF activity, and in whose hands decision-making powers and responsibility were concentrated. Until the death of its Chairman, Menachem Ussishkin, in October 1941, the composition of the Directorate

---

1   See above pp. 28–29.
2   CZA, KKL5/10565, letter from H. Levin, Secretary of the JNF to JNF members 2.6.1940, and minutes of JNF Directorate meeting, 25.6.1940; CZA, S53/437j, Report by the JNF Directorate to the Annual General Meeting, 25.6.1940; CZA, KKL5/10565, letter from Mohilewer, secretary of JNF to Y. Ken, member of the JNF Company 1.12.1941; CZA, S53/43j, Report by JNF Directorate to the Annual General Meeting, 24.12.1941; CZA, KKL5/11860, minutes of JNF Annual General Meeting, 28.12.1941; CZA, S53/437f, Report by JNF Directorate to the Annual General Meeting, 17.9.1942; CZA, KKL5/11860, letter from Mohilewer to members of the JNF 30.8.1942; CZA, S53/437i, Report by JNF Directorate to the Annual General Meeting, 17.9.1942; CZA, KKL5/11860, minutes of JNF Annual General Meeting, 4.10.1942; CZA, S53/437j, Report by JNF Directorate to the Annual General Meetings, 23.12.1943, 11.3.1945; CZA, KKL5/13979, minutes of JNF Annual General Meeting, 21.10.1945; CZA, KKL5/22307, Report by JNF Directorate to Annual General Meeting to be held on 3.11.1946; CZA, KKL5/13979, minutes of JNF Annual General Meeting, 3.11.1946; CZA, KKL5/15905, minutes of JNF Annual General Meeting, 30.12.1947, Report by JNF Directorate to the Annual General Meeting, 30.12.1947.

remained unaltered. It included, aside from Ussishkin, Yitzhak Vilkansky, Shmuel Zuchovitzky, Avraham Granovsky (who served as both a director and the head of the Financial Department), Rabbi Meyer Berlin, Herman Stroock, Berl Katznelson, David Ben-Gurion and Zalman Schocken. The latter two served as Governors. Members, who according to the by-laws had to resign annually, presented their candidacy for re-election and this was ratified by the Directorate, the Zionist General Council and the Annual General Meeting of the JNF Company.[3]

Immediately following the death of Ussishkin, a few members of the Directorate, led by Katznelson, demanded greater involvement in the work of the JNF's Executive. They criticized the situation that prevailed during Ussishkin's time, when certain issues were decided and determined by the Executive and Ussishkin without involving them sufficiently, but

> during the entire time that Ussishkin headed the JNF, the directors did not request additional rights in directing the activities and the institution because they had consideration for Ussishkin's attitudes and his nature, despite the fact that such a state of affairs regarding the Board of Directors of an institution which governed a national project was totally unsatisfactory. However, now, after the death of Ussishkin, a change in these matters was perforce necessary. It was essential to involve the JNF Board of Directors more and intensify the collaboration of the Directors in managing its affairs and taking decisions in important matters.

Katznelson demanded a series of changes in the work of the Directorate and its ties with the Executive: The Directorate should be convened more frequently "once or twice a month" (instead of once every few months as previously) in order for it to be more involved in both the receipt of information and in decision–making. No president or permanent chairman should be elected during the year of mourning for Ussishkin, and the Directorate meetings would be chaired by the body's members according to rotation. Two members of the Directorate who would be chosen

---

3   See, e.g., CZA, KKL5/13979, list of members of JNF Directorate during 1940–1946, prepared by Y. Aricha, 5.5.1946; CZA, KKL5/11860, copy of the proceedings of Smaller Zionist General Council session held on 26.8.1941; CZA, S8/92, letter from the JNF to World Zionist Organization Executive 4.8.1942, see also Appendix 1.

alongside Granovsky would serve as a quasi-executive committee of the Directorate (subsequently the "Directorship") which would convene once a week and whose function was to steer the JNF's activities. The practical import of this change, demanded by Katznelson was to expand the JNF's Executive (consisting of Weitz and Granovsky responsible for land and settlement matters; and the Directors of the Organization and Information Departments, together with Granovsky regarding topics in these spheres) by two members of the Directorate in place of Ussishkin.[4]

The proposal to establish a new management framework that would occupy a position between the Directorate and the Executive encountered criticism from both members of the Directorate as well as from some of the department heads. The former feared that the status of the Directorate plenum as the JNF's supreme decision–making body would be impaired, while the department heads feared a blow to their status and prerogatives and the routines of their departments. Only after it was guaranteed that the new body would not bring about any changes that would harm the Directorate, the department heads and the departments themselves, the Directorate authorized the changes in the spirit of Katznelson's proposals. It desired to finalize changes as quickly as possible, to stave off adverse comment in Palestine and abroad to the effect that "the disputes have started in the JNF as well" which would have caused grievous harm to the JNF's activities precisely at the time when unanimity was most needed.[5]

Hence it was decided not to elect a president or chairman for the moment. The Directorate would convene once a month; a "Directorship" was chosen from among the Directorate members, comprising Granovsky, Katznelson and Rabbi Berlin. This Directorship's role was "to examine current matters, sort out proposals and determine the questions that would be submitted to the Directorate and decide upon matters which were in its purview as well as on matters which could not be postponed until the meeting of the Directorate." The Directorship would convene as required, but no less than once a week and its members would chair its meetings by rotation. The Directorate reaffirmed its choice of Granovsky as a managing director.[6]

---

4   CZA, KKL10, minutes of JNF Directorate meeting, 9.10.1941 – quotation from there; Weitz (1951), p. 15.
5   CZA, KKL10, minutes of JNF Directorate meetings, 9.10.1941, 21.10.1949.
6   Ibid., 21.10.1941 – quotation from there.

The executive framework, as established at the end of 1941, lasted for a year, although it is not clear whether during that year as well it convened at the frequency that was determined at the time of its establishment. In the years 1943–1944 this framework was weakened either due to Rabbi Berlin's trips abroad in the course of 1943 or due to the illness and death of Katznelson in summer 1944, and the protracted illness of Rabbi Berlin during that year. Nevertheless, until Granovsky was elected Chairman of the Directorate in September 1945, the Directorship framework was not formally rescinded, and its members conducted its meetings by rotation. In practice, it was Granovsky who managed the bulk of the matters and in light of the aforementioned conditions, he chaired most meetings of the Directorate.[7] No minutes of the meetings of the Directorship are available, and it is therefore unclear what was the nature of the Directorship's deliberations, beyond those of the Executive prior to the establishment of this framework.

Nonetheless, a perusal of the minutes of the Directorate's meetings reveals that its status was not impaired. While the frequency in which the Directorate was convened averaged once every two months rather than once a month as stipulated in the reorganization, this frequency still exceeded the prevailing norm prior to Ussishkin's death. The Directorate remained the supreme body that decided upon land purchase policy and the specific purchases to be made. Attempts on the part of Executive to constrict the power of the Directorate, and to allow the Executive wider freedom of action, encountered opposition from the Directorate. Thus, at the end of 1941, Granovsky sought the Directorate's authorization for an annual land purchase work plan submitted by Weitz, and to allow the JNF Executive freedom of action within the framework of this plan "without recourse to an occasional decision at a Directorate meeting." Members of the Directorate turned down this request. Rabbi Berlin, for example, stressed: "Every purchase proposal must come before the Directorate for a decision after prior deliberation in the meetings of the JNF's Directorship which convenes no less than once a week, and if need be even more frequently. Although the Directorate convenes once a month, it can be convened if necessary for extraordinary meetings outside the fixed time." Indeed,

---

7   CZA, KKL5/13979, list of members of the Directorate (above, n. 3); Weitz (1951), p 15; CZA, KKL10, minutes of JNF Directorate meetings, 9.11.1943, 13.7.1945.

until the end of 1944, the Directorate not only discussed and ratified the annual work plans for land purchases submitted to it at the beginning of the year, but also deliberated on each specific purchase proposal. At the end of 1944, given the situation which compelled the JNF to act quickly and consummate purchases immediately after they appeared feasible, Weitz again requested freedom of action when operating within the framework of an annual purchase plan. His request was turned down.[8] Nonetheless, Weitz reported to the Directorate in March 1945, concerning a purchase that he had to implement urgently and requested retroactive authorization for this purchase.[9]

Visit of the Executive Members of JNF in the South, 1942

8 Ibid., 25.11.1941 – quotation from there. See also, ibid., 14.11.1944. In personal interviews with S. Ben-Shemesh (Jerusalem, 8.10.1997) and H. Danin (Jerusalem 8.10.1997) the central role of the Directorate in determining policy and decisions for land purchases was stressed.
9 Ibid., 20.3.1945.

The stability that prevailed in the Directorate's make up until the death of Ussishkin, did not continue subsequently. During 1941–1945, two additional members died: Herman Stroock at the beginning of 1944 and Berl Katznelson in August of that year. The vacancies resulting from these deaths were not readily filled.[10] Menachem Ussishkin was replaced by his son, Attorney Shmuel Ussishkin. The younger Ussishkin was the candidate of the General Zionist Federation which demanded a place for him on the Directorate to succeed the elder Ussishkin who was a member of the General Zionists. Shmuel Ussishkin, who served as the JNF's salaried attorney, was requested by the Directorate to forego his position as a JNF employee as a precondition for joining the Directorate. However, given the economic situation in Palestine, the Directorate allowed him to choose the date when he would leave his work in the JNF. Shmuel Ussishkin joined the Directorate in December 1941.[11] Ben-Gurion participated infrequently in the Directorate sessions due to his many concerns, first and foremost as Chairman of the Jewish Agency Executive, and his travels abroad. In order to preserve its ties with the Jewish Agency Executive and strengthen them, the JNF and the Jewish Agency agreed at the beginning of 1942, following a prolonged trip by Ben-Gurion abroad, to appoint Eliezer Kaplan, a member of the Jewish Agency Executive, as a temporary replacement for Ben-Gurion until the latter would return to Palestine. Kaplan participated in a few meetings, whereas Ben-Gurion attended the Directorate's meetings on rare occasions.[12] Zalman Schocken was outside the country from 1939 and did not participate in a single meeting during 1940–1945. However, the Directorate refrained from recommending his replacement due both to his vast seniority in the Directorate and because he served as a Governor–Director. Rabbi Berlin also was absent from meetings during 1944 due to illness. Hence during this period, the Directorate meetings took place with five and sometimes only four members participating and there was a perceptible need to fill the ranks, although the presence of only two members constituted a legal quorum for meetings. Demands to

10   CZA, KKL5/13979, list of members of the Directorate (above, n. 3).
11   CZA, KKL10, minutes of JNF Directorate meetings, 25.11.1941, 18.12.1941, 20.1.1942; ibid., proceedings of the session of the Smaller Zionist General Council, 6.1.1942. See also Appendix 1.
12   Ibid., minutes of JNF Directorate meeting, 20.1.1942; CZA, S8/92, letter from the Organization Department to the Jewish Agency Executive 22.1.1942.

appoint new members in lieu of the deceased emanated from the Mizrachi (of which Stroock was a member) and from Mapai (of whom Katznelson was a member).[13] All this produced a situation whereby in April 1945 the Directorate decided to recommend to the Zionist General Council the election of Avraham Hartzfeld as the representative of Mapai and Avraham Kestenbaum as the representative of Hapoel Hamizrachi (the Mizrachi had deferred its place to it). Hashomer Hatza'ir's demand, which was already raised at the beginning of 1942, as well as the demand of the South African Zionist Federation to appoint representatives on their behalf, thus expanding the number of Directorate members from 9 to 11, was in the meantime rejected by the Directorate.[14]

The Regional Offices, the Himnuta Company and Relations with the Palestine Land Development Company

During 1936–1940, the JNF's Land Department headed by Weitz had ceased implementing its purchases exclusively via the PLDC and increasingly implemented its purchases through affiliation with additional bodies, private individuals and private companies alike. The successful experience with such affiliations, the aggravations of the mutual recriminations between the JNF and PLDC, which deepened the rift between the two bodies, and first and foremost between Weitz and Hankin, the severe decline in the PLDC's involvement in agricultural purchases (see below) and the JNF's constraint to appreciably expand land purchase activities due to political and settlement considerations over many areas simultaneously – all these constituted the basis for the formulation of the "regional method" in the work of the JNF Lands Department. The policy was formulated towards the end of the period covered by the previous chapter, and at the beginning of the period being dealt with in the present chapter.

---

13   CZA, KKL10, minutes of JNF Directorate meetings, 20.1.1942, 23.8.1944, 14.1.1944, 19.12.1944, 20.3.1945. See also Appendix 1.
14   Ibid., 23.8.1944, 14.11.1944, 24.4.1945; CZA KKL10, proceedings of the session of the Smaller Zionist General Council, 6.1.1942; CZA, S8/92, letter from Ya'ari (Hashomer Hatza'ir) to Jewish Agency Executive 2.1.1942.

The method essentially delegated purchase activity and all that it entailed, to the JNF offices (branches) and agents exclusively affiliated with the JNF, spread over the country and with each in charge of a given area whose boundaries were defined and delineated by the Lands Department. In this manner, Weitz sought to create a situation where in each district of the country there would be a single Jewish purchaser exclusively affiliated with the JNF. Weitz thus reverted in practice to a former policy of the WZO that had previously designated the PLDC to act as the exclusive purchaser for all Jewish requirements of land, with all the policy's inherent advantages. Weitz and his assistants in the Lands Department in Jerusalem, maintained control, coordination, decision making and supervision of the offices' and agents' activity. Weitz himself made frequent surveys and visits to the offices where policy and methods of implementations were delineated. Weitz was ably assisted by a battery of attorneys (such as Aharon Ben-Shemesh, Mordechai Eliash, Yosef Stromeza and others), who were entrusted with the handling of all legal matters that were especially complex during this period and to a large extent because of the Lands Law.[15] Weitz summed up the method in a letter to Yisrael Teiber on August 1943 as follows:

> The principle of regionality is the basis upon which the apparatus for purchasing agricultural land for the JNF acts. According to this principle the land is divided into certain regions and in each and every one a permanent organization functions responsible for supply and demand, for implementation and activity in all that appertains to the purchase and maintenance of land in that region. It is not to deal in any form whatsoever, even passively, with any proposal in another region, unless it is explicitly called upon to do so. Of course, every regional organization is subordinate to the Head Office of the JNF regarding the determination of policy lines, etc. This method, entailing centralization and decentralization within this

---

15   CZA, KKL5/12715, letter from Weitz to Teiber 27.8.1943; CZA, S5/10641, letter
     from Hankin to JNF 11.8.1940; Weitz (1951), pp. 16–17, 553–556; Bistritsky (1950a),
     pp. 157–165; CZA, KKL5/12803, minutes of matters discussed at the Haifa Office
     with the participation of Ben-Shemesh, 15.6.1944; CZA, KKL5/12809, summary of
     deliberations at the Galilee JNF Office on 22.6.1944–25.6.1944; S. Ben-Shemesh,
     personal interview, Jerusalem 27.11.1996.

same apparatus, has already clearly demonstrated its utility, since in my opinion, as a result the JNF has managed to obtain in recent years a successive increase in its purchases reaching an annual quota of 50,000 dunams and beyond, despite the difficulties which are intensifying from year to year.[16]

Aside from the aforementioned considerations which led to the development of the regional policy and the reasons underlying the JNF's affiliation with bodies other than the PLDC – affiliations which constituted the basis of the regional policy and which were described in the previous chapter – through this method Weitz gained full control over all matters entailed in land purchases where the JNF was involved. This was a situation which Weitz, the person charged with this area in the JNF, aspired to. The Lands Law and other restrictions and difficulties in implementing purchases which characterized the years 1940–1945, and which will be discussed below, also mandated the regional policy.[17] Furthermore, Weitz hoped that through this method he could secure the elimination of brokers and land dealers from the market. These in his opinion only caused the JNF difficulty in implementing purchases and drove up prices. On those occasions when such people approached him with purchase proposals, he generally refused to enter into negotiations with them and referred them to the regional appointees acting on his behalf and sometimes he even demanded that they cease their involvement in land purchases.[18] For example, in response to a proposal by the Mifal Ubinyan Company to make purchases for the JNF in various regions of the country, Weitz responded to the company:

16 CZA, KKL5/12715, letter from Weitz to Teiber 27.81943. For further information on the importance of the regional offices see the comments of Weitz and Granovsky in Bistritsky (1950a), pp. 10–12 (Granovsky's statement); Daily bulletins, Information Service from JNF Head Office, 14.5.1945 – address by Weitz at the Agricultural Conference, pp. 5–6.

17 Weitz (1951), pp. 16–18; S. Ben-Shemesh, personal interview, Jerusalem 7.4.1997.

18 CZA, KKL5/12715, the following letters: Weitz to Teiber 27.8.1943, Weitz to Pinhasevitch 14.12.1941; CZA, KKL5/11822, letter from Weitz to the Tsur Co. 15.7.1941; CZA, KKL5/12715, letter from Weitz to P. Yosef 2.2.1943; CZA, KKL11871, JNF Head Office circular to the JNF Office 23.3.1943 "On the situation regarding land purchases during the fourth year of the War" (also in files S53/437f, S8/92, KKL5/10072); CZA, KKL5/13921, letter fron Weitz to JNF Haifa Office 14.11.1943, letter from Weitz to Y. Abulafia 18.4.1944; CZA, KKL5/12715, letter from Weitz to Teiber 20.1.1942.

You are undoubtedly aware that the JNF has a complete apparatus dealing with land purchases in all regions of the country and we don't have any need for agencies and go-betweens outside our apparatus. Furthermore, in our opinion, all handling of lands purchases outside the JNF's apparatus can cause damage to land matters which are in any case difficult and severe.[19]

The Lands Department had five regional offices, although their formal status was not identical. Two of them were JNF branches and the others were offices of agents who were not formally JNF employees but were affiliated with it on an exclusive basis. The Galilee Office was situated in Tiberias and headed by Yosef Nahmani who joined the JNF. At first the Office was called "JNF Ltd.–The Lands Department Northern District" and subsequently "JNF Ltd. – The Galilee Office." The office was responsible for the Tiberias and Safad Districts. Haifa had the "Haifa and its Environs Office" which opened at the beginning of 1943, pursuant to an agreement between the JNF and the PLDC under which the local PLDC office was closed and its employees (Yosef Stromeza, Zvi Wolf, Aharon Danin and Eliahu Dura) became JNF workers. Previously, the principal activity of this PLDC branch in Haifa was connected with the JNF's purchase activities. The office of Haifa and its vicinity was in charge of the Haifa, Acre, Nazareth, Beisan, Jenin and Shechem districts. JNF agents Gad and Moshe Machnes, whose office was in Tel Aviv, were in charge of the Sharon region which included the districts of Tulkarm, Jaffa, and part of Ramle. Yoav Zuckerman was another agent whose office was in Tel Aviv and his area of responsibility was the southern region and the Negev which comprised the Gaza, Hebron and Beersheba districts and part of Ramle. JNF agent Pinhas Margalit was responsible for activity in the Jerusalem, Jericho, and Ramallah districts as well as part of Ramle. In 1942 at Weitz's initiative, a partnership was formed between Margalit and Yisrael Teiber (an owner of the Tsur Company) which subsequently adopted the name "Marom" and served as the JNF's agent in charge of the aforementioned districts.[20] The employees in the JNF branches of Haifa and Tiberias were

19 CZA, KKL5/13921, letter from Weitz to Mifal Vebinyan 17.8.1945.
20 CZA, KKL5/11901, the following letters: Weitz to Stromeza, Wolf and Danin 5.3.1940, Mohilewer to Granovsky 24.3.1943 – the latter concerning JNF Offices; CZA, KKL5/12809, list of employees in JNF offices; CZA KKL5/12809, list of employees in

JNF officials in every respect and received their salaries according to rank
from the Head Office. The offices of the JNF's agents were independent
and under the terms of affiliation with the JNF they received their salary
as regular commission in advance.[21] In 1937, a JNF branch, the Zebulun
Valley Office, was opened in Haifa but its activity was restricted to the
preservation and development of JNF lands in the Zebulun Valley.

Weitz had demanded from the persons in charge of the regional offices,
not to deviate from the territory he had fixed for them in order to prevent
duplicate negotiations with the Arabs, price increases and harm the
purchase process. However, despite this, sometimes deviations did occur,
to the displeasure of Weitz and the offices relevant to the matter.[22] The
offices were expected "to acquaint themselves with the land owners, the
relations between them and authorities and between them and the Arab
leaders, to be familiar with their property and economic conditions and
to enter into negotiations with them in all matters that pertained to land
dealings, whether it concerned their own lands or those of others. In this
manner, they became friendly with various Arabs who served our interests
at every juncture and opportune moment." Thus it was the offices that
implemented the purchases. A perusal of many files from the Galilee Office
for example, reveals that the office painstakingly assembled a vast amount
of data concerning the landowners in its region, carried out measurements
and mapping, transferred purchase proposals to the Lands Department in
Jerusalem, conducted negotiations with the sellers, dealt with all matters
relating to the tenant farmers, furnished the relevant materials to the
lawyers, in the case of litigation, and was active in trials. It was the office
that presented JNF demands to the Government's Land Arrangements
officials.[23]

Alongside the regional offices, the JNF also used the services of the
Himnuta Company which during the period covered by this chapter
expanded its sphere of activities. Himnuta continued to fill the functions
it had filled since its establishment in 1938 as well as executing new

---

Galilee Office; CZA, KKL5/13921, memorandum by Weitz on "Proposal for Land
Purchase Activities in 1945" 30.10.1944; Weitz (1951), pp. 16–17; Katz (1992), pp.
45–46.

21   CZA, KKL5/7408, letter from Borochov to Zebulun Valley Office 5.4.1937; CZA,
KKL10, minutes of JNF Directorate meeting, 29.1.1946.

22   See, e.g., CZA,KKL5/12377, letter from Weitz to G. Machnes 2.8.1942; CZA, KKL9/

functions which arose in light of new necessities. These activities discussed in the previous chapter, were to serve as the body in whose name the JNF continued to register land given over to it as living bequests in which the JNF's interest was only in the financial proceeds from that parcel of real estate and which it intended to sell at the opportune time. Within this framework, measures were taken to liquidate the Meheiman Company and register its remaining properties in the name of Himnuta. A second task of the Himnuta Company was to register in its name those lands purchased within the framework of the cooperation project with private capital. Part of the land the JNF purchased within the framework of this project would pass to the ownership of private capital. Indeed, as will be explained later in this chapter, during the first half of the 1940s the cooperation project with private capital expanded and included a plan for "garden cities."

There were primarily five new tasks within the sphere of land registration that were imposed on the Himnuta Company since 1940, in light of the particular needs of the hour: first task was the purchase of two citrus groves, the one Jewish–owned and the other Arab–owned which were in a unique strategic location. The size of the citrus groves did not permit the establishment of a new settlement at the location, nor could they constitute a supplement to an existing settlement. The JNF was induced to respond favorably to the pressures applied upon it to make the purchases, but from the very outset, it intended to sell the citrus groves to Jewish bodies, and therefore the purchases were registered under the name of the Himnuta Company. The second task was to serve as a body in whose name complex and complicated purchases could be registered on a temporary basis (some were from Jews registered as companies, associations and individuals), when the JNF foresaw at the time of purchase that it would have to transfer or exchange part of the purchases in the future with other bodies. The third task was to serve as a body under whose name lands were transferred to the JNF in restitution for outstanding debts, and which from the outset the JNF intended to convert into cash. The fourth task was to register urban

443, letter from Nahmani to the Haifa Office 8.12.1944, letter from Weitz to the JNF Haifa Office 25.1.1945.

23   See, e.g., Weitz (1951), pp. 17–18 – quotation from there; CZA, KKL9/22, letter from Nahmani to Hankin 12.3.1940; CZA, KKL5/11822, letter from Tsur Co. to JNF Head Office 15.4.1940; CZA, KKL9/21, letter from Weitz to Nahmani 6.6.1940; CZA, KKL5/12715, letter from G. Machnes to Weitz 17.8.1942. See also KKL9/443,

lands purchased with a view of accommodating some institution, but at the time of purchase the JNF was uncertain that it was actually suitable for the purpose intended, and wished to reserve the option of selling the plot in the future. The fifth task was to assist when necessary in circumventing the Lands Law (on the law see below) in a manner that the land that the JNF purchased would be registered in the names of Arabs who took out security mortgages in favor of the Himnuta Co.[24]

In summer 1944, the Directorate decided to expand the Himnuta Company's activities beyond the task of formal registration of ownership over certain lands. The JNF transferred to the Himnuta Co. all the capital that had accumulated to the JNF's credit in its capacity as trustee over the monies of various projects in which it was involved (such as housing projects), or that were transferred to it (such as pension funds and provident funds of public institutions). The JNF also credited the Himnuta Company with capital which donors had entrusted to the JNF for specific purchases (such as life bequests for certain purposes or funds that were opened by donors for specific purposes). This amounted to the appreciable sum of P£620,000 to which an additional P£150,000 were subsequently added. The actual request to separate these funds from the JNF's regular income account was presented to the JNF Executive by its accountants. It would appear that the JNF Executive was uneasy about the mixing of these spheres. In any case, a transfer of this appreciable capital from the JNF's possession to the Himnuta Co., necessitated the drafting of an agreement that left full control over the sum in the JNF's hands, and thus in this matter as well, the

---

KKL9/178, KKL9/238, KKL9/339, KKL9/386, KKL9/356, KKL9/290, KKL9/446, KKL9/308, KKL9/246, KKL9/184. These files contain numerous details about the functioning of these offices in many areas. See also Bistritsky (1950), pp. 10–13.

24   CZA, KKL10, minutes of JNF Directorate meetings, 30.7.1940, 31.8.1943, 7.12.1943, 20.6.1944; CZA, S25/6546, joint letter from Weitz and Granovsky to Hankin 18.8.1940 (also in file CZA, KKL5/10641); CZA, L51/596, letter from APC to Auster 23.12.1940; CZA, KKL5/12809, summary of deliberations held in the Tiberias Office on 22.6.1944–25.6.1944, the following documents: letter from Granovsky to Bart and Kamini 7.5.1941, report of the Himnuta Co. 11.5.1941, letter from Granovsky to Bart 14.4.1942, minutes of the Himnuta Co. Annual General Meeting 30.12.1941, letter from Granovsky to the Directorate of Himnuta Co. 19.12.1942. As will be explained below, the Himnuta Co. was given the additional task during 1945–1948 of registering in its name the lands owned by Jews defined as "missing" after the Holocaust. After the Second World War arrangements were made for the transfer of these lands to the JNF.

Himnuta Co. was no more than a legal body controlled, managed and fully owned by the JNF.[25]

The organization of regional offices exacerbated the relationship between the JNF and the PLDC in general and between Weitz and Hankin in particular. The PLDC increasingly realized that the re-organization in the JNF was voiding the PLDC of its principal activity, but it was unable to change matters.[26] In the previous chapter, we alluded to the economic crisis which the company faced during the latter half of the 1930s, and this crisis deepened in the 1940s. It led to the PLDC's decreased engagement in agricultural land purchases and contributed to its a changed focus on urban purchases. It should be noted that the following factors contributed toward this crisis: The PLDC had invested an appreciable portion of the company's capital in purchasing the Hula Concession, and efforts to redeem this investment had failed; the Arab disturbances and the Second World War led to a drastic decline in land purchases from the company by private capital in Palestine and the world over, and left the PLDC with a substantial inventory of real estate. Complications arose in a number of purchases that involved the company in appreciable expenses over an extended period; bank credit was reduced as a result of the Second World War; purchases for the JNF declined, once the JNF adopted the regional method for its operations, resulting in an appreciable drop in PLDC income.[27]

---

25   CZA, KKL10, minutes of JNF Directorate meetings, 23.8.1944, 20.2.1945.

26   CZA, KKL5/10641, letter from Hankin to JNF Head Office 11.8.1940 (also in S25/6546); CZA, KKL5/10641, joint letter from Weitz and Granovsky to Hankin 18.8.1940 (also in S25/6546); CZA, S53/1682, "Report of the situation in the Palestine Land Development Company Ltd.," 15.11.1940 drawn up by S. Hirsch; CZA, S53/1682b, memorandum "On the Tasks of the PLDC," no date, but apparently from the end of 1942 or beginning of 1943.

27   On the crisis in the PLDC and the reasons for it, see p. 48 above; PLDC (1938), PLDC (1939), PLDC (1940), PLDC (1941), PLDC (1942), PLDC (1943), PLDC (1945), PLDC (1946); CZA, proceedings of the session of the Smaller Zionist General Council, 6.1.1942; CZA, microfilm CM428/2, minutes of PLDC Executive meetings, 19.8.1940, 5.9.1940; CZA, S53/1682a, "Report on the situation of the Palestine Land Development Compnay Ltd." 15.11.1940 prepared by S. Hirsch; CZA, S53/1682b, minutes of PLDC Executive meeting, 21.12.1941; CZA, KKL5/11917, the following letters: Thon of the PLDC to Kaplan 18.1.1942, 1 PLDC to JNF 12.6.1942; CZA, S53/1682a, memorandum prepared by S. Tal of APC concerning the developments of the PLDC financial affairs during 1941 and comments by A. Ashbel on 29.7.1942; A. Cohen, "The Palestine Land Development Co. Ltd. and its Tasks," *Ha'aretz*,

Although the JNF's detachment from the PLDC contributed in no small measure to the latter's crisis, Hankin viewed it as the **exclusive** reason and demanded that the JNF assume responsibility. He also accused the JNF of subverting the existence of the PLDC, which expressed itself among other things in employing the Himnuta Co. for the purchase and sale of lands on behalf of private capital – a task that formerly belonged to the PLDC. In this context, Hankin demanded in summer 1940 that the JNF "remedy the terrible injustice perpetrated by you against our company" by the immediate transfer of a grant to the PLDC in the sum of P£20,000 which the company needed to pay pressing debts.[28] In an explanatory letter, Weitz and Granovsky rejected Hankin's accusations and demands while holding the PLDC, and in effect Hankin, responsible for a major share of the reasons which induced the JNF to progressively detach itself from the PLDC. They also accused the PLDC of the complications and damages inflicted on the JNF: "We totally reject any blame for the evil which has befallen your Company, just as we are not willing to accept credit for the good which it enjoyed in better days.... The JNF's interests take precedence for us over anything else and in no respect will we be prepared to inflict burdens on the JNF under which it could God forbid collapse."[29] The JNF was indeed prepared in the course of 1940–1945 to assist the PLDC by means of postponing the payment of debts owed by the PLDC to the Company, but refused to come to its assistance with grants, especially given the proliferation of cases where PLDC shareholders ceased their contributions to the JNF because the latter had not assisted the PLDC.[30]

Despite the deterioration of relations between the two bodies, the exchange of accusations, etc.,[31] contacts between them did not cease. The

---

19.11.1941; M. Ater, "The Palestine Land Development Company and its Prospects," *Ha'aretz*, 25.8.1943.

28   CZA, KKL5/10641, letter from Hankin to JNF Head Office 11.8.1940 (also in file S25/6546).

29   Ibid., joint letter from Weitz and Granovsky to Hankin 18.8.1940 (also in file S25/6546).

30   CZA, KKL5/10641, letter from JNF National Committee in Palestine to JNF Head Office 23.7.1941, letter from Granovsky to JNF National Committee in Palestine 13.8.1941; CZA, KKL10, minutes of JNF Directorate meeting, 24.12.1942.

31   See, e.g., CZA, KKL5/11821, letter from Weitz to PLDC Haifa Office in which he complains about the high commission taken by the PLDC and that it sold lands to the JNF calculated according to the Turkish dunam and not the metric dunam. See also

PLDC had an interest in reaching an agreement with the JNF that would extricate it from the problem posed by the inventory of agricultural land in its possession and likewise to receive reimbursement from the JNF for PLDC investments in transactions that had not been completed, and in return turn over these contacts to the JNF. But the JNF as well, had an interest to reach an arrangement with the PLDC as the latter was indebted to it at the end of 1940 in the sum of P£45,000. The trend which discussions between the two institutions took was that the JNF would purchase the agricultural lands in the PLDC's possession and likewise its rights in uncompleted affiliations and the return would be partially covered by PLDC's debts to the JNF. At the end of 1942, agreements were signed between the bodies transferring the PLDC's rights to the JNF for lands in the Beersheba vicinity (about 6,200 dunams) north of Jerusalem (1,200 dunams) in the Zebulun Valley (Damun Dirva – about 2,700 dunams) and in Transjordan (about 17,000 dunams which the PLDC purchased in 1934 from Richard Hughes of Jerusalem). It was clear to the JNF that the purchase of this latter area was a departure from its sphere of activity, since there was no intention of settling there, but its agreement to make this purchase also stemmed from the political value of the purchase in Transjordan and the chance to use this land in the future as a barter commodity in exchange for Arab lands in the Beisan Valley.[32]

Following the signing of these agreements, the feeling in the PLDC was that the JNF had in practice exploited the predicament of the PLDC. An internal company memorandum noted:

---

the exchange of letters between Weitz and Ashbel of the PLDC, CZA, KKL5/12824, Weitz to PLDC 21.4.1944, Ashbel to JNF 25.4.1944, Weitz to PLDC 1.5.1944, Ashbel to JNF 4.5.1944. See also S. Ben-Shemesh, personal interview, Jerusalem 7.4.1997.

32   CZA, KKL10, minutes of JNF Directorate meeting, 24.12.1942; CZA, microfilm CM428/2, minutes of PLDC Executive meetings, 19.8.1940, 5.9.1940; CZA, KKL5/10641, letter from Granovsky to JNF National Committee in Palestine 13.8.1941; CZA, S53/1682b, minutes of PLDC Executive meetings, 14.12.1941, 27.2.1942; CZA, microfilm CM428/2, minutes of PLDC Executive meetings, 5.5.1942, 11.12.1942; CZA, KKL5/11917, letter from Ashbel to JNF 12.6.1942; CZA, S53/1682b, minutes of PLDC Executive meetings, 5.7.1942, 11.10.1942, 3.12.1942, 5.1.1943, 18.2.1943; CZA, KKL5/11917, supplement to the agreement between JNF and PLDC, 28.12.1942, minutes of the joint meeting of JNF and PLDC Executives 17.1.1943 (also in KKL5/11901). See also Ilan (1984), pp. 409–410.

As for the tendency to free us from investments in agricultural lands, the JNF did purchase from us certain lands as well as rights over uncompleted purchases. These were primarily lands which under the present legal conditions could not be purchased, and it was only thanks to our preparations years ago made through tremendous efforts, that the JNF could obtain these important areas. Nonetheless, in certain cases we had to transfer our rights to the JNF at a veritable loss relative to our investments.[33]

At the end of 1943, the JNF agreed to purchase the balance of the PLDC's lands in Yoqne'am and also assumed responsibility for evacuating the tenant farmers. In the wake of this agreement, the PLDC sensed an appreciable relief.[34]

Another matter in which contacts were maintained between the two parties concerned the transfer of the staff of officials engaged in agricultural land purchases in the PLDC to the JNF. This was a mutual interest of the two parties given the dwindling agricultural purchases on the part of the PLDC, the intensified agricultural purchases on the part of the JNF and the development of the regional method. These contacts led to an agreement between the two bodies transferring to the JNF the PLDC's Haifa Office with its employees – an office specializing in agricultural purchases in the North. Pursuant to this agreement, the JNF opened its Haifa Office with the responsibility for purchases in the Haifa area and its vicinity.[35] It should be noted that it was the PLDC's contention that this agreement was linked to an unwritten understanding between the two bodies to transfer to the PLDC a monopoly over purchases of urban lands – an understanding which the PLDC contended was violated. It is not clear whether such an understanding existed, but we have not encountered a written agreement

---

33   CZA, S53/1682, memorandum on "The tasks of the Palestine Development Company," not dated, but apparently from the end of 1942 or beginning of 1943.

34   CZA, S53/1682b, minutes of PLDC Executive meeting, 10.11.1943. See also CZA, microfilm CM428/2, minutes of PLDC Executive meetings, 19.8.1940, 5.9.1940.

35   CZA, S53/1682b, memorandum on "The tasks of the Palestine Development Company," not dated, but apparently from the end of 1942 or beginning of 1943; CZA, KKL5/11917b, summary of the joint meetings of JNF and PLDC Executives 17.1.1943 (also in file KKL5/11901); CZA, S53/1628b, minutes of PLDC meeting, 18.2.1943.

to this effect, and in any case the JNF in those years engaged in urban purchases as well and not necessarily through the PLDC.[36]

Hankin himself did not transfer to the staff of the JNF, although his status in the PLDC was on the decline. In April 1941, he proposed that Weitz should employ him as an independent worker without any connection to the PLDC and entrust him with purchases in the Sharon on behalf of the JNF in the sum of P£60,000. Weitz did not agree to the proposal. In his response to Hankin he wrote:

> I hereby inform you that after a thorough discussion of your proposal we unfortunately cannot guarantee your esteemed self-employment in purchasing land in the Sharon. Our current involvements intended in the most part for private capital and only a small fraction for the JNF, guarantee us a sufficient area to the extent that we will not have need of any additional purchases for about a year. Whereas regarding purchases in other regions, our financial situation has deprived us of any ability to implement additional involvements during the current period. [37]

As will be seen below, at least the latter part of the letter was inaccurate to say the least. Given the facts as noted in the previous and present chapter, Weitz's response avoided the issue. He had no interest in tying Hankin to substantial work in his Department. Nonetheless, the JNF entrusted Hankin with the evacuation of tenant farmers from Wadi Kabani, but in the first half of 1943, due to Hankin's state of health, the JNF was compelled to assume the job itself.

Obligated by his wife's will and testament to engage in redeeming the land until the age of 80, at the beginning of 1943 Hankin demanded that the JNF assume the expenses of his office in the sum of P£50 a month for a period of two years (until he would attain the age of 80) so that he could remain involved in land purchases. Weitz and Granovsky refused but suggested that he engage in writing his memoirs which would be financed

---

36 CZA, S53/1682b, memorandum on "The tasks of the Palestine Development Company," not dated, but apparently from the end of 1942 or beginning of 1943; CZA, KKL5/13861, letter from Weitz to Granovsky 6.5.1944; JNF Report (1947), pp. 54–59.

37 CZA, KKL5/10641, letter from Weitz to Hankin 5.4.1941.

Olga and Yehoshua Hankin

by the JNF. These memoirs, they explained in their proposal, "when they will be put in order will have current historical–educational value which will appreciate in the future. Cognizant of its value for the JNF's affairs, the JNF will be prepared to implement this proposal." Hankin refused the offer and remained adamant in his demand. As a result, the entire matter was brought up for discussion in the Directorate. Although no formal tie remained between the JNF and Hankin, and from the JNF's standpoint this was a superfluous expense (and in Granovsky's words: "a waste from a practical and financial standpoint"), the Directorate decided unanimously out of consideration for Hankin's past and his merits in the redemption of the lands, to consent to his demand, even if the JNF did not succeed in persuading the PLDC to participate in the expense. Members of the Directorate added as well: "we cannot be put into a situation which could speed up his demise and…in this manner [agreeing to his demand] we will spare ourselves subsequent tongue wagging and remorse." Indeed until Hankin's death at the close of 1945, the JNF maintained his office.[38]

The Economic Background of the Period and Land Supply Trends on the Part of the Arab Sellers

The years of the Second World War, 1940–1945, were characterized by an economic reality in Palestine that was closely connected with the War. The free movement of goods and money was abrogated when supervision and rationing were imposed both on foreign currency as well as on the volume use of transport vessels. In order to guarantee vital supplies to the civilian population and the participation of the country's manufacturing potential in the British war effort and in supply arrangements throughout the Middle East, the Palestine Government abandoned its liberal policy and began far-reaching intervention in manufacturing and consumption. For that purpose, a system of price supervision and rationing of raw materials and commodities was imposed. All in all, the War period was a period of economic boom and prosperity for most residents of Palestine, especially in light of the huge demand on the part of the army and the neighboring countries on the one hand, and the sharp restriction on imports on the other. The boom also expressed itself in an inflationary price spiral.[39] For example, inflation in the country was part of a broader process passing over the entire Middle East which found its expression in a decline in the value of the Pound Sterling, intensified demand for gold and an appreciable increase in the price of food as a result of a decline in supply, shortage of goods and intensified demand. To demonstrate the severity of the inflation, it should be noted that since the outbreak of the War in summer 1939 until June 1943 the cost of living index rose from 100 points to 250.[40]

---

38   CZA, KKL5/11902, the following letters: Hankin to JNF 17.3.1943, Weitz to Hankin 18.6.1943 – quotation about writing his memoirs from there; CZA, KKL10, minutes of JNF Directorate meeting, 1.7.1943 – quotation from Granovsky and others members of the Directorate from there. See also CZA, KKL5/11902, letter from Weitz to Hankin 4.7.1943; CZA, KKL5/12805, letter from Granovsky to Hankin 19.7.1944.

39   Gross & Greenberg (1994), p. 38; idem (1993), pp. 59–82.

40   Gelber (1995), p. 407.

Four basic factors determined the development of the economy in the course of the War years: (1) full employment of people and the industrial system; (2) inflationary trends with a large increase in national income, a rise in purchasing power, increase of prices, a favorable balance of payments; (3) autarchic trends which intensified as a result of the country's detachment from sources of supply, restriction in the volume of ships, the rise in shipping prices, etc.; (4) the increased involvement of the public sector in the economy.

The investment economy, i.e., building and new plants – agricultural and industrial – was hard hit at the start of the War because it was dependent on the import of capital and the market created by immigration. It is clear that the investment economy was harder hit by the contraction of capital import and investor apprehensions, hence an appreciable number of workers and those supported by the investment economy were ejected from it at the start of the War. This was compounded by the repercussions caused by the withdrawal of deposits from the banks and the severe blow to the building and orchard sectors. The economic depression on the eve of the War not only did not ease but also actually worsened at the beginning of that period in summer 1939, but slowly the economy transposed itself to a war economy, with all the unique phenomena characteristic of such an economy. First and foremost, the influence of the military buildup in the country intensified in three areas: Firstly, it generated a large volume of public works which absorbed the unemployed who had been ejected from the building and citrus economy. Secondly, orders of increasing magnitude were placed with industry by the military authorities as the pace of the War intensified; Thirdly, the soldiers as consumers influenced the service and industrial branches. All this, produced a situation that after the shock of the first war years a period of recovery ensued that was perceived in all branches of the economy stimulating their substantial expansion and leading to a drop in unemployment, with the exception of the citrus orchard economy. Thus, for example, there occurred a perceptible rise in building activity, a rise in bank deposits, an expansion of industrial and agricultural manufacture, and the development of industrial entrepreneurship in a number of new branches. But these trends were arrested when apprehensions grew regarding war in the Mediterranean at the beginning of summer 1940. A process of paralysis and decline overcame the recovery trends when war with Italy became a fact and the downturn continued until September 1940.

It was only in Spring 1941 that the process of recovery began when the population began to become used to the new situation arising from the war economy. The depression in the orchard industry and in building activity remained in effect, but the vast changes in mixed agriculture, in industry and the various services led to an improvement in the situation. The army served as a quasi import market absorbing not only merchandise but also labor, and various services. Thus similar to the role played by the massive immigration and export of capital at the beginning of the 1930s in the tremendous expansion of the building industry and investment economy, the war economy during the first half of the 1940s served as a stimulating and revitalizing factor.

Due to difficulties in importing during the War period, there ensued an expansion of production in the intensive branches of the mixed agricultural economy and despite various difficulties this economy, as in all the countries involved in the War, was on the upsurge. In contradistinction, the citrus branch was harder hit by events of the War. The difficulties of transport and the high shipping costs provoked a severe crisis, and expenses rose steeply. Cultivation of the orchards was neglected and the citrus crop declined appreciably, although some alleviation to citrus cultivation resulted from Government loans to the branch, from the citrus products industry and the sale of fruits to the armed forces. During the War years, the area of citrus groves contracted by 60,000 dunams and the crop dropped from 18 million crates to 5 million crates. With the end of the War, the export of citrus rose and the branch returned steadily to its former status in the country's economy. The condition of the citrus growers themselves that was grave at the beginning of the War was alleviated due to the diversification of the economy and its reliance on a mixed agricultural economy as well as the improvement of the country's economic situation which enabled the citrus growers to turn to other professions.

A great expansion ensued in the industrial sector during the course of the War and the growth of industrial production in the country was appreciable also in comparison with other countries. Accounting for this growth was the elimination of competition with the European countries which had previously satisfied the bulk of the country's demand for industrial products, the rise in shipping and insurance costs which made foreign imports more expensive, the retooling of the industrial plants in many countries for the war effort, the imposition of restrictions on the import of merchandise by the Mandatory Government, increased purchases by the army in Palestine and the opening of more favorable markets for the export of merchandise.

Those branches related to the war effort and the huge military orders expanded in particular; in contradistinction those sectors tied to building declined. Beyond the expansion of production in existing plants, there were many initiatives to establish new plants. The vast amount of capital that did not find other investment outlets – citrus growing and the mixed agricultural economy were not attractive to it, and building activity was almost completely paralyzed – turned primarily to industry.

Profound and far-reaching changes occurred in the Arab economy during the course of the War and the differences between the Jewish and Arab sector diminished. The main reason for these developments in the Arab economy was related to accumulation of capital which occurred in this sector. True, even before the War, part of the import of Jewish capital flowed to the Arab economy but during the War, the flow of capital to the Arab economy accelerated, and an appreciable portion of the tremendous military and governmental expenditures was absorbed by the Arab sector. The principal reason for accumulation of capital in the Arab sector was related to the fact that 60 percent of the Arab community was employed in agriculture, and during the War the prices of agricultural produce, and especially the prices of grains rose steeply. It should be emphasized that the increase in prices for agricultural produce surpassed the general price increase during this period. Together with the rise in grain prices, the prices of other Arab agricultural produce (aside from citrus groves) also increased, such as milk, eggs, vegetables, cheese, olives, fruits, etc. In general, prices in the Arab market rose faster than in the Jewish market. An additional source for accumulation of capital by the Arabs was the sale of lands. Although the sale of lands to non-Arabs dwindled during the course of the War, the price of lands for a territorial unit rose drastically during the War years. Part of the intensified accumulation of capital in the Arab economy was reflected also in an appreciable demand for land by Arab purchasers, and in the purchase of lands by Arabs from Arabs.

The Arab peasant farmers and hired workers benefited greatly from the wartime economic prosperity in the Arab economy, and their income rose appreciably. Their standard of living rose and this allowed them to pay off debts from previous periods. The preponderance of capitalist factors in the Arab sector increased concomitantly.[41]

---

41   Horowitz (1948), pp. 180–257; Gelber (1995), pp. 388–411; Banker (1977), pp. 166–169, A. Cohen (1978).

The economic prosperity that came to the Arab economy during the War years reduced the Arab sellers' need to sell land, especially given the most substantial role of agricultural production – particularly grains – in the economic prosperity in general and the appreciation of land prices in particular. This also induced an appreciable drop in the supply of land by Arab sellers, and to expectations on their part for an additional appreciation in land prices, which again tended to limit supply. In the continuation of this chapter, where the special difficulties besetting JNF land purchasing during these years will be examined, details will be provided regarding the issue of contracted supply and the sharp increase in land prices, which was higher than the general price increase in the economy.[42] The pressures applied by the Arab leadership and its institutions against the sale of lands to the Jews played an important role in these developments. "Matters reached the stage where even those Arabs who had already initiated negotiations over land sales, given the inducement of ever-increasing prices, were compelled to terminate these negotiations and refrain from selling land to the Jews." On the other hand, the Arab landowners could sell their land to other Arabs, including Arabs from abroad, given their demand due to a drop in the value of the pound sterling and to capital accumulation amongst the Arab population. "They [the Arabs] urgently wished to convert their money into gold or to real estate, especially land which they viewed as a secure and stable investment. And since they could not easily obtain gold, they invested their cash in land."[43]

Difficulties in Land Purchases

In the years 1940–1945 the difficulties the JNF encountered in purchasing agricultural land intensified. The hardships stemmed first and foremost from the political restrictions imposed by the British on land purchases by Jews through the Lands Law and from the battle waged by the "Arab Land Fund" against the purchase of land by Jews. The difficulties which these factors imposed, were compounded by the problems of evicting tenant farmers, protracted and complicated land trials, the intensification of Arab

---

42 See below.
43 Granot (1952), pp. 97–98; Karnenu (September 1942), p. 34.

demand for agricultural land and a drop in the supply, a substantial increase in land prices, etc. The following section provides details concerning the difficulties besetting land purchases which the JNF confronted in its work during this period.

The Lands Law and government policy
After a period of waiting, a period characterized by no small degree of uncertainty regarding the eventual Government restrictions on Jewish land purchases which began with the promulgation on 18 May 1939 of the White Paper, the High Commissioner McMichael published the Lands Law (or under its original name, Ordinances Regarding the Transfer of Land) on 28 February. They went into effect retroactively from the day the White Paper was promulgated. According to the Law, the land was divided into three zones from the standpoint of Jewish land purchase options: Zone A (the prohibited zone); Zone B (the restricted zone) and the Free Zone. In Zone A, a prohibition was imposed against the transfer of lands to anyone who was not a Palestinian Arab. The prohibition did not apply to transfer of lands which resulted from carrying out a court decision or court order for paying off a mortgage that was registered before the Lands Law went into effect, or to carry out other court decisions rendered prior to the promulgation of the Law. Likewise, the High Commissioner had free discretion in the following cases: Granting authorization to transfer to a person who was not a Palestinian Arab in the case where the transfer request was presented to the Land Registration Office prior to the promulgation of the Lands Law; granting authorization to transfers lands that were owned by a Palestinian Arab to religious or charitable institutions; authorizing the mortgaging of lands to companies and associations; authorizing the transfer of lands to persons who were not Palestinian Arabs, in case the transfer was needed for the purpose of consolidating existing farms or to transfer Musha lands into Mafruz; authorizing a transfer to those who were not Palestinian Arabs in the event that the land transferred did not belong to a Palestinian Arab. In Zone B a prohibition applied to the transfer of lands by Palestinian Arabs, unless the land was to be transferred to other Palestinian Arabs. Here, however, the commissioner had the authority to allow the transfer of lands to any other person.

In Zone B, the High Commissioner could not prohibit transfers to those who were not Palestinian Arabs in the event that this transfer was intended to execute a verdict of the court in order to pay off a mortgage that was registered before the Law went into effect, or to implement other court verdicts rendered before the promulgation of the Law. In the Free Zone, no restrictions were imposed on the transfer of land. Likewise, the Law did not apply within municipal boundaries or to Government lands. It should be emphasized that under the Law identical conditions applied to other transfer of rights to the land such as leasing, tenant farmers, and even water usage.[44] All in all, the area prohibited or restricted for Jewish purchase (Zones A and B) comprised 95% of Western Palestine (about 25,665,000 out of 27,000,000 dunams). Zone A comprised 17,132,000 dunams, constituting 63% of Palestine – the entire mountain region in Judea, Samaria and the Galilee, the Upper Western Galilee, areas south and east of Haifa, a small portion of the Jezreel Valley, the bulk of the Beisan Valley, the southern region, the Northern Negev and part of the Central Negev (See map 17).

Zone B included about 8,533,000 dunams, constituting 32% of the area of Palestine including the Upper and Eastern Galilee, the Jordan Valley, part of the Beisan Valley and the major part of the Jezreel Valley, part of the Coastal Plain, parts of the Central Negev, and the entire southern Negev (see Map 17).

In the Free Zone, only 1,344,000 dunams remained, constituting 5% of the areas of Palestine, including non-contiguous areas in the Coastal Plain in the vicinity of Haifa, and from Tantura until the vicinity of Gedera (see Map 17). Whereas in this area about half the land was already owned by Jews (688,000 dunams), in Zone B the Jews owned only 6% (about 529,000 dunams) and 2% in Zone A (about 326,000 dunams). The area that remained unfettered by the restrictions of the Lands Law for purchase by Jews totaled only 656,000 dunams, concentrated in the Coastal Plain which was densely populated.[45] It is not surprising that given these statistics,

---

44 Details of the Law appear in supplement no. 2 of the official publication, special edition, no. 988 of 28.2.1940. See also the Law: JNF Report (1947), supplement a, pp.140–142; Weitz (1951), pp. 19–21. See also: CZA, S53/437, memorandum by Granovsky, "The Law that Turns Back the Wheel of History – on the New Lands Law in Palestine," 28.2.1940 (also in file A202/167); Weitz (1941); CZA, proceedings of Smaller Zionist General Council session, 29.2.1940; CZA, KKL10, minutes of the joint meeting of JNF Directorate, with Jewish Agency and Va'ad Le'umi Executives, 3.3.1940; ibid., proceedings of Smaller Zionist General Council session, 14.3.1940; CZA, A402/166, memorandum from Jewish Agency Information Department "On the Lands Law," 17.3.1940.

45 CZA, KKL5/11782, details on the division of the various areas in Palestine as set

Granovsky termed the Lands Law upon its promulgation as "the most severe blow the Jews had received during the twenty years of British rule in our country both from a national political standpoint and from a human moral standpoint.... A new measure for the implementation of the White Paper."[46]

The British were quite punctilious about the observance of the Lands Law.[47] Although the letter of the Law left loopholes both in Zone A and Zone B through which the Jews could make land purchases, from the Jewish standpoint, the British took a strict interpretation of these loopholes. Thus, under the Law the Commissioner could allow sales within Zone A necessary for the consolidation of existing farms. In practice "the interpretation accorded to this paragraph was that exchanges of territory for consolidating farms would be permitted, but not purchase. This is an encumbrance because it opens the way for incessant blackmail and strews obstacles on the path of developing an existing settlement which will not be able to develop its economy for many years."[48] In general, not only were requests for the purchase of lands from Arabs which were needed for the consolidation of existing farms denied authorization, but the British also refused to permit the sale of Government lands needed for this purpose.[49] Requests for leasing Government lands in Zones A and B were also turned down on the grounds that this contravened the Lands Law, irrespective of the fact that the Lands Law did not apply to Government lands regarding

---

down by the Lands Law and the memorandum "What is the Lands Law: Facts and Figures," no date (also in CZA, KKL5/15556); CZA, S3/437f, manifesto by Ussishkin to "The Jewish World and the Zionist World," 28.2.1940; A202/167, memorandum by Weitz: "Allocation of Jewish-owned Lands in Accordance with the Constituted Areas," 27.2.1940; CZA, KKL5/11782, from an address by Rabbi Berlin at a celebration in Jerusalem on 11.3.1940; CZA, A402/166, memorandum from Jewish Agency Information Department on "The Lands Law," 17.3.1940; ibid., proceedings of Smaller Zionist General Council session, 29.2.1940; JNF Report (1947), pp. 20–24.

46   Granovsky (1940), pp. 86–87 – quotation from there; Granot (1952), pp. 120–121; idem (1951b), p. 212.

47   Ibid.

48   CZA, KKL5/13848, memorandum "Regulations for the Transfer of Lands 1940."

49   CZA, KKL10, minutes of JNF Directorate meeting, 29.4.1943; CZA, KKL5/13848, "Memorandum on the regulations concerning the transfer of lands 1940"; Granot (1952), p. 102.

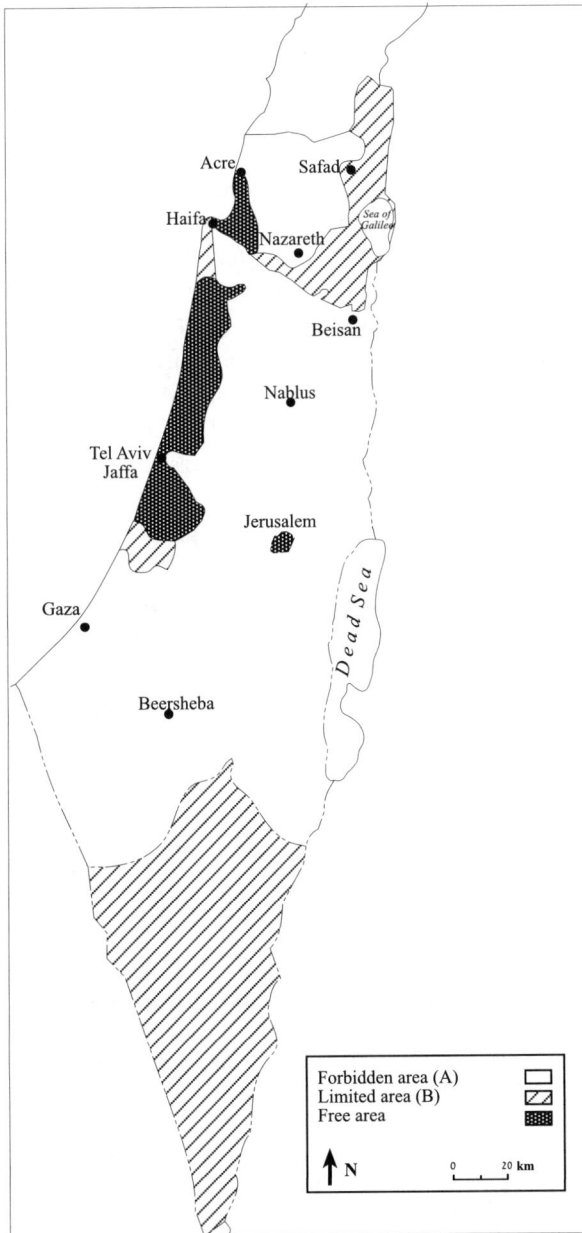

Map 17: "Lands Law" map, February 1940
Source: CZA, file S25/6937

neither sale nor leasing. In contradistinction, the Government leased and sold Government lands to Arabs. Thus, for example, the settlements in the Beisan Valley which yearned for territorial expansion suffered from the Government's refusal to sell or lease to the JNF state lands in the Valley, where at the same time such lands were given over to Arabs.[50] At the beginning of 1945 rumors abounded regarding the Government's intention to distribute among the Arabs Government lands in Zones A and B "whether in perpetuity or by recognizing the rights of the Arabs to land for pasture, etc. A number of Government officials explicitly gave the explanation that Jewish immigration might intensify and this would lead to a demand by the Jews first and foremost for Government lands, and therefore it should be ensured in advance that the Government will not own land."[51] Indeed, already in 1941, Ben-Gurion observed that the Government's behavior regarding state lands was consistent with its policy toward a Jewish national home rather than arising from its interpretation of the Lands Law. He did not hesitate to call a regime that upheld this policy "semi-Nazi regime."[52]

In most instances the High Commissioner tended to deny authorization to JNF requests for implementing transfers.[53] But the very fact that despite the Lands Law, the JNF managed in the beginning of the 1940s to purchase a relatively large number of plots by exploiting the loopholes in the law (in ways which will be detailed below) produced a situation whereby "'the government's eye' is monitoring us increasingly. The central Government has imposed upon the senior officials of the Government Lands Department to investigate and snoop around any JNF land activity in the Land

50 CZA, KKL5/13904, letter from the group at Ma'oz Hayim to JNF Haifa Office 21.11.1944, letter from Weitz to Jewish Agency Political Department 12.12.1944; CZA, KKL5/15556, article by Weitz, "The Lands Laws and the Struggle for Redemption of the Soil," not dated, but would appear to have been written in 1945; CZA, KKL5/13904, the following letters: Stromeza of JNF Haifa Office to JNF Jerusalem 23.1.1945, Weitz to Prag of the Agricultural Center 4.5.1945; CZA, minutes of Jewish Agency Executive meeting, 29.12.1940; CZA, KKL10, minutes of JNF Directorate meeting, 27.2.1941; JNF Report (1947), pp. 22–26; Granot (1952), p. 96.

51 CZA, KKL5/13904, letter from Weitz to Jewish Agency Political Department 28.1.1945 – quotation from there, letter from Stenreiser to Weitz 24.1.1945.

52 CZA, minutes of Jewish Agency Executive meeting, 2.3.1941.

53 JNF Report (1947), p. 25.

Registration Offices and the Government Lands Department."[54] "Matters whose handling in Government offices should take a few weeks are now stuck for a number of months and sometimes the months accumulate to a year, two years, without any results."[55] Thus, the JNF's land purchase options diminished increasingly.[56] Given the apprehensions over the government's tendency to close the loopholes in the Lands Law and the difficulties the government imposed, Weitz reported to the Directorate at the end of April 1943 and it is worthwhile citing his words verbatim:

> There is apprehension that the narrow legal loopholes through which we operated in Zone A could be closed in the near future, be it in a legal manner by a supplement to the Lands Law or in an administrative manner. Over the last three months, the Government Lands Department has displayed particular vigilance concerning JNF land purchases. The "question" arose as to exactly how did it occur that in the past two years the Jews have bought lands in the south in Zone A, which is prohibited to them, and established settlements there. It searched through the land transfers and when it did not find any irregularity there, an order went out from the main office to bring to Jerusalem for inspection the land registries of the Gaza Land Registration Office for the last two years. The special officials sat and scrutinized the details of the entries and looking for transgressions against the paragraphs of the Lands Law. In the past few months, the central government is causing us difficulties and strewing obstacles on the path of our land activities in the south and north, which it would previously authorize without special delay. Here are two examples: All these facts clearly demonstrate that in the higher reaches of the government there are people whose entire interest is to play "let's outsmart the Jewish national home, lest it multiply" and they are plotting schemes and cooking up stratagems to hold up, hinder, prevent and sabotage.[57]

54   CZA, KKL10, minutes of JNF Directorate meeting, 20.8.1942; see also ibid., 12.11.1942.
55   Ibid., 29.4.1943.
56   Ibid., 20.8. 1942.
57   Ibid., minutes of JNF Directorate meeting, 29.4.1943.

In the end, the Government also appointed a special committee to ascertain if the Jews were violating the land edicts.[58] It should be noted that the Arab national bodies made copious use of the Lands Law to present protests and file legal suits to prevent the transfer of lands to the JNF.[59]

The Arab National Chest and Arab National Activity Against Selling Land to Jews

The Arab National Chest which was established in the mid-1930s at the initiative of the Istiqlal Party as a company for "redeeming land," operated from Summer 1943 with great vigor in order to prevent Jewish land purchases in general and JNF purchases in particular.[60] In October 1944, Weitz termed the Chest as "an evil decree that is sevenfold more severe than the Lands Law decree" and he viewed it as the principal factor responsible for the contraction of JNF land purchases in 1944.[61] Weitz added further: "Even if the Lands Law had not existed, the National Chest in its form and means of operation today could pose a serious and severe obstacle for us. But this is ever more the case when it comes on top of this Law."[62]

The renewed activities of the Chest in the 1940s found expression first in widespread agitation against the sale of lands to the Jews, but speedily passed to the initiation of law suits which would prevent the completion of purchases by Jews and activities that from the outset would block the sale of land to Jews. The Chest entered into competition with the JNF at public auctions (one of the few loopholes through which the JNF could purchase lands in the prohibited zones) and raised prices "to a level which the Jews

58 JNF Report (1947), p. 26; CZA, KKL5/15556, memorandum by Weitz, "The Lands Laws and the Struggle for Redemption of the Soil," not dated, but would appear to have been written in 1945.

59 S. Ben-Shemesh, personal interview, Jerusalem 27.11.1996.

60 CZA, KKL5/13846, a comprehensive review of the Arab National Chest apparently written by Jewish Agency personnel on 28.7.1944; CZA, S25/7949, memorandum prepared by the Jewish Agency Political Department on the Arab National Fund, 11.3.1945.

61 CZA, KKL5/13921, "Proposal for a Program of Land Acquisitions During 1945," prepared by Weitz 30.10.1944. See also CZA, KKL10, minutes of JNF Directorate meeting, 14.11.1944.

62 CZA, KKL5/13921, "Proposal for a Program of Land Acquisitions During 1945," prepared by Weitz 30.10.1944.

could not meet." The Chest intended to withdraw the lands it purchased from the real estate market either by breaking them up into small and numerous parcels or by leasing them. The Chest financed lawsuits and land cases against the JNF and instructed the Arabs who had signed contracts with the JNF (but the transfer of which had not yet been completed in the Land Registration Office) or had transferred power of attorney in return for a down payment to cancel the contracts or the power of attorney. The Chest did not hesitate to resort to threats against Arab owners who refused to yield to its authority, and the JNF found it difficult to contend with this. Emissaries of the Chest reached landowners who resided outside of Palestine, in order to prevent them from selling land to the JNF, thus sealing off another loophole in the Lands Law.[63]

The pressure which the Chest applied on the Government also bore fruit on more than one occasion. Thus, for example, sales contracts to the JNF were annulled, appeals were presented, by the Government against a Land Arrangement official's ruling regarding JNF ownership rights and the head of the JNF's Galilee Office, Yosef Nahmani, was denied a visa to Syria and Lebanon where he sought to travel in order to conduct negotiations with Arab landowners. In addition, Arab Government officials were active in the Chest and assisted it in attaining its goals. Beyond all the damage the Chest inflicted, its general activity contributed to a rise in land prices which caused difficulty to JNF activity from another direction.[64] It should be noted that aside from the National Chest, the "Company for Rescuing

---

63 CZA, KKL5/12803, summary of deliberations held in JNF Haifa Office on 20.7.1944; CZA, KKL5/13846, extensive review of the National Chest, 28.7.1944; CZA, S25/1892, memorandum "We will Extend the Borders of Our Country," 1.10.1944; CZA, KKL5/13894, letter from Nahmani to the JNF Lands Department 2.3.1945; CZA, KKL10, minutes of JNF Directorate meeting, 6.7.1944 – quotation from the address by Weitz. Up to the middle of 1945 purchases by the National Chest totalled 10,300 dunams. On this see CZA, KKL5/17134, memorandum on "The Arab National Chest."

64 CZA, KKL10, minutes of JNF Directorate meeting, 20.2.1945, 6.7.1944; CZA, KKL5/12803, summary of deliberations in JNF Haifa Office on 15.6.1944; CZA, KKL5/13846, comprehensive review of the National Chest, 28.7.1944; CZA, KKL5/12809, letter from Weitz to Shertok 2.1.1945; CZA, KKL5/13904, letter from Gilboa Regional Council to Weitz 24.1.1945; CZA, KKL5/13894, letter from Nahmani to Lands Department in JNF Head Office 2.3.1945; S. Ben-Shemesh, personal interview, Jerusalem 27.11.1996.

Lands in the South" operated in the southern region with similar objectives and similar methods, while the Arab press aired various proposals on how to rescue lands of the motherland.[65]

Weitz and Granovsky summarized the particular difficulties which the activities of the National Chest caused the JNF, at a meeting of the Directorate in July 1944:

> As a result of all this, our activity in redeeming land from the Arabs has almost been brought to a standstill. We could perhaps overcome the high prices which the Chest is paying out, but how are we to overcome its threats toward Arab sellers?.... Up to now we have invested special efforts in the 'prohibited zones,' and this constituted our response to the land decrees. But today we are unable to make these efforts on the previous scale because a new factor that thwarts our activity in these regions has emerged – the Arab Chest. Hitherto, political activity against us was carried out by the English – from a legal perspective. Now the activity is conducted by the Arabs – from a practical standpoint and apparently with the encouragement of an authoritative party. The major danger inherent in the bank's [the National Chest] land activities is the hindrance to purchase arrangements and the elimination of territorial areas from our grasp. There is also apparently a tendency being pursued by the Chest's directorate not to sell the lands but to arrange "something along the lines of the JNF's activities," that is to maintain ownership of the land by the Chest and to lease it to Arab lessees. In such an event it will prove impossible to buy these lands back and those residing on them would be thorns in our eyes.[66]

The JNF's Report to the 22nd Zionist Congress in 1946 added:

> Circles close to the Arab leadership have established an espionage network that has also penetrated the Government offices. They have gotten on the tracks of Arabs who maintain business relationships with Jews, threaten them, vandalize their property and do not recoil from acts of murder. Arab pressure has become widespread and has reached beyond the boundaries of Palestine and especially to Syria

---

65   CZA, KKL5/13846, comprehensive review of the National Chest, 28.7.1944.
66   CZA, KKL10, minutes of JNF Directorate meeting, 6.7.1944.

and Lebanon. With the encouragement of the Arab League, their governments have used legal measures to prevent the Arabs from selling their lands located in the areas of Palestine. The incitement against selling land to Jews also emanates from other circles and the Mandatory Government apparatus at all its levels is not free of it. This pressure of course has frightened many of the land owners.[67]

Reduction of supply, Arab demand for land and the rise in land prices
The reduction of supply and Arab demand for land which competed with the JNF, and the rise in agricultural land prices during the period under discussion, were caused not only by the activity of the "National Chest" and Arab national activity against the sale of lands to Jews, additional factors also contributed. Firstly, prices rose generally in Palestine during the War period, and especially grain prices which influenced the rise in land prices; secondly, there were expectations that property prices would record further increase in the future; thirdly capital accumulated by Arabs during the War period resulting from the vast demand by the British army for food supplies and labor; additionally there was a fall in the purchasing power of the Pound Sterling and a lack of confidence in its stability.

This induced, on the one hand, a contraction in the supply of lands offered for sale and on the other hand, stimulated increased investments by Arabs in land purchases and especially on the part of dealers and contractors including those residing in Syria and Egypt. Thus as opposed to the initial period of the War, and during the decline of the Arab disturbances in Palestine, when there was an upsurge in supply, immediately afterwards, an accelerated process set in where supply contracted, Arab demands for land expanded and land prices increased drastically. It should be noted that private Jewish parties evinced an increased demand for agricultural land, mainly for reasons similar to those enumerated above (especially in the vicinity of Tel Aviv and the Sharon) and they too entered into competition with the JNF.[68]

---

67   JNF Report (1947), p. 30. See also Israel National Archives, 138/3132c (1298b), "The Land Problem and the Plans of the National Chest Company," internal document 1944.

68   JNF Report (1947), pp. 27–28; Granot (1952), pp. 97–98; Ater, "The Palestine Land Development Company and its Prospects," *Haaretz*, 25.8.1943; Granovsky, "At the End of 1942: Summaries and Dangers": *Karnenu* (November 1943); Weitz, address

178 *Chapter Three*

The following report transmitted to the JNF offices in the beginning of 1943 by the Head Office expresses the competition over land posed by Arab demand and not necessarily from nationalist motivations, which the JNF contended with in the course of the 1940s, a situation which the JNF had not encountered in the past.

> We were negotiating for the purchase of 1,000 dunams in the Northern Hula. Contracts had been drawn up several years ago. It was necessary to receive a permit from the Commissioner in order to transfer to our name the land belonging to an Arab, as required for Zone B by the Law. As a result of our efforts the authorities were constrained to issue the permit. However, when the time came to implement the purchase, competition arose on the part of the peasants of the neighboring Moshava who presented a claim regarding the rights of adjoining land, since the land that was about to be purchased was Musha with the land of the Moshava. The monies available to the peasants of this poor Moshava sufficed in order to offer the seller an increase of P£3 per dunam. The JNF [generally] paid P£7 per dunam and they [the villagers] proposed P£10 and deposited almost the entire sum of P£10,000 in the bank. How could these Arabs offer such a high price? It emerges that they owned herds of buffalo which wallowed in the swamps and a head of buffalo which before the War fetched P£5–8 currently sells for P£50–60. It was sufficient, therefore, that every peasant would extract 2–3 heads of cattle from

---

to Agricultural Conference on 14.5.1945, daily reports, p. 16; CZA, S53/437f, article by Granovsky, "A Law that Turns Back the Wheel of History," 28.2.1940; CZA, S53/437f, manifesto by Ussishkin "To the Jewish World and the Zionist World," 28.2.1940; CZA, KKL5/10580, excerpt from the address by Weitz at JNF National Committee meeting, 7.11.1940; CZA, S53/437f, letter from Granovsky to Kaplan at Jewish Agency 15.7.1942; CZA, KKL5/11871, *Information Bulletin*, no date, but apparently in 1942; CZA, KKL5/11871, circular from JNF Head Office to JNF offices, 23.3.1943, "On the Situation Regarding Land Purchases in the Fourth Year of the War" (also in files S53/437f, S8/92, CZA, KKL5/10072); CZA, KKL5/12830, letter from Weitz to Hakibbutz Hame'uhad Secretariat 5.12.1943; CZA, S25/1892, activities in 1945, especially p. 4; CZA, KKL10, minutes of JNF Directorate meetings, 24.3.1942, 25.6.1942, 20.8.1942, 12.11.1942, 18.2.1943, 23.4.1943, 9.11.1943, 25.4.1944, 6.7.1944, 19.12.1944, 20.2.1945, 20.3.1945.

his herd in order to obtain the required sum for purchasing the land. The competition between us is still continuing.[69]

The average price of lands purchased by the JNF rose from P£4 per dunam in 1940 to P£20 in 1945 – i.e., an increase of about 500 percent! This should be viewed in comparison to the wholesale price index which rose in that period by 2.2%, and the cost of living index which doubled.[70] In the Gaza vicinity, for example, the JNF purchased lands in the year 1942 at a price of P£11 per dunam, and in the end of 1944 it was required to pay for lands in that same vicinity P£25 per dunam. In the vicinity of Beit Eshel in the Negev, the JNF was required to pay P£11–12 per dunam, whereas "a few years ago we paid P£2–2.50 per dunam for land in this vicinity."[71] The same applied to a purchase proposal in Abu Gosh which was submitted to the Directorate at the beginning of 1945. Granovsky reported that

> A few years ago Mr. Yehoshua Hankin conducted negotiations for the purchase of the land area under discussion at the price of P£5–7 per dunam, but for various reasons not dependent on us, it was not implemented. About three quarters of a year ago we entered into negotiations to purchase this area at a price of P£15–17 per dunam and because of various delays the purchase was not implemented. Now a price of P£25–26 per dunam, including various expenses is being quoted.[72]

The problem of tenant farmers

Prior to the publication of the Lands Law, the JNF viewed land held by tenant farmers as a major drawback. In the event that it considered the option of purchasing such lands, it ensured that the purchase contract with the selling party would include an obligation to transfer to the JNF lands which were vacant. It almost totally abstained from purchases when the responsibility

---

69 CZA, KKL5/11871, circular letter from JNF Head Office to JNF Offices 23.3.1943 "On the Situation Regarding Land Purchase During the Fourth Year of the War," 23.3.1943 (also in S53/437f, S8/92, KKL5/10072, which include other examples of this competition).
70 JNF Report (1947), pp. 28–29. On the rise of the wholesale price index and the rise in the cost of living index, see Ettinger (1947), p. 39.
71 CZA, KKL10, minutes of JNF Directorate meeting, 19.12.1944.
72 Ibid., 20.2.1945.

for eviction remained that of the JNF.[73] After the promulgation of the Lands Law the JNF found it difficult to remain selective, and implemented purchases where the eviction of tenant farmers was its direct obligation. In order to transfer lands to its full ownership, it had to contend with all the difficulties in the matter, be they difficulties created by the Ordinance for the Protection of Tenant Farmers,[74] or with difficulties attendant upon the actual eviction process. Among the difficulties the JNF confronted due to the ordinance were the award of rights to a person holding the land even though he had not leased the land with the consent of the owners; the award of tenant farmer rights to a person holding any area whatsoever; the rights of tenancy were not restricted to a maximum defined area; the possibility that the tenant farmer would obtain rights over both plots if he had transferred from one plot to another, but on lands belonging to the same owner; the exploitation of the ordinance as a means for extorting money from the owners. The JNF's direct obstacle was created by the tenant farmers, since both parties preferred almost in all circumstances the option of financial compensation for eviction over the option of the mandatory one year eviction notice, and the provision of a new place for livelihood with the assent of the High Commissioner. Thus, the ordinance stimulated a substantial rise in the price of the land being purchased. However, the eviction process itself was also complex and complicated and took a long time, and sometimes involved protracted court cases. Tenant farmers who received the agreed upon compensation refused in the end to vacate the area and sometimes the lands which were vacated were seized by new tenant farmers. In cases where the number of tenant farmers was especially large, their eviction even within the framework of a financial arrangement was almost impossible.[75]

---

73 See above p. 42.
74 On this Ordinance and the rights of tenant farmers see in detail Granovsky (1949), pp. 295–301; Halperin (1944), pp. 107–111; Katz (in press); Avneri (1980), pp. 108–109, 114, 123, 209–212.
75 CZA, KKL10, minutes of JNF Directorate meeting, 18.1.1944; CZA, KKL5/13847, letter from Weitz to Kravel 25.7.1944; CZA, KKL5/12697, letter from Stromeza to Weitz 31.5.1942 concerning the "Amendment of the Tenant Farmers Law"; CZA, KKL5/12697, letter from Eliash to the JNF Executive "Re the Committee for the Tenant Farmers Law," 24.61942; CZA, KKL9/244, letter from Nahmani to Maharshak 22.7.1940; CZA, KKL5/12697, letter from Stromeza to JNF 6.8.1942; H. Danin, personal interview, Jerusalem 8.10.1997.

The Rise in JNF Income: A Ray of Light in a Period of Difficulties

In the years 1940 to 1945, JNF income increased appreciably. This increase in income explains to a large extent the magnitude of JNF land purchases despite all the limitations described above, although it should not be inferred from this that the JNF was absolved from all fiscal constraints. The increase in income occurred despite the war situation and the European Holocaust which led to a drastic decrease in JNF income from this continent (excluding Britain), and did not exceed 1.6% of JNF income world-wide. The European countries (excluding Britain), which since the establishment of the JNF were the leading providers of JNF income had since the outbreak of the War, dropped to last place. However, the JNF's general annual income rose from P£560,000 in 1939, to nearly P£2.3 million in 1945. A year later JNF income rose by an additional million Palestine Pounds. In 1940 the JNF's income totaled P£ 617,000, in 1941 – P£620,000, in 1942 – P£681,000; in 1943 – P£1.146 million and in 1944 – P£1.766 million (see Appendix 15). Over 60% of income during 1940–1946 derived from the United States, the balance from Britain (10%), South Africa (about 10%), Palestine (about 9.4%), Latin America (about 3.2%) and Canada (about 3%). Thus given the rise in the JNF's income, Granovsky could contend at the close of 1943 "that from a fiscal standpoint there has been no impediment to land purchases in recent years: no purchase was turned down 'for reasons of lack of money.' If there will be a possibility to realize all portions of the land purchase program for the year 1943–1944 we will not refrain from implementing them, and the question of resources will not serve as an impediment or obstacle."[76]

A source for the increased income was an appreciable growth in contributions of various types which were bestowed upon the JNF including wills, living bequests, indirect taxes on various services in Palestine, etc. Undoubtedly the rise in contributions was linked to the heightened sense of

---

76 JNF Report (1947), pp. 74–78; CZA, KKL10, minutes of JNF Directorate meeting, 30.5.1940. On the JNF's financial constraints that did not enable it to implement all its programs in 1940 see KKL10, minutes of JNF Directorate meetings, 3.3.1940, 26.9.1940, 25.12.1940; CZA, KKL10, proceedings of Smaller Zionist General Council session, 14.3.1940. For Granovsky's address at the end of 1943 see minutes of JNF Directorate meeting, 9.11.1943.

obligation to Palestine felt by that part of World Jewry which was distant from the area of conflict because of the War, the Holocaust and identification with the Jewish Community in Palestine's struggle against the White Paper and the Lands Law: "A turnabout has occurred in the sentiments of the Jewish public. Previously, the Jew would give only financial assistance to building the land and its redemption, whereas, in recent years, this participation has become deeper and more personal."[77] However, the JNF had since 1940 significantly expanded its propaganda, organizational and educational activity abroad (excluding countries under the Nazi conquest) as well as in Palestine. Amongst other things this activity included the establishment of a network of emissaries who were the responsibility of the Head Office, frequent visits of JNF leaders abroad where they participated in conferences on the JNF's behalf. Various projects were established by the JNF in Palestine and throughout the Jewish world including North Africa, whose purpose was to expand by every means the volume of contributions. The JNF coordinated fund-raising activity (but never collaborations that might diminish the JNF's independence) with appeals of various other Zionist bodies and this also increased the volume of contributions.[78]

However, the JNF worked to increase its resources not only by contributions but also by tapping additional financial sources. Firstly, upon the outbreak of the War, measures which had proved successful were taken to transfer to Palestine sums of money that had accumulated to the JNF's credit in its European offices (save for Poland). In this manner, about P£167,000 were transferred to Palestine. Secondly, the JNF offered

---

77   JNF Report (1947), p. 94 – quotation from there; CZA, proceedings of Smaller Zionist General Council session, 14.3.1940.

78   JNF Report (1947), pp. 78–117; CZA, KKL5/11866, memorandum by Czernowitz, 23.5.1943 "Regarding the work of the JNF in the future: Proposals for Drawing up a Program"; CZA, S25/1892, "JNF activities during 1945"; CZA, KKL10, minutes of JNF Directorate meetings, 26.9.1940, 14.8.1941, 25.11.1941, 24.3.1942, 23.4.1942, 29.5.1942, 25.6.1942, 12.11.1942, 24.12.1942, 18.2.1943, 29.4.1943, 17.6.1943 – the latter report stresses that there was an increase of 66% in the JNF's income from contributions from September 1942 to April 1943 as compared with the same period during the previous year. See also CZA, KKL10, minutes of JNF Directorate meeting, 27.9.1943 (especially on activities in Britain and the income from there), 27.9.1943 (distribution and activities of the emissaries in English-speaking countries), 18.1.1944 (about the visit of Rabbi Berlin to America), 25.4.1944 (Granovsky points out with satisfaction the tremendous increase in the JNF's income).

for sale in Palestine and the United States interest-bearing bonds for an intermediate term which were earmarked for financial institutions in Palestine, capitalists and the middle class. In the United States alone bonds were issued in the volume of over $3.2 million (P£1.06 million). Thirdly, long-term loans were taken directly from banks. Fourthly, the JNF sought to gain control of capital that was intended for various public purposes which had generally been lying dormant in the banks. The JNF guaranteed bank interest rates to the institutions that had made these deposits, and this in return allowed the JNF to use the actual monies for purchasing lands. Thus, at the end of 1943, an agreement was signed between the JNF and the Supervisory Union of the Provident and Pension Funds regarding the deposit of pension funds with the JNF. "For the first time an economic and financial connection was established with the pension and provident funds of the workers whose capital increased annually and whose investments would undoubtedly appreciate in the future. To cover their current expenses, these funds require but a small portion of their income, whereas the balance will remain deposited with the JNF. Therefore, these investments should be construed as long-term deposits." At the end of 1943, until September 1946, the JNF received from the pension and provident funds more than P£500,000. Additional public bodies such as the Hebrew University as well as private bodies such as insurance companies also deposited with the JNF several hundred thousand Palestine Pounds.[79]

The JNF continued to operate the program for cooperation with private capital in land purchases and even expanded it to the Garden City Projects.[80] These projects which had been in operation since 1940, primarily in Britain, were intended first and foremost to increase the JNF's income and enable it to meet its primary objective – purchasing agricultural lands. An additional source of income were land purchase plans for urban housing, under whose terms the future home owner shared in financing land purchases as an advance leasing fee and deposited with the JNF an additional interest-bearing sum that would be returned with the start of construction. It should be emphasized (as we shall see below) that in the purchases of agricultural

79   JNF Report (1947), pp. 120–126 – the quotation from p. 125; CZA, KKL10, minutes of JNF Directorate meetings, 27.2.1941, 24.12.1942, 18.2.1943, 29.2.1944 (on the loan of P£300,000 the JNF received from a consortium of Palestine banks led by APC Ltd.), 25.4.1944 (including the transfer of the pension fund monies to the JNF).

80   These two projects are described in detail below.

land that were intended to complete the territorial quota of existing settlements, there was a considerable participation by the settlements themselves or of their settlement movements when this participation was credited to the account of the leasing fee.[81] Since 1940, there was impressive growth in JNF income from leasing fees on its urban and rural lands, and they constituted an important additional source of JNF income. During 1940–1946, leasing fees totaled over P£250,000 – an almost fourfold increase in total JNF income from leasing fees from the establishment of the JNF until 1939. Amongst the factors accounting the rise in income from leasing fees was: the growth in the number of settlements; the growth in the number of settlements which entered the category obligating them to pay full leasing fees; efficiencies in the collection apparatus; and the drop in delayed payments and debts, resulting from the improvement in the situation of the agricultural settlements and the rise of the standard of living in Palestine during the War period.[82] Furthermore, the authorities consented to the JNF's demand that the agricultural tax should be collected directly by the Government from the settlements, rather than from the JNF, which also resulted in decreased JNF expenditures.[83]

Decisions Following the Publication of the Lands Law: Continued Activity Within the Framework of the Law and Preference for Zones A and B

The promulgation of the Lands Law at the end of March 1940, with all its implications, obligated the JNF to decide on a number of important issues and determine policy lines regarding its future land purchase activity. Indeed, a meeting of the Directorate in the course of 1940 was devoted to thrashing out questions which arose in the wake of the Lands Law, as well

81 JNF Report (1947), pp. 42–55, 129–130; CZA, KKL5/11871, *Information Bulletin*, no date, but apparently from 1942; CZA, KKL10, minutes of JNF Directorate meetings, 24.3.1942, 23.4.1942, 20.8.1942, 12.11.1942, 27.9.1943.

82 JNF Report (1947), pp. 68–70; CZA, S25/1892, JNF Activities in 1945; CZA, KKL10, minutes of JNF Directorate meetings, 23.4.1942, 28.5.1942, 25.6.1942, 20.8.1942, 12.11.1942, 18.2.1943, 29.4.1943, 17.6.1943, 27.9.1943, 25.4.1944.

83 JNF Report, p. 71; CZA, KKL10, minutes of JNF Directorate meeting, 29.4.1943.

as to adopting decisions and formulating policy foundations as necessitated by the new conditions created with the promulgation of the Law. The vast importance which the Directorate attached to the deliberations concerning the significance of the Lands Law to future JNF activity is attested to by the fact that the Directorate's meeting which convened a few days after the Law's promulgation, had a single topic on the agenda – "The JNF's activity following the promulgation of the new Lands Law by the Mandatory Government." Members of the Jewish Agency Executive and members of the Va'ad Leumi Executive were invited to participate in the deliberations. Joint meetings of the JNF Directorate with the Jewish Agency Executive were rare, and it would appear that aside from the session that took place after the promulgation of the Lands Law no joint session of the JNF Directorate with the Jewish Agency Executive and the Executive of the Va'ad Leumi was ever held again.

The JNF was faced with three concerted issues arising from the promulgation of the Lands Law: The first, were there grounds to consider a halt to purchases in order to create economic pressure on the Arabs – pressure which would in the end result lead to the revocation of the Law? The second issue was whether future JNF purchases would take place within the framework of the Law (while exploiting the few options permitted by the Law), or would purchases be made in contravention of the Law? The third issue was what would be the priorities in land purchases in light of the fiscal constraints?

Although the President of the Va'ad Leumi, Pinhas Rutenberg, and apparently other members of the Zionist General Council, favored a halt for a specific time to land purchases in order to generate economic pressure on the Arabs which would induce them to vigorously demand the repeal of the Law, the JNF's position as well as that of the Jewish Agency Executive was that land purchases should not cease for even a single moment.[84] The decision to continue purchases in any case constituted a continuation of the JNF policy pursued both after the outbreak of the Arab disturbances in 1936 as well as after the promulgation of the White Paper in 1939, when

---

84   Arthur Ruppin, who served as head of the Jewish Agency Settlement Department, considered the proposal to cease land purchases for the above reasons as being logically sound, but in the end reached the decision that purchases should be made wherever possible within the confines of the Law. See CZA, KKL10, minutes of JNF Directorate meeting, 3.3.1940.

opinions were voiced within the Jewish community to cease purchases in order to create pressure on the Arabs.[85] Now, as in the past, the JNF leaders did not believe that a cessation of purchases would exert pressure on the Arabs that would lead to the repeal of the Law. Additionally, they felt that the land ownership and settlement on it constituted a tangible asset in the future political struggle, especially when it was demonstrated that one could not rely on Britain and it was also difficult to rely on Diaspora Jewry. A halt to purchases, in order to obtain Arab pressure to repeal the Law was as Rabbi Berlin stated:

> Political speculation and one could not anticipate its results with confidence. Whereas, by refraining from land purchases and putting down territorial and settlement stakes in Zones A and B even within the framework of the few possibilities open to us under the new Lands Law, we are by our own hands forfeiting these positions for many years and perhaps forever.... What is axiomatic for the JNF today is: You don't lay down the arms of redeeming the land for a "retaliatory" calculation or for a "political" calculation whatsoever, not for a single day. No "calculation" will satisfy us as much as another territorial position and another settlement point.

Moreover, apprehension was expressed in the JNF that with a halt in purchases, a cessation of contributions would also occur, as stated by Ussishkin: "The donor today is prepared to give money to the JNF only if one can demonstrate to him concrete day to day land purchases and land redemption." In general, Ussishkin and other members of the Directorate felt that the cessation of practical Zionist activity in Palestine would lead to the decay of the entire Zionist Movement. The decision on the first issue was therefore clear. The JNF should continue purchases without interruption, not even temporarily.[86]

---

85 See above, p. 63, on the dispute with Hankin.
86 CZA, KKL10, minutes of JNF Directorate meeting, 3.3.1940; address by Ussishkin at the session of the Smaller Zionist General Council, 14.3.1940 in CZA. See also Weitz (1941) concerning the importance of immediate land acquisition for the political struggle for Palestine which would certainly arise at the end of the War. He stressed: "What will be the situation at the end of the War? I believe with all my heart that justice will win out, and that the allies will be victorious. The national issue will then be raised once more. Following the First World War, we received the Balfour Declaration which

Despite the tremendous anger in the Zionist institutions against the Lands Law, the general opinion formulated in the JNF and the Jewish Agency Executive was that the former should continue its activity in land purchases within the framework of the new Law and not in contravention of it. It was to do so while taking advantage of the purchase options which the Law allowed and exploiting all existing legal and political venues (by the Jewish Agency and the JNF together) in order to exploit the opportunities that permitted purchases within the framework of the law and perhaps bring about its total repeal. Ruppin, for example, proposed appealing the Lands Law before the Jerusalem court, and if the appeal would be turned down to address the Kings Council in London.[87] Ben-Gurion suggested examining measures that would bring about an assault on the Law in the House of Commons, including immediate settlement on the lands recently purchased by the JNF in Zones A and B. Kaplan, the Jewish Agency Treasurer, was the most practical. He suggested the establishment of an experts' commission of legal and land specialists who would examine in depth the legal means for making purchases within the framework of the Law, and they would amass data on the ownership of the lands and their status, data that would improve the chances of successfully completing purchases within the framework of the Law. These proposals were also adopted as decisions ratified by the Directorate. It would appear that Kaplan was also the first who suggested circumventing the Lands Law by purchasing from Jewish owners who were not residing on their lands, purchases that would also be a springboard for purchases from Arabs in their vicinity. Likewise, Kaplan suggested identifying those farms in Zone

---

brought us back to our land and gave us our homeland. Today we are witnessing the results of this Declaration. One of the obstacles for implementation is that we did not settle the land, that we did not stand firm on it and in such a situation a major change can come about tomorrow. The extent to which we will settle the land will determine the extent to which we will gain our freedom."

87   Ussishkin also demanded a political struggle against the Lands Law, see CZA, proceedings of Smaller Zionist Council session, 14.3.1940. See also proposals for a political struggle against the Law: CZA, S53/437, memorandum by Granovsky, "The Law that Turns Back the Wheel of Jistory – on the New Lands Law in Palestine," 28.2.1940 (also in file A202/167); CZA, S53/437j, manifesto by Ussishkin, 28.2.1940, "To the Jewish and Zionist World."

A which required consolidation and expansion, for in such a case this could be exploited as one of the loopholes in the Lands Law.[88]

There were three primary reasons advanced in the Directorate and the Jewish Agency Executive for implementing purchases within the framework of the Law: Firstly, the attendant financial risk in implementing land combinations that would be carried out in violation of the Law, i.e., JNF ownership would not be guaranteed irrespective of the fact that the JNF in practice would invest monies. The land would not be registered in its name and the courts would not authorize the transfers of official powers of attorney in favor of the JNF. Secondly, there was apprehension that the loopholes in the existing Law would be sealed. Likewise, restrictions could be imposed on options to purchase in the Free Zone, in the event that the English discovered that transfers were being effected outside the framework of the Law. Thirdly, in the event that loopholes in the Lands Law were exploited, the JNF could implement some purchases in both region A and region B and definitely in the Free Zone. The total of these combined purchases was estimated at 500,000–750,000 dunams which could be purchased over ten years "and after ten years we will wage our decisive political battle at the close of the period of the White Paper."

The JNF indeed examined various options for transfers outside the framework of the Law, but pursuant to a legal opinion it was made clear "that these possibilities are adventures," and the JNF should not be drawn into them despite the fact that they had political value and merited consideration "also from the standpoint of the psychological impact on Jews." Indeed, the possibility of implementing a number of experimental purchases outside the framework of the Law was not rejected, but "the work" decreed Ussishkin, "should continue in a legal manner."[89] In the

---

88 CZA, KKL10, minutes of JNF Directorate meeting, 3.3.1940 (joint meeting with Jewish Agency and Va'ad Leumi Executives), 11.4.1940.

89 Ibid. – the first quotation is from Ruppin's address as recorded in the first minutes, the second quotation is from Granovsky's comments as recorded in the second minutes and the third quotation from Ussishkin's statement recorded in the second minutes. See also ibid., Ussishkin's address in the proceedings of Smaller Zionist General Council, 14.3.1940; CZA, S53/437, Granovsky, "The Law that Turns Back the Wheel of History – on the new Lands Law in Palestine," 28.2.1940 (also in A202/167), Granovsky's analysis of the manifold possibilities remaining for JNF purchase of lands within the confines of the Lands Law.

minority opinion were Yitzhak Gruenbaum (a member of the Jewish Agency Executive), Dov Joseph (Legal Adviser to the Executive) and Berl Katznelson who believed that the JNF should adopt every measure that would sabotage the Lands Law. They maintained the opinion that one should implement purchases even in contravention of the Law and without receipt of the deeds. Jewish settlements would be established on the purchased lands while formal partnerships would be arranged with the registered Arab owners.[90]

A uniform position regarding the order of priorities in land purchases did not emerge among the members of the Directorate and members of the Jewish Agency Executive at the joint session of the Directorate held after the promulgation of the Lands Law. Ruppin believed that preference should be given precisely to the permitted zone, although he did not reject purchases in every area within the framework of the Lands Law. He contemplated that it would be advantageous if an appreciable portion of the productive lands in Palestine would be owned by Jews. A substantial concentration of these lands was located in the Free Zone. Vilkansky contended that purchases should be made in all zones for two reasons: First, he feared that in the future the British would impose restrictions in the Free Zone as well; secondly, the Jewish community in Palestine needed to free itself from the burden of expenditures implicit in the import of various foodstuffs and therefore it required a variety of lands for a variety of crops. Katznelson was of the opinion that it was imperative to purchase in Zones A and B but felt that purchases in the Free Zone should still be made. Therefore, he rejected any thought of waiving the large territorial blocs in Wadi Kabani and Wadi Samara in the vicinity of the Hefer Valley, which was part of the permitted zone. "We must purchase lands," explained Katznelson, "not only for political reasons but also for reasons of fortification, reinforcement and consolidation. Any portion of Palestine is important, sometimes from this standpoint and sometimes from another." As opposed to Ruppin, Vilkansky and Katznelson, Gruenbaum and Joseph rejected any purchase in the permitted zone. They believed that the objective of purchases

---

90 CZA, KKL10, minutes of JNF Directorate meetings, 3.3.1940 (joint meeting with Jewish Agency and Va'ad Leumi Executives), 11.4.1940. See also CZA, KKL5/ 15556, Weitz's memorandum "The Lands Law and the Struggle for the Redemption of the Land" (apparently from 1945) that shows that the purchase of lands during the period the Lands Law was in force were generally made according to the Law.

should be political–strategic, both to abolish the Lands Law and to allow settlement on widespread areas of Palestine with all its inherent importance to the future political fate of of the country. Therefore, purchases should be concentrated first and foremost in Zone A. Within this zone, Gruenbaum sought to concentrate on the Western Galilee.[91]

Ussishkin believed that priority should be accorded to Zones A and B because of the political importance entailed and in the event that an important land purchase would be made in the Free Zone, and the requisite resources would be available, this purchase should be implemented as well. Shmorek, as well as Kaplan, Granovsky, Zuchovitzky, Rabbi Berlin and Weitz were of a similar opinion. Granovsky emphasized the severe error committed by the JNF in that it had neglected the Upper Galilee until recent years, as well as its total neglect of the South and the Negev.[92] However, given the new conditions, Ussishkin proposed that a new objective be assigned to the JNF: the penetration of the towns. He contended that since the Lands Law would in any case not allow a broad Jewish foothold in the agricultural areas of Zones A and B, a tangible Jewish penetration into the urban communities of Zones A and B (the Lands Law did not apply to the towns) was warranted. By this evasion, there would still be substantial Jewish presence in the prohibited and limited zones. Regarding the penetration of the towns, Ussishkin emphasized the following:

> In all my years of Zionist activity, I fought for the Jewish villages and did not consider the cities, save for one city – Jerusalem, which is our capital, and to a certain extent Haifa, which is the key to Palestine as well. But under today's conditions, when there are to be complete areas without any Jewish foothold, we have to break this by taking hold of some of the Arab towns. We must penetrate Gaza, Jericho, Hebron, Nazareth, Shechem, Jenin, and Tulkarm…. In all these and other towns, we must create the nucleus of a Jewish community.

---

91   CZA, KKL10, minutes of JNF Directorate meetings, 3.3.1940 (joint meeting with Jewish Agency and Va'ad Leumi Executives) – quotation by Katznelson from there, 11.4.1940. On the activities of the JNF in the first half of 1940 regarding the purchase of lands in Wadi Kabani and Wadi Samara, see, e.g., S53/437j, *Information Bulletin*, 9.6.1940 issued jointly by JNF, Jewish Agency Executive and Keren Hayesod.

92   Ibid., 3.3.1940, 11.4.1940, and the proceedings of Smaller Zionist General Council meeting, 14.3.1940; CZA, KKL5/11782, address by Rabbi Berlin at a celebration in Jerusalem on 11.3.1940.

Regarding Jerusalem and Haifa, there is general assent that we must concentrate our strength on the expansion of Jerusalem and Haifa. There are Arab towns close to Jewish settlement points, such as Acre which is near Nahariya and to Shavei Tziyon, and which must be considered as well. As for Hebron in general, we must return to it, it is to our tremendous shame that we allowed this name to be erased from the map of Jewish Palestine. We must return to urban settlement points. [93]

It should be noted that both Gruenbaum and Berlin supported penetrating the towns,[94] but Ussishkin's ideas were vigorously rejected by Katznelson and Vilkansky. Katznelson explained:

What value can these land purchases have? They will create another ten to fifteen ghettos in Palestine. What will the Jews do in these Arab towns? If they are to be shopkeepers – there are enough Arab shopkeepers in these towns and they are as skilled in buying and selling as Jewish merchants, and if they are to be industrialists in these cities, they will be forced to employ Arab workers – that is, to funnel Jewish capital, vigor and venture to an Arab city. Furthermore, from a physical standpoint, there will never be security for a small Jewish community in a large Arab city. From a nationalist standpoint, it will lead to Arab assimilation of the worst possible sort. This translates into disaster from a national and economic standpoint. Perhaps, the idea of creating a Jewish urban settlement framework, surrounding the Arab towns, can be considered, but not Jewish neighborhoods within the Arab towns. However, it should be stated here that nothing was done for the sake of Jerusalem and Haifa, in a Jewish settlement sense, that could have been carried out up to now, and we have not attained what it was possible to attain, and we must correct this defect at the earliest possible moment.

Vilkansky put forward similar arguments, but he rejected even the establishment of new towns adjacent to the Arab towns.[95]

---

93 Ibid., proceedings of Smaller Zionist General Council session 14.3.1940. See also Ussishkin's statement at JNF Directorate meeting (jointly with Jewish Agency and Va'ad Leumi Executives) held on 3.3.1940, CZA, KKL10.
94 Ibid. Also address by Rabbi Berlin at a celebration in Jerusalem on 11.3.1940.
95 Ibid., minutes of JNF Directorate meeting, 3.3.1940 – quotation from there.

The Directorate's decision regarding the order of priorities for land purchases reflected the opinion of the majority of speakers in the joint session. It stipulated that the utmost priority would be awarded to purchases in Zones A and B, while in the Free Zone only necessary purchases or those where the JNF had already incurred obligations would be implemented.[96] The assumption was that the JNF would be the sole party prepared to implement purchases in Zones A and B; regarding private capital "there is no doubt that it will concentrate only in the permitted zone because there transfers do not involve particular difficulties....The redemption of lands in these regions [A and B] will involve dangers and risks which private capital cannot withstand. National capital, on the other hand, which has fulfilled a pioneering role from time immemorial, would not recoil before these new obstacles as well."[97] Ussishkin's proposal to penetrate the Arab cities was rejected, but his demand to reinforce Jerusalem and Haifa was adopted.

Already during the Directorate's meeting which followed the promulgation of the Lands Law, and similarly at the Directorate's meetings which took place in 1940, the underlying political–strategic objective behind the purchases and settlements that would be erected upon them was emphasized again and again. The consequence was the need to prefer Zones A and B (including places where no Jewish settlement foothold existed at all) in order to prevent their detachment from the boundaries of a future Jewish State. The guiding assumption was that the Palestine issue would also be resolved at the end of the War and indeed, the JNF's activity during the 1940s was characterized by a desire to realize the territorial policy within this time limit. Hence increased importance was attached to purchasing lands in the southern and northern Negev, where up to 1940 no Jewish settlement foothold had existed, and the same applied to penetrating other places where no Jewish presence existed. Likewise, it was urgent to expand and consolidate the Jewish hold in other frontier areas where Jews had already settled, such as the Hula Valley, the Western Upper Galilee and the Beisan Valley.[98] Ussishkin would subsequently emphasize

---

96 Ibid.
97 Granovsky, minutes of JNF Directorate meeting, 11.4.1940. See also Ben-Gurion's statement, CZA, KKL10, minutes of JNF Directorate meeting, 11.4.1940.
98 Ibid., 3.3.1940, 11.4.1940, 30.5.1940, and minutes of Jewish Agency Executive meeting, 12.3.1940; CZA, S53/437, Granovsky, minutes of JNF Directorate meeting,

in Autumn 1941: "Today the decisive factor in our activity throughout the country is the political factor."[99] At the same time Weitz added: "We have the important task of expanding the boundaries of our settlement in order to provide for the present needs of the Jewish community and to ready ourselves for future developments, for the decisive political activities which we will confront at the end of the War."[100] Whereas at the close of 1943, Ben-Gurion explained that:

> The period we are experiencing now is vastly different from other periods. In normal years land purchases would be measured according to their economic value and according to their political value. However, in this emergency period in which we are living today, the principal consideration for purchasing this piece of land or the next is first of all the political value. We are living in a period of decision which can determine our fate for generations. Facts and deeds indeed will be of tremendous importance. In the present state of affairs, nothing will carry greater importance than Jewish settlements, and we must implement all land purchases which are important to us from a political standpoint – we are duty bound to take hold of the land.

At the same time Granovsky added that:

> Both the territorial and financial areas of our activity in the past years were determined by the political strategic line. Our primary purpose must be to enter new regions. We have performed a double activity: diversification and concentration amidst diversification. Diversification – we have gone in all directions: to the region of the North, the Hula, the Beisan Valley, to the Hills of Ephraim and the South. By concentration amidst diversification – we have amassed blocs of territorial purchases and blocs of settlements in all parts

---

11.4.1940; Weitz (1941); CZA, S25/1941, address by Shertok at JNF national convention – "The Voice of the Land," 22.9.1942; CZA, S25/1892, JNF Activities in 1945; Katz (1992), p. 9.

99   CZA, KKL10, minutes of JNF Directorate meeting, 2.9.1941.

100   CZA, KKL5/10580, memorandum by Weitz, "What's New in the Activities of the JNF," 17.10.1941.

of the country in a systematic manner. In the South we have gone
further and further south, and all this because we are approaching the
hour of resolve. [101]

It should be noted that the lands purchased in Zones A and B were
earmarked already in the period covered by this chapter to be part of a
settlement project that was an outcome of the War, namely, the project of
settling discharged veterans in communities of their own.[102]

The sum total of JNF purchases from the promulgation of the Lands
Law until mid-1946 also indicates that 75% of the lands purchased during
that period were in Zones A and B and the balance in the permitted zone.[103]
Concomitantly, as will be shown in detail below, since the promulgation
of the Lands Law, the Directorate also decided to implement in Zones A
and B purchases of Jewish-owned land. This constituted a break of sorts
with the "dogma...that the JNF had no need to purchase land from Jews
because this does not represent 'redemption of the land.' However, today,
such purchases do constitute 'redemption of the land' because if the JNF
did not redeem the lands they could totally be lost to Jewish ownership."
In other words, purchase from Jews was one of the means through which
it was possible to penetrate into Zones A and B within the framework of
the Lands Law.[104]

101 CZA, KKL10, minutes of JNF Directorate meeting, 9.11.1943 – both quotations from
     there. See also CZA, S44/60d, Ben-Gurion's address to the "Voice of the Land"
     convention, 28.9.1944.
102 CZA, KKL10, minutes of JNF Directorate meetings, 20.8.1942, 25.4.1944,
     20.2.1945; CZA, KKL5/12677, letter from Granovsky to Liberman 26.5.1943, letter
     from JNF to the Veterans Association 22.7.1943; CZA, KKL5/13849, memorandum
     from Granovsky "Preparation of Land for Discharged Soldiers," May 1944; CZA,
     S44/60d, Ben-Gurion's address to the "Voice of the Land" convention, 28.9.1944.
103 JNF Report (1947), p. 31. For the division of the purchases according to regions
     and years see, e.g., CZA, KKL10, minutes of JNF Directorate meetings, 25.11.1941,
     20.1.1942, 24.3.1942, 23.4.1942, 2.11.1942, 29.4.1943. See also, CZA, KKL5/11821,
     letter from Weitz to Stroock 18.5.1941 concerning Weitz's rejection in May 1941 of
     the proposal to purchase 3,000 dunams in the Sharon, since priority was given to
     purchases in the North and the South.
104 Ibid., minutes of JNF Directorate meeting, 11.4.1940 – Ussishkin's address. See also
     minutes of JNF Directorate meetings, 30.5.1940, 26.9.1940.

Additional Components in the Policy of Preference
for Purchases in Zones A and B

The JNF policy to give priority to the implementation of land purchases in
Zones A and B, the policy that was formulated upon the promulgation of
the Lands Law, continued in practice until the establishment of the State of
Israel. It was necessary to take into account a variety of considerations when
deciding upon the order of preferences within the aforementioned zones
and setting priorities among the lands offered for sale, when it appeared
possible to purchase them within the framework of the Lands Law. Members
of the JNF Directorate and the Executive presented diverse opinions. The
following principal considerations were weighed when contemplating a
purchase: reaching places where Jewish settlement had not yet penetrated;
the feasibility of winding up the purchase quickly and settling promptly;
connecting the purchased land to existing blocs or uniting blocs as a result;
the option for additional purchases in the wake of the concrete purchase
when in this matter the JNF adopted a policy of concentration amidst
diversification, i.e., expanding its hold around new areas into which the
JNF penetrated; the territorial needs of existing agricultural settlements,
i.e., expanding existing agricultural settlements (details below); the need
to expand the settlement foothold in a particular region for security and
settlement reasons; the very possibility for establishing a new settlement
on the land about to be purchased; the location of the purchase along
especially vital transportation arteries, such as the road between Jerusalem
and the Coastal Plain or the Tel Aviv–Mikve Yisrael and the Moshavot
in the South; the price of land which occupied a marginal place in
considerations (if considered at all) when the purchases in Zones A and
B were considered, but occupied a central position in considerations when
addressed to purchases in the Free Zone (in the words of Rabbi Berlin:
"In the prohibited zone, we agree to any price")[105]; activities related to
"Land Arrangement" in a particular location where Jewish rights to land
had existed in the past and the JNF intended to transfer these rights to itself
in order to guarantee the confirmation of Jewish ownership under a land
arrangement; preventing occurrences where lands offered for sale by Jews
would fall into Arab hands; reinforcing the Jewish hold over lands around

105   Ibid., minutes of JNF Directorate meeting, 25.4.1944.

cities, such as Safad and Jerusalem (the last three considerations will be expanded later in this chapter); purchase for the purpose of exchanging a plot in the future for other land in which the JNF had an interest, for one of the reasons mentioned above.[106] The supreme consideration was the political (rather than the economic) importance of the purchase. Indeed, Weitz would subsequently contend that "it is possible that were it not for the Law, we would not have come to those places we did reach by circumvention of the Law. It is possible that in normal situations of free bargaining, we would not have purchased certain areas and would have preferred more desirable lands and particularly from the standpoint of economic settlement on them. But it was the Law which guided us precisely to these purchases through which we sought the possibility of obtaining a foothold and penetration into areas where we had not previously been present."[107] It would appear that the policy of awarding preference within Zones A and B to purchases in those areas where Jewish settlement had not

---

106   Ibid., minutes of JNF Directorate meetings during 1940–1941 and minutes of JNF
      Directorate meetings, 20.1.1942, 23.4.1942, 28.5.1942, 20.8.1942, 12.11.1942,
      26.11.1942, 24.12.1942, 18.2.1943, 29.4.1943, 17.6.1943, 31.8.1943, 9.11.1943,
      7.12.1943, 18.1.1944, 24.2.1944, 25.4.1944, 20.6.1944; 6.7.1944, 14.11.1944,
      19.12.1944, 20.2.1945, 20.3.1945. See also CZA, KKL5/11822, letter from the Tsur
      Co. to JNF Head Office 19.4.1940, letter from Weitz to the Tsur Co. 25.4.1940;
      CZA, KKL9/373, letter from Nahmani to JNF Head Office 20.1.1941; CZA, KKL5/
      10580, JNF circular, 17.2.1941; CZA, KKL5/11822, letter from Weitz to Tsur Co.
      17.8.1941; CZA, S53/1689, Jewish Agency circular "Increased Land Purchases by
      JNF," 20.8.1941 (also in file S25/6559); CZA, KKL5/10380, memorandum by Weitz
      "What's New in the Activities of the Jewish National Fund," 17.10.1941; CZA,
      KKL5/11872, from a talk with Weitz on 9.11.1941; CZA, KKL9/59, letter from
      Nahmani to the Lands Department in JNF Head Office 21.11.1942; CZA, KKL9/374,
      letter from Nahmani to the Agricultural Workers Union, 13.2.1942; CZA, S25/1941,
      address by Shertok at JNF national convention, "The Voice of the Land," 22.9.1942;
      CZA, KKL5/373, letter from Nahmani to Stromeza 26.11.1942; CZA, J15/5338,
      letter from Weitz to PICA 24.1.1943; CZA, KKL9/373, letter from Nahmani to JNF
      Lands Department 19.2.1942; CZA, KKL9/374, letter from Nahmani to JNF Lands
      Department 3.1.1944; CZA, KKL5/12809, summary of deliberations on current
      matters that took place in Galilee office in Tiberias on 22.6.1944–25.6.1944; CZA,
      KKL5/374, letter from Nahmani to Kolnsher 6.5.1945; CZA, KKL5/11822, letter
      from Weitz to Margalit 22.8.1941.
107   Weitz (1947), p. 15; the Oral History Institute, interview with Weitz, Jerusalem
      16.1.1969. See also CZA, KKL10, minutes of JNF Directorate meeting, 12.11.1942.

yet penetrated is clearly exemplified in penetrations in the South and the Negev. Already in September 1940, the Directorate decided in principal to carry out a purchase of 30,000 dunams in the South when for budgetary reasons this purchase meant that a previous decision to purchase 1,000 dunams in the Beisan Valley would have to be abandoned. Both purchases were in Zone A.

In the Directorate's deliberations there was no unanimity on the issue. Granovsky believed that the purchase in the Beisan Valley should go through even at the cost of purchases in the South because he feared that if the present opportunity were not exploited it would not be possible to purchase the area in the Beisan Valley in the future. Furthermore, the cost of the purchases in the South, were in his opinion beyond the JNF's budgetary capacity. Katznelson as well opposed forgoing the Beisan Valley purchase, because it connected Ma'oz and Neve Eitan and was owned by an Arab company whose by-laws prohibited the sale of lands to Jews. In contradistinction, in the South this was not a contiguous bloc but a number of blocs that in his opinion mandated a separate discussion on the purchase of each and every one. Ussishkin, in contrast, was most insistent that the purchases in the South took priority

> because by doing so we are about to create something new and open a broad passageway to "conquering a new region" and establish an important center of activity for territorial settlement from a political–communal standpoint, and we can issue encouraging and glad tidings to the Jewish people in Palestine and in the Diaspora who sorely need them today. In contradistinction, in the "sum total" 1,000 dunams more or less in the Beisan Valley will not alter our situation regarding this region, where the JNF controls about 37,000 dunams today.

Zuchovitzky, Vilkansky, and Weitz also supported Ussishkin's position and it appears that Granovsky and Katznelson were won over. In any event, the Directorate's decision was not to purchase in the Beisan Valley, but in contrast "the Directorate finds that the creation of a territorial center in the South is most vital from a communal–national–political standpoint and the necessity to create such a center is a pressing need." The Directorate therefore decided on the purchase of 30,000 dunams in the South.[108]

---

108   Ibid., minutes of JNF Directorate meeting, 26.9.1940 – quotations from there. See

It should be emphasized that in general the South and the Negev occupied a central position in the JNF's activity during the 1940s.[109] It appears that the purchases made south of Jerusalem (Gush Etzion) originated amongst other reasons in a policy of extending preference within Zones A and B to places where the Jewish presence was non-existent or nearly non-existent.[110]

Purchase Policy in the Free Zone

As stated above, only a quarter of the JNF's land purchases during 1940–1946 were located in the Free Zone. These generally included purchases where the JNF had assumed obligations before the Lands Law went into effect, purchases of unusual importance such as: those which contributed to the formation of large territorial JNF-owned blocs which could facilitate the development of a broad-based settlement project; purchases which supplemented the territorial needs of existing settlements; purchases that were designed to prevent speculative activity in the vicinity of the those lands; purchases that were intended to forestall damage to settlements in the event that a non-Jewish factor would make the purchase; purchases that were earmarked for housing needs in the vicinity of towns and villages. Other lands in the Free Zone were not purchased despite their availability for sale. The decisive preference awarded Zones A and B, the high price of land in the Free Zone, and the assumption that private capital would find its way to purchases in this region, accounted for the diminished volume

---

also CZA, S53/1689, Jewish Agency Information Department circular 20.8.1941 concerning "Increased Land Purchase by the JNF" (also in S25/6559); CZA, KKL5/10580, memorandum by Weitz "What's New in the Activities of the JNF," 17.10.1941; CZA, KKL5/11872, from a talk with Weitz on 9.11.1941 – summation of purchases made until then in the South and in which he stated that "the settlement in the South opens the way to conquer the Negev in the future." See also JNF Report (1947), p. 40.

109 See, e.g., CZA, KKL10, minutes of JNF Directorate meeting, 12.11.1942; Katz (1999), pp. 144–159; Porat (1996), pp. 91–131; in detail CZA, KKL10, minutes of JNF Directorate meetings, 25.12.1940, 14.8.1941, 2.11.1941, 18.12.1941, 24.2.1942, 25.6.1942, 12.11.1942, 26.11.1942, 24.12.1942, 18.2.1943, 29.4.1943, 9.11.1943, 7.12.1943, 19.12.1944, 20.3.1945.

110 CZA, KKL10, minutes of the meetings of the JNF Directorate held on 24.2.1942, 23.4.1942, 28.5.1942, 31.8.1943, 10.1.1944.

of JNF purchases in this region.[111] Among the major agricultural purchases that were carried out in the Free Zone were the purchase of the Wadi Kabani and Wadi Samara blocs and the purchase of the Falik Concession south of Nathanya. Likewise, significant purchases were implemented in the vicinity of Kadima in the Sharon, which connected between the settlements and promoted the territorial consolidation of existing settlements.[112] Some lands were earmarked for the future settlement of army veterans.[113] The purchase of Wadi Kabani, which the JNF had launched before the promulgation of the Lands Law, and the purchase of Wadi Samara together with Wadi el-Hawarith, created a cluster of tens of thousands of nationally-owned dunams of land in the heart of the Sharon which were suitable for an integrated settlement project, including agricultural settlements, housing, industry, trade and tourism. The JNF had intended already in the 1920s to purchase these blocs due to their importance for creating territorial contiguity under Jewish ownership in the Coastal Plain, but this plan was realized only in the 1940s.[114] The Directorate decided in mid-1942, on the purchase of the Falik Concession, an area of 5,000 dunams, from the Jewish-owned Nathanya Development Company. Although the deal involved a lease rather than purchase, and the land was owned by Jews and located in the Free Zone, the JNF Executive and all members of the Directorate save for one, viewed this purchase as supremely important and described its advantages in detail. Granovsky, who inter alia viewed the purchase's inherent potential on a par with the situation that obtained when the JNF purchased the Zebulun Valley, emphasized:

> The purchase of the concession area is important from numerous standpoints: It is a large area on the seacoast. It connects between Jewish areas in general, and the JNF's areas in particular into a total area of 22,000 dunams in one bloc. It opens the possibility

---

111   See above, n. 98; CZA, KKL5/10641, letter from Weitz to Hankin 3.4.1941; CZA, KKL5/11821, letter from Weitz to Stroock 18.5.1941; CZA, KKL5/12715, letter from Weitz to G. Machnes 24.12.1941; CZA, KKL5/12832, letter from Foeder to JNF 31.7.1944, letter from Weitz to Rassco 21.8.1944; CZA, KKL10, minutes of JNF Directorate meetings, 23.4.1942, 28.5.1942, 18.2.1943, 7.12.1943, 25.4.1944, 17.6.1943, 20.6.1944.
112   Weitz (1941); CZA, KKL10, minutes of JNF Directorate meeting, 28.5.1942.
113   Ibid., minutes of JNF Directorate meeting, 20.2.1945.
114   Weitz (1941); CZA, KKL10, minutes of JNF Directorate meeting, 26.9.1940.

of realizing large-scale plans and establishing manufacturing and industrial projects. Here there is room for developing a large-scale plan for urban housing and manufacturing and industrial structures. Where between Tel Aviv and Hadera does such a large area for factories, plants and large warehouses exist along the sea coast to accommodate the export and import of merchandises for a country which is developing in normal years and affording fine conditions for shipping and marketing? In assuming the concession from these Jews, we are removing the obstacle to the sound economic development of the project. This obstacle existed when the concession was in the hands of a private Jewish company that was interested first and foremost in its profits.

Zuchovitzky dwelled on the possibility of paving a second road between Tel Aviv and Haifa along the coast, as a result of purchasing the concession. Weitz like Granovsky viewed the concession area "as the 'key' to this entire vicinity from Herzliya to Nathanya [comprising 100,000 dunams][115] and it was critical that this key should be in the JNF's possession. Control of this concession will lead to the development of this area and even if this development will be slow, it will be healthy." Vilkansky feared that if the JNF would not purchase the concession, it would revert to the hands of the Government which could transfer most of it to non-Jewish hands with all the anticipated damages to the area's future.[116]

Indeed, the fear of irreversible damages to settlement, in the event that the JNF did not embark on the purchase, motivated the JNF to purchase, for example, an Arab-owned orchard with an area of 800 dunams located very near the Moshava Nes Tziyona and offered for sale at a public auction. It was clear that if the JNF would not make the purchase, the orchard would be sold to an Arab party who would establish an additional Arab neighborhood at the location in addition to the already existing neighborhood on the other side of the Moshava. This could have created a tangible threat to the Moshava's security as well as imperiling its Jewish character. Despite the vast sum that was demanded in the vicinity of about P£25,000, a price level at which "one could obtain land not far from Tel

---

115 Ibid., 23.4.1942.
116 Ibid., 28.5.1942 – quotation from there. See also the matter of the Falik concession, ibid., 23.4.1942, 18.2.1943, 23.8.1944.

Aviv," it was decided after deliberations to make the purchase, irrespective of the fact that the participation of the Moshava committee in sharing the expenses was not guaranteed in advance.[117]

Methods of Circumventing the Lands Law

In order to implement the purchase of lands in Zones A and B within the framework of the Lands Law, the JNF's Lands Department had to find the loopholes in the Law as well as devise sophisticated legal ideas which would permit the implementation of the purchase. It also forced a change in the JNF's traditional concepts such as the decision not to purchase from Jews. In any case, it was clear that the matter had to be delegated first and foremost to lawyers fully versed in the field. Indeed, upon the publication of the Lands Law, the JNF widened its affiliations with lawyers who were entrusted with finding solutions to allow purchases to go through and with handling the many legal complications that typified the 1940s. Among these lawyers were Aharon Ben-Shemesh, Mordechai Eliash, S. Horowitz and the employees in his office, Yakov Olshan, Yirmiyahu Feiglin, Yosef Stromeza and Avraham Weinshal. It was Ben-Shemesh, who was very close to Weitz, who primarily coordinated the legal activity. The work of the legal staff operating alongside the Lands Department – a staff which subsequently received the sobriquet, "the juridical underground" – led to the formulation of a series of methods through which lands in Zones A and B were purchased. It should be noted that some of the methods were "outside the legal framework" that is, the purchases were not completed by transferring the land in the Land Registration Office to the JNF's name; but the volume of such purchases was limited, and already at the beginning of 1940, the Directorate allowed the implementation of a few such purchases.[118]

The method by which many purchases were made exploited the passage in the Lands Law which stipulated that the Law would not apply to

---

117   Ibid., 18.2.1943, 17.6.1943, 20.6.1943 – the quotation is from Granovsky's comments as reported in the minutes of the meeting on 20.6.1943.

118   S. Ben-Shemesh, personal interview, Jerusalem 27.11.1996; Weitz (1951), pp. 553–556. Bistritsky (1950a), pp. 553–556; Katz (in press).

transfers that were executed in carrying out a court order by an auction in
order to defray a mortgage that was registered before the Law went into
effect. Therefore the JNF took the trouble to locate such court decisions.
There were many such decisions and it was not difficult to find them. The
years of the Arab disturbances had wrought injury and impoverishment
upon the Arabs and landowners were burdened with debts which were
secured by mortgages and court decisions on their lands. The JNF reached
agreements with the landowners'creditors and with those suing them in
a manner calculated to ensure that the end result was that the land was
put up for sale by public auction. The JNF participated in these auctions,
it proposed the highest prices and thus bought land in Zones A and B.
Since the indebted landowner was not always prepared to put up his lands
for public auction, the JNF sought to create conditions that obligated the
indebted person to offer his lands for sale. Generally it would do so by
paying off the creditors in order to compel the debtors to offer their land for
sale by public auction. Subsequently the "juridical underground" perfected
the purchase method through public auctions in a technique where the JNF
aligned itself with debt-ridden borrowers who had no land, but against
whom a court decision had been rendered before the Lands Law had gone
into effect. These persons served as fictitious land purchasers on behalf of
the JNF. The moment the lands were registered in their names, the JNF
sought to galvanize the creditors to compel the landowner to sell his lands
at a public auction where the JNF would make the purchase. Another way
to implement the purchases was limited to Musha lands where the JNF held
a certain percentage. It banded together with Arabs who were considered
reliable, and requested that they purchase other sectors of the Musha. After
these Arabs completed the purchase, the JNF as the owner of adjoining
land sued them and received verdicts in its favor in accordance with the
Law. Of course, all these purchases utilizing the aforementioned methods
obligated the JNF not only to reach prior agreement with quite a number
of Arabs, but also compounded its expenses. The method relying on public
auction of lands which were encumbered by a mortgage and securing a
verdict in favor of the creditors, was put into operation for the first time
shortly after the promulgation of the Lands Law. By this method the JNF
then purchased lands in the vicinity of Gaza which were owned by the
previous Mayor of Gaza, Fathi El Husseini.[119]

119   Katz (1999), pp. 146–147; idem (1996a), pp. 202–226; idem (1990b), pp. 109–135;

In the Negev, the JNF exploited the accepted local custom where transfers were implemented and recognized on the basis of contracts with the Bedouins and registered in record books maintained by the Sheikhs and Mukhtars without the need to register the transfers in the Lands Registration Office. These were "external transactions" of the type the PLDC had implemented in the Negev already at the beginning of the 1930s, and now the JNF went the same route. It should be noted that in areas other than the Negev, as well, the JNF made purchases through a number of methods that were not concluded by transfers in the Lands Registration Office. In practice these were exceptional purchases outside the framework of the Lands Law and their number was limited. Three principal methods of implementation were utilized: receiving non-revocable powers of attorney from Arab sellers who provided the JNF with a security mortgage on other lands in their possession; registering the land in the name of Arabs who were loyal to the JNF, and who provided the JNF with mortgages on lands in their possession, generally in the city, where the Lands Law did not apply; and registering the sellers as a company, with the JNF purchasing shares in that company.[120]

Bistritsky (1950a), pp. 157–165; Weitz (1951), pp. 553–556; CZA, KKL10, minutes of JNF Directorate meetings, 3.3.1940, 11.4.1940, 30.5.1940, 14.8.1941 (in which Granovsky summed up: "We found legal ways 'to break down the wall' of the Lands Law regarding purchases in Zone A... These ways open up many possibilities for the purchase of lands in Zone A, even from Arabs"). See also ibid., minutes of JNF Directorate meetings, 25.11.1941, 18.12.1941, 12.11.1942, 26.11.1942, 29.4.1943, 17.6.1943, 29.7.1943; ibid., proceedings of Smaller Zionist General Council session, 14.3.1940; CZA, KKL5/11821, letters Yekutieli to JNF Head Office 8.4.1940, 30.4.1940; CZA, KKL5/10580, memorandum by Weitz "What's New in the Activities of the JNF," 17.10.1941; CZA, KKL5/15556, memorandum by Weitz, "The Lands Laws and the Struggle for Redemption of the Soil," not dated, but would appear to have been written in 1945; CZA, KKL5/12810, letter from Weitz to JNF Haifa Office 25.6.1944; CZA, KKL5/12809, letter from Weitz to Shertok 2.1.1945; Weitz (1941).

120   See above n. 119. The Arab owned Ali Beck Company was established in Haifa by the JNF and served as a "cover company" for the purchase of lands on behalf of the JNF. See CZA, KKL5/12810, letter from Weitz to JNF Haifa Office 25.6.1944. See also CZA, KKL5/14305, letter to Weitz in connection with the matter of Ali Kassem, no date but apparently from the beginning of 1946. Lands belonging to the German monastery in Kefar Etziyon were purchased through the creation of a company whose shares were registered in the name of the sellers. These shares were bought by the

Purchase from Jews was an additional method for implementing purchases within the framework of the Law in Zones A and B. In general these lands were registered under the name of Jews who in fact did not retain them. In Zone B there was no need for any authorization by the High Commissioner whatsoever, but in Zone A such authorization was required. It was easy to obtain the necessary authorization either because of prior Jewish ownership or because the JNF was able to prove a previous link to the land through agreements with the sellers. The JNF used similar methods for purchases from non–Palestinian Arabs – purchases which required the authorization of the High Commissioner only in Zone A.

Approaches to the High Commissioner to authorize transfers from Arabs in general (either Palestinian or non–Palestinian) – transfers that were required for the consolidation or expansion of existing Jewish farming settlements, or to authorize transfers when the negotiations on them had been initiated prior to the promulgation of the Law, were additional methods for implementing purchases within the framework of the Law. In a similar fashion, the JNF obtained purchase contracts between Arabs and Jewish individuals (where the transfer had not been completed) – purchases that were made before the promulgation of the Lands Law. On the basis of these contracts, the JNF sought to receive the High Commissioner's authorization for completion of the transfers, or it relied on the work of a "land settlement" to recognize its rights (something which did not involve the testimony of the previous landowners regarding the JNF's link prior to the promulgation of the Law), and register ownership in the JNF's name. The "land settlement" was also exploited for agreements between the JNF and Arab land sellers, agreements which underpinned the JNF demand from the "land settlement" to recognize purchase contracts between it and the Arabs and to register the lands under its name in the Land Registration Office.[121]

JNF without the land being transferred through the Lands Registration Office. See Katz (1992), pp. 47–48. On purchase methods used in the Negev, see in detail Porat (1996), pp. 115–118.

121   See n. 120. See also CZA, KKL51/596, letter from APC to Auster 23.12.1940 – regarding the chances of obtaining the High Commissioner's authorization in Zone A for transfer of land from one Jew to another. Also regarding mitigation in transferring land in Zone A from one Jew to another, see CZA, KKL5/12666, letter from Nahmani to the JNF Lands Department 5.2.1942, concerning transfer of Sharona in Lower Galilee from PICA and the sale to JNF.

Map 18 sums up the Jewish–owned lands at the beginning of 1946 subdivided according to the Zones of the Lands Law, while Appendix 6 details JNF purchases during the years 1940–1947 according to the Zones of the Lands Law.

A Turnabout in JNF Policy in Purchasing Land from Jews

Chapter Two explained that the JNF's policy was to abstain from purchasing Jewish–owned lands. However, with the publication of the Lands Law, this policy was altered, and land purchases from Jews became widespread. These purchases included purchases from private individuals as well as from companies, including PICA. Already in the Directorate meetings which took place immediately following the publication of the Lands Law, as well as in Ussishkin's address to the Smaller Zionist General Council in March 1940, reference was made to the need to modify the historic policy on purchasing exclusively from non–Jews. In April 1940, Weitz stated: "and if up to now the JNF's practice was not to purchase land from Jews, henceforward it would be worthwhile for the JNF to change its custom and to award special attention to these aforesaid Jewish–owned lands in Zone A."[122] Ussishkin summed up "this does constitute a break from the dogma which it [the JNF] had maintained up to now, that the JNF should not purchase lands from Jews since this did not represent 'redemption of land,' but today these purchases as well constitute 'redemption of the land,' because if the JNF will not redeem the lands they could totally be lost to Jewish ownership."[123] Other Directorate members agreed on the fundamental need to change policy.[124] However, as will be seen below, the fear that the land would be lost to Jewish ownership was not the sole reason for the shift in policy. There were additional reasons. On the other hand, it will also be pointed out below that the change in policy was not sweeping, and in other words, not every land purchase offer from Jews received authorization for purchase by the JNF.

---

122   CZA, KKL10, minutes of JNF Directorate meeting, 11.4.1940.
123   Ibid.
124   Ibid., 11.4.1940, 30.5.1940; see also ibid., proceedings of Smaller Zionist General Council session, 14.3.1940.

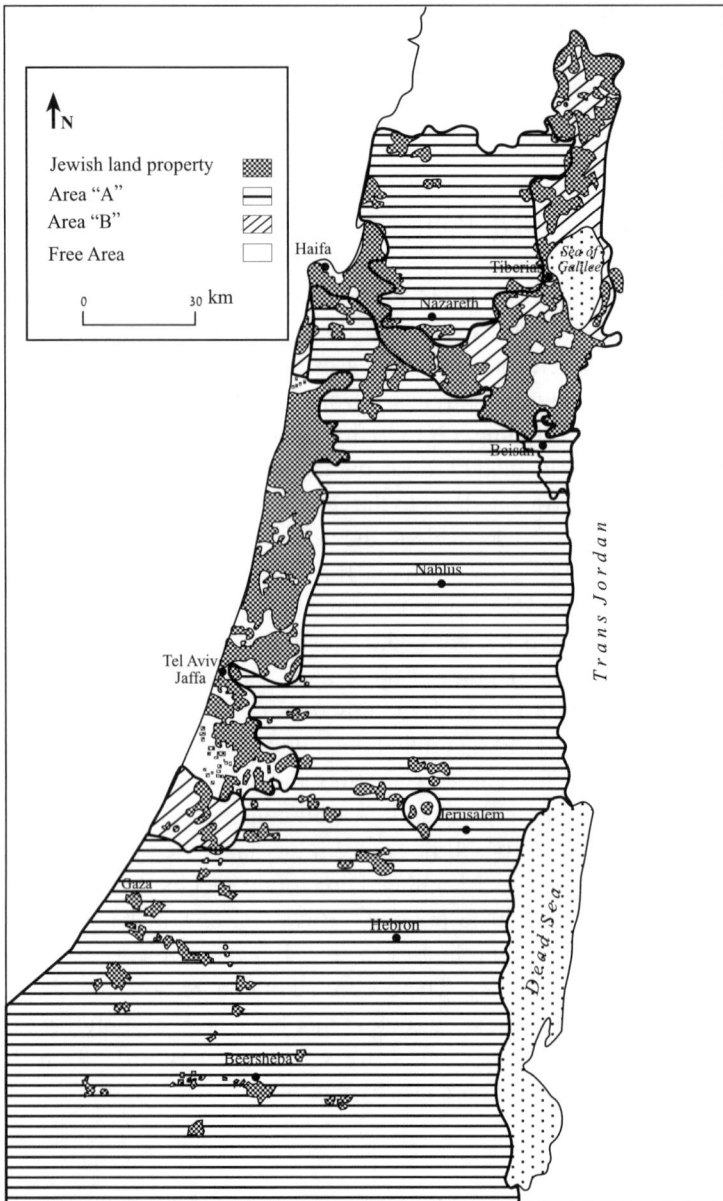

Map 18: Jewish land property according to the Lands Law zones
in the beginning of 1946
Source: JNF map archives, Map 4097

The Directorate's decision to purchase from Jews in the South, in Gezer and Nahhalin – decisions that were adopted in the course of the first year following the publication of the Lands Law, were among the first purchases which the JNF Directorate authorized for purchase from Jews.[125] Over the course of time, the volume of purchases from Jews increased. Thus for example, in the budgetary year 1941–1942 they constituted 28% of the JNF's total purchases (13,675 dunams out of 49,000 dunams).[126] In the first seven months of the 1942–1943 budgetary year was 38% (30,000 dunams out of 80,000 total dunams of purchases which the JNF budgetary year the volume of purchases from Jews reached 42%,[127] and during that entire maintained but had not yet received deeds of sale for them).[128] In the first half of 1944 the volume of purchases from Jews totaled 71% (!) (16,954 dunams out of 24,041), and it was with no small measure of disappointment that Granovsky noted this statistic when he reported to the Directorate that "the distribution of land according to their owners is not satisfactory to us. Most of the lands have not been redeemed from Arabs but were purchased from Jews. This constitutes redemption of sorts, for in this manner we managed to save property that was going to be lost to Jewish ownership, but there is no unalloyed redemption here."[129]

At the beginning of 1945, the opinion that "seemingly the JNF is not proceeding with its main activity of redeeming the land and the lands which it does purchase, it purchases only from Jews," gained currency in the public. These comments were disagreeable to the JNF and it opposed them, and justifiably so since they were not accurate,[130] but they reflected to no small extent the reality which prevailed since the publication of the Lands Law. Not only had a change ensued in the JNF's policy, but also purchases from Jews proliferated in a significant manner. The total balance which the JNF drew up for its purchases in the years 1939–1945 demonstrated

---

125 Ibid., minutes of JNF Directorate meeting, 26.9.1940; Katz (1992), pp. 20–21; idem (1996c), pp. 145–150.
126 CZA, KKL10, minutes of JNF Directorate meeting, 12.11.1942.
127 Ibid., 17.6.1943.
128 Ibid., 27.9.1943. From the minutes it becomes apparent that extent of lands for which deeds of sale had been received reached 52,000 dunams, thus the relative volume of lands purchased from Jews reached 58%.
129 Ibid., 25.4.1944.
130 Ibid., 20.3.1945.

that 40% of the lands were purchased from Jews (135,000 dunams out of a general total of 340,000 dunams).[131]

A number of factors combined to prompt the shift in JNF policy on making purchases from Jews. First of all, there was apprehension that Jewish-owned lands would fall into Arab hands. This apprehension was based either on fear that in the event that the JNF would not implement the purchase, the Jewish owners who offered their lands for sale would sell them to Arabs, or due to the fact that for various reasons those actually controlling the lands were not the Jewish landowners but tenant farmers who could demand recognition of ownership due to effective control. This fear was most tangible in view of current activity by British land settlement officials who could recognize such claims. The Jewish settlers found it difficult to handle on their own everything that was involved in protecting their rights.[132]

Secondly, the very possibility of making purchases in Zones A and B first within the framework of the Law, necessitated the shift. As mentioned above, it was easy to obtain the authorization of the High Commissioner in Zone A in the event that these were transfers from one Jewish party to another Jewish party, and in Zone B this authorization was not required in purchases from Jews. Given the difficulties of penetrating into Zones A and B it was necessary to explore every loophole in the Lands Law. Purchases from Jews was one of the loopholes and constituted a necessary evil under conditions of the time, and which offered the additional advantage of laying the basis for expanding the Jewish hold in the vicinity by purchases from non-Jews. Thirdly, the need to implement some purchases from Jews arose because of the importance of the land, be it in terms of their strategic location, in that they were crucial to secure the territorial completion of existing farming settlements, their contribution toward creating the requisite territorial bloc to establish a new settlement, or as a connecting element between blocs and significant Jewish territorial contiguities, with all the inherent strategic and political importance. Given the difficulties described in detail above, besetting purchases in general during those years, and the political objectives that were tied to the specific purchases,

---

131 CZA, S25/1892, memorandum "Activities of the Jewish National Fund in 1944–1945."

132 For example, see below on the Yavneh Co. at Ulam and Madar.

such purchases attained further importance, and they too were considered a necessary evil.

Fourthly, the need arose to strengthen and buttress the Jewish hold in the cities of Jerusalem and Safad through purchasing land in their vicinity as a reserve for agricultural settlement. It was precisely Jewish–owned lands that were offered for sale in the vicinity of these cities.

Fifthly, the land purchases, including those from Jews, were required to strengthen the veteran Moshavot which had been abandoned by some of their residents over the years. Land purchases aided their resettlement. Sometimes the decision to purchase from Jews was supported by a reality which comprised a combination of the factors mentioned above. It should be noted, that in implementing purchases from Jews, the JNF was not content with awaiting sale proposals from Jewish owners. It also operated through its regional offices to locate Jewish–owned lands that it had an interest to purchase in light of the factors detailed above, and it conducted, on its own initiative, negotiations with the Jewish owners regarding the possibility of purchasing the land.[133]

Below are examples of purchases that were implemented from Jews given the aforementioned factors.

Despite the change in JNF policy concerning the purchase of property from Jews, offers that did not fall into the categories detailed above, and especially those which were most expensive were rejected by the JNF. The JNF also turned down proposals when it was not convinced that the lands would be sold to Arabs in the event that the JNF would not implement the purchase. These were false threats which could lead to similar extortion in the future, or it was evident to the JNF that the Arab purchasers would in the future re-sell the land to the Jews. It also had an interest that the political bodies in the Moshavot should feel a similar obligation to prevent the transfer of real estate from Jews to aliens because the JNF was not prepared from both a budgetary and moral standpoint to view its task as the sole "redeemer" of any real estate that was offered for sale in the Moshavot. Given this background, the JNF in general rejected proposals to purchase orchards from Jews and especially those located in the Free Zone. Indeed, the persistent refusal led to a decline in sales proposals by Jews.[134]

---

133 See, e.g., on the matter of Ein Zeitim below.

134 CZA, KKL5/11814, letter from Weitz to the Association of Sons of the Moshavot in Palestine 7.4.1941; CZA, KKL5/11781, letter from JNF to Yachman 18.5.1941;

The JNF's decision, a number of months after the publication of the Lands Law, to purchase the Sugarman Orchard near Beit Dajan on both sides of the Tel Aviv–Jerusalem road and in the vicinity of the junction to the South Judean Moshavot, could serve as an example of purchase from Jews which the JNF implemented in Zone A, given the severe apprehension that the orchard which was located in a most strategic location would be sold to Arabs. This 130 dunams orchard owned by the Sugarman family was offered for public auction because it served as collateral for a mortgage extended by Barclays Bank and the Credit Bank – debts which the Sugarman family could not pay off. Purchase proposals were presented by a number of Arab bodies and requests to implement the purchase were channeled to the JNF by the Va'ad Leumi and the Agricultural Center. Despite the steep monetary cost and the JNF's current economic distress, and at a time when its order of priorities dictated penetrating into the South, the Directorate decided to implement the purchase. Ussishkin explained the grounds for the decision:

> The importance of purchasing the land under discussion is extensive. The orchard is located in Zone A at the junction of the Tel Aviv–Jerusalem road to the South Judean villages. It is adjacent to Jewish land. If the land would not be purchased by the JNF, there is a danger that the orchard would pass into Arab hands, and it is superfluous to emphasize the danger of the propinquity of an Arab orchard to Jewish lands and orchards and to the highway where there is the frequent traffic of Jewish private and public vehicles both day and night. This danger outweighs all other considerations against purchasing the orchard.

CZA, KKL5/11821, letter from JNF to Rabinowitz 29.8.1941, memorandum concerning the request of A. Hari 8.9.1941; CZA, KKL5/12715, letter from Weitz to Eliash 17.11.1941; CZA, KKL5/12830, letter from Weitz to Hakibbutz Hameuhad Secretariat 12.10.1943; CZA, minutes of Jewish Agency Executive meetings, 14.9.1941, 31.5.1942, 16.8.1942. At the end of 1940, the JNF rejected the request of the Har Tuv Moshava committee to purchase an 8-dunam plot of land offered by one of the farmers who threatened to sell it to the local Arabs if the JNF did not effect the purchase. The JNF feared that submission to such a threat would bring in its wake similar action by other farmers. On this, see S25/6559, letter from Weitz to Jewish Agency Political Department 25.11.1940; see also CZA, KKL10, minutes of JNF Directorate meeting, 11.4.1940.

The JNF decided that the orchard would be registered under the name of the Himnuta Company rather than under the JNF's name so that at the appropriate time it could sell the lands to other Jewish parties.[135]

Decisions to purchase from Jews in order to prevent the land from being lost to Jewish ownership were also taken in other locations. Two examples of such decisions were: from the first taken at the end of 1944 to initiate the purchase of 700 dunams near Masmiah owned by the Jewish company Kana'im and since the Arab disturbances had been maintained in Arab hands.[136] The second is a decision from the end of 1943 to purchase over 2,000 dunams in Zone A between Afula and Kefar Zababuba to the south – the lands were actually held by Arabs and "constituted a bridge between the land of Afula and the land of Zababuba where we have been conducting purchase negotiations for years."[137]

The purchase of lands in the South and in the Negev exemplify purchases from Jews which were motivated by two factors: the one, the option of penetrating into Zone A and expanding the Jewish hold there and the second, the fear that the land would be lost to Jewish ownership. In the South (the Western Negev), in the vicinity of Beersheba and the Rafiah region, over 100,000 dunams were purchased by Jews (private

---

135   CZA, KKL10, minutes of JNF Directorate meeting, 30.7.1940; CZA, KKL5/11822, letter from Weitz to A. Braude of Africa–Palestine Investments Ltd. Company 1.4.1940; CZA, KKL5/11821, letter from Weitz to Bunim 15.4.1940; CZA, S25/6559, letter from Credit Bank to Jewish Agency 2.7.1940 concerning the Sugarman orchard, memorandum by Y. Gvirtz "The Sugarman Orchard" 4.7.1940; CZA, L51/596, letter from APC to Auster 23.12.1940. See also re the Sugarman Orchard: CZA, files KKL5/11317, KKL5/12281, esp. KKL5/11317, letter from Granovsky to Schocken 15.7.1940; CZA, KKL5/12281, letter from S. Schlain to JNF 28.8.1940, letter from JNF Head Office to JNF National Office 15.2.1943.

136   CZA, KKL10, minutes of JNF Directorate meeting, 14.11.1944.

137   Ibid., 7.12.1943. See also the decision to purchase Jewish–owned property in Peqi'in – a settlement that symbolized the longtime Jewish presence in the Galilee and that had been evacuated by nearly all its inhabitants – in the apprehension that this property would fall into the hands of the Druze. On this see CZA, KKL10, minutes of JNF Directorate meeting, 18.1.1944. See also on the decision to purchase Jewish–owned property in Hebron and Tiberias so that it would not fall into Arab hands, CZA, KKL10, minutes of JNF Directorate meetings, 23.1.1945, 20.2.1945. On the decisions to participate in the Nechess Company, the purpose of which was to prevent the transfer of Jewish–owned property to Arabs in the Haifa area, see CZA, KKL10, minutes of JNF Directorate meeting, 23.8.1944.

companies and individuals from abroad and from Palestine) prior to the Arab disturbances. Only part of the lands was registered in the name of the Jewish purchasers. Additionally, with regard to some of the lands registered in the name of Jews, the registration process was not completed, and in cases were the lands were already registered in the name of Jews they had not been maintained by Jewish organization since the Arab disturbances. In such a situation, unless the lands were transferred to the JNF and it maintained them de facto, Arabs actually holding them could claim ownership.[138] Thus, for example, in the early 1940s, when the JNF sought to penetrate the South and consolidate its position there, it became interested in purchasing Ruhama – an estate that had been established by the Russian–based She'arit Yisrael Company already prior to the First World War. Due to that war and the Russian Revolution, Ruhama had lost contact with its owners and the financial resources needed for its existence. The Anglo–Palestine Company (APC) that maintained the estate after the War tried to restore it, but in the Arab disturbances of 1929 the orchards were ruined and not replanted. From then on the neighboring Bedouins cultivated the lands. In the second half of 1942, the JNF reached a complex agreement to purchase the land with a number of the owners of rights to Ruhama, members of She'arit Yisrael whose company was in the process of liquidation. In summing up the details of the complicated purchase and the JNF's readiness to invest substantially at the site, Granovsky emphasized: "I don't think that the transaction is an excellent one and one must 'call a spade a spade': it involves purchasing land from Jews. However, this purchase has a number of positive factors: (a) we are saving the land of Ruhama from the dangers of cession to Arab tenant farmers; (b) this area expands the JNF's lands in that vicinity and are contiguous to our lands, both those we have purchased and others that we are about to purchase."[139]

The JNF's decision to implement purchases from Jews in Nahhalin and Kefar Etziyon south of Jerusalem, where the JNF had refused to enter

---

138   See, e.g., CZA, KKL10, minutes of JNF Directorate meetings, 26.9.1940, 25.6.1942, 12.11.1942, 26.11.1942; CZA, KKL5/10580, memorandum by Weitz, "What's New in the Activities of the JNF," 17.10.1941; CZA, KKL5/12678, agreement between Smilansky on behalf of the "Judea Lands Purchasing Company" and JNF, 27.7.1943.

139   CZA, KKL10, minutes of JNF Directorate meeting, 26.11.1942 – quotation from there.

prior to 1940 – clearly exemplify purchases from Jews that originated from a combination of factors. Firstly, there was the danger that lands would be lost to Jewish ownership (either because Arabs would settle on them – in Nahhalin, or they would be purchased by Arabs – in Kefar Etziyon). Secondly, it afforded the possibility of penetration into Zone A. Thirdly, it would strengthen Jewish Jerusalem.[140] A combination of identical factors underpinned the JNF Directorate's decision in 1941 to implement purchases from Jews in Rama-Mitzpeh north of Jerusalem. Regarding the Mitzpeh purchase proposal and the role of the reinforcing Jerusalem factor, Granovsky emphasized:

> The purchase proposal under discussion is more problematic in many respects – the price, maintaining the land after its purchase, etc. – than the first purchase proposal of 6,000 dunams in the area of Kefar Etziyon. The price is definitely unjustified in economic terms. However, this purchase proposal constitutes one of the few proposals for purchasing lands around Jerusalem, and one should view it as an activity for strengthening Jewish Jerusalem and it cannot be performed according to the accepted yardstick of a normal real estate transaction. It is imperative that this land purchase should be implemented.

Rabbi Berlin added:

> We must discuss this from an overall viewpoint. In the past we have sinned against Jerusalem and its daughter towns. We cannot say that we didn't want to redeem land in the Jerusalem vicinity. All of us wanted it and particularly the late Menachem Ussishkin. However, we didn't do this adequately while employing calculations that may have been justified at the time. But there comes a time when calculations that derive from an economic viewpoint are canceled out by the loss which derives from a national–political standpoint, and if not now, when?

Shmuel Ussishkin summed up:

> If we are not prepared to forego the Jerusalem region for various reasons, we have no other option but to purchase land in the vicinity

140   Katz (1990b).

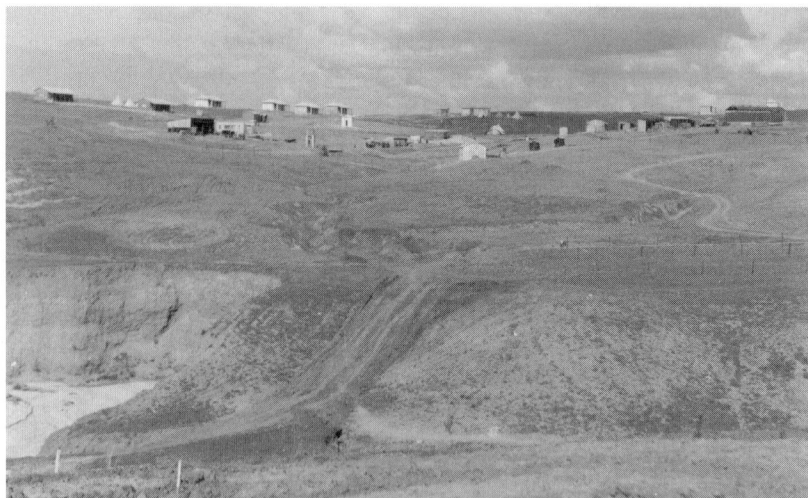

Ruhama, 1945

of Jerusalem except by such means. It is necessary to purchase small plots of land and as well as larger tracts that are not Arab–owned, as long as a change will not ensue in the Lands Law. In the vicinity of Jerusalem there are three to four territorial areas in Jewish hands – Nachalat Yitzchak, the Arazim Valley, Kefar Etziyon and Rama-Mitzpeh. If we forego Rama-Mitzpeh the upshot will be that we are closing down activity around Jerusalem.[141]

The JNF's initiative at the end of 1941, in purchasing lands from Jews in the adjacent villages of Ulam and Madar in the Lower Galilee, can furnish examples of Jewish purchases in the context of two factors: the fear that the land would be lost to Jewish ownership, and the special importance attached to purchases near extensive Jewish territorial blocs, while strengthening the Jewish hold in Zone B. This was a most complex purchase of Musha

---

141   CZA, KKL10, minutes of JNF Directorate meeting, 24.3.1941. See also CZA, KKL5/
      11782, letter from Va'ad Leumi Executive to Ussishkin 8.3.1940; CZA, S25/9839,
      letter from the Va'ad Leumi to JNF Executive 20.3.1940 (also in file A246/402);
      CZA, S53/1689, memorandum from Jewish Agency Information Bureau "Increased
      Land Purchase by the JNF," 20.8.1941; CZA, KKL5/11872, from an interview with
      Weitz, 2.1.1942.

rights registered in the name of the private Yavneh Company – a Company for Settlement in Palestine founded in 1934, one of whose shareholders was Lord Melchett. Yavneh itself had purchased two-thirds of the land from Agudat Israel which had the Musha rights on half of the areas in the villages. These rights Agudat Israel had in turn purchased from Mugrahbi peasants already in 1926. PICA as well had Musha rights on portions of the village. Neither Agudat Israel nor Yavneh ever received the lands into their control. They did not arrange the conversion of the lands into Mafruz, and in practice the peasants continued cultivating the lands and obtained by this the rights of tenant farmers. In addition, there was no correlation between the registration in the deeds books regarding the area of the Moshavot (17,270 dunams) and the measurements in practice as they were also marked on the maps (29,980 dunams). The arrival of the "land settlement" officials in the Moshavot at the end of 1941, raised a dual apprehension. First of all, the "land settlement" would correspond to tenant farmers' demands for recognition of their ownership over the entire area by virtue of effective control, and secondly, the Government could claim for itself the discrepancy between the area registered in the deeds books and what was registered on the maps. The Yavneh Company possessed neither the capability nor the talents to handle the issue by itself in order to preserve its rights, evict the peasants, effect Mafruz and receive the areas as they appeared in the maps. Therefore it proposed that the JNF purchase its lands in Ulam and Madar, while turning over to the JNF the entire handling connected with securing Yavneh's rights. Weitz decided that "JNF was obligated to salvage this land" in the hope that after the JNF implemented Mafruz and freed the land from the peasants, PICA would carry out similar activity to obtain its lands in the Moshavot, and in such a manner the lands effectively in Jewish hands would total 15,000 dunams. The importance of this area was immense for unifying the areas of Kefar Tabor, Yavni'el and Menahamia, and creating a single contiguous territorial bloc between the Moshavot and the Lower Galilee in particular, and in Zone B in general. "And here we can establish a settlement position that will serve as a bulwark for all our settlements in the Lower Galilee."[142]

---

142   CZA, KKL10, minutes of JNF Directorate meeting, 18.12.1941 – the first quotation from there; CZA, KKL5/12537, Weitz report on Ulam and Madar 28.11.1941 – the second quotation from there. See in detail on this purchase: ibid.; CZA, KKL5/13675; CZA, KKL5/15321; CZA, KKL5/13675, letter from Weitz to PICA 2.2.1942. See

At the end of 1943, when the purchases from the Yavneh Company were completed, the directors of that company did not hesitate to express their appreciation to the JNF regarding the way it had handled the complex issue. From this it can be deduced that special expertise was required in order to prevent lands held by Jewish owners who did not control them in practice from being lost. Private Jewish parties lacked such expertise, but the JNF possessed it. The directors of the Yavneh Company wrote the following inter alia to the JNF:

> Now that we have completed with you all the matters regarding this sale of the lands in Madar and Ulam we feel compelled to express our satisfaction and appreciation regarding the way your representatives Messrs. Weitz and Nahmani handled the negotiations. The entire activity of obtaining and selling the lands involved many difficulties and only thanks to talent and tact in the conduct of the negotiations displayed by Weitz, it was concluded to the satisfaction of all the interested parties. We could only express our sense of admiration over the way Mafruz was arranged by your representative in the presence of the settlement official. We, as you, are aware of the many obstacles which stood in the path of our obtaining rights to the land and only the vast experience and talent of your representatives, whom you placed at our disposal, availed us in obtaining our rights and facilitated the purchase of a large area which adjoins the JNF's property.[143]

The fear that land would slip from Jewish ownership into Arab hands, the desire to penetrate Zone A within a legal framework, strengthening the Jewish foothold in the Upper Galilee and reinforcing Jewish Safad, "which is decaying from an economic and settlement standpoint,"[144] were the factors underlying the JNF's decision to implement purchases from Jews in Ein Zeitim, Birya, Meiron, and Mt. Cana'an. All in all this was a matter of the purchase possibility of 12,400 dunams surrounding Safad which could

---

also ibid., minutes of JNF Directorate meeting, 27.9.1943. See also CZA, KKL9/59, the agreement between Yavneh Company and JNF on 8.2.1942; CZA, KKL9/59, letter from Nahmani to JNF Lands Department 13.2.1942.

143   CZA, KKL5/13675, letter from Gridinger and Kaminetsky of Yavneh Company to JNF 18.10.1943.

144   CZA, KKL10, minutes of JNF Directorate meeting, 23.4.1942.

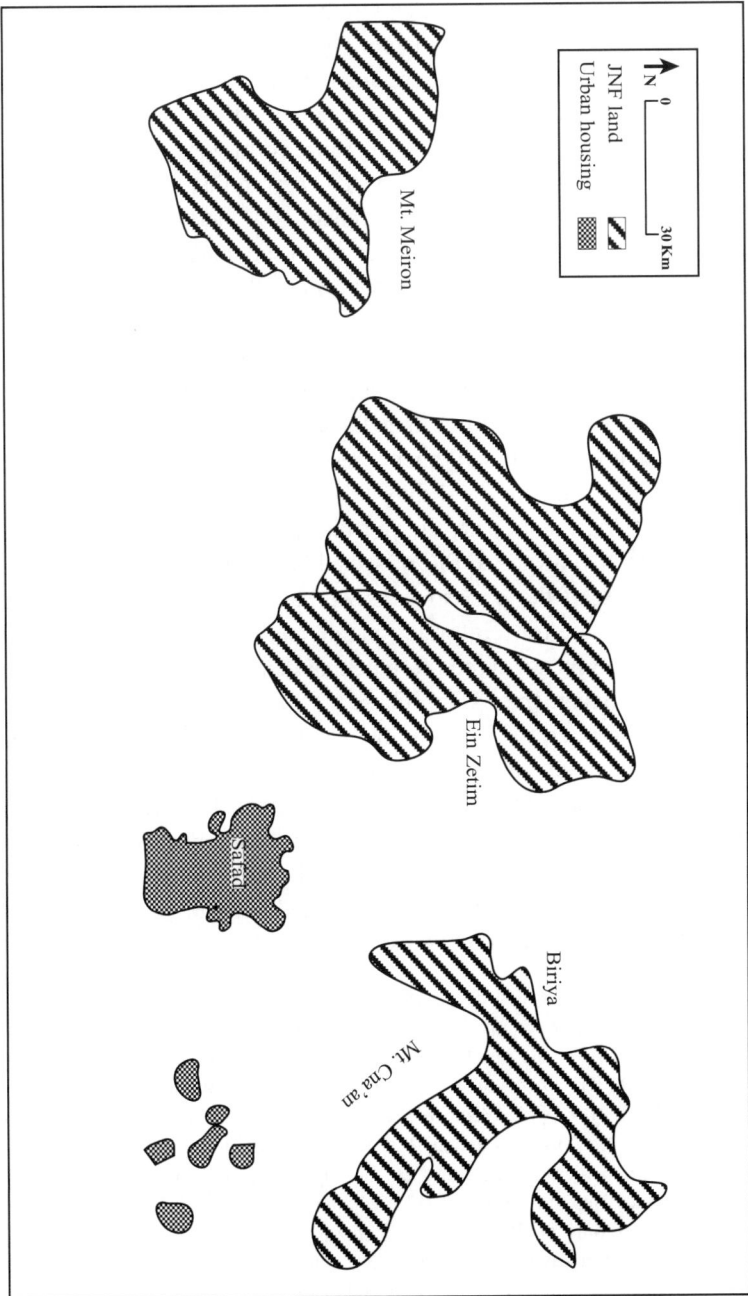

Map 19: JNF lands in the Safad area at the end of 1944
Source: JNF map archives, Map 476

serve as an agricultural hinterland to the Jewish community in the city and assist its economic and settlement revival (see Map 19).

In Ein Zeitim the ownership was registered in the name of PICA, but in practice and according to an agreement made following the First World War signed by PICA, the lands of Ein Zeitim were sub-divided between 30 Jewish landholders. During the 1929 Arab disturbances, the Moshava was abandoned by a number of its inhabitants and those who remained left during the disturbances of 1936. Some of the landholders left the country and the fate of others was unknown. Since the Moshava was abandoned, the land was cultivated by Arab leasers, but part of the lands were taken over by neighboring Arabs. The "land settlement" intended to enter the region at the beginning of 1942, and this occasioned severe apprehension in the JNF's Galilee Office that those actually holding the area would demand that the "land settlement" recognize their ownership on the basis of effective ownership, and thus Jewish ownership over this area would be lost. PICA, for its part, did not display any interest in preserving the rights of Jewish owners ("PICA is shedding responsibility for this place"). In the context of these reasons, as well as Ein Zeitim's location in Zone A, its importance for reinforcing Safad, and the prospects for reviving the village, the JNF endeavored to reach agreement with the landholders and with PICA to have the JNF purchase the site. Some of the landholders also expressed an interest in selling their plots to the JNF. After negotiations, PICA also agreed that the plots of the owners abroad, whose fate was unknown, would temporarily be transferred to JNF ownership. Thus the JNF consolidated its hold on Ein Zeitim and continued activity to purchase the remaining plots from those who initially were not interested to sell their plots. At the same time, the JNF succeeded in freeing the site from claims to ownership raised by the Arabs.[145]

---

145   Ibid., 24.2.1942 – quotation from there. For details on the negotiations carried out by the JNF for the purchase of Ein Zeitim and the complex difficulties involved, see CZA, KKL9/374, the following letters: Jewish Community Committee in Safad to Weitz 10.4.1942, Weitz to Jewish Community Committee in Safad 15.4.1942, 24.5.1942, Weitz to Nahmani 24.5.1942, Nahmani to Lands Department 25.5.1942 with the agreement regarding Ein Zeitim, Weitz to Nahmani 22.2.1943, Nahmani to Lands Department 13.2.1942 (Nahmani wrote: "Ein Zeitim is in Zone A which is closed to us and it would be a sin not to use the means at our disposal to prevent losing Jewish–owned land. The JNF is dutybound to redeem this land and to bring it under its authority"), Weitz to Nahmani 28.2.1943, Weitz to PICA 28.2.1943

Ein Zeitim

In Birya, near Safad, a similar situation obtained: 4,900 dunams were registered in PICA's name, parts of which PICA sold to a number of Jews in Safad without the transfer being registered in the Lands Registration Office, and another part (1,000 dunams) was transferred in barter deals with the Arabs, also without registering the transfer. In practice, the village Arabs held on to the land and claimed ownership over all those areas that were registered in the name of PICA, and they intended to sell these areas. The "land settlement" was also about to enter the area and again it was

(also in file J15/5856), Nahmani to Lands Department 7.3.1943, to Elihu 23.7.1944, Nahmani to Lands Department 3.1.1944, Nahmani to Kolnshar 6.5.1945. See also on the difficult situation of the Jewish community in Safad and the readiness of the JNF already in 1941 to assist the resettlement of Ein Zeitim and Mt. Cana'an (to the extent that the landholders would donate part of their lands to the JNF) and thus assist in the resettlement of Safad, CZA, KKL5/10257, KKL5/11622, KKL5/12548, KKL5/13691. See in detail the letters in CZA, KKL5/ 8645; KKL5/10340; KKL5/11380.

feared that the lands would be lost to Jewish ownership. After negotiations with the JNF, agreements were reached both with PICA and with Jews from Safad to sell these lands to the JNF.[146]

In Kefar Meiron, which comprised 12,000 dunams, the Abu family in Safad had about 25 percent of the area in the village, which was purchased by the family's father already prior to the First World War. These areas also included the tomb of Rabbi Shimon Bar Yohai. The family did not effectively maintain the lands for a long time and the Arabs who took control of the land could ask the "land settlement" authorities to recognize their rights of ownership by virtue of effective ownership. In this context, the Abu family offered its lands for sale to the JNF. It was clear to the JNF that if it would not implement the purchase, the lands would be lost to Jewish ownership. Likewise, the JNF believed that through this purchase and legal combinations it would be able to purchase lands from the Arabs, and thus obtain a consecutive land holding of 4,500 dunams in the village. For these reasons the JNF decided to implement the purchase in Meiron.[147]

The purchases of land from Jews, when the land was earmarked to complete JNF-owned territorial blocs, to establish new settlements, to serve the requirements of existing settlements or of special settlement projects, were implemented on various occasions. Thus, 400 dunams were purchased in the land of Masmiah from a farmer in Rehovot in order to unite them with JNF lands in Bashit, in such a manner that the unified area could serve for establishing a new settlement point.[148] In Gezer, about 2,000 dunams were purchased from the Hanoteah Company and from other

---

146   CZA, KKL10, minutes of JNF Directorate meeting, 23.4.1942; CZA, KKL5/12277, the following letters: Nahmani to the Lands Department 14.7.1942, PICA to the JNF 30.11.1942, Nahmani to Lands Department 20.12.1942, PICA to the JNF 11.1.1943, Weitz to PICA 12.1.1943, 20.1.1943, PICA to JNF 26.1.1943, Weitz to PICA 4.7.1943.

147   CZA, KKL10, minutes of JNF Directorate meeting, 23.3.1942; CZA, KKL5/12480, the following letters: Nahmani to Lands Department 2.2.1943, JNF to Va'ad Leumi 31.12.1944. See also CZA, KKL5/16817, letter from Ra'anan Weitz to Settlement Department and JNF 19.10.1947.

148   CZA, KKL10, minutes of JNF Directorate meeting, 2.11.1941; CZA, KKL5/12310, letter from Weitz to Agricultural Center of Hapoel Hamizrachi 26.3.1942; CZA, KKL5/12485, letter from Weitz to Miller 19.10.1941, agreement between JNF and Miller 2.3.1942.

Land Preparations of JNF in Birya

private individuals[149]; 1,140 dunams were purchased from the Nahalat Ya'akov Company in Hartia in order to expand the housing plan of Kiryat Amal.[150] It was decided to purchase some of the Mahane Yisrael lands in the Jezreel Valley in order to complete the territorial quota urgently required for Kibbutz Mizra[151]; likewise, it was decided to purchase from Jews near Kefar Nordau. A decision was taken at the beginning of 1942 to purchase land from Jews near Gan Shmuel in order to complete the territorial quota for the Kibbutz.[152] It was similarly decided in the beginning of 1943 to purchase land from Jews in order to complete the quota for Kefar Piness.[153]

The JNF decided in December 1944 to exchange its lands on Mt. Cana'an for lands in Poriya, owned by Yisrael Teiber, and join them to lands

---

149   CZA, KKL10, minutes of JNF Directorate meeting, 26.9.1940, 14.8.1941.
150   Ibid.
151   Ibid., 19.12.1944.
152   CZA, KKL5/11821, Mohilewer to A. Curtiss 10.7.1941; CZA, KKL10, minutes of JNF Directorate meeting, 24.3.1942.
153   Ibid., 18.2.1943.

offered for sale by the farmers of Yavni'el and Kinneret. The intention was to establish in Poriya a semi-agricultural semi-urban community based on vacation centers, because in the summer it could also host Jewish campers interested in enjoying the hot springs of Tiberias and in this manner assist the development of Tiberias. The strategic location of the settlement that would be established "that would command the entire vicinity," as well as the relatively limited investment that was involved in the purchases, also assisted the adoption of the decision.[154]

The necessity for action to save the veteran Moshavot induced the JNF to purchase lands from Jews in the Moshavot or near them. Such were the cases in Har Tuv and Sejera, although the background in both cases was different. In Har Tuv, at the beginning of the 1940s there remained only 11 families who cultivated some of the Moshav's lands. Some of the lands were cultivated by tenant farmers – some were leased to Arabs in perpetuity and some were in the process of being sold by the farmers to Arabs. The efforts invested by the Zionist institutions to revive the place by bringing in new settlement groups did not succeed because they encountered opposition from the Moshava committee. Nonetheless, the JNF did not give up the possibility of saving the Moshava, and when farmers approached it in 1944 with offers to sell their patrimony, it decided to make the purchase "in order to prevent the loss of this settlement." In the long run the JNF intended to concentrate all the lands of Har Tuv in JNF hands "to revive Har Tuv and convert it into a truly Jewish Moshava...this is not an issue of redeeming the land but of saving a veteran Moshava."[155]

The JNF had taken a decision in 1944 to purchase the Sejera farm (an area of 6,550 dunams) from the APC. The bank had held on to it for many years because it had assumed ownership as a result of the debts of the Neta'im Association which had purchased the land prior to the First World War from the Jewish Colonization Association, and since the War, it had created a huge debt to the APC and was unable to meet the payments.[156] In practice, the Neta'im Association had gone bankrupt and its properties

---

154   Ibid., 7.12.1943, 6.7.1944. Rabbi Berlin objected to this purchase on the grounds that this project could be carried out by private capital without the JNF. On this, see minutes of JNF Directorate meeting, 6.7.1944 – quotation from there; CZA, KKL5/ 11872, talk with Weitz on 26.12.1941.
155   CZA, KKL10, minutes of the JNF Directorate meeting, 25.4.1944.
156   Katz (1994a), pp. 176–186; idem (1990a), pp. 391–393.

Poriya, 1946

passed to the APC. Over the years, the lands of the farm were seized by the Arabs and from 1940 onwards the APC transferred the maintenance of the site to Mitzpeh Hagalil, a settlement of the Hapoel Hamizrachi Moshav organization, which numbered 40 families. During the years that the organization held the farm, it became increasingly interested in permanently settling the site and it conveyed its request to the JNF. The Moshava which bordered the farm also had a major interest in having this settlement group settle the site on a permanent basis.[157] For many years this Moshava had fought for its existence when the root of its problem was the small number of inhabitants. In 1944 the number of families at the site did not exceed 25. It was clear that if there would not be a substantial increase in the number of the Moshava's residents, it faced the danger of extinction. It viewed the settlement of the Mitzpeh Hagalil settlement group, which

---

157   CZA, KKL10, minutes of JNF Directorate meeting, 20.6.1944; CZA, KKL5/11594, letter from Hazani of Hapoel Hamizrachi Agricultural Center to executive of Bitzaron Fund 13.6.1940.

was willing to merge with the Moshava, as the way to enlarge and save the Moshava, and was prepared to allocate 1,250 dunams from the land of the resident farmers for this purpose. In this context, the Moshava also approached the JNF to purchase the land of the farm from the APC.[158] This was not the first time that proposals to purchase the farm were addressed to the JNF – such approaches had already been made by the APC in 1940 but were turned down by the JNF.[159] Now the JNF gave its assent.

In explaining his recommendation to the Directorate to purchase the farm in Sejera, Weitz emphasized: "By purchasing the 'land of the Bank' and in its wake a certain area from the 'land of the farmers,' we will save one of the veteran Moshavot in the Galilee from decay." He also relied upon precedents where the JNF purchased lands from Jews when they were in danger of being lost to Jewish ownership and he did not consider Sejera as being a different case because "the lands of the 'Sejera Farm' were also held captive by foreigners and only thanks to the 'Mitzpeh Hagalil' organization it was redeemed and is being cultivated. Will the JNF lose by this? Especially since we are confronted by a case of saving a Moshava [Sejera] which has been oscillating between life and extinction for decades." Most members of the Directorate supported the decision for reasons similar to those which Weitz raised, and principally saving the Moshava. Granovsky also feared that the land would be sold by the APC to private parties who would use the land for speculation. In the course of discussion he requested "not to establish a 'principle' that land should be purchased from Jews only if there was a danger that it would be sold to foreigners. If the land went uncultivated by Jews for a number of years there was also a danger that it would be lost." Katznelson sought to emphasize "the pioneering aspect of Sejera and the national duty to save it from decay." The sole dissenter to the purchase was Vilkansky. He was confident that the APC, as a national bank rather than a private bank, would most definitely "ascertain that the patrimony would not come under alien

---

158 CZA, KKL10, minutes of JNF Directorate meeting, 20.6.1944; CZA, KKL5/13905, minutes of a meeting at Sejera Farm on 14.6.1944 with the particpation of representatives of JNF, Settlement Department, Hapoel Hamizrachi Agricultural Center, Farmers Association, Mitzpeh Hagalil and Sejera Moshava Committee.

159 CZA, KKL5/11594, the following letters: APC to JNF 4.12.1940, 8.12.1940, Granovsky to APC 6.7.1941; CZA, KKL5/11595, letter from APC to Granovsky 10.7.1941.

Sejera, 1928

ownership." He feared that other Moshavot would raise similar requests, when the JNF's current duty is to invest its capital in purchasing from non-Jews before it engaged in transferring lands from private Jewish ownership to national ownership.[160]

The Directorate's decision was to implement the purchase of the Sejera lands for the expansion and salvation of the Moshava. The details of the agreement with the APC and the Sejera farmers were finalized in the course of the latter half of 1944 and in the course of 1945.[161] It should be

160   CZA, KKL10, minutes of JNF Directorate meeting, 20.6.1944.
161   Ibid., 20.6.1944; CZA, KKL5/13905, letter from Weitz to APC 21.8.1944; CZA, KKL5/15625, memorandum "Veteran Moshavot are Being Restored to Life," 1947; CZA, KKL5/13661, the following letters: JNF Lands Department to Galilee Office 5.7.1944, Hapoel Hamizrachi Agricultural Center to Granovsky 13.7.1944, Weitz and Granovsky to APC 17.7.1944, APC to JNF 20.7.1944, 20.7.1944, Ahuzat Sejera Ltd. to Mitzpeh Haglil Association, 20.7.1944, Weitz to Jewish Agency Settlement Department 25.7.1944, Weitz to PICA 23.8.1944, Weitz to Settlement Department 28.12.1944, Ra'anan Weitz to Yosef Weitz 8.1.1945, the Sejera Village Council to Agricultural Research Station 25.4.1945, Weitz to Settlement Department 13.5.1945, Weitz to Galilee Office in Tiberias 7.8.1945.

emphasized that the JNF purchase of Har Tuv and Sejera did not constitute precedents for implementing purchases from Jews in the Moshavot.[162] Indeed, at the beginning of 1945, a bitter debate erupted in the Executive and Directorate when the Jewish Farmers Organization of Lower Galilee approached the JNF to purchase 15 farmsteads that were offered for sale in Menahamia after PICA had refused to agree to the Organization's request to take control of the farmsteads and to arrange new settlements there. The Jewish Agency had agreed in principle to organize a new settlement comprised of scores of army veterans' families on the lands about to be purchased, and in this way revive the small Moshava and consolidate it. In the JNF, on the other hand, opinions were divided. The opponents headed by Granovsky could not agree to a financial investment that was double than that of Sejera, especially given the apprehension expressed that the Jewish Agency would attempt to impose upon the JNF the financing of the farmers' houses and the equipment needed. Granovsky and his associates viewed PICA as responsible for the entire affair. "Indeed, Menahamia is in a difficult situation. But is it the JNF's obligation to extricate it from its penury? Here you are not dealing with redeeming the land."[163] There was great apprehension, precisely at this juncture, about setting a precedent in the event that the JNF would purchase the lands from the farmers. "This" – emphasized Vilkansky – "is a new land policy – the transformation of private settlements; and if we agree to this inroad, then this breach can widen and embrace three quarters of private Jewish settlement in Palestine."[164] Shmuel Ussishkin added: "This can recur in other Moshavot and there will be no end to the matter." In contradistinction, Weitz as well as Zuchovitsky, supported the purchase. Aside from the fact that the JNF had already initiated purchases in the Moshavot, Weitz emphasized:

> The existence of an entire Moshava in the Galilee is in jeopardy, and it is the obligation of the central Zionist institutions to enter into the crux of the matter. Not that we want to help PICA abscond from its obligation. PICA itself has abandoned this obligation.... Land areas are being lost from PICA to the Arabs and the Mandatory

---

162 Granovsky hinted at this at the Directorate meeting that deliberated on the purchase of the Sejera Farm, see CZA, KKL10, minutes of JNF Directorate meeting, 20.6.1944.
163 Ibid., 20.3.1945.
164 Ibid., Vilkansky's address.

Government, and the company is not exerting itself to save them. There are no central institutions in Palestine save for the Jewish Agency and the JNF and if these two don't enter the picture to save Menahamia from its difficult predicament, the end result will be that the JNF will have to return and redeem Menahamia but at a much steeper price than is quoted today.

Weitz also attached vast importance to deepening the hold of national capital in the Lower Galilee. "Menahamia dovetails with the JNF's land holdings in the Galilee. Adjacent to it is the JNF area on the 'Madar' lands, and together they will constitute one bloc of JNF lands up to Degania. The JNF also has an interest in possessing lands on both sides of the Jordan River. If the JNF does not enter into the crux of the matter there is a danger that Menahamia as an agricultural settlement will be wiped off the map of Palestine."[165] Under Granovsky's pressure, no decision was reached on the purchase. It was decided to await the receipt of clear information regarding the Jewish Agency's intentions on the entire matter.[166] A few months later, when it became clear that the price of the lands could be reduced and that the Jewish Agency promised to finance the houses and equipment, the opponents in the Directorate dropped their objections to purchasing the farmsteads. They were persuaded by Weitz's arguments to the effect that on the one hand, in the event that the JNF did not purchase the farmsteads they would be used for speculation. On the other hand, as a result of the purchase, a vast settlement project of national capital would be facilitated with territorial contiguity beginning with the JNF lands in Madar and Ulam from the West, running through Menahamia in the center, and perhaps even to the east bank of the Jordan River. Thus Menahamia would fit into a belt of intensive Jewish settlement in the Jordan Valley.[167]

The JNF's efforts to prevent Jewish–owned lands from being lost, as well as its efforts to strengthen footholds in Zone A, especially in strategically important locations – where the lands connected Jewish–owned land, or were required for forming territorial blocs for the establishment of new

---

165 Ibid.
166 Ibid.
167 Ibid., minutes of JNF Directorate meetings, 29.10.1945, 13.11.1945; CZA, KKL5/ 15551, summary of Weitz's comments on the lands purchase program and the new immigration, 31.10.1945; CZA, KKL5/15625, memorandum "Veteran Moshavot are Being Restored to Life," 1947.

Menahamia, 1920

settlements or supplementing existing settlements, etc. – induced the JNF
to approach PICA on this matter. It sought either to ascertain that Jewish
ownership over these lands which were owned by PICA but in practice had
been seized by Arabs was safeguarded, or to persuade PICA to allow the
JNF to purchase such lands from it. Furthermore, the JNF also requested
PICA to make an effort to have dispersed lands under its ownership clustered
in locations of similar importance or to entrust the entire task to the JNF.
The JNF was critical (alluded to above) regarding the fact that "areas of
land are been wrested away from PICA by the Arabs and the Government,
and the company is not exerting itself to save them." Thus, for example,
the JNF had a vast interest in purchasing the PICA lands in Kefar Subarin
east of Zikhron Ya'akov due to "the need to erect a Jewish bridge between
the Jezreel Valley and Zikhron Ya'akov in Samaria that would include
Yoqne'am, Reihaniya, Ein Hashofet, Daliat a-Rucha and Subarin." The
PICA lands in Subarin were dispersed and they had to be clustered in order
to create a single territorial bloc before the lands settlement operations
could begin work in the region. PICA did not display a notable interest in
carrying out the work by itself. In any case, the JNF concerned itself with

this land owned by PICA whose importance derived from the needs of the hour, which induced the JNF to enter into areas previously associated with PICA activity and where the JNF had not ventured before. Negotiations with PICA on the aforementioned matter were complex, and on more than one occasion the JNF encountered difficulties in receiving PICA's assent to its proposals.[168]

From the exchange of correspondence between JNF and PICA it is not difficult to detect the attitude of suspicion which PICA displayed toward the JNF, verging on the growing JNF's domination and perhaps suspicion of a JNF take-over. Characteristic is PICA's response to the JNF request of Summer 1943 to provide it with data on PICA lands which were not settled or cultivated as well as their agricultural quality. It is almost certain that behind the request lay the JNF's concern for preserving the Jewish

---

168   CZA, KKL10, minutes of JNF Directorate meeting, 20.3.1945 – first quotation from there; CZA, KKL5/12703, letter from Weitz to PICA 16.4.1943 – second quotation from there. See also CZA, KKL10, minutes of JNF Directorate meeting, 12.11.1942; CZA, KKL9/21, letter from Weitz to Nahmani 6.6.1940, letter from Nahmani to JNF Head Office 9.6.1940; CZA, KKL9/244, the following letters: Maharshak to Nahmani 21.7.1940, Nahmani to Maharshak 22.7.1940, Nahmani to Wolfsohn 23.7.1940; CZA, J15/5153, letter from Weitz to PICA 7.1.1941; CZA, KKL9/21, memorandum between PICA and JNF, 25.12.1941; CZA, KKL5/12715, Meyerowitz to Kaplan 26.1.1942 (also in file S53/1675f), CZA, KKL5/12703, letter from Weitz to Wolfson of PICA 23.8.1942; CZA, J15/5338, letter from Weitz to PICA 24.1.1943; CZA, KKL5/12703, letter from Nahmani to JNF Lands Department 21.3.1943; CZA, KKL5/11433, the following letters: Weitz to Nahmani 6.6.1940, Nahmani to JNF Head Office 9.6.1940, Weitz to Nahmani 13.6.1940, Weitz to PICA 10.7.1940, Weitz and Granovsky to PICA 26.7.1940, Wolfsohn to JNF 6.8.1940, Wolfsohn to Weitz 19.9.1940; CZA, KKL5/16697, memorandum between PICA and JNF 25.12.1941; CZA, KKL5/12403, letter from Nahmani to Lands Department 10.5.1942; CZA, KKL5/13661, letter from PICA to JNF 28.8.1944. The JNF purchased Ahuzat Sharona in Lower Galilee at the beginning of 1942 from the Histadrut–owned Nir Co. which had purchased it from PICA in 1940. On this see CZA, KKL5/10580, for internal information prepared by Tschernowitz, 7.3.1941; CZA, KKL5/11821, letter from Yehuda to JNF Head Office 22.6.1941; CZA, KKL5/11872, from a conversation with Weitz, 29.12.1941; CZA, KKL5/11765, letter from Weitz to Histadrut Agricultural Center in June 1941; CZA, KKL5/12666, letter from Weitz to Histadrut Agricultural Center 7.12.1941; ibid., letter from Weitz to PICA 30.1.1942; CZA, KKL5/12666, the following letters: the Agricultural Center and Nir Co. to PICA, not dated, Nahmani to JNF Head Office 5.2.1942, draft agreement between PICA and JNF, 11.2.1942, letter from Weitz to PICA 11.2.1942.

ownership of these lands. PICA's reply was far from business like. "Until
the settlement of all the land affairs in the areas in which you are taking
an interest has been completed we will not be able to provide you with the
details you are requesting." Weitz viewed the answer as a "pure evasion"
and could only express his displeasure with it.[169]

Territorial Supplements for Existing Agricultural Settlements

Aside from the JNF's principal activity in purchasing agricultural lands
earmarked for the establishment of new agricultural settlements, the JNF
had to make land purchases intended to supplement the territorial quotas
of agricultural settlements – Kibbutzim and Moshavim alike – which had
been established prior to the period covered by this chapter.[170] Demands for
land increments were addressed to the JNF by the settlements themselves,
the institutions of their settlement movement, by the Agricultural Center of
the Histadrut and by the Settlement Department of the Jewish Agency.[171]
To the JNF's vast displeasure, on more than one occasion the settlements,
settlement movement institutions, and the Histadrut Agricultural Center,
maintained contacts with the sellers of those lands in which they were
interested, and then presented the JNF with the results of these feelers. As
may be recalled, such "mishaps" occurred before 1940 as well, and the JNF
protested. Since they recurred and encumbered JNF purchase activities,
the JNF made it clear to the Agricultural Center in 1944, that it would not

---

169   CZA, KKL5/12703, the following letters: letter from Weitz to PICA 2.7.1943, PICA
      to JNF 1.8.1943 – quotation from there, letter from Weitz to PICA 15.8.1943.
170   CZA, S25/1892, JNF activities in 1945.
171   See, e.g., CZA, KKL5/11821, letter from Hartzfeld to Granovsky 8.9.1940, together
      with the list of urgent purchases in the Sharon needed to fulfill the land requirements
      in existing settlements; CZA, KKL9/238, letter from Kibbutz Dafna to Jewish Agency
      1.9.1942; CZA, KKL9/373, letter from Nahmani to Histadrut Agricultural Center
      6.1.1941 concerning additional lands for Hitien, letter from Hartzfeld to Nahmani
      14.1.1941; CZA, KKL5/11872, excerpts from the Moshav movement's magazine
      Telamim 10.2.1942. Concerning the need to supplement units in the Moshavim: CZA,
      KKL5/12830, letter from Weitz to Hakibbutz Hameuhad Secretariat 12.10.1943;
      CZA, KKL5/12830, the following letters: the Histadrut Agricultural Center to Weitz
      3.11.1944, Hartzfeld to Weitz 7.1.1945, Weitz to Hartzfeld 14.1.1945; CZA, KKL10,
      minutes of JNF Directorate meeting, 25.6.1942.

purchase lands necessary for territorial supplements to the settlements in the event that the negotiations for the purchase in their entirety or partially had not been conducted by itself or by parties which it had authorized to handle the purchase.[172]

During the course of the years 1940–1945, requests for supplements were addressed by agricultural settlements in Judea, Samaria and the Sharon. The requests of these settlements for land supplements stemmed from two principal reasons: Firstly, at the time when they had settled on the land they had not yet received their full territorial allocation needed for a farm (family) unit, as determined in the original settlement plan. Secondly, the total number of families in the settlements had increased over the years. The fact that the land had been settled before securing the stipulated territorial quota under the original settlement plan derived, on the one hand, from the difficulties which the JNF encountered in purchasing the entire requisite area, and on the other hand, the settlement institutions assumed that in the interim the settlements could suffice with the territorial quota in their possession, since some of them could also earn an income from work outside the settlement, and others could subsist on citrus groves which afford a livelihood even from the limited areas that were originally allocated. However, the Arab disturbances that began in 1936, the depression in citrus growing, the political–economic depression in Europe in 1937–1938, and the War that broke out in 1939 led to a demand by the settlements to change the farm structure to a mixed economy. Pursuantly, requests for additional lands and for completing the land quota, as determined in the original settlement plan, arrived. Such demands were already presented to the JNF beginning with the period covered by this chapter, and even earlier than that. "However at that juncture, the JNF confronted very important land purchases, from a settlement, strategic and national–political standpoint in the South and in the North, and the JNF

---

172   Ibid., 2.11.1941; CZA, KKL5/12830, letter from Weitz to Histadrut Agricultural Center 2.7.1944. See also CZA, KKL5/12830, the following letters: Hartzfeld to Weitz 23.10.1943, Dayan of Agricultural Center to JNF Executive 5.4.1944, Weitz to Histadrut Agricultural Center 24.4.1944; CZA, KKL5/13861, letter from Weitz to Granovsky 6.5.1944; daily pages to *JNF Weekly Bulletin* 14.5.1945 – address by Yosef Weitz at the Agricultural Convention, esp. pp. 6–7. All these documents reflect the tension between the Agricultural Center and other Histadrut institutions and the JNF – among other reasons the former's direct involvement in land purchases.

could not find the time to handle the question of completing the territories of existing settlements."[173]

The intensified demands for supplements and pressures on the JNF at the same time as the steep rise in land prices and the current priority which the JNF accorded to purchases calculated to furnish a response to political strategic necessities,[174] combined in June 1942 to raise the issue of completing land quotas in the Judea, Samaria and Sharon settlements on the Directorate's agenda in order to adopt a definitive decision. Deliberations on this matter took place later as well. In general, both the Executive and the Directorate agreed on the need to provide the territorial supplements of the settlements, and the JNF did act in a number of instances to implement such purchases prior to the fundamental discussion.[175]

But now the Directorate had to decide on four main issues: Firstly, how to implement the purchases intended for supplements without depleting the resources earmarked for implementing purchases in accordance with the order of priorities that had been determined upon the publication of the Lands Law, i.e., implementing purchases whose major purpose was political–strategic. According to the plan presented by the Executive to the Directorate, this involved supplementary purchases totaling 11,500 dunams for 24 settlements, the cost of which totaled P£200,000.[176] "Purchasing areas of land in accordance with the aforementioned list did not amount to redeeming the land 'one hundred percent,' and if we devote our entire efforts to this activity, over the course of one year we will lack resources for genuine redemption of the land in other places, in all regions of the country." On this matter the JNF had to decide on a ceiling price that it was willing to assume for land required for supplement, and beyond that price the settlements and their institutions would have to fend for themselves. Secondly, the Directorate had to decide whether to adopt the

---

173 CZA, KKL10, minutes of JNF Directorate meeting, 25.6.1942 – quotation from Weitz's address; see also CZA, KKL5/11871, *Information Bulletin*, apparently from 1942.

174 CZA, KKL5/11872, quotations from *Telamim*, 10.2.1942; CZA, KKL10, minutes of JNF Directorate meeting, 25.6.1942.

175 Ibid., 24.3.1941, 25.11.1941, 20.1.1942 – accession to the requests of Giv'at Hashlosha, Kvutzat Schiller and Gan Shmuel.

176 For details see CZA, KKL5/13921, supplementing a land unit on existing farms, 1943.

Executive's recommendation (as presented by Weitz) to restrict the size of the farm units, i.e., the area per family, to 20–25 dunams, a calculation that was predicated on the findings adopted by the Institute for Agricultural Research and the Executive's desire to refrain, to the extent possible, from very expensive purchases, as well as purchases from Jews. Thirdly, was the JNF responsible for assuring land supplements even to settlements which had increased their number of families beyond the total set forth in the original plan? In other words, should they be allotted a land supplement not only to complete the units determined in the original settlement plan, but an increment as well for new units to accommodate families who had joined in the intervening years.[177]

In June 1942, the Directorate decided that to avoid impairment to financing JNF lands purchase activity following the order of priority set after the publication of the Lands Law, the financing of purchases earmarked for supplements according to the Executive's aforementioned plan would be spread over the course of six years. The upshot of the matter was that supplement purchases would take place over a number of years, and it was necessary to have patience. The Executive received a directive to attempt to make supplementary purchases primarily from Arabs, and the Directorate was united in a decision to impose upon the JNF the task of financing purchases whose total that did not exceed P£20 per dunam. The price differential was imposed on the settlements and their movement institutions. It should be emphasized that in any case, the entire land purchase would be registered exclusively in the JNF's name, and the settlements' share in the cost would be considered in some cases as an advance on leasing fees, in other cases as a contribution to the JNF. There were even cases where the settlements' share was considered as part contribution and part an advance on leasing fees.[178] A year later, given the

---

177   CZA, KKL10, minutes of JNF Directorate meeting, 25.6.1942 – quotation from the remarks of Granovsky.

178   Ibid., 25.6.1942. See also ibid., regarding the following matters: purchase of supplementary land for the Womens' Farm at Hadera; minutes of JNF Directorate meeting, 20.8.1942, concerning the purchase of supplementary land for the "Girls Farm" in the Galilee and the Training Farm in Talpiyot, Jerusalem; minutes of JNF Directorate meeting, 20.11.1942 concerning the purchase of supplementary land for Giv'at Hashlosha; minutes of JNF Directorate meeting, 12.2.1943 concerning the purchase of supplementary land for Kefar Piness. See also CZA, KKL5/12714, list of land purchases – transfer of land to the JNF in 1942. Cf. purchases made by the

general rise in land prices, the Directorate raised the JNF's maximum share in land supplement purchases to P£25 per dunam (but not retroactively).[179] In the beginning of 1945 it raised the ceiling by an additional P£10.[180]

With regard to the settlements' request for territorial increments explained by their absorption of additional families beyond the quota that had been agreed upon in the original settlement plan, the Directorate in June 1942 adopted Weitz's position which stated that

> The JNF purchases land only for completing a farm unit, but the JNF does not purchase land in order to raise the number of families in every settlement beyond the number agreed upon by the settlement institutions. This proviso will prevent the practice that has recently become widespread whereby the settlements repeatedly increase the number of families in contravention to the plan agreed upon by the settlement bodies, and subsequently pressure the JNF to purchase additional land in consideration of the increased number of families.[181]

Two and a half years later, pursuant to a discussion that arose in the Directorate regarding the request by Kibbutz Ramat Hakovesh for a territorial increment, the Directorate amended its decision. While it still adhered to its original decision not to agree to the settlements' demands for additional land due to an increase in the number of families without the agreement of the settlement institutions, the Directorate decided that in the event that the increase in the number of families was justified by security reasons, the JNF was obliged to accede to the land increment necessitated by the population increase.[182]

JNF for settlements in the Jezreel Valley where the price of land was less than P£10 per dunam, and the JNF arranged a significant loan by the settlements to cover the purchase. See also ibid., minutes of JNF Directorate meeting, 2.11.1941.

179   Ibid., 1.7.1943.

180   Ibid., 23.1.1945.

181   Ibid., Weitz's statement at the JNF Directorate meeting, 25.6.1942. See also CZA, KKL5/12830, letter from Weitz to Hakibbutz Hameuhad Secretariat 12.10.1943, and letter from Hakibbutz Hameuhad Secretariat to Weitz, no date, but obviously from October 1943 – from which it is possible to appreciate the deep dissension between the JNF and Hakibbutz Hameuhad regarding the supplementary lands for kibbutzim where the number of families had increased beyond the original settlement plan.

182 CZA, KKL10, minutes of JNF Directorate meeting, 23.1.1945.

Differences of opinion arose in the Directorate regarding the question of the "standardized" size of units which constituted the basis for the supplement. Regarding the Executive's recommendation regarding 20–25 dunams per unit ("and in the case where the land of the settlement is very fertile, and can be exploited further, the unit will remain at 20 dunams per family.... In any place where the settlement's land is poor and less fertile the size of the unit will increase up to 25 dunams net per family"),[183] there was no agreement. The difference of opinion reflected divergent approaches among the Directorate members regarding the farm structure and the sources of income upon which the farms should support themselves for the long term. In other words, should the agricultural character of the settlements be maintained, or should the changes that had already occurred in some of the farms which had introduced non-agricultural occupations be consolidated, thus sparing the JNF the need to finance the requested supplements? Weitz, whose recommendation formed the basis for the discussion, believed that

> The basis for every agricultural settlement is that it should sustain itself from agriculture. If in Giv'at Brenner there is a jam factory today due to the War, we should ascertain that there should be a sufficient territorial unit quota at the time when there will not be scope for a war industry following the War. And if in Yarkona, some of the settlers have to earn a living as officials, because they do not have an adequate farming unit, we have to provide them with land that will suffice for the requisite unit so that they can support themselves exclusively from agriculture to which they aspired from the outset and to which they aspire today as well.[184]

It was only natural that Weitz's opinion was sustained by Katznelson. In general, the latter was perplexed by the very fact that a debate had arisen within the Directorate concerning the subject. "What is the point of the question? We desired and still desire to create in Palestine an agricultural economy. If due to a lack of land to maintain an adequate economic unit, some settlements are engaged in a jam or shoe industry, it is not our duty to compel them to remain confectioners of jam and sewers of shoes for

---

183   Ibid., 25.6.1942 – quotation from Weitz's statement.
184   Ibid.

others. It is our desire that Giv'at Brenner and Giv'at Hashlosha and their like should be genuine farmers." Shmuel Ussishkin, in contradistinction, presented an opposite approach and negated the need to supplement quotas and definitely not in the size of the territory that was recommended by the Directorate in those settlements where the non-agricultural occupations had been consolidated.

> Let us agree in principle that the farming unit should be supplemented **where the matter is necessary** without establishing hard and fast rules whether we have completed the supplement of 20–25 dunams per farming unit or not. In contradistinction there are settlements to which such a supplement should not be awarded. Let us take for example two settlements, Kibbutz Giv'at Hashlosha is part of the Moshava Petah Tiqva and it has a shoe industry or similar; why shouldn't we leave Givat Hashlosha as an industrial suburb of Petah Tiqva? In Moshav Yarkona most of the settlers support themselves as officials. Why shouldn't they support themselves in the future as officials as well? If today we were to purchase land for new settlements, it would be necessary to take as a basis the farming unit of Vilkansky's organic farm. But when we are dealing with an already existing community, including settlements which subsist on outside work then these settlements in the future as well can subsist on outside work.

Zuchovitzky and Vilkansky requested the Executive to discuss together with the Settlement Department the territorial needs of each and every settlement on an individual basis, and they did not embrace the yardstick proposed by the Executive. Indeed, in view of the various opinions expressed regarding the size of the units, the Directorate did not succeed in adopting a decision on the subject but left the matter inconclusive. In June 1942, it authorized only the general framework of the total amount of lands to be purchased in the vicinity of the settlements, but it requested that the Executive determine together with the Settlement Department the details of the supplement, while considering the opinions voiced in the Directorate.[185] These decisions guided the Executive and Directorate in principle during 1942–1945, when they discussed specific requests for supplements presented by farming

---

185   Ibid.

settlements in Judea, Samaria and the Sharon. An examination of the deliberations and resultant decisions regarding these requests yields the following findings: (1) There were cases where the JNF was prepared to pay a price for the supplementary purchases that was higher than the ceiling established in the Directorate's meetings.[186] (2) The JNF did not agree to requests for territorial supplements in the event that the reason for the request was tied to the increase of families beyond the original settlement plans, unless the increase was warranted by security reasons.[187] The JNF also refused to agree to requests for territorial supplement when according to the JNF's concept the settlement requesting the supplement was not by its very character an agricultural settlement. Thus, for example, the JNF turned down the request of Hakibbutz Hameuhad Organization to assure the territorial expansion of Kibbutz Ramat Rahel "because this is an urban neighborhood and one cannot house an agricultural settlement within an urban neighborhood when the land is not available and its current price was P£50–60 per dunam. The JNF's role is to redeem agricultural land and not to facilitate agriculture within the city."[188] For similar reasons, the requests of Kibbutz Gelil Yam, which the JNF viewed as a "semi-urban kibbutz" and contended that this was how the Kibbutz itself had portrayed the situation to it, were denied. "There is no basis for your demands or complaints to the JNF. The opposite is the case. We have much more severe and fundamental complaints against you. Why didn't you disclose from the outset your plan

---

186   Ibid., 1.7.1943, 29.2.1944.
187   See CZA, KKL5/12830, letter from Weitz to Hakibbutz Hameuhad Secretariat 12.10.1943 in which Weitz wrote: "We, too, wish to comment regarding the 'self determination' and the number of families in the kibbutz at 120: We have nothing against this number and we are prepared to support it, if this relates to the period prior to 'settlement on the land' and at the time the settlement plan is determined. However, we must object when you come to force this determination in relation to settlements prior to the settling and then the JNF is required to increase the land resources for those settlements even when land is not available in the area or to purchase it from Jewish owners and at high prices. In such cases it must be remembered that the definition set by the JNF comes before that of Hakibbutz Hameuhad."
188   Ibid. – quotation from there. See also CZA, KKL5/12830 from Hakibbutz Hameuhad Secretariat to Weitz, no date, but probably from October 1943. However, the JNF was prepared to purchase for Ramat Rachel about 130 dunams from the PLDC, not above the price of P£50 per dunam and the kibbutz was required to pay the difference. On this, see CZA, KKL10, minutes of JNF Directorate meeting, 1.7.1943.

that the Kibbutz wishes to be an agricultural settlement? If you had said so we would have prevented you from going there, because it was already then clear to us that a location that was so close to the city cannot cluster an area of 1,200 dunams which would serve for agriculture."[189] (3) Even before the principles for supplements in Judea, Samaria and the Sharon had been determined in 1942, the JNF implemented "follow-up purchases" which were intended for supplements at other locations where settlement was being consolidated, such as in the Harod bloc, Beisan Valley and the Upper Galilee. Nonetheless, at the time when the JNF implemented purchases of large territorial blocs, it preferred that these lands should be used to establish new settlements "due to a desire to multiply settlement points for political–strategic reasons" and not for the sake of supplementing existing farms. In this connection, the JNF found itself in certain cases in disagreement with the Settlement Department from whose perspective land supplements for existing settlements took priority.[190]

Requests for supplements were also addressed to the JNF by middle class settlements that were established during this period on private lands, such as Ramat Hadar and Yoqne'am. They encountered a sympathetic response from the Executive and Directorate.[191] In Ramat Hadar, for example, the settlers living there in 1942 found it difficult to sustain themselves from the family unit of 3–7 dunams they possessed. The JNF agreed to complete the quota to 15 dunams per unit because "there is immense value from a national–settlement perspective to assist members of the middle class to take root in the country and fit into an agricultural settlement." The JNF posed two conditions: (1) The transfer of private lands to the JNF's name when the JNF's payment for this would be written off against the leasing fees which Ramat Hadar would have to pay in the future to the JNF; (2) One-third of the cost of the land supplement would be financed by the settlers, on condition that the price per dunam would not exceed P£40. In the event that the price would exceed this sum, the difference would also be defrayed by the settlers. Ramat Hadar's share in financing would be

189 CZA, KKL5/12830, letter from Weitz to Hakibbutz Hameuhad Secretariat 12.10.1943.
190 CZA, S53/689, letter from Weitz to Jewish Agency Settlement Department 17.8.1941; CZA, KKL5/11872, information, 9.11.1941, from a talk with Weitz – quotation from there.
191 CZA, KKL10, minutes of JNF Directorate meeting, 26.11.1942, 29.7.1943.

considered a contribution to the JNF.[192] Decisions in a similar vein were adopted regarding the request from Yoqne'am where the JNF decided to purchase from the PLDC a bloc of land in the size of 3,500 dunams (held by Arab tenant farmers), which was intended to serve as a supplement to Yoqne'am and Hazorea, and in this manner "it would save the Moshava Yoqne'am and consolidate Kibbutz Hazorea."[193]

Increased Cooperation with Private Capital

Chapter Two discussed in detail how the JNF initiated the creation of frameworks of collaboration with private capital based on plans for cooperation in land purchases. These frameworks were intended to increase the JNF's income in order to enable it to finance land purchases, which expanded at the close of the 1930s.

Since 1940, although joint purchases with the AMICA and Africa–Palestine Companies were no longer implemented and they even sold to the JNF lands which they had purchased jointly with the JNF,[194] the cooperation with private capital intensified. Now, as before, cooperation was intended first and foremost to provide a source of income which would assist the JNF in implementing the goal of widespread purchases centered on Zones A and B. The bulk of the effort was devoted to involving private capital in England and Ireland, since in Rumania activity had declined because of the War, and attempts to operate the plan in South Africa and other places outside of Britain did not succeed.[195] The motto of activity in Britain no longer spoke of charity, and especially for European refugees, but on the summons: "You, the Jews of Britain, you yourselves are obligated to invest money in Palestine and assure your future."[196]

---

192   Ibid., 26.11.1942 – quotation from the statement by Granovsky.
193   Ibid., 29.7.1943 – quotation from Weitz's statement.
194   Ibid., 12.11.1942; CZA, KKL9/22, letter from Weitz to Nahmani regarding lands in the Hula, 9.3.1941; CZA, KKL5/10580, *Information Bulletin*, 12.5.1941; CZA, S53/1675f, letter from Weitz to Hakibbutz Hameuhad, Sha'ar-Hanegev–Kefar Szold, 10.5.1942.
195   CZA, KKL10, ibid., 25.11.1941.
196   Ibid., 27.9.1943.

The involvement of private capital in Britain was to be accomplished within the framework of two plans: (1) A plan for purchasing lands which was similar to the one originally operated at the end of the 1930s in Rumania described in the previous chapter, and (2) A plan explained below called "Farm Cities."[197] Subscribers to these programs were people of means in England and Ireland who "have earned well and are looking for secure investments for their money. In order to 'diversify the risk' they are prepared to invest part of their capital in Palestine. On the other hand, they are worried about the intensification of anti-Semitism in Britain (and there are many manifestations of this) and they are seeing to their future and the future of their children."[198]

The program operated in Britain for involving private capital in purchasing lands resembled that which had operated in Rumania at the end of the 1930s. However, in light of accumulated experience, a number of changes were introduced. The plan for operations in Britain, as ratified by the Directorate at the beginning of 1941, included the following components: (1) The JNF purchases land and registers it under the name of the Himnuta Company as Musha common to it and to private individuals. The contract between the JNF and the private individual was drawn up regarding land that had just been purchased, or was in the process of being purchased. (2) At the appropriate time the land would be parceled (into Mafruz), between the JNF and the private individuals. Until that time, the JNF would be responsible for preserving the lands, when the private purchaser would finance expenses in a manner proportional to the size of his plot. (3) The private purchaser has to pay in cash for the land he purchases (a cost which is not less than P£500) a price comprising the JNF's principle plus expenses. (4) The private purchaser reserves the option to forego his purchase during a period of three years from the time the land is registered under his name. In such an event, the JNF is obligated to buy back the land, but it can spread the reimbursement payments over five years at an interest rate of 3%.[199]

---

197   Ibid., 24.3.1942; JNF Report (1947), pp. 127–129.
198   CZA, KKL5/12688, discussion with Kollek concerning Garden Cities and the involvement of private capital, with the participation of Granovsky, Weitz, Mohilewer and Epstein on 1.2.1942.
199   CZA, KKL5/11788, letter from Granovsky to JNF Office in Brussels regarding "Cooperation with private capital in purchasing land in Palestine," 9.5.1940; CZA,

The plan therefore awarded the JNF appreciable advantages. Monies in cash would flow into its treasury to serve its current needs in redeeming the land, but in the case that the purchaser would seek to invoke the buy-back option, the JNF could spread payments over a number of years. Indeed, the Directorate raised the possibility that the JNF would face financial difficulties in the event that a large number of purchasers would simultaneously wish to exploit the resale option to the JNF. However, the likelihood that such a request would arrive simultaneously from many people seeking to exercise the option appeared slim. "In practice, the state of affairs would undoubtedly be as follows: Part of the land purchased for the partners would remain in the hands of the purchasers. Part of the land would pass to the JNF in the form of life bequests. On part of the land it would be necessary to implement the right of preferential obligation, however, these monies could be returned over a protracted period of time."[200] Additional advantages mentioned included the very possibility of "extracting the capital from the pockets of its owners and investing it toward redeeming the land" through an investment plan in the Sharon region which touched the hearts of owners of private capital, as well as freeing the JNF to invest the bulk of its capital in Zones A and B, while nonetheless maintaining a joint presence in the Sharon with private capital which would bear an appreciable portion of the burden in this zone. Most Directorate members assumed upon the plan's ratification that land prices in the Sharon would not significantly change, and thus the JNF would not be harmed in the event of price declines and demands by private purchasers

---

L51/596, letter from Granovsky to Bart 5.6.1940; CZA, KKL5/11790, letter from Ranovsky to S. Ussishkin 25.6.1940; CZA, KKL5/11791, memorandum "Joint Land Purchase Scheme," July 1940; CZA, KKL5/11786, JNF memorandum 4.1.1941 signed by Bistritsky and Tschernowitz regarding cooperation between the JNF and private capital in purchasing land; CZA, KKL5/11286, memorandum "The Program for the Involvement of Private Capital in the purchase of land in Palestine by the Jewish National Fund Ltd.," 26.1.1941; CZA, KKL5/15605, sample purchase deeds Himnuta Co. gave private individuals who purchased land together with the JNF (Himnuta); CZA, KKL5/15599, draft report to the Congress regarding "The program for involving private capital in the purchase of agricultural land," 18.5.1946; CZA, KKL10, minutes of JNF Directorate meeting, 27.2.1941; JNF Report (1947), p. 127. It should be pointed out that later the period of option was extended to one year after the War.

200   CZA, KKL10, minutes of JNF Directorate meeting, 27.2.1941.

to realize the option at a price they had paid the JNF, or in the case of price increases when the JNF would be asked by those exercising the option to refund the price differential.[201]

The JNF endeavored to ascertain that those British Jews who signed contracts "had an affinity with the land in Palestine and did not base their investments solely on economic motives. Regarding this circle, we are certain, for example, that they would not sell their land to non-Jews, come what may."[202] The JNF expected that the plan would draw the JNF closer to private capital, leading to an increase in the volume of contributions from this sector. Granovsky did not even hesitate to contend (and act in this spirit) that

> The land purchase together with the award of an option is a service which the JNF provides the investor gratis, and it was therefore logical that the investor should note his appreciation in a tangible fashion. In Britain matters have reached the stage where investors allot a certain percentage (and a very high one – up to 15%!) of their investment as a contribution to the JNF. It is clear that this contribution should not be construed as a fee to the JNF for its activity on behalf of the investor, but in a number of cases the investment opens up an avenue for donations, especially as regards this new circle which was not accustomed to donate to the JNF.[203]

At the end of 1941 the JNF decided to stop the original plan for cooperation in the purchase of land with private capital from Britain. This decision followed the meteoric rise of land prices in the Sharon, where the plan had been put into operation, and difficulties that arose in implementing purchases there in general. Furthermore, the JNF feared that it would have to pay out substantial amounts in the event that the investors would wish

---

201   Ibid., 24.3.1942; see also CZA, KKL5/11787, letter from Mohilewer to Hoofien 22.1.1941.

202   CZA, KKL5/12693, letter from Mohilewer to de Shalit 8.7.1942, which shows that in the case of Jews in Egypt, the JNF was apprehensive of implementing this program of cooperation with private capital for the purchase of land because it was not certain that in the future the land might be sold to non-Jews, and were convinced that joining this program would be solely for the purpose of economic benefit.

203   CZA, KKL5/12693, letter from Mohilewer to Bistritsky in Buenos Aires 14.5.1942 regarding collaboration between JNF and private capital from South America for the purchase of land in Palestine.

to exercise their buy-back option. The JNF offered an alternative plan under which contracts would be signed and money would be paid by the participants, not for specific purchases already implemented or that were in the process of being implemented, but on account of future purchases to be made by the JNF. Only after the purchases had been implemented, would it be determined whether the private purchaser wished to receive a share of the purchase or await future purchases by the JNF. It is clear that this plan was less attractive than the original one, and the JNF itself was aware of this, and it did not attract many subscribers.

At the end of 1943, the JNF decided to revert to the original plan, but to transfer it to Zones A and B where land prices were cheaper, but this was not carried out. Thus, cooperation with private capital did not go beyond the Sharon area. In 1944, the plan for collaboration with private capital in purchases came to an end, due to the aforementioned reasons and because the JNF's income increased to an extent that enabled it to implement purchase without requiring the involvement of private capital.[204]

In 1940, JNF income from the cooperation plan with private capital in land purchases totaled P£83,000.[205] A year later, income totaled P£67,000,[206] and Granovsky could report with satisfaction to the Directorate at the end of 1941 that "if these land owners should exercise their option under their contract with the JNF, after a number of years the JNF will have to return these sums. However, in the meantime, these monies have entered the JNF's cash flow and can be employed to redeem the land."[207] A few months later, he added: "Raising money through this plan affords us the possibility of purchasing land from non-Jews in both the prohibited zone... as well as in the permitted zone. If the lands...will pass subsequently to

---

204   JNF Report (1947), pp. 127–129; CZA, KKL10, minutes of JNF Directorate meetings, 26.9.1940, 27.2.1941, 21.10.1941, 25.11.1941, 24.3.1942, 27.9.1943, 9.11.1943; KKL5/12693, the following letters: Mohilewer to JNF National Committee's Department for Special Projects 14.12.1942, Mohilewer to Ricks 28.2.1943, Mohilewer to JNF National Committee's Department for Special Projects 28.2.1943; CZA, KKL5/13885, JNF memorandum "Annulment of the JNF's Commitment to provide land in keeping with the plan for collaboration with private capital," 16.7.1945. See also CZA, KKL5/10641, letter from Weitz to Hankin 3.4.1941; CZA, KKL5/11821, letter from Weitz to Stroock 18.5.1941.

205   CZA, KKL10, minutes of JNF Directorate meeting, 26.9.1940.

206   Ibid., 25.11.1941.

207   Ibid., 25.11.1941.

Jewish owners of private capital, so much the better; If they will remain in our hands, this is fine as well."[208] From September 1941, until March 1942 the JNF coffers were enriched as a result of this plan by P£90,000. JNF income from operating the plan in Britain until then totaled P£250,000.[209] In December 1946, the JNF reported to the 22nd Zionist Congress that the organization's total income from operating the plan involving private capital in Britain reached P£350,000.[210]

The plan for cooperation in purchases with private capital in Britain was implemented in the following Sharon locations: Wadi Kabani (on 5,000 dunams), in an area south of Nathanya (on 1,100 dunams), the Falik Concession (on 2,000 dunams), in the areas near the Moshava Kadima, southeast of Nathanya (on 3,700 dunams), in Beth Lid, south of Nathanya (2,000 dunams), in Zeta, east of Hadera (on 1,500 dunams), and in Atil, south of Zeta (on 1,500 dunams).[211] In addition, 700 dunams were purchased in the vicinity of Kefar Yona, Geulim and Ramat Hakovesh, within the framework of the new program that was put into operation at the end of 1942, under which at the time contracts with private individuals were signed the locations of purchase were not specified (see Map 20).[212]

208 Ibid., 24.3.1942.
209 Ibid.
210 JNF Report (1947), p. 127.
211 CZA, KKL5/11824, internal memorandum from Mohilewer on "Planning and Development," 25.12.1940; CZA, L51/597, report from the Himnuta Co. 11.5.1941; CZA, KKL5/11786, supplement to the plan for collaboration with private capital, 30.7.1941, signed by Mohilewer (also in file KKL5/ 12692); CZA, KKL5/12691, memorandum from Mohilewer: "Collaboration with Private Capital," 16.8.1942 with details of the lands purchased within the plan for collaboration with private capital; CZA, KKL5/12693, memorandum "Purchases for Private Capital Without Restrictive Conditions," 26.7.1943; CZA, KKL5/13855, memorandum "Annulment of the JNF's Commitments Regarding Provision of Land Under the Plan for Involvement of Private Capital," 16.7.1945.
212 CZA, L51/596, letter from Granovsky to Bart 11.11.1940 (also in KKL5/11789); CZA, KKL5/11789, Mohilewer, "Internal Memorandum on Planning and Development," 26.12.1940; CZA, KKL5/11787 letter to Toibman 3.1.1941; CZA, KKL5/11786, letter from Weitz to Smilansky 15.1.1941; CZA, KKL5/12692, report on the Atil land 6.4.1941; CZA, KKL5/11793, letter from Granovsky and Ezrahi to D. Joseph 16.4.1941; CZA, KKL5/12693, memorandum "Purchases for Private Capital Without Restricting Conditions," 26.7.1943.

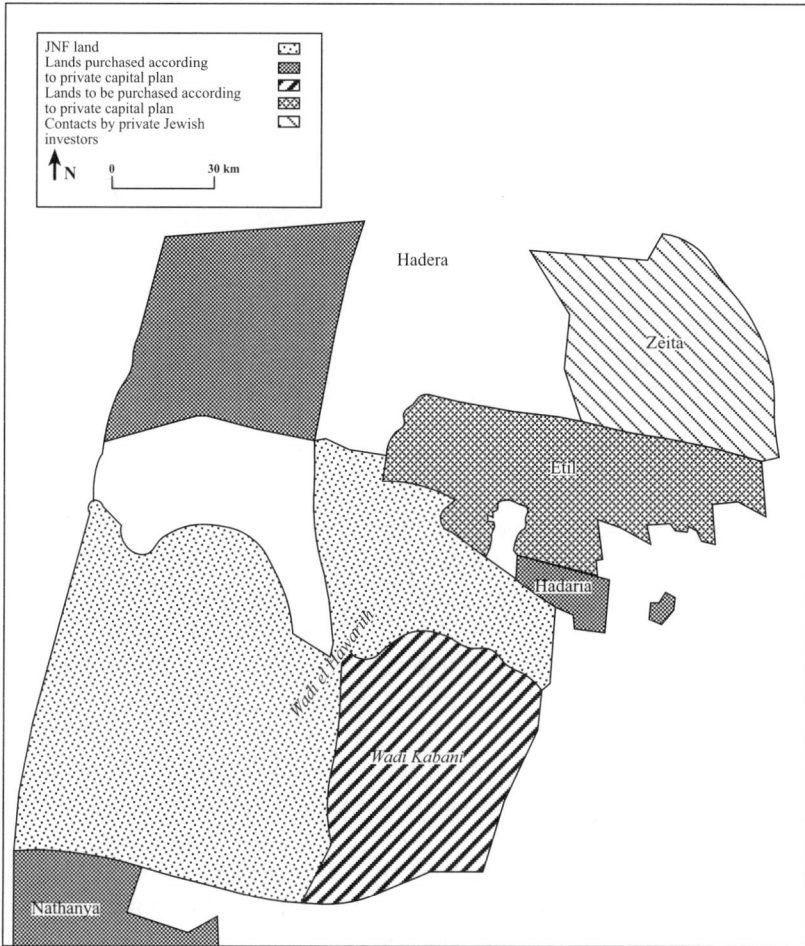

Map 20: JNF land purchases between Nathanya and Hadera
in the framework of cooperation with private capital, 1941
Source: CZA, file KKL5/12692 (April 1941)

The involvement of private capital in the purchase of Wadi Kabani in 1940 was of particular importance. This was part of the JNF's expanded program begun in the 1920s to purchase the land blocs of Wadi el-Hawarith (about 33,000 dunams), Wadi Kabani (12,000 dunams), and Wadi Samara (5,000 dunams) in order to create a large nationally owned territorial bloc in the heart of the Sharon. However, when the JNF was about to complete the purchase of 9,000 dunams in Wadi Kabani, it emerged that it could not sustain the heavy financial burden by itself. The solution was to involve private capital from Britain which was allotted about 5,000 dunams (as Musha out of the total 9,000 dunams) for which the private individuals transferred P£75,000 in cash to the JNF treasury. It was this sum that enabled the JNF to complete the purchase of 9,000 dunams in Wadi Kabani (see Map 21).[213]

The plans for collaboration with private capital from Britain to purchase lands brought in an appreciable sum to the JNF treasury and assisted land purchase objectives. On the other hand, from the mid-1940s and even prior to that, the owners of the private capital expressed their discontent over the delays in receiving a return on their investment. This followed repeated postponements by the JNF in parceling the lands for the owners of the private capital (which were registered as Musha with the Himnuta Co.) and delaying the allocation of specific plots to the investors. The delays stemmed from various reasons: Delays in the actual completion of purchases; concentration and parceling the lands that were Musha owned by both the JNF and Arabs; demands on the part of farming settlements in the area (which received the backing of the Settlement Department and the Agricultural Center) to receive lands that were allotted to private capital, as well as the territorial needs posed by the settlement of army veterans; the JNF's intention to exchange lands and make changes in the lands which were assigned to private capital; the taxes which the Himnuta Co. was to pay upon the transfer of ownership registration from its name to the names of the private purchasers. Indeed, it emerges that only after the establishment of the State of Israel allocations were made and the plots registered in the

---

213   CZA, KKL10, minutes of JNF Directorate meeting, 26.9.1940; CZA, KKL5/12691, memorandum "Involvement of Private Capital," with details of the places where land was purchased within the plan for involvement of private capital, 16.8.1942; Weitz (1941).

names of the private investors. Even before that, the investors exploited their option and sold their rights back to the JNF.[214]

As mentioned previously, the second plan for involving private capital that operated in Britain from the beginning of the 1940s was called "Garden Cities." As opposed to the plan for involving private capital in purchasing lands which was intended to stimulate investments, the Garden Cities plan was intended to produce a direct increase in contributions to the JNF from owners of private capital, and especially those who had previously not been involved in JNF projects. The JNF was aware of the widespread movement for establishing Garden Cities and garden suburbs in various locations throughout the world – a movement that had been established in Britain at the beginning of the 20th century following the publication of Ebenezer Howard's work *Garden City of Tomorrow*[215] which aroused great interest. It is not inconceivable that the very use of the term Garden City by the JNF, despite the differences between the original British plan,[216] and the model which the JNF sought to develop, was intended to increase the number of subscribers to the JNF plan.

214   CZA, S15/9920, letter from Stern to JNF Head Office 5.6.1941; CZA, KKL5/13886, discussion with the participation of Granovsky, Weitz and Mohilewer on 21.4.1942 regarding Wadi Kabani; CZA, KKL5/12693, letter from Granovsky to Bistritsky 14.5.1942; CZA, KKL5/13892, letter from Mohilewer and Weiss to Talitman 31.7.1945, concerning involvement of private capital from Britain in the purchase of land; CZA, KKL5/13885, memorandum "Annulment of the JNF's Commitments Regarding Provision of Land Under the Plan for Involvement of Private Capital," 16.7.1945; S. Ben-Shemesh, personal interview, Jerusalem 7.4.1997; JNF Report (1947), p. 127. At the beginning of 1943, the Histadrut Agricultural Center endeavored to exert pressure on the JNF to allocate lands to supplement the farms in the Sharon, including those purchased under the plan for collaboration with private capital. The argument put forth by the Agricultural Center was that "These Jews [owners of the private capital] are still – or Heaven Forbid no longer alive – living in the Diaspora." Weitz rejected this request vehemently. On this see CZA, S53/1687, letter from Weitz to the Agricultural Center 24.1.1943. However, in reply to the lawyer of one of the investors who complained in 1945 that he had not yet received his specified plot, the JNF stated that "In accordance with the agreement between the investor and the JNF, the JNF would do its best, but it had not undertaken to provide the investors with 'parceled' plots if it were unable to do so." See on this CZA, KKL5/13892, Mohilewer and Weiss to Talitman 31.7.1945.
215   Howard (1970).
216   On the original idea of the Garden City and the great interest it aroused, see Katz (1986a), pp. 406–408; Howard (1970), pp. 343–346.

Under this plan, the JNF would grant to those contributing sums of no less than P£250 (to be paid in 7 annual installments) the option of receiving a 49 year lease on a plot of land 2.5 dunams in size which was intended for building a house and a small auxiliary farm. The JNF assumed responsibility for drafting plans for such settlements as well as linking them to main roads, and planting trees in suitable areas, but the expenses involved in site preparation and preparing the area for settlement would devolve on the contributors.[217] The small farm in the Garden Cities was not intended to support its owners, but was suitable for a vegetable garden and fruit trees which would provide the family's needs, and perhaps enable it to sell the surplus and enjoy an income in addition to their regular income. In some cases the farm was not intended to generate any income for its owners "and their entire work in the garden would be only a leisure activity and a source of spiritual satisfaction."[218] The contributor had to decide whether he intended to establish his house in the Garden City within 10 years from the time of his contribution. He also had the option of turning the house over to relatives or to rent it out. Aside from the attractiveness of the plan, it constituted a reliable source of income for the JNF, and as Vilkansky did not hesitate to emphasize at one of the Directorate's meetings "'in return' for a net 2.5 dunams valued at P£60, the contributor donates P£250 in a manner that leaves a profit of P£190 to the JNF."[219]

The JNF's Garden City plan was enthusiastically received in England and in Ireland. At the beginning of 1942, hundreds of families had already subscribed and at the end of 1943 it was reported that 1,115 families had joined the plan and had organized within the framework of regional and national associations affiliated in the majority to the Palestine Farm City

---

217   JNF Report (1947), pp. 128–129; CZA, KKL5/13860, letter to the Agricultural Research Station 24.11.1941; CZA, KKL5/512689, letter from Borochov to Epstein, E. Danin and Matrikin concerning the Honorary Committee of the Garden Cities on JNF land 15.2.1943; CZA, KKL5/13884, letter from JNF to Berlowitz 15.11.1943; CZA, KKL5/13870, First Garden City Limited, 15.1.1944.

218   CZA, KKL5/12689, in n. 217; CZA, files KKL5/13870, KKL5/13862, various publications on Garden Cities; JNF Report (1947), pp. 128–129.

219   CZA, KKL10, minutes of JNF Directorate meeting, 21.10.1941; CZA, KKL5/12688, "Discussion with Kollek on Garden Cities and the involvement of private capital," 1.2.1942; CZA, KKL5/13862, letter from Weiss and Mohilewer to Kaplan 25.10.1944.

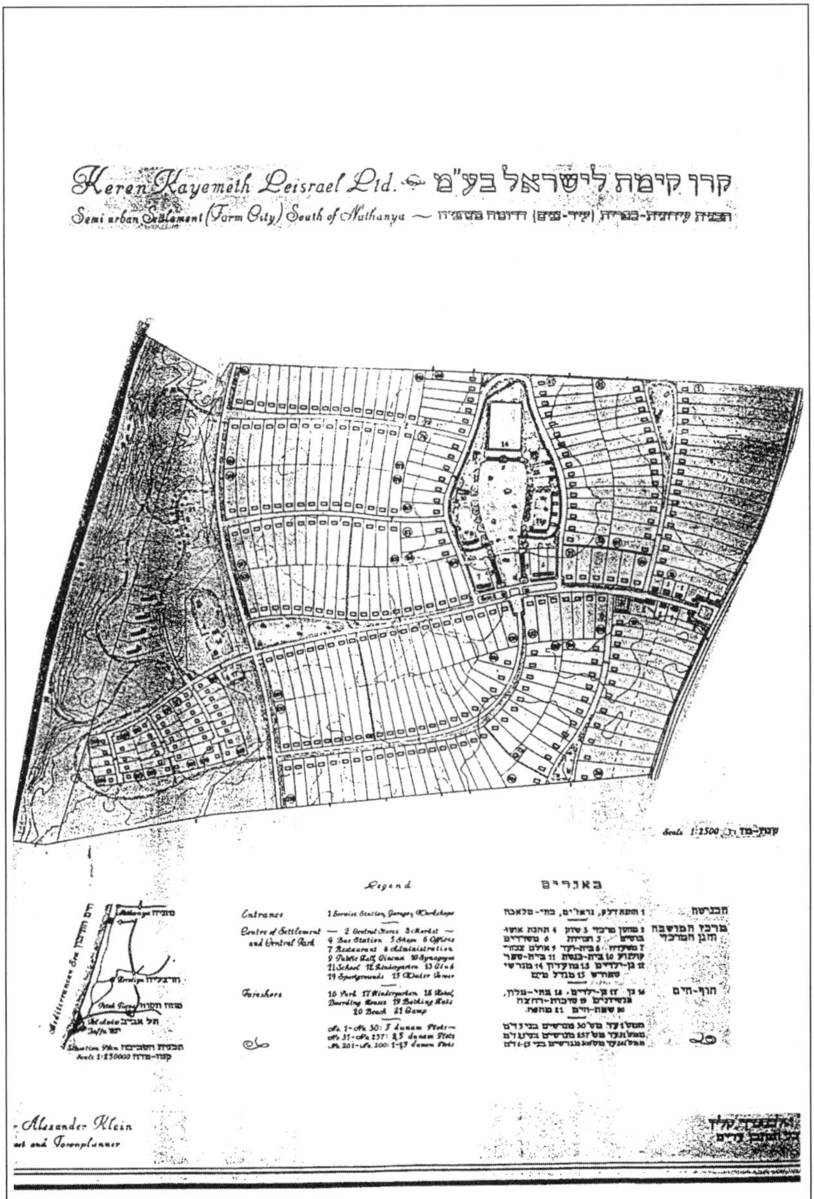

Map 21: "Garden City" plan, south of Nathanya
Source: KKL5/13860

Association Ltd. (hereafter PFCAL), headed by Fred Nettler, who in 1946 would chair the Committee for Urban Settlement at the 22nd Zionist Congress. Most of the subscribers came from London (310), Glasgow (170) and Manchester (166). The total area of plots ordered in the Garden Cities totaled 1,245 dunams at the end of 1944.[220] At the end of 1943, JNF income from the plan totaled P£145,000.[221] The program was a vast success in Britain despite the opposition of the local Keren Hayesod personnel who feared that "the matter could harm their interests," i.e., their fundraising activity.[222] Nonetheless, in the latter half of 1944, pursuant to clarifications of the military situation in Europe and the feeling that the end of the War was approaching, the interest in Britain of private individuals in the plan declined.[223] It is conceivable that the JNF also was no longer interested in another expansion of the plan, whether for the reasons that had brought to a halt the collaboration schemes with private capital, or due to the apprehension that confusion would be created between its fundamental goal of raising contributions and the commercial component implicit in the plan – even if the JNF sought not to view it in this manner.[224]

The JNF decided to allocate areas in five locations which it owned for the establishment of Garden Cities on the seacoast south of Nathanya (1973 dunams), on the seacoast north west of Kefar Vitkin (1970 dunams), east of the Moshava Even Yehuda (965 dunams), in the Zebulun Valley near

---

220   CZA, KKL5/12688, talk with Kollek concerning Garden Cities and collaboration with private capital 1.2.1942; CZA, KKL5/15571, Ir Ganim "C," no date; CZA, KKL5/ 12687, letter from Mohilewer to Granovsky 12.5.1943, concerning the collection of the agreements, lists and accounts of the Garden Cities; CZA, KKL5/13884, letter from Mohilewer to Berlowitz 15.11.1943; CZA, KKL5/13870, Extract from Report 3703 of the JNF for Great Britain and Ireland; CZA, KKL5/ 13862, letter from Weiss and Mohilewer to Kaplan 25.10.1944; see publications (n. 218 above); CZA, KKL5/ 11871, "Information circular," no date, but apparently 1942.

221   CZA, KKL5/13870, memorandum from Mohilewer "The Garden City plan," end of 1943.

222   CZA, KKL5/13860, letter from Mohilewer to Weitz, Borochov and Haezrahi 24.11. 1941 – quotation from there; CZA, KKL10, minutes of JNF Directorate meeting, 25.11.1941.

223   CZA, KKL5/13862, letter from Weiss to Granovsky 13.10.1944; JNF Report (1947), pp. 128–129.

224   This was implied in CZA, KKL5/15598, letter from Weiss and Mohilewer to JNF National Office in Buenos Aires 21.11.1946.

Kiryat Bialik (847 dunams), and near Beit She'arim (665 dunams).[225] The JNF began to examine programs for Garden Cities only at the beginning of 1943, and only then did it seek to clarify issues relating to the very essence of this entity. Were the Garden Cities to be independent urban units or would they rely on other cities? Were the places allocated for Garden Cities suitable for this purpose? Could the JNF's concept of Garden Cities be put into practice? From the deliberations it became clear that not all sites were suitable for this purpose. Furthermore, it emerged that in principle the cities would be independent units with all the required services. As a consequence, the JNF realized the need for a minimum total of 500 families in each city to create the requisite conditions for developing educational institutions, food markets and maintaining infrastructure on an economically feasible basis, without encumbering the residents. Other questions which arose concerned the date for starting development work in the Garden Cities. Would this be before or after the owners had immigrated to Palestine; are the lands at the various locations suitable to the types of gardens planned; what would be the income level derived from the gardens, etc.?[226]

Solutions were not found to all these issues, but in the beginning of 1944 the JNF entrusted the implementation of detailed planning for the Garden Cities to the architect Alexander Klein (see Maps 21–22).[227] At the same

---

225 See publications (n. 218 above); maps in CZA, KKL5/11789, KKL5/13867, KKL5/13860; Ir Ganim "C," no date; CZA, KKL5/12689, letter from Borochov to Epstein, Danin and Matrikin 15.2.1943; CZA, KKL5/13870, the following documents: "The Garden Cities Plan," end of 1943; data on the Garden Cities near Nathanya, near Even Yehuda, in the Zebulun Valley, near Kefar Vitkin, 22.2.1944; parceling of the plots in the Beit She'arim project, 1944. See also CZA, KKL5/13862, memorandum "Garden Cities: List of Areas and Plot Numbers," 2.11.1944, letter from Borochov to Klein 14.12.1944; CZA, KKL10, minutes of JNF Directorate meetings, 27.9.1943, 23.8.1944.

226 CZA, KKL5/12689, letter from Borochov to Epstein, E. Danin and Matrikin 15.2.1943; CZA, KKL5/12687, the following documents: summaries of meetings regarding Garden Cities 28.4.1943, "Opinion of the Honorary Committee Regarding Garden Cities," 7.4.1943, letter from Mohilewer to Borochov 24.6.1943.

227 CZA, KKL5/13870, the following documents: Data on Garden Cities near Nathanya, near Even Yehuda, in the Zebulun Valley, near Kefar Vitkin, 22.2.1944; parceling of the plots in the Beit She'arim project, 1944; letter from Klein to Borochov 28.2.1944. See also CZA, KKL10, minutes of JNF Directorate meeting, 23.8.1944; CZA, KKL5/13867, plans drawn up by A. Klein.

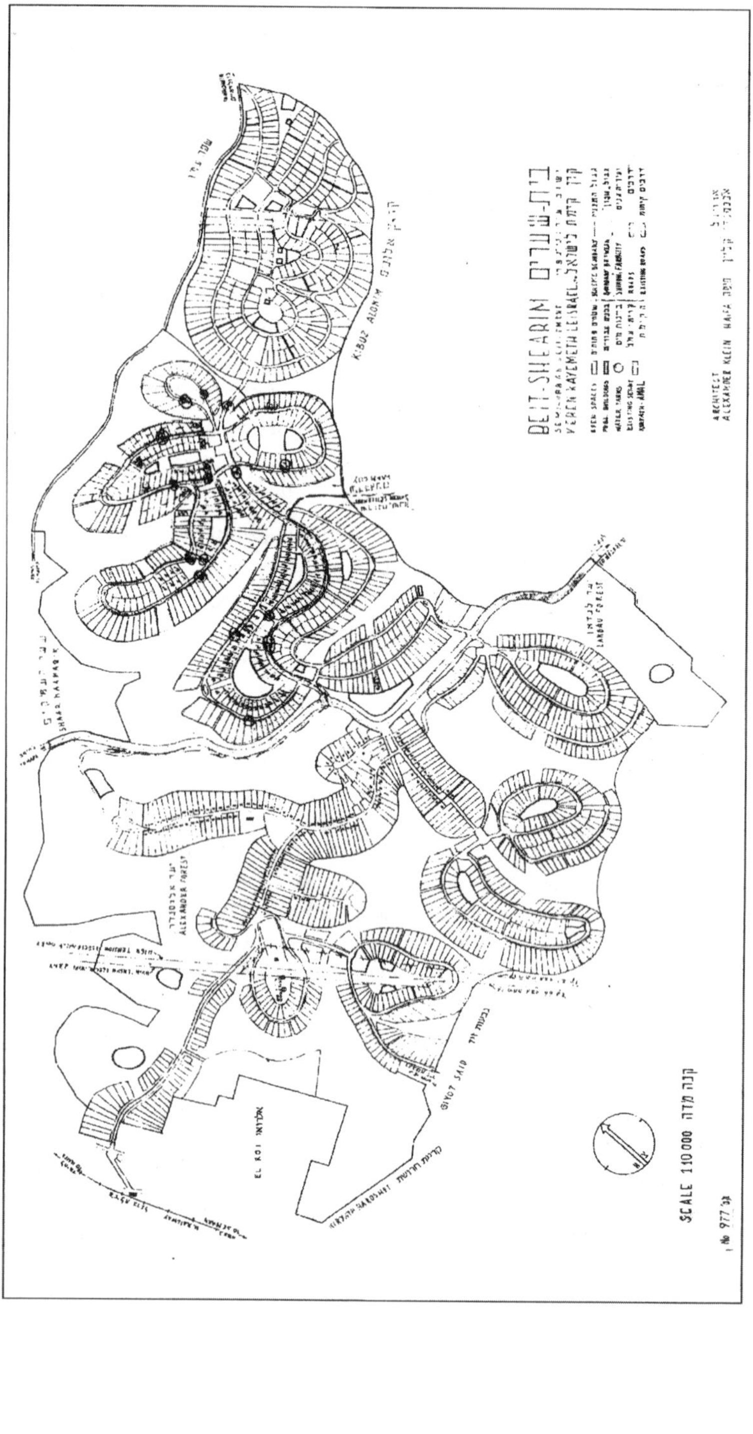

Map 22: Plan of "Garden City" in Beit She'arim (Tivon)
Source: JNF map archives, Map 226

time, the PFCAL began negotiations with the Rassco Company regarding the actual construction of the cities, negotiations that were concluded only in 1946.[228] Furthermore, it emerged that most participants in the program had not decided if they would actually immigrate and build their houses in the Garden Cities. "The activity in its entirety suffers from a lack of clarity. Not all the participants, especially those in the outlying towns, are aware of all the details involved in their contracts, and especially the obligations incumbent upon them. Furthermore, two companies – Farm City Association and the Company headed by Mr. Shen are conducting parallel activity which causes difficulty."[229] The JNF itself decided not to be directly involved in implementing the plans, because it feared the confusion that would be created in the public's mind regarding its goals and it could cause damage to gathering contributions. It only assisted in connecting the organizations in Britain with the construction companies in Palestine.[230] In fact, until the end of 1946, only the garden city of Beit She'arim reached the stage of completion and construction. In Beit She'arim, near Kiryat Amal, about 200 houses were erected up to the end of 1946, mostly by British Jews.[231]

228   CZA, KKL5/13867, letter from Mohilewer and Weiss to Ussishkin 17.4.1944; CZA, KKL5/13862, letter from Weiss and Mohilewer to Kaplan 25.10.1944; CZA, KKL5/15571, report by Foeder on his visit to Britain and Holland in May–June 1946, July 1946; CZA, KKL5/15598, letter from Mohilewer and Weiss to JNF National Committee in Buenos Aires 21.11.1946.

229   Leopold Shen was responsible for the circulation of the plan in Britain on behalf of JNF and he initiated the establishment there of the Keret Company whose purpose was similar to that of the PFCAL.

230   CZA, KKL5/13867, letter from Mohilewer and Weiss to S. Ussishkin 17.4.1944; CZA, KKL5/13862, letter from Weiss to Granovsky and Epstein 13.10.1944; CZA, KKL5/15571, report by Foeder on his visit to Britain and Holland in May–June 1946, July 1946 – quotation from there; CZA, KKL5/15598, letter from Mohilewer and Weiss to JNF National Committee in Buenos Aires 21.11.1946.

231   JNF Report (1947), pp. 58, 128–129; as in n. 224 above.

CHAPTER FOUR

From the End of the War and Toward the Establishment of the State of Israel, 1945–1948

Changes in the Composition of the Directorate and in Its Work Methods

As in previous years, the General Assembly of the Jewish National Fund Ltd. continued to serve as the JNF's supreme institution and in the years that preceded the establishment of the State continued to be no more than a formal body. The Assembly convened once a year at a time and place set by the Directorate, for the purpose of ratifying land purchases that had already been implemented, accepting the financial reports, and approving the members of the Directorate whose candidacy had already been predetermined by the Directorate and the Zionist General Council. No more than four to five members (out of nine) participated in the Assembly, and the last meeting prior to the establishment of the State of Israel took place at the end of December 1947.[1]

During this period, important changes took place in the composition and manner of functioning of the Directorate. This institution was entrusted with determining policy in the various spheres of JNF activity and retained the decision-making powers and responsibility for those activities. At the beginning of 1945, the Directorate was constituted of seven members: Avraham Granovsky, Rabbi Meyer Berlin, Shmuel Zuchovitzky, David Ben-Gurion, Zalman Schocken, Yitzhak Vilkansky and Shmuel Ussishkin. In April 1945 the Directorate decided to recommend to the Zionist General

---

1   CZA, KKL5/13979, proceedings of the JNF General Assembly, 21.10.1945; CZA, KKL5/22307, Report of the JNF Directorate to the General Assembly, 3.11.1946; CZA, KKL5/13979, proceedings of JNF General Assembly, 3.11.1946; CZA, KKL5/15905, proceedings of JNF General Assembly, 30.12.1947.

Council that it ratify the appointment of Avraham Hartzfeld and Avraham Kestenbaum as members of the Directorate replacing the deceased Berl Katznelson and Herman Stroock, but rejected the demand of the Hashomer Hatza'ir movement as well as of the South African Zionist Federation to appoint representatives on their behalf to the Directorate.[2] Formally it was agreed upon in the Directorate to turn down the demand of the aforementioned groups, because it involved the expansion of the Directorate from 9 to 11 members, "and this is not the time to discuss and decide upon the expansion in the number of Directorate members but we should wait until after the Zionist Congress."[3] However, in reality, opposition to the expansion of the Directorate was rooted in the vigorous opposition of Rabbi Berlin to allocating a seat on the Directorate to the Hashomer Hatza'ir movement. Shmuel Ussishkin also opposed the addition and thus expressed the position of his party, the General Zionists. Rabbi Berlin's opposition could not be ignored, not only because of his seniority in the Directorate, but primarily because of his status as rotating Chairman since the death of Menahem Ussishkin. His antagonism to the idea not only derived from Hashomer Hatza'ir's political stance, which ran counter to positions embraced by the majority in the World Zionist Movement, but primarily because of Hashomer Hatza'ir's position on religious affairs which represented an antithesis to that of Mizrachi and Hapoel Hamizrachi. Rabbi Berlin feared, on the one hand, that a Hashomer Hatza'ir representative could influence the JNF policy shift regarding Sabbath observance in the settlements that were established on its land, while on the other hand, the very addition of a place for Hashomer Hatza'ir would lead to a removal of religious Jewish support for the JNF.[4]

Hashomer Hatza'ir was determined to demand that the Zionist General Council immediately elect a representative on its behalf to the Directorate, and to this end it applied strong pressures on the WZO. These pressures had their effect, and while in mid-May 1945 the Jewish Agency Executive was also prepared to submit to the Smaller Zionist General Council, a recommendation in the spirit of the decisions taken by the JNF's Directorate,

---

2   See above, p. 150.
3   CZA, KKL10, minutes of JNF Directorate meeting, 24.4.1945.
4   Ibid., 31.5.1945, 10.7.1945.

i.e., to postpone expanding the Directorate for the time being, and to suffice with the addition of Avraham Kestenbaum and Avraham Hartzfeld, at the end of that month, Moshe Shertok, who was at that time Acting Jewish Agency Chairman, had already clarified to Granovsky that the Executive could not oppose the addition of Hashomer Hatza'ir. It was evident to the Executive that a discussion in the Zionist General Council confirming the addition of Hartzfeld and Kestenbaum would necessarily have to deal with Hashomer Hatza'ir's request and with the expansion of the Directorate. Nonetheless, Granovsky and Shertok agreed that if Hashomer Hatza'ir would be added, it would be balanced by a representative of the South African Zionist Federation, and this would also constitute a response to the latter's demand.[5] Granovsky had no recourse save to assent to the expansion of the Directorate in such a manner. It was clear to him "that it was an illusion that the Hashomer Hatza'ir movement could be excluded from the World Zionist Organization"[6] and that their demand for a representative on the Directorate would be authorized by the Zionist General Council. Granovsky strongly feared the repercussions of anti-JNF activity on the part of Hashomer Hatza'ir, if the JNF openly opposed their addition. It appears that he recalled the words of his fellow Directorate member, Shmuel Zuchovitzky, when he contended: "Is it possible that we should be the authors of a major act of schism and exclude Hashomer Hatza'ir? Hashomer Hatza'ir also is on the presidium of the Zionist General Council."

A delay in the discussion in the Zionist General Council regarding all the personnel changes in the JNF Directorate (including appointments in place of the deceased) was also problematic, because only four to five members were active, and it was not feasible to postpone deliberation on the issue of appointments till autumn because Granovsky would be overseas at that time. Nonetheless, given the vigorous opposition by Rabbi Berlin, seconded by Shmuel Ussishkin's opposition, Granovsky preferred recommending to the Directorate that it support a resolution under which, while not backing down on its previous decision the Directorate would accept without opposition a decision by the Zionist General Council, as long as a balance would be preserved in the expansion of the Directorate.

---

5   CZA, KKL10, ibid., minutes of the Jewish Agency Executive meeting, 17.5.1945 and
    minutes of JNF Directorate meeting, 31.5.1945.
6   Ibid., minutes of JNF Directorate meeting, 31.5.1945.

It would appear that both Rabbi Berlin and Ussishkin realized that an expansion centering upon the introduction of a Hashomer Hatza'ir representative was unavoidable, especially as they themselves did not dispute the major role which this movement had played in furthering the Zionist settlement projects and volunteering for pioneering activity. It is equally logical to assume that they sought to operate behind the scenes in an attempt to change the "evil decree" or to allay their suspicions regarding the repercussions of Hashomer Hatza'ir's entry into the Directorate. This was the apparent reason behind the Directorate's decision to seek a delay on a decision on this issue in the Zionist General Council, but for a period that would not exceed one month.[7]

In the latter half of June 1945, the Smaller Zionist General Council ratified the addition of Avraham Kestenbaum and Avraham Hartzfeld to the JNF Directorate and decided on two members – Yaakov Hazan of Hashomer Hatza'ir and Yosef Yanover of the South African Zionist Federation, who had recently immigrated to Palestine.[8] Members of the Smaller Zionist General found it difficult to accept the objection to Hashomer Hatza'ir's participation in the Directorate. "It runs counter to our tradition and to the structure of the Zionist movement to deny representation to a Zionist party because of its views," emphasized Moshe Sneh, the chairman of the Zionist General Council, especially as nobody disputed the pioneering role of Hashomer Hatza'ir and its vast contribution in the area of settlement. It was difficult to withstand the argument of Hashomer Hatza'ir's leader, Meir Ya'ari, in the Zionist General Council regarding the right of his movement to representation on the Directorate in proportion to its representation in settlement praxis. This was especially true given his clarification "we have agreed to the constitutional framework which enjoins Sabbath observance without coercion." S. Z. Rubashov upbraided Mizrachi for its objection to the addition of Hashomer Hatza'ir which ran counter to its tradition, since "the Mizrachi never rejected cooperation with other parties within the World Zionist Organization whose opinions on national, religious and Zionist thought were the opposite to its own." With 17 members of the Smaller Zionist General Council in favor and only one opposed, a

---

7   Ibid. – quotation from Zuchovitsky from there, and ibid., 10.7.1945.
8   CZA, KKL5/13979, list of members of the JNF Directorate during 1940–1946, 5.5.1946.

resolution was passed to expand the Directorate and approve the addition of the aforementioned persons.[9]

The four new members, who joined the seven veteran members, were well versed in JNF activity and its work methods. Hartzfeld headed the Histadrut's Agricultural Center, Kestenbaum was a member of the Hapoel Hamizrachi Executive Committee and worked alongside Michael Hazani in managing the agricultural center of this movement. Ya'akov Hazan headed the Hashomer Hatza'ir movement together with Meir Ya'ari, whereas Yanover was an active Zionist in South Africa deeply involved in promoting the JNF's work.[10] It should be noted that the agricultural settlement movement was represented by three members on the Directorate, of whom two were members of the Kibbutz Moshav movement which belonged to the framework of the Histadrut[11]

At the beginning of July 1945, the first meeting of the Directorate took place with the four new members in attendance. This was also the first meeting where all members of the Directorate, except Ben-Gurion and Schocken, were present and in this fashion the new members constituted almost half of participants there (4 out of 9). It is not by chance that Granovsky saw fit to emphasize both in his greetings at that meeting and in his summation the obligation of the JNF and its Directorate members to the lease agreement with the settlers which spoke inter alia about the commitment "to observe the Sabbath and Jewish festivals by abstaining from any construction activity, work in the fields and vineyards, and trade and industry projects." Hazan in response emphasized the support of his movement for the Zionist Congress' resolution regarding the observance of the Sabbath and Festivals on JNF land: "and...we will all remain steadfast and united behind this decision." Rabbi Berlin restated the obligation of Sabbath observance on JNF lands and the need to find ways to enforce these by-laws, and alluded to his opposition for this reason to

---

9   CZA, KKL10, proceedings of Smaller Zionist General Council session, 19.6.1945.

10   Ibid., minutes of JNF Directorate meeting, 10.7.1945; CZA, KKL5/12830, letter from Granovsky to the Histadrut 26.6.1945; Tzahor (1997), *Encyclopedia of Religious Zionism*, V, pp. 481–484.

11   On the expectations of the Histadrut's Agricultural Center following upon the addition of Hartzfeld and Hazan to the JNF Directorate, see, e.g., *Agricultural Center Bulletin*, Nov. 1945, pp. 9–15; also CZA, KKL5/12830, letter from Granovsky to the Histadrut 26.6.1945.

Ya'akov Hazan

adding a representative of Hashomer Hatza'ir to the JNF Directorate. He emphasized: "that [Menachem] Ussishkin as well as Berl Katznelson of blessed memory, were filled with apprehension over the libertinism which exists in JNF settlements regarding the Sabbath. I would be happy if all the members here would be permeated with that same apprehension for the sanctity of the Sabbath which the late blessed Katznelson felt in his heart." However, after he heard the words of Hazan, Berlin unhesitatingly announced: "If Hazan agrees to the Congress' resolution and wants to assist in its realization, it makes no difference what is the ideological platform underlying that assistance. It is practice which unites all of us and therefore, I am happy that we should have another supporter and another person who can stir the hearts, and another guardian who will stand watch over our principles and activities."[12]

Up to the establishment of the State of Israel, no changes ensued in the composition of the Directorate, save for the retirement at the end of 1947 of Zalman Schocken, due to health reasons. His place as Director-

12　CZA, KKL10, minutes of JNF Directorate meeting, 10.7.1945.

Governor was taken by Daniel Auster, who during the 1930s served as the Deputy Mayor of Jerusalem and in the mid-1940s served as a permanent replacement to the Mayor and as acting Mayor.[13] Both Schocken and Ben-Gurion, two Governors on the Directorate, hardly ever participated in Directorate meetings from the time the new members joined it. It a logical assumption that Ben-Gurion's manifold political involvements and his frequent travels abroad during that year, made his participation in meetings of the Directorate difficult.[14]

Immediately following the task of renewing the composition of the Directorate, the matter of selecting a permanent chairman arose. After the death of Menachem Ussishkin an executive framework was established, but now it was decided not to elect a chairman. Members of the executive (Katznelson, Granovsky and Berlin) chaired the meetings of the Directorate on a rotating basis. The executive framework functioned in an orderly fashion for no more than one year, although formally it was never rescinded and the principle of rotation in chairing meetings was preserved. Due to the illness and death of Katznelson and the absence of Berlin, either because of his trips to America or because of his prolonged illness, Granovsky was the guiding spirit in managing the affairs of the Directorate. He chaired most of the sessions in 1941–1945,[15] and was the natural candidate for the post of Chairman. Berlin who had chaired the meeting of the Directorate in mid-June 1945, where the matter of choosing a chairman arose for the first time on the agenda, believed that Granovsky was the most suitable and natural candidate for the job, but sought to postpone the decision until after the Zionist Conference had convened in London in December 1945. He had two reasons for delaying the decision: Firstly to allow discussion on the candidacy within the various Zionist institutions and perhaps also at the London Conference, because in his opinion "the public won't understand how the Directorate itself was choosing a replacement for Ussishkin. The Zionist public believes that this is a matter for the entire movement. In this fashion Granovsky's candidacy would win broad Zionist support, which

---

13 Ibid., 7.10.1947, 18.2.1948; CZA, KKL5/15905, proceedings of JNF General Assembly session, 30.12.1947; D. Tidhar, *Encyclopedia of Pioneering Settlers* I, pp. 165–166.

14 See, e.g., CZA, KKL10, minutes of JNF Directorate meeting 15.10.1946.

15 See above, p. 147; see also CZA, KKL10, minutes of JNF Directorate meeting, 13.7.1945.

was of importance for the JNF's continued activity. Secondly, he feared, and there were grounds for this suspicion,[16] that at the London Conference the Executive of the World Zionist Organization would apply pressures on the JNF, thus impairing the JNF's independence. He believed that if the JNF would appear at the Conference without a chairman, this would complicate matters for those planning to constrain the JNF's independence because they would have to deal with a large number of Directorate members and not only with the chairman. However, from a subsequent expression by Rabbi Berlin,[17] it emerges that he was possibly interested in postponing the decision not only for the aforementioned reasons but also to hint to Granovsky that he was in fact dependent on the Directorate and in order to prevent him excessive dominance as had been the case during the period of Ussishkin's chairmanship.[18] In any case, Granovsky disagreed with Rabbi Berlin and believed that the matter of electing a chairman was a matter for the Directorate alone (as mandated by the by-laws) which should be concluded immediately and even before the London Conference. He believed that the very absence of a permanent chairman played into the hands of those who wanted to strike at the JNF's independence, and he suspected that "one of these days they will honor us with a candidate for the post of chairman with any Jew whom they wanted to get rid of from some other place."[19] The other members of the Directorate also believed that the decision should be made within the Directorate, and any attempt to take it to London to "graft a head upon us, should be forestalled." Nonetheless, they contended that the election be postponed until after the London Conference in order to obtain broad support for the candidacy in the parties whose members were represented on the Directorate. In the event, the decision of the Directorate was to elect the chairman immediately following the London Conference.[20]

In September 1945, exactly four years after Ussishkin's death, the Directorate elected Granovsky to the post of Chairman. He was the sole candidate and his election was ratified unanimously. Nonetheless, to

---

16   Ibid – quotation from there.
17   See below.
18   See above, p. 144.
19   CZA, KKL10, minutes of JNF Directorate meeting, 13.7.1945.
20   Ibid., 13.7.1945 – quotation from the statement of Hartzfeld.

Granovsky's displeasure, the Directorate limited his term to only one year. It can be assumed that the common suspicion of all seven Directorate members present at the meeting where Granovsky was elected, was that their power would be weakened and this is what motivated them to limit the term of office. It was not by chance that Rabbi Berlin chose to emphasize the following in his summation of the discussion preceding the vote: "Let us hope that this chairmanship will not lead to excessive absolutism as was the case with the deceased Menachem Ussishkin, who overstepped the bounds without anyone restraining him."[21] A year and a half later, in February 1947, the Directorate renewed its choice of Granovsky for a period till after the following Congress.[22] In the period of Granovsy's absence from the country, Rabbi Berlin was to serve as his deputy.[23]

Upon his election as Chairman, Granovsky sought to introduce changes in the work of the Directorate with a view toward involving more members of the Directorate in practical matters, but without causing any impairment in the decision-making powers and the delineation of policy by the Directorate itself or restricting the Executive's power of implementation. He suggested establishing five permanent directorial committees and two ad hoc ones that would function as quasi-advisory committees and that would bring to the Directorate plenum their recommendations on the subjects with which they were entrusted. The permanent committees would deal with general land policy (the "objectives committee" whose members were Berlin, Hartzfeld, and Vilkansky); the issues of urban housing ("the committee for urban housing"); issues of agricultural housing (the committee for rural housing); the issues of propaganda and organization (the committee of organization and propaganda) and ensuring that contracts were honored (by the committee for ensuring implementation of contracts). The ad hoc committees were intended to deal with various budgetary issues within the general range of JNF activity, and they were to convene prior to the annual budgetary deliberations. These proposals made by Granovsky were possibly connected to agreements made previously with members of the Directorate with a view to pacifying them and allaying their fears of being neutralized. The Directorate ratified the Chairman's proposals and the

---

21   Ibid., 18.9.1946
22   Ibid., 12.11.1946, 4.2.1947.
23   Ibid., 29.10.1945, 12.11.1946, 27.5.1947.

committees were established. The Chairman of the Directorate by token of his post, as well as the Director or senior personnel of the appropriate departments, participated in the committee's sessions.[24] Until the conclusion of the period covered by this book, these committees remained in force.[25]

The powers of decision, responsibility and policy determination in all spheres of JNF activity, remained as before, in the hands of the Directorate which generally met once a month. The Directorate deliberated upon and ratified the annual framework plan for purchases that were presented to it by Weitz at the beginning of each year. But every single purchase whose possible implementation became relevant was to be submitted by the Executive to the Directorate for discussion and authorization. On this matter, Granovsky for example, emphasized when the Directorate deliberated on the purchase plan for the year 1945–1946: "the [annual] plan demonstrates what the territorial options would be should the resources become available. Upon authorization of the plan, we do not authorize in advance every purchase. Every specific purchase proposal will be submitted to the Directorate for a detailed deliberation in order for a decision to be taken."[26] Regarding the purchase plan presented to the Directorate in 1946–1947, the Directorate decided that "the aforesaid plan is only a 'framework' for the JNF's territorial activities in the present year and within its limit the JNF Executive can act in accordance with the needs of time and place. However, every purchase proposal whose implementation is in the offing should be brought in advance to the Directorate for detailed deliberation and a definitive decision."[27]

Increase in JNF Income, the Threat to Its Independence and Its Response to the Financial Demands of the Jewish Agency

The trend of a progressive increase in JNF income explained in Chapter Three continued with greater force in the period covered by the present

---

24 Ibid., 18.9.1945, 2.10.1945; CZA, S44/230, letter from Aricha to Ben-Gurion 18.11.1947.
25 CZA, KKL10, minutes of JNF Directorate meetings, 7.10.1947, 11.11.1947, 18.2.1948.
26 Ibid., 29.10.1945.
27 Ibid., 12.11.1946.

chapter. In 1946, income totaled P£3.3 million – more than P£1 million over the previous year.[28] In the first half of 1947, income totaled P£2.1 million, an increase of 60% as compared to income in the parallel period in the previous year, and the estimate in 1947 was that total anticipated income for the year 1947 would reach P£5 million (see Appendix 9). The increase in income for the first half of 1947 merited special emphasis in the Directorate, which in its decisions noted "with great satisfaction the huge increase in JNF income during the first half of the current year (1946–1947) in general, and as opposed to the first half of the previous year."[29] It is not clear what the total JNF income was for the entire year of 1947, but from one of the reports presented to the Directorate at the beginning of 1948, it emerges that from contributions alone about P£1.2 million entered the JNF's treasury in the period between October–December 1947. The increase in contributions continued also in the first half of 1948, although their exact amount is not clear.[30]

The increase in income stemmed primarily from contributions of various sorts (including life bequests), first and foremost from the United States where a widespread and active JNF fund-raising apparatus had developed. "'Its net is cast' throughout all corners of the United States. All political organizations are involved in it and it has thousands of volunteer functionaries. Heading the departments of the apparatus in the New York central office are devoted and loyal appointees and it is headed by a devoted chairman who is respected by the American public." Representatives of the Head Office in Jerusalem including members of the Directorate, made many visits to the United States in order to enhance the collection of contributions. Without the artificial ceiling for the JNF's total independent income set for the JNF by the United Jewish Appeal in the United States at $1.8 million, the JNF estimated that it could raise still greater sums. Yisrael Rokach, Mayor of Tel Aviv, who together with Avraham Hartzfeld visited the United States at the beginning of 1948 on a JNF mission, emphasized in summing up his visit the vast fund-raising potential for the JNF in the

---

28 JNF (1947), p. 77; CZA, KKL10, minutes of JNF Directorate meetings, 29.1.1946, 23.7.1946; Report WZO (1946), pp. 374–375 – quotation from Granovsky's statement.

29 CZA, KKL10, minutes of JNF Directorate meeting, 29.4.1947.

30 Ibid., 16.3.1948. In his report to the Directorate, Granovsky stated only that: "in the JNF's income there has been an increase in the second quarter of 1948 as well."

The "Blue Boxes" from Various Periods

United States. He added: "American Jewry has not yet made a major effort that would enable the Land of Israel and the Jewish community there the opportunity to stand fast."[31] At this time, there was an increase in JNF income also in Canada, South America (especially in Argentina), South Africa, Australia and Western Europe. The JNF's emissaries and its leaders visited these places and worked on an intensive basis to increase the volume of contributions. In Palestine as well, the volume of income rose appreciably, both from contributions and from leasing fees.[32]

In order to augment its resources, the JNF continued to raise long-term credit, especially through the issuing of bonds and by encouraging provident funds to invest their monies in the JNF. Generally, the JNF undertook obligations to repay within no less than 10 years and at an interest of at most 4% per annum. In 1946 the JNF agreed to receive from the provident funds short-term deposits for one year, on condition that these would not

31 Ibid., 16.3.1948 – all quotations from there.
32 Ibid., 10.7.1945, 7.10.1947, 3.2.1948; CZA, KKL5/15568, summary of the meeting held on 5.5.1946 in JNF Head Office with the participation of Granovsky, Cohen, Weiss, Mohilewer and Konikow; Schenkolewski (1996), pp. 198–203.

exceed more than one quarter of the volume of deposits. Furthermore, the JNF raised loans from banks and from private individuals abroad and in Palestine, and reached various agreements with the insurance companies.[33] The JNF made special efforts, some of which met with success, with the British authorities and the local banks that would allow it access to the deposits in Palestine of European Jews who were defined in the wake of the Holocaust as missing.[34] These accounts had been blocked since the Second World War by the Custodian of Enemy Property or by the Supervisor of Foreign Currency. The intention was to receive these monies as long-term loans.

On the other hand, as noted above, collaboration with private capital in land purchases ceased and the "Garden Cities" plan was also in decline. During this period, the JNF's professional administration, which controlled the financial system, developed rapidly. This made an important contribution toward developing plans for obtaining resources and ways for investing them. Especially worthy of mention was the work of Dr. Yosef Weiss as well as Dr. Adiya Konikow, director of the JNF Finance Department. The fact that Granovsky, who for years had served as the JNF's financial administrator now headed the Directorate, most likely contributed to the upgrading and professionalization of the Finance Department.[35] In any event, the JNF enjoyed vast confidence in among World Jewry as a financial institution as well as a charitable cause, and by the use of various methods this led to an increase in the number of depositors and the volume of deposits.[36]

Proof of the appreciable increase in the JNF's income and in its financial resources in general, can be adduced from its engagement from 1947 in collaboration with the Municipality of Tel Aviv in the purchase of the German Colony Sharona (see in detail below). In this purchase project which Granovsky termed "a land project without prior precedent in the

33 JNF (1947), pp. 122–126; CZA, KKL10, minutes of JNF Directorate meeting, 10.7.1945; CZA, KKL5/15568, summary of the meeting.
34 Ibid.; CZA, KKL5/14320, letter from JNF Department of Special Projects to JNF Head Office 3.9.1947.
35 CZA, KKL5/15568, summary of the meeting; Adiya Konikow, personal interview with S. Ben-Shemesh and G. Alexander, Jerusalem 16.10.1992.
36 JNF Report (1947), p. 126; CZA, KKL10, minutes of the meeting of the JNF Directorate held on 15.4.1948.

JNF's history and I believe in the entire history of Palestine," the JNF and the Tel Aviv Municipality agreed to purchase about 4,400 dunams out of the total 7,000 dunams of the entire German Colony. The amount required for this purchase totaled P£2.1 million of which the JNF undertook to cover P£1.16 million (!). In the end result, the joint JNF–Tel Aviv Municipality purchases in Sharona increased to a total of 6,000 dunams, with the JNF's share in the purchase amounting to P£2.117 million (!).[37] Furthermore, during this period, the JNF transferred to the Jewish Agency special allocations not directly connected with the purchase of land or to settlement activity. The JNF served as a guarantor to the Jewish Agency for very expensive loans which the latter assumed and which were related to the special efforts necessitated upon the eve of the establishment of the State of Israel. The JNF contributed substantial sums toward financing the vast majority of the Negev Project, and also took a substantial share in financing the security needs of the Jewish community in general on the eve of the establishment of the State.[38]

It was precisely, however, the increase in JNF income and its financial resources in general which prompted unprecedented Jewish Agency pressure on the JNF for a "share of the pie." This share was needed by the Jewish Agency as a result of the financial exigencies which arose during

37 CZA, L51/2669, letter from Granovsky to Bart 1.6.1948; CZA, KKL10, minutes of JNF Directorate meeting, 4.2.1947 and see below for further details.
38 CZA, KKL10, minutes of JNF Directorate meeting, 1.4.1947 on the Directorate's decision to participate to the extent of a half million dollars of the United Jewish Appeal to cover the costs of the Jewish delegation to the United Nations session that was to pass a resolution on the future of Palestine; idem, minutes of Jewish Agency Executive meeting, 29.8.1947 regarding JNF participation in the security budget; idem, minutes of JNF Directorate meetings, 29.7.1947, 18.2.1948, 16.3.1948; Report WZO (1951), p. 595 concerning the Negev Project and participation in the security budget of the Jewish community in Palestine; CZA, KKL10, minutes of JNF Directorate meeting, 16.3.1948, at which Ben-Gurion stated that "The Executive [of the Jewish Agency] is unable to undertake not to approach the JNF for an amount above P£2.3 million." The minutes show that the Directorate approved JNF participation in the Negev Project in the amount of P£2.65 million; idem, minutes of JNF Directorate meetings, 3.2.1948, 16.3.1948, 18.3.1948 concerning the lien of P£1.25 million of JNF monies from the United Jewish Appeal as a guarantee for a Jewish Agency loan in the United States; ibid., 15.4.1948 concerning a JNF guarantee for half the Jewish Agency loan in the amount of P£5 million.

the years preceding the establishment of the State of Israel. The Jewish Agency sought to formally anchor its right to this share through resolutions adopted in the institutions of the World Zionist Organization – decisions which would subordinate the JNF to the Jewish Agency bodies in everything that related to the expenditure and employment of JNF monies. The JNF was thus confronted with a severe threat to its independence, as since its establishment it was exclusively responsible for both its fundraising and expenditure. Furthermore, the JNF's primary purpose – the purchase of lands – also was now threatened.

On the eve of the Zionist Conference in London in December 1945, news reached the JNF to the effect that the Jewish Agency Treasurer, Eliezer Kaplan, planned to submit to the Conference resolutions in the spirit mentioned above which would undermine the JNF's independence. This information also provided the background to deliberations in the Directorate, in mid-July of that year, regarding the election of a Chairman and the date for his appointment.[39] They provoked an angry response in the Directorate. Granovsky noted that

> For some time now, Mr. Kaplan has cast a covetous eye on the JNF's development and growth. For understandable reasons he is an ardent supporter of the Keren Hayesod which allocates to him as the Treasurer of the Jewish Agency the financial resources. He plans to increase them [the financial resources] by putting the income of both funds, per his proposal, into one pot. The United Jewish Appeal has to exist as a permanent institution, and the division of monies will be carried out by the institutions, and they would like to prohibit any special activity of the funds. I am not certain that the matter will be placed on the agenda of the London Conference, but we must be prepared for any difficult eventuality.... It is important that we should stand guard and be prepared for tactics to defend the JNF's rights.

Indeed, the Directorate adopted an unambiguous resolution "to do everything to preserve the JNF's complete autonomy in its activities and in the management of its affairs."[40] In an emotional letter to Ben-Gurion,

---

39 See above, p. 259.
40 CZA, KKL10, minutes of JNF Directorate meeting, 13.7.1945 – quotation from there.

Eliezer Kaplan

immediately after the session of the Directorate in July 1945, Granovsky expressed his apprehensions regarding Kaplan's intentions and beseeched Ben-Gurion to prevent such action. Granovsky wrote as follows:

> Information has reached us from the United States that Kaplan presumably intends to table before the Zionist Conference in London, proposals which can be to the detriment of the JNF. We don't know the exact content of these proposals, for Kaplan did not find it necessary to inform us of their content. However, the little we have heard from Judge M. Routtenberg in New York, suffices to arouse grave apprehension. It emerges that what we are confronting is a repetition of the previous attempt to curtail the JNF's independence by subordinating it to the supervision of another body which can also decide on the use of JNF monies. In the 43 years of its existence, the JNF Directorate has decided on its activities – whether in raising monies or expending them for redeeming the land and other activities. The efficiency of this principle has been totally demonstrated by the major achievements recorded by the JNF in these two spheres of activity. Any diminution of the JNF's authority – be it by merger with

other bodies, or by its subordination to other authorities, will restrain its activities and growth potential. It will weaken the hands of scores of functionaries the world over, slacken their energy and enthusiasm by dint of which the JNF has attained what it has achieved up till now. At the last session of the Directorate which took place in Jerusalem, with participation of all its members in the country – all those present expressed their apprehension regarding the JNF's fate in light of the renewed attempt to undermine its integrity and independence. It was resolved to object to these proposals with all possible force, not only for the JNF's sake but for the sake of the Zionist Movement as a whole whose activities are crucially dependent on the JNF's redemption of the land. I have been requested to convey these apprehensions to your knowledge in the name of all members of the Directorate and request that you take a stand and guarantee that these aforementioned proposals should be stricken from the agenda. Let it be emphasized that we have not received any formal notification regarding the intention to raise these proposals for discussion, but it is possible that they will be raised at the London Conference without prior notification. The Directorate hopes and is certain that you will favorably accede to its request.[41]

In the end result, a formal change in the JNF's status and independence did not occur during the period of our discussion. Nonetheless, it was subjected to heavy pressures on the part of the Jewish Agency not only to increase its share in funding settlement activities, (the JNF had previously been dragged in as a result of Jewish Agency pressures) but also to earmark substantial funds for purposes to which it had not allocated funds in the past. These purposes included security needs, and the guarantee of substantial loans subscribed to by the Jewish Agency, purposes which digressed from the JNF's principal goal – the purchase of lands. The closer the date for the establishment of the Jewish State approached, and the security situation deteriorated, pressures on the JNF were intensified. In mid-March 1948,

---

41   CZA, KKL5/12759, letter from Granovky to Ben-Gurion in London 17.7.1945; CZA, A107/834, letter from Epstein of the JNF to Ruppin 10.5.1942. See also Granovsky's statement regarding the need to defend the independence of the JNF and to prevent any restriction of the possibility of obtaining contributions in various countries, in his address to the 22nd Zionist Congress in 1946, Congress (1947), pp. 374–375.

Ben-Gurion made it plain to the Directorate in one of the few meetings in which he participated in the period covered by this chapter, that the JNF would have to share in every financial burden that would be required, such as extending guarantees to large financial loans which the Jewish Agency assumed.[42] In addition, the Jewish Agency by-passed the JNF and brought a resolution before the Zionist General Council without the JNF's knowledge to allocate specific sums from the United Jewish Appeal in the United States before they were divided between the funds.[43]

The JNF was aware that it had to shoulder its share of the financial burden in funding the special needs which confronted the Jewish Agency at the end of the Mandate and upon the eve of the State's establishment. But it was also aware that these expenditures would come at the expense of its options to purchase land, and as Granovsky emphasized in his address before the delegates to the 22nd Zionist Congress at the end of 1946:

> We can't ignore the fact that any sum of JNF monies that is expended on settlement activities of necessity constricts the resources that were intended for the purpose for which the JNF was founded – the redemption of the land. We must re-emphasize here that any attempt to increase the JNF's expenses for activities which are outside its purview, or to reduce through all sorts of arrangements its income quota in the United States, signifies constricting the possibilities for redeeming lands.[44]

Therefore the JNF tried to curb the pressures to the extent possible, but while gritting its teeth and protesting the very pressures themselves – the impairment in practice of its independence, the imperilment of its economic existence and its diversion from the JNF's primary objectives to purchase lands – it was forced to give in.[45] As stated above, it could not be oblivious to the exigencies of the time:

> The JNF's Directorate recognized the pressing necessity to assist the war effort of the Jewish people in the Land of Israel. Cognizant of

42 CZA, KKL10, minutes of JNF Directorate meeting 29.8.1947; ibid., 1.4.1947, 29.7.1947, 3.2.1948, 18.2.1948, 16.3.1948, 15.4.1948.
43 Ibid., 11.6.1946.
44 Congress (1947), p. 375.
45 See in detail, CZA, KKL10, minutes of JNF Directorate meetings, 12.11.1946, 4.2.1947, 3.2.1948, 18.2.1948, 16.3.1948.

this, the Directorate is willing to impose on the JNF special tasks
connected to security needs and which also include activities of
economic and settlement benefit in the present hour and in the future,
whereby their fulfillment by the JNF would alleviate the burden of
the war effort on the Jewish Agency and would free certain financial
resources for the defense system.[46]

Nonetheless, it would appear that the JNF realized that if it "persisted in
its refusal" it would bring upon itself those very same formal measures by
the Jewish Agency which could have annulled the JNF's independence.
Therefore, the JNF decided to consent to the Jewish Agency's demand[47]
and accept de facto the ideological solution which Ben-Gurion offered it
–"the JNF's task doesn't alter, but it responds to the needs of the hour in
a manner which will not impair its principles."[48] Furthermore, it emerges
that also from the perspective of public relations and fund-raising activity
abroad, it was worthwhile for the JNF to demonstrate that it too was enlisting
in the overall Zionist settlement needs of the hour and undertaking special
projects:

> The JNF's work [in raising contributions] has been shunted aside
> due to the security problems which preoccupy World Jewry first
> and foremost. It is difficult to demand precedence for JNF activity
> at a time the campaign is taking place, when every Jew be he in the
> Diaspora or Palestine, realizes that the fate of the entire Zionist project
> is dependent on the results of the struggle. Therefore, it would greatly
> facilitate the public relations activity and the JNF's fundraising if we
> can point to an important security area, such as the conquest of the
> Negev which would be under the JNF's responsibility.[49]

Indeed the "Negev Project" for the consolidation and expansion of the
settlement projects in the Negev and its security reinforcement which the
JNF financed in the sum of P£2.3 million (!) – a sum which constituted

---

46   Ibid., 18.2.1948.
47   This is hinted at in ibid., 16.3.1948.
48   Ibid.
49   CZA, KKL5/17143, memorandum signed by Czernowitz on 13.2.1948 concerning
     "The change in the extent of the JNF's task in light of the situation" – quotation from
     there.

the major part of the required budget was the center piece of the special projects in which the Jewish Agency enlisted the JNF on the eve of the establishment of the State of Israel. Substantial sums were included not only for settlement needs but also for security needs, supply, creating a transport infrastructure, etc. It should be noted that beyond the necessity for undertaking the project, given the reasons detailed above, as well as the JNF's hope that its response would forestall additional financial demands by the Jewish Agency for needs that were remote from its spheres of activity– an additional explanation was raised within the JNF to justify its budgeting of the project.

> Because the Negev is the largest repository of land and settlement in the near future when the Jewish State will come into being. These investments, aside from the JNF's normal activities, will create for it permanent assets. This will not be the case if the JNF's monies will be handed over for general security matters. Then it will have no control over them and it will not be appreciated that the JNF had a share in them.[50]

Still prior to this, the Directorate ratified the Jewish Agency's request for JNF participation in the sum of half a million dollars to finance the expenses for preparatory work and briefings by the Jewish delegation to the special session of the United Nations General Assembly in 1947. The sum that the JNF was requested to provide constituted half the sum required for the work of the delegation, and when authorizing this, the Directorate emphasized that "it should not be viewed as a precedent for the granting of allocations in the future by the JNF for the expenses of Jewish Agency political activity."[51] In August of that year, the JNF assented to the Jewish Agency request that it contribute to the security budget due to the security situation. Once again it emphasized that "such participation could not serve as a precedent for similar demands upon the JNF." However, the JNF continued to make allocations to the Jewish Agency budget for these needs.[52]

---

50 Ibid.; CZA, KKL10, minutes of JNF Directorate meetings, 29.7.1947, 3.2.1948 – quotation from Weitz's statement in the latter meeting, 18.2.1948, 16.3.1948; Report WZO (1951), pp. 595–596.
51 CZA, KKL10, minutes of JNF Directorate meeting, 1.4.1947.
52 Ibid., 29.8.1947 – quotation from there; ibid., 16.3.1948.

Half a year later, the Directorate authorized the Jewish Agency's request to extend a JNF guarantee to the substantial loans it had taken in the United States, and for this purpose a lien was placed on $3 million of the JNF's share on income from the United Jewish Appeal in the United States.[53] The JNF also extended a guarantee in the sum of P£750,000 for a loan of P£2.5 million which the Jewish Agency took in Palestine from the Anglo-Palestine Bank.[54] This guarantee was increased a month later by P£500,000. With regard to this guarantee, Ben-Gurion did not hesitate to point out to the Directorate, that it would be preferable for the JNF to authorize the guarantee because if it did not do so the Jewish Agency would find it difficult to obtain the loan – a situation that would compel the Jewish Agency to demand the required funds in the form of a JNF allocation.[55] Less than a month later, the JNF authorized the Jewish Agency request to extend a guarantee to a special loan project which the Jewish Agency conducted in Palestine in the sum of P£5 million – the JNF was required to grant a guarantee on half the amount. The JNF, as mentioned, assented to this but not without criticism, contending that its hands were tied from the option of investing in "other large national projects connected with the JNF's main activity and which mandate large financial investments." The JNF had no resort other than to accept the Jewish Agency's explanation that the general public had vast confidence in the JNF and "without the JNF's participation in the responsibility for paying off the loan, the whole matter could fail."[56] In addition, aside from extending the large-scale guarantees, in March 1948, the Directorate authorized the allocation of the sum of P£850,000 to strengthen the weak settlements in various parts of the country (apart from the Negev), including over twenty settlements which remained outside the partition boundaries set by the United Nations' resolution. This allocation also included sums for purchasing vehicles, equipment and security needs.[57]

---

53   Ibid., 3.2.1948.
54   Ibid., 16.3.1948.
55   Ibid.
56   Ibid., 15.4.1948 – quotation from there; ibid., 1.7.1948 – it transpires from these minutes that with the establishment of the State the JNF allocated to the Jewish Agency a sum of $12.5 million and to the Government of the State of Israel a loan of $6 million, half of which apparently became a grant.
57   Ibid., 18.3.1948; Report WZO (1951), p. 596.

The Economic Background of the Period and Offers of Land by Arab Sellers

The period from the end of the Second World War in mid-1945, up to the outbreak of the War of Independence in May 1948, began with relative prosperity thanks to the renewal of exports and civil construction, despite the renewal of imports and a boycott imposed by the Arab countries. The period closed with severe disturbances to the development of production given the security events which preceded the War and the background of the War itself. Inflation continued during these years, but at a slow pace.[58]

When the War came to an end, on the one hand, there were still signs of the artificial autarky, and on the other, there were signs of a favorable balance of payments. Tens of millions of Palestine Pounds were credited to the Palestine banks abroad, as opposed to a few millions prior to that. Money supply and the total deposits in Palestine itself, also grew by an appreciable volume. As may be recalled, during the Second World War period an artificial expansion occurred in industry, and it was not required to adjust to conditions of competition. It was the market which adjusted to costs of production rather than the reverse. These factors greatly encumbered industry's transition to peacetime conditions. Mixed agriculture had also, as may be recalled, augmented its production in an appreciable fashion while the citrus branch which was harmed by the War, saw its markets re-opened.

The changes and processes which occurred in the country's economy during the War, left their imprint on the entire domain of economic activity, and placed before the country new economic problems with a transition to a peacetime economy. The huge demand during the wartime period created by the army and the intensified purchasing power ostensibly isolated the country from the influence of a sound economy. The principal factors of feasibility, competition, profit and price were seemingly annulled and their place was taken by the factor of pure consumption. The economy passed from a finance economy to an economy of men and materials. Certain sectors expanded without any correlation to the economy in normal times, and in contradistinction other sectors contracted. Under these conditions, the country entered a period of transition from a war economy to a peace economy.

58   Gross & Greenberg (1994), p. 38.

Two years after the conclusion of the War, the industrial production capacity was still fully utilized, despite the drop in the volume of government and military orders, and there was no sign whatsoever of unemployment. This phenomenon stemmed from the pent-up demand during the War, which didn't find an outlet due to the scarcity in merchandises on the world market and the difficulties which the import trade encountered. The appreciable purchasing power which had accumulated and which originated in the expenses connected to the management of the War, galvanized demand, stimulated production and exerted a salutary influence on the level of employment. The volume of imports and its composition, were a decisive factor in the country in peacetime as well, and upon the conclusion of the War, their importance grew because price levels and the expansion of production were dependent to a large extent upon them, as were indirectly employment conditions. The imports during these years sustained the existence of an economy which had not developed stable and permanent sources of income, and likewise facilitated the renewal of part of the equipment which had become dilapidated, given its intensive use during the period of the Second World War.[59]

In practice, in the period immediately following the War, both the apprehension about unemployment and hopes for renewed construction and large-scale Jewish immigration proved groundless. Therefore, import substitution for local production was postponed. Due to political conditions in the country, the decline in orders from the army was much smaller than anticipated earlier. The world-wide shortage in basic commodities prevented the extensive renewal of construction, also given the high level of activity in industry, the labor force which had been ejected from the building trades during the War years showed no inclination to return to them.

The process of deflation tarried, but was not totally prevented. Competition from abroad intensified and this was now accompanied by the Arab boycott. In the latter half of 1946, intensified marketing difficulties began to manifest themselves in a number of sectors. Especially hit was the diamond sector, plagued by a combined sharp drop in worldwide demand and the rehabilitation of the industry in Belgium. In 1947, the deflationary trend strengthened, and the number employed in industry declined, compared to the previous year, primarily it would appear, as

---

59   Horowitz (1944), pp. 125–126.

a result of competition from imports. The growth of competing imports influenced price levels both directly as well as by reducing liquidity in the economy, and in the second half of 1947 a drop in the price index manifested itself.[60]

Trends in the supply of lands for sale from Arab sellers during the period covered by this chapter were mixed. The economic prosperity in the Arab economy, a product of the War period did not disappear when the War ended, but persisted afterwards. Thus the capital accumulated by Arabs was not exhausted. These factors as well as the high land prices (for reasons which we explained in Chapter Three, and for other reasons which we will dwell upon below), resulted in a general trend of reduction of supply.[61] Thus for example, the Arab landowners could offer for sale a small portion of their lands in the urban areas "and they don't want to sell us their rural land anymore unless we pay an exorbitant price."[62] Alternatively, these sellers themselves invested their money in the purchase of agricultural lands. The high income from agriculture, especially in the relatively close vicinity to urban centers, produced a situation where "the owners don't need to sell their land except for high prices and in a paltry amount."[63] However, the conditions described above applied particularly to the Free Zone for land trading according to the Lands Law. In the prohibited zones matters were different. The supply was much greater, although even there land prices were high and as Weitz explained it at the end of 1945:

> These areas served and will always serve as easily negotiable merchandise. Even in these years, when income from cultivating the lands and agriculture is high and pays a dividend, the land sellers are from the circle of large or small effendis. The price that they can receive for their land is still higher in comparison to the

---

60 Banker (1977), p. 206.
61 CZA, KKL5/15556, minutes of JNF Directorate meeting with the participation of Jewish Agency Executive overseas members, 13.12.1945; ibid., report of the meeting on land purchases 20.11.1945; CZA, KKL5/1551, meeting regarding JNF land purchases held on 10.11.1945; CZA, KKL5/15635, increase in land prices during 1940 to 1946; *Karnenu* (October 1947), p. 14.
62 CZA, KKL5/15551, meeting of persons involved in land purchase on behalf of the JNF held on 10.11.1945.
63 CZA, KKL5/15556, minutes of the meeting of the JNF Directorate with the participation of Jewish Agency Executive overseas members, 13.12.1945.

ample income they can receive from their property – whether they cultivate it themselves or lease it to tenant farmers. In this category can be included the agricultural lands that belong to the Christian communities.... These too are negotiable commodities and sooner or later they will be sold to the highest bidder "on the market are small plots of land, offered either by owners with an area of less than 500 dunams or by Moshavot in complete blocs by the allocation of part of their lands for sale in order to improve their agricultural situation, and compelled by the need to develop their existing economy."[64]

It was assumed that in the future, when there would be a change for the worse in economic conditions – apparently as a result of the distancing from conditions of the war economy – supply would increase and with it there would be a resultant drop in land prices.[65] It should be emphasized nonetheless and we shall dwell upon this in detail below, in practice land supply and their prices were influenced to no small extent by a reality that was not related to economic conditions, namely the threats of terror against the actual sellers and the activities of the "National Fund."[66]

Difficulties in Purchasing Land and Efforts to Overcome Them

The Lands Law and its repercussions on possibilities for purchasing lands, described at length in Chapter Three, remained in effect until the end of the Mandate. Furthermore, during the period covered by the current chapter, the British made greater efforts to close the loopholes in the Law and persisted in their refusal to transfer state lands to the JNF, even for the benefit of settling army veterans.[67] In mid-1945 the British also established,

---

64 Ibid.
65 CZA, KKL5/15551, meeting of persons involved in land purchase on behalf of the JNF, 10.11.1945.
66 See above, n. 61; see also CZA, KKL5/14042, letter from Nahmani to JNF Head Office 24.10.1946.
67 Congress (1947), pp. 370–371; CZA, KKL5/15556, memorandum by Weitz: "Human Justice and the Lands Law," 25.11.1945. See also, CZA, KKL5/13904, letter from Weitz to Jewish Agency Political Department 22.5.1945; CZA, KKL5/14042, summary of discussions with Nahmani, and Alexandrovsky held in Jerusalem on 25–26.6.1946, during which the intention of the Government to allocate to the Arabs the remaining lands in the Beisan Valley and in other locations became apparent.

under the pressure of Arab activists, a special committee to examine the violations against the Lands Law from the time it was legislated in 1940.[68] It was clear to the JNF that the purpose of the committee was "to seal the loopholes in the Law regarding the sale of land, in order to pay off a previous debt."[69] "To add restriction upon restriction, to add new laws and to prevent Heaven forbid, our reaching Zone A and even Zone B."[70] The conclusions of the Committee did not justify the severe apprehensions which accompanied the start of its activity, but the cracks in the field itself were narrowed further and further.[71] Requests which the JNF submitted to the Government to authorize transfers for various reasons (for example unification of areas) were almost invariably turned down.[72] Furthermore, in the course of 1946, the Governments of Lebanon and Syria legislated laws prohibiting their inhabitants from selling land in Palestine to Jews, and thus an additional loophole was closed to the JNF, one that the JNF had previously exploited skillfully. The Lands Law had not prohibited the transfer of lands to Jews by non–Palestinian Arabs.[73]

68 CZA, KKL10, minutes of JNF Directorate meeting, 10.7.1945; CZA, KKL5/13848, letter from Weitz to Granovsky 15.6.1945; CZA, KKL5/13894, letter from Nahmani to Lands Department in JNF Head Office 18.6.1945; CZA, KKL5/13848, letter from the Chairman of the Land Transfers Inquiry Committee to JNF 5.7.1945, letter from Granovsky to Land Transfer Inquiry Committee 10.7.1945.

69 CZA, KKL5/13848, letter from Weitz to Granovsky 5.6.1945.

70 *Agricultural Center Bulletin* (Nov. 1945), p. 14 – quotation from the statement of Hartzfeld.

71 CZA, KKL5/15556, the following documents: Report of a gathering concerning land purchases with the participation of directors of JNF regional offices and JNF lawyers, representatives of Jewish Agency Political Department and representatives of Information Department, 20.11.1945 – the quotation from the comments of A. Ben-Shemesh; Weitz's statement at the meeting of JNF Directorate with the participation of Jewish Agency Executive overseas members, 13.12.1945. See also CZA, KKL5/15559, meeting of persons involved in land purchase on behalf of JNF, 10.11.1946 with the participation of Granovsky, Weitz, Zuckerman, Nahmani, Yisrael Teiber, G. Machnes, H. Danin, A. Danin, M. Machnes, Stromeza, Wolff, Margalit, Yehiel Teiber, and A. Ben-Shemesh.

72 CZA, KKL5/15556, Weitz's statement at the meeting of JNF Directorate with the participation of Jewish Agency Executive overseas members, 13.12.1945; CZA, KKL5/15557, the reasons for the requests for transfer of lands which were turned down by the Government, 1946.

73 CZA, KKL5/15551, summary of Weitz's statement on the plan to purchase lands and the new waves of immigration, 31.10.1945; CZA, KKL5/14042, lands purchase plans

In 1946, the Anglo–American Enquiry Commission recommended annuling the existing Lands Law and replacing it with other laws which were not discriminatory and whose purpose was to protect small farmers, but this was never implemented. Furthermore, on the basis of their experience, the JNF's leaders were certain that talk about the abolition of the Law or making it more flexible, was no more than an illusion. In any case "in the hands of the present administration any other law presumably predicated on a general order of land affairs in the country, would turn into a new tool of the very same purpose, to seal off the avenues for the agricultural territorial expansion of the Jewish community. This is what the Palestine administration aspires to in all its legislative activities."[74] Disgruntlement was expressed by the JNF over the fact that the struggle of the WZO since the promulgation of the White Paper in 1939, concentrated on the decree barring immigration and very little was done in the area of a political battle against the decrees on land purchases.[75] The JNF's independent activities in this sphere, whether in publications, in the press and protests to the British, did not produce results.[76] In mid-1945, a joint committee of the Jewish Agency's Political Department and the JNF was established, whose purpose was to promote a political struggle against the Lands Law, but the JNF did not entertain great hopes for any results "and it remains for us

for 1947; CZA, KKL5/15556, Weitz's statement at the meeting of JNF Directorate with the participation of Jewish Agency Executive overseas members, 13.12.1945; CZA, KKL5/15637, letter from Nahmani to Lands Department in JNF Head Office 14.3.1946; CZA, KKL5/13995, letter from Czernowitz 26.2.1947.

74   Congress (1947), pp. 370–371 – from Granovsky's statement; CZA, KKL5/15557, announcement concerning the Anglo–American Enquiry Commission's recommendation regarding the Lands Law, 1946 (no specific date); CZA, KKL5/15551, meeting of persons conducting land purchase on behalf of JNF, 10.11.1946.

75   Congress (1947), pp. 370–371; CZA, KKL5/13894, letter from Nahmani to JNF Head Office 18.6.1945 in which Nahmani demands the carrying out of a political struggle against the Lands Law; CZA, KKL5/15556, Report of a gathering concerning land purchases (see above, n. 71); CZA, KKL5/15551, meeting of persons conducting land purchase on behalf of JNF, 10.11.1946.

76   CZA, KKL5/13848, letter from Weitz to Granovsky 16.6.1945; CZA, KKL5/15556, report of a gathering (see above, n. 71); meeting of persons conducting land negotiations on behalf of JNF, 10.11.1946; ibid., memorandum by Weitz: "Human Justice and the Lands Law," 25.11.1945; CZA, KKL5/15557, announcement concerning the Anglo–American Enquiry Commission's recommendation regarding the Lands Law, 1946 (no specific date).

to continue our day-to-day activity in the future despite all the obstacles, and to try to progress toward our goal with great efforts."[77] The scope and duration of this committee's activity is not clear, but apparently it was not of any significance. In June 1947, the JNF and the Political Department of the Jewish Agency again decided on joint activity in order to facilitate the creation of suitable conditions for land purchases by the JNF.[78]

The activity of both the Arab National Fund and the Supreme Arab Council sharply intensified in the last years prior to the establishment of the State of Israel. The JNF viewed such activity during those years as a far more serious obstacle to its purchases than that posed by the Lands Law. The JNF was less concerned about the National Fund's activity in purchasing lands, because this activity never reached significant proportions. It was much more concerned about the Fund's activity in intimidation and terror against the Arab land seller and against all those Arabs who assisted the JNF by various means to implement purchases. From 1946, the National Fund no longer contented itself with intimidation and harassment, but on more than one occasion it actually perpetrated the murder of land sellers and others who collaborated with the JNF. There were dual repercussions to all these activities: First of all, supply of lands for sale constricted appreciably and secondly the prices rose, caused by both the scarcity and the vast risk entailed in selling lands.[79]

At a special meeting convened by the JNF in November 1946, attended by all the heads of the regional offices, Yosef Nahmani (who managed the JNF Tiberias Office) dwelt in detail upon the activity of the Arab National Fund and its repercussions, while directing criticism on this matter to the JNF as well. He emphasized, inter alia:

---

77   CZA, KKL5/13894, letter from Weitz to JNF Galilee Office 28.6.1945.

78   CZA, KKL10, minutes of JNF Directorate meeting, 2.6.1947.

79   Congress (1947), pp. 370–371; CZA, KKL5/15556, Weitz's statement at the meeting of JNF Directorate with the participation of Jewish Agency Executive overseas members, 13.12.1945; CZA, KKL5/14042, lands purchase plan for 1947, 24.10.1946; CZA, KKL5/15551, meeting of persons purchasing lands on behalf of JNF, 10.11.1946; CZA, KKL5/13885, letter from Czernowitz 26.2.1947; CZA, KKL10, minutes of JNF Directorate meetings, 10.7.1945, 3.2.1948; ibid., proceedings of Smaller Zionist General Council session, 30.10.1945 (p. 12); CZA, KKL5/15556, report of a gathering (see above, n. 71); CZA, KKL5/15551, meeting of persons purchasing lands on behalf of JNF, 10.11.1946 – in which the argument is put forward that if there had not been any terror the extent of offers of land for sale would have been much greater.

The situation is becoming increasingly grave. While the National Fund, as a competitive element in purchases, is not particularly serious due to the meager resources of this Fund, however, in lieu of financial competition, there are threats of murder – threats that were also carried out. The arguments which we so long maintained, namely that the protection of Arabs who worked shoulder to shoulder with us is their own affair and concern, are false arguments and a serious mistake. The Arab camp is gathering strength and is becoming organized. This has spawned the Hanegada organization with branches in every village; it is making a marked impact on the Arab public and its strength is becoming intensified from day to day. Those who work with us are in mortal peril, and there is no one to save them. The Government is doing nothing to protect their lives, and murders that were committed have remained a mystery, and the criminals were not apprehended. The Arab working with us contends that he is not prepared to continue working with us unless we are able to give him the necessary security. This is one explanation for the steep rise in land prices. The Arabs working with us, whose lives are endangered, demand monetary compensation, part of which they spend for their inadequate protection.[80]

Similar sentiments were expressed by other JNF office heads who demanded the extension of protection to land sellers and JNF collaborators.[81] As the months passed, the terror activity and murder intensified. "A number of Arab notables were murdered because of their assistance in selling land to Jews or because they opposed the ruling gang in the Arab national movement.... And these are but manifestations of a widespread terror network organized by the Supreme Arab Council and by the National Fund, who have spies in every place and who are assisted by the tacit consent of the Government."[82]

---

80 CZA, KKL5/15551, meeting of persons involved in land purchase on behalf of JNF, 10.11.1946 with the participation of Granovsky, Weitz, Zuckerman, Nahmani, Yisrael Teiber, G. Machnes, H. Danin, A. Danin, M. Machnes, Stromeza, Wolff, Margalit, Yehiel Teiber, and A. Ben-Shemesh.
81 Ibid.
82 CZA, KKL5/13995, letter from Czernowitz 26.2.1947.

The prices of land during 1945–1948, continued to skyrocket "at a pace, and at an extent not witnessed in any period, or in any country, with regards to agricultural land."[83] The tempo of price increases was disproportionate to the rise in JNF income. As stated above, the terror against Arab land sellers and collaborators with the JNF contributed in no small measure to price rises. But there were additional reasons.

First of all the appreciable rise in the purchase of urban lands and those adjacent to the cities which the JNF bought in the years before the termination of the Mandate, in return for which the Arab sellers received "fabulous sums," induced the sellers to invest part of the proceeds in the purchase of agricultural land. In this manner, competitors to the JNF in the purchase of agricultural lands entered the market, contributing to price rises. This factor was compounded by the terror that motivated the sellers to prefer sales to Arab investors over sales to the JNF.

Secondly, the appreciable rise in Zionist settlement activity that found expression either in the physical settlement of the land (albeit in the form of encampments, conquest points and observation posts, etc.), by its very nature promoted higher land prices in the immediate vicinity of the settlement point. This was not a novel phenomenon in the history of the Jewish settlement project in Palestine, but now it expressed itself most forcibly as the result of the intensive settlement activity.

Thirdly, both the Agricultural Center and the settlements themselves, did not desist, to the JNF's displeasure, from maintaining contacts with land sellers with a view to completing their land quotas. In fact, the settlements had no intention of implementing purchases by themselves and they inevitably asked the JNF to step in, but by dealing independently with the sellers they contributed to price increases.

Fourthly, agricultural development persisted in the Arab economy, under the influence of Jewish settlement or spurred by the economic prosperity and capital accumulation of the Arab economy during the War. An opinion was raised within the JNF itself that, the extensive publicity which the JNF

83 Congress Report (1947), p. 371 – quotation from there. See also JNF Report (1947), pp. 26–30; CZA, KKL5/15635, "The level of land price rises in 1940–1946," 28.10.1945; CZA, KKL5/15556, statement by Weitz at JNF Directorate meeting with the participation of Jewish Agency Executive overseas members, 13.12.1945; ibid., proceedings of Smaller Zionist General Council session, 30.11.1945; *Agricultural Center Bulletin* (Nov. 1945), pp. 14–15.

gave "in full public view regarding our achievements in redeeming the land despite the Lands Law, worked to our detriment."[84]

All these difficulties compounded by the problem of evicting tenant farmers and the security occurrences which followed the United Nations declaration concerning the establishment of a Jewish State,[85] influenced the extent of JNF land purchases during 1945–1948. This situation was further aggravated by pressures exerted upon the JNF by the Jewish Agency to channel major resources to finance various needs not directly connected to land purchases.

To overcome some of the difficulties, the JNF persisted with methods similar to those it had employed from the time of the promulgation of the Lands Law, such as purchasing lands in Zones A and B at public auctions necessitated by arrears on a mortgage or purchases from foreign subjects – both Syrian and Lebanese. Nonetheless, especially during this period, the JNF stepped up its efforts to locate collaborators from among the Arab population who would perform various functions in the purchase process, and under whose name the JNF would register its purchases while seeking maximum guarantees from these "intermediaries." As the loopholes remaining in the Lands Law narrowed increasingly, and amidst a tendency to purchase the greatest possible amount, the JNF had no recourse but to rely on this method despite the very high risk involved.[86] The measures which the JNF employed to reduce such risks included the receipt of a non-revocable power of attorney from the Arab "purchasers," or establishing companies in the name of the "purchasers," whose securities were bought

---

84 See in detail CZA, KKL5/15551, minutes of the meeting of members of the JNF Executive and Directors of the regional offices held on 10.11.1946 which discussed the difficulties the JNF was facing at that time in purchasing land and analyzed the reasons for the sharp rise in prices of land – all quotations from there. See also on the individual attempts to purchase land by the Agricultural Center and the settlements: *Agricultural Center Bulletin* (Nov. 1945), p. 14; CZA, KKL5/KKL9/334, letter from Kibbutz Amir to Nahmani 6.5.1945; CZA, J15/5856, letters from Hartzfeld to R. Gottlieb of PICA 26.12.1945, 29.12.1945.

85 See e.g., CZA, KKL10, minutes of JNF Directorate meeting, 29.10.1945; CZA, KKL5/ letter from Lands Department in JNF Head Office to JNF Tiberias Office 15.8.1947.

86 CZA, KKL5/14035, concerning JNF connection with Ali Kassem 13.1.1946, letter from Shimoni to H. Danin 9.1.1947; CZA, KKL5/15556, comments by Weitz at the JNF Directorate meeting together with the Jewish Agency Executive overseas members, 13.12.1945.

by the JNF.[87] The directors of the regional offices insisted that the JNF guarantee the security of the collaborators which was mandated not only by a moral obligation, but constituted a major precondition for continued purchase activities and checking price appreciation.

At the same time, the JNF sought to persuade the Jewish Agency to enter into joint activity in the information, political and legal areas in order to break through the Lands Law barricades and reduce the scope of terror targeted against land sellers and to attenuate the sharp increase in land prices. The JNF allocated resources for this purpose, but the limited extent of the joint efforts did not reward the hopes entertained.[88] It was clear to the JNF that it could influence land prices by ceasing purchases even for a limited time, "but we will never be able to do this, since redemption of the land is a most important political factor and one cannot dare to even think of ceasing land purchases as the present time."[89] In view of the situation that had materialized, the directors of the regional offices insisted on

87 CZA, KKL5/14044, letter from Zuckerman to JNF 14.2.1946, letter from Zuckerman to JNF 5.4.1946; CZA, KKL5/14043, memorandum of a meeting with Margalit 24.4.1946; CZA, KKL5/14037, meeting in Haifa with the participation of Weitz, Stromeza, Wolff and A. Danin, 8.5.1946, summary of discussions in Haifa on 29–30.5.1946; CZA, KKL5/14042, summary of discussions with Nahmani and Alexandrovsky on 25–26.6.1946; CZA, KKL5/15555, meeting of persons dealing with land purchases, 10.11.1946; CZA, KKL5/15927, minutes of meeting with Stromeza, Wolff and A. Danin, 5.11.1947; CZA, KKL5/15929, letter from JNF Lands Department to Zuckerman 4.1.1948, from which it transpires that one of those Arabs who collaborated with the JNF was Darwish Dahoudi who was given the code name of "King David" by the JNF. See also on this matter Katz (1992), pp. 15–52.

88 CZA, KKL10, minutes of JNF Directorate meetings, 2.6.1947, 3.2.1948; CZA, KKL5/15556, the following documents: report from the gathering regarding land purchases, 20.11.1945; letter from JNF Head Office to attorneys Eliash, Yosef, Levin, Olshan, Ussishkin, Weinshal, Solomon, Feiglin, Ben-Shemesh, Hamburger, and Dunkelblum – concerning consultation with Jewish Agency Political Department about steps to be taken in the struggle against the Lands Law; Weitz's comments at meeting of JNF Directorate with the participation of Jewish Agency Executive overseas members, 13.12.1945. See also, e.g., CZA, KKL5/15557, announcement concerning the recommendation by the Anglo–American Enquiry Commission about the Lands Law, 1946; CZA, KKL5/15551, meeting of persons dealing with land purchases, 10.11.1946.

89 The quotation is from Granovsky's statement; CZA, KKL5/15551, meeting of persons purchasing lands on behalf of the JNF, 10.11.1946. Cf. comments of Wolf CZA, KKL5/15556, report of a gathering concerning land purchases on 20.11.1945.

implementing purchases almost at any financial cost. However, Granovsky, and apparently Weitz as well, found it difficult to assent to this policy. "He [Granovsky] is prepared to accept the formula proposed by a number of those present to the effect that prices should not constitute a deterrent, but a limit be set, for there has to be an economic limit, a commercial limit, or a logical limit."[90] Nonetheless, while the JNF had no option but to purchase land even at exorbitant prices, no clear-cut policy was established regarding the price boundaries the JNF was prepared to pay.[91]

An additional method proposed within the JNF during those years as a means for augmenting land supply and lowering prices, was the "development route." The intention was to achieve Jewish–Arab cooperation on an economic profitability basis which would focus on the JNF. Under this plan, the JNF would attempt to establish various development projects – chiefly water pipelines – and the Arab population would benefit as well from such projects. The Arabs could pay their share in the project by selling off lands rendered surplus by the development projects. Nonetheless, it was clear that "the development approach will take years, undoubtedly," and did not offer an immediate solution.[92]

In those last years prior to the establishment of the State, the JNF Lands Department continued to operate through the regional offices in Haifa and Tiberias, whose personnel were in all respects JNF officials. In the other regions it functioned through independent agents who were affiliated to the JNF and worked on a commission basis. Through the offices of these agents purchases were implemented for the JNF in the Jerusalem region, the Sharon region, and in the South and Negev region. Weitz was totally involved in the work of the regional offices. He guided them directly, supervised them, helped them in adopting decisions, and his authorization

90   CZA, KKL5/15551, meeting of persons purchasing lands on behalf of JNF, 10.11.1946.
91   Ibid.
92   CZA, KKL5/15556, report of a gathering concerning land purchases on 20.11.1945 – quotation from Weitz's statement. In the course of time, Weitz raised the idea of the "development route" as a method of land purchase by the JNF in the Negev and other locations in the country, when the Jewish State would be established. On this see: CZA, A246/699, letter from Weitz to A. Ben-Shemesh 26.1.1948; for a detailed account see Katz (1998a).

was a pre-condition for the completion of purchases by these offices.[93] Intensified cooperation between the regional offices was proposed as one of the required methods for overcoming the difficulties which beset land purchases during those years.[94]

Purchase Policy from Mid–1945 to Summer 1947

During 1945–1947, the JNF expended vast efforts to complete purchases commenced previously, although due to various difficulties not yet completed (including the eviction of tenant farmers if required) and to create territorial blocs. It implemented land exchange requisite for creating these blocs and connecting between them.[95] The underlying general

---

93 CZA, KKL5/13921, letter from Weitz to Levy 17.8.1945, letter from Weitz to the Haifa Regional Office 21.8.1945; CZA, KKL5/14042, letter from Weitz to the Tiberias Office 4.2.1946; CZA, KKL5/14040, letter from Zuckerman to JNF 4.2.1946; CZA, KKL5/14037, letter from Weitz to Haifa Office 17.3.1946; CZA, KKL5/14042, letter from Nahmani to JNF Head Office 20.5.1946; CZA, KKL5/15638, memorandum of Weitz's meeting with Haifa Office personnel 28.7.1946; CZA, KKL5/14042, meeting with Weitz at Galilee Office 2.3.1947; CZA, KKL5/14043, letter from Weitz to Meron Company 11.5.1947; CZA, KKL5/14042, letter from Nahmani to JNF Lands Department 21.5.1947, letter from JNF Lands Department to JNF Tiberias Office 15.8.1947; CZA, KKL5/14037, letter from the JNF Lands Department to Haifa Office regarding the "Work Schedule of the Office Personnel" 15.8.1947, letter from Weitz to Tiberias Office 29.8.1947; CZA, KKL5/14040, letter from Weitz to Zuckerman 5.9.1947; CZA, KKL5/15929, letter from Weitz to Zuckerman 5.9.1947; CZA, KKL5/15929, letter from Weitz to Fisher 29.9.1948; CZA, KKL10, minutes of JNF Directorate meeting, 29.1.1946. Purchases were also made by the PLDC, but these were very few. On this see CZA, S53/1682a, the following documents: minutes PLDC Executive meeting, 21.8.1945, PLDC Report January–May 1946, minutes of Executive Committee meeting, 31.10.1946.
94 CZA, KKL5/15551, meeting of persons involved in land purchases on behalf of JNF, 10.11.1946.
95 CZA, KKL10, minutes of JNF Directorate meetings, 15.5.1945, 29.10.1945, 5.2.1946; CZA, KKL5/12809, letter from Weitz to JNF Tiberias Office 13.5.1945; CZA, KKL5/15551, summary of Weitz's statement on purchase plans and new waves of immigration, 31.10.1945; CZA, J15/5856, letters from Hartzfeld to Gottlieb of PICA 21.12.1945, 26.12.1945; CZA, KKL5/140435, memorandum – meeting between Weitz and Margaliot, 24.4.1946; CZA, KKL5/14037, meeting in Haifa between Weitz and Stromeza, Wolf, and A. Danin, 8.5.1946; CZA, KKL5/14037, summary of matters

JNF agricultural land purchase policy from mid–1945 until the close of Summer 1947 when the UNSCOP[96] Report was published, represented a continuation of the purchase policy adopted in the first half of the 1940s. The political objectives to which the purchase and settlement of agricultural land were targeted were placed in sharp relief during this period. The Zionist institutions clearly perceived that they stood on the verge of international decisions concerning the Palestine Question, and the institutions sought to secure the optimal territorial objectives from the standpoint of the future Jewish State, within the framework of these decisions. This anticipation of imminent decisions was rooted in the end of the Second World War, the beginning of United States involvement in the Palestine Question, the recommendations made by the Anglo–American Committee, the feverish discussions in the international arena regarding the Palestine Question which revived plans for partition and cantonization, and the transfer of responsibility for the Palestine Question from Britain to United Nations adjudication. By accelerating lands purchase and settling them, the JNF and the Jewish Agency believed they could thwart plans that had been formulated in the international arena which were unacceptable to the Zionist institutions.

Such a scheme was the 1946 Morrison–Grady Plan (see Map 23) which sought to implement the decisions of the Anglo–American Committee. Under this plan, only 17 percent of the area in Palestine was to be allotted to the autonomous Jewish entity and included the eastern and lower Galilee, the Jezreel and Beisan Valleys and the Coastal Plain from Haifa to Be'er Tuvia. The Arab entity would incorporate the central Galilee, the mountain

---

discussed in Haifa on 29–30.5.1946; CZA, KKL5/14042, the following documents: summary of discussions with Nahmani and Alexandrovsky at meetings, 25–26.6.1946, resume of a meeting held in Safed on 12.9.1946, lands purchase plan for 1946–1947, 24.10.1946; CZA, KKL5/15551, meeting of persons purchasing lands on behalf of JNF, 10.11.1946; CZA, KKL9/24, letter from Weitz to Gvati of Agricultural Center 20.8.1947; CZA, KKL5/14042, letter from JNF Lands Department to JNF Office in Tiberias 15.8.1947; CZA, KKL5/14040, letter from Weitz to Zuckerman 21.8.1947.

96 UNSCOP = United Nations Special Committee on Palestine submitted its report to the United Nations General Assembly on 31.8.1947 recommending the partition of Palestine into independent Jewish and Arab States linked in economic union, and the internationalization of Jerusalem. The Committee was composed of representatives of Australia, Canada, Czechoslovakia, Guatemala, India, Iran, Netherlands, Peru, Sweden, Uruguay and Yugoslavia.

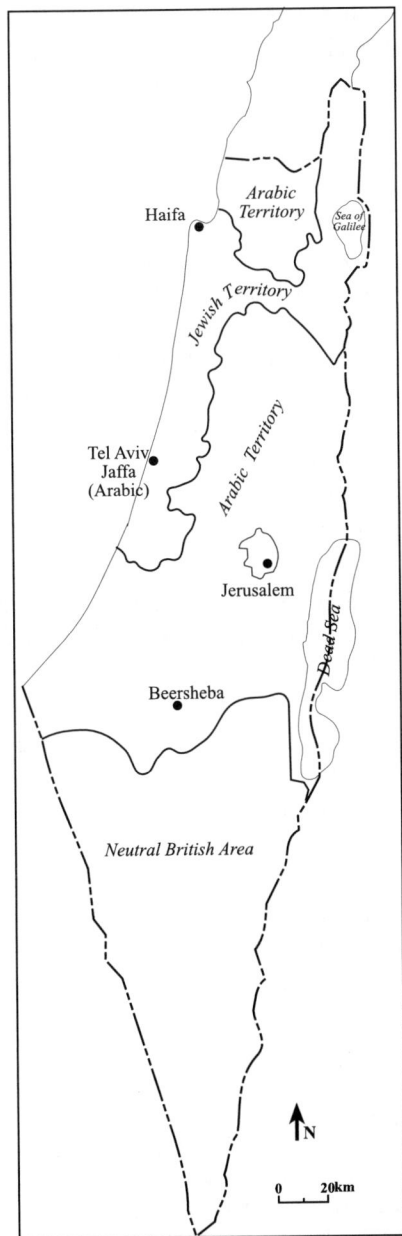

Map 23: Morrison–Grady Plan, 1946
Source: CZA, file S25/6937

region of Samaria and Judea, the southern Coastal Plain and the northern Negev.[97] The JNF's continued penetration into Zone A where Jewish purchases were totally banned by the Lands Law,as well as to the restricted Zone B, was therefore necessary in order to forestall such plans, and obviate a situation where future Jewish penetration into these areas would be rendered totally impossible. Indeed the vast majority of JNF purchases in these years represented expansions around lands that had already been purchased in Zones A and B, or new purchases in these zones with a view towards expanding purchases around them in the future. The South and the Negev continued to occupy a central place, and inter alia it was decided to implement purchases for the purpose of establishing an urban center in the Negev. It should be noted that in the South and the Negev fewer obstacles were strewn in the path of land purchases because the registration of land transfers were not effected through the Lands Registration Office, the incitement against selling to Jews was comparatively benign as opposed to other regions, and due to their living conditions the Bedouin were forced to offer quite a few lands for sale.[98] It should be added that the exigency to obtain land for political reasons, combined with a sense of urgency, induced the JNF to adopt greater flexibility with regards to the land prices it was willing to pay.[99]

There were cases in which in addition to the location of lands in Zones A and B, there were further advantages and qualities to recommend purchase. Thus for example, it was decided in summer 1945 to purchase about 2,500 dunams in the vicinity of Mishmar Hayarden because "from the standpoint of the national water plan, this region has immense value."[100] A few months later it was decided to expand purchases in the area for the very same reasons. "The importance [of the purchase] is in the location. It is located on the route of the master plan to convey water from the north to the south. The main pipeline will pass through this land."[101] Immense importance was

---

97   Dothan (1983), pp. 307ff.; Orren (1978), pp. 169ff., Katz (1992), pp. 222–224.

98   Porat (1996), pp. 151,152,158, 159, 167–171, 192, 198, 199; CZA, KKL10, minutes of JNF Directorate meetings, 24.4.1945, 10.7.1945, 29.10.1945, 25.3.1947; CZA, proceedings of Smaller Zionist General Council proceedings, 30.10.1945 (p. 13); minutes of Jewish Agency Executive meeting, 5.5.1947; CZA, KKL5/13995, letter from Czernowitz 26.2.1947; Congress (1947), pp. 370–371, 377.

99   CZA, KKL10, minutes of JNF Directorate meeting, 29.1.1946.

100   Ibid., 10.7.1945.

101   Ibid., 2.19.1945.

also attached to purchase proposals located on the Jerusalem–Tel Aviv Highway.[102]

In addition to the political objective of purchasing lands, the JNF had to implement purchases necessary for consolidating existing farms (including the farms run by female workers), either because the predetermined land quotas for these farms had not been allocated completely or because the JNF was persuaded of the necessity for territorial increments. The arrangements for dividing payments between the JNF and the farms for this purpose, were similar to those which were observed in Chapter Three.[103] The need to settle army veterans also arose, especially as the Government (except for isolated cases) refused to allocate state lands for this purpose.[104]

Similar to the pattern of the early 1940s, in the latter half of the decade and for similar reasons, an appreciable portion of JNF purchases were from Jewish sellers. Thus for example, JNF purchases from Jews at the end of 1946 and the beginning of 1947 approached nearly 50 percent of the total purchases of that time.[105] However, in expensive locations within the Free Zone, such as the Sharon, the JNF objective was to avoid land purchases from Jewish owners because of both the issue of ownership and price. Nonetheless, there was prominent support for implementing such purchases expressed by the settlement movement representatives in the

---

102 Ibid., 24.4.1945.

103 See, e.g., CZA, KKL10, minutes of JNF Directorate meetings, 14.5.1946, 11.6.1946, 20.8.1946, 15.10.1946, 1.4.1947, 18.2.1948; CZA, KKL9/334, letter from Kibbutz Amir to JNF Tiberias Office 6.5.1945, letter from Weitz to JNF Tiberias Office 22.6.1945.

104 See, e.g., CZA, KKL10, minutes of JNF Directorate meetings, 29.10.1945, 13.11.1945, 11.6.1946, 20.8.1946, 18.2.1948; CZA, KKL10, proceedings of Smaller Zionist General Council proceedings 30.10.1945 (p. 5); CZA, KKL5/13904, letter from Weitz to Jewish Agency Political Department 22.5.1945; CZA, KKL5/15566, letter from Ben-Gurion to Kaplan, Granovsky, Weitz, Hartzfeld and Horin 8.5.1947; CZA, S14/4992, letter from Weitz to Ben-Gurion 14.5.1947 (also in KKL5/15566); CZA, S25/6915, letter from Rosenberg of Jewish Agency Political Department to Ben-Gurion 28.11.1947.

105 CZA, KKL10, minutes of JNF Directorate meetings, 29.1.1946, 29.4.1947. See also CZA, KKL5/14040, letter from JNF to Zuckerman 26.9.1947, from which it transpires that from September 1946 to September 1947 purchases from Jewish owners comprised one third of the total (21,000 out of 63,000 dunams); CZA, KKL5/17213, "Details of purchases in 1948," 12.5.1948.

Directorate – Hartzfeld, Kestenbaum and Hazan – because these purchases could serve the needs of existing settlements.[106]

The Expansion of Land Purchases in the Moshavot

During the first half of the 1940s, the need to rescue veteran Moshavot and prevent the sale of Jewish-owned land to non-Jews, prompted the JNF to engage in the purchase of land that had been place on the market by Jewish farmers in other Moshavot. In Chapter Three, the JNF's involvement in the purchase of lands offered for sale in Har Tuv. Sejera and Menahamia were described in detail.[107] During 1945–1948, land purchase by the JNF in the Moshavot expanded. Lands were purchased in Mishmar Hayarden, Yesud Hama'ala and Rosh Pinna (See Map 24), Beit Gan, Giva't Ada and Ekron. In most cases these were Moshavot which held a large supply of land, while their total membership and especially those engaged in agricultural work, was dwindling as the result of the outflow of young people, the death of adults and the farmers' relocation to the cities. Moshavot such as Beth Gan, and Giva't Ada, from the outset had small populations. In any case, the diminution in the population of the Moshavot caused stagnation and crisises, and spurred additional emigration of waves of young people. Those who remained in the Moshavot found it very difficult to bear the public burdens. Introducing efficiencies into agricultural labor and developing the farms on a rational basis was not possible, and the percentage of Arab laborers was particularly high.[108]

Thus for example, with regard to Mishmar Hayarden, Weitz reported in 1947:

> This Moshava totals only 23 families…. Such a Jewish community cannot sustain all the public needs which repose on a Jewish

---

106   CZA, KKL10, minutes of JNF Directorate meetings, 13.7.1945, 13.11.1945.
107   See above, p. 222.
108   JNF Conference (1947), pp. 26–32; CZA, KKL5/15625, internal information bulletin, "Veteran Moshavot are being revived," 1947; CZA, KKL9/267, irrevocable power of attorney granted to JNF by farmers of Mishmar Hayarden; CZA, KKL5/15921, summary of matters discussed with Weitz in JNF Tiberias Office on 7.11.1947; CZA, KKL5/17139, letter from Levin to the Custodian of Enemy Property 18.1.1948; CZA, KKL10, minutes of JNF Directorate meetings, 11.6.1946, 20.8.1946, 24.9.1946, 15.10.1946, 16.12.1947, 18.2.1948; personal interview with Adiya Konikow, Jerusalem 16.10.1992.

Mishmar Hayarden

community. Such a small group cannot develop the farm economy in a rational manner so it can subsist from it.... This farm economy remains stagnant, just the way it was 30–40 years ago, an arid grain farm economy lacking water not only for irrigation but also for sufficient drinking purposes, and therefore it cannot provide an existence for its workers...and the young people have been leaving the Moshava for a number of years, and only the elderly and the weaklings remain...and Mishmar Hayarden is not alone. This picture emerges as well in Yesud Hama'ala, Rosh Pinna, Sejera and Menahamia, as well as Ekron (Mazkeret Batya).[109]

Regarding Rosh Pinna he reported at the time that:

The Moshava is facing a crisis today. Members of the younger generation have abandoned it. A number of farms have been

109   JNF Conference (1947), p. 27.

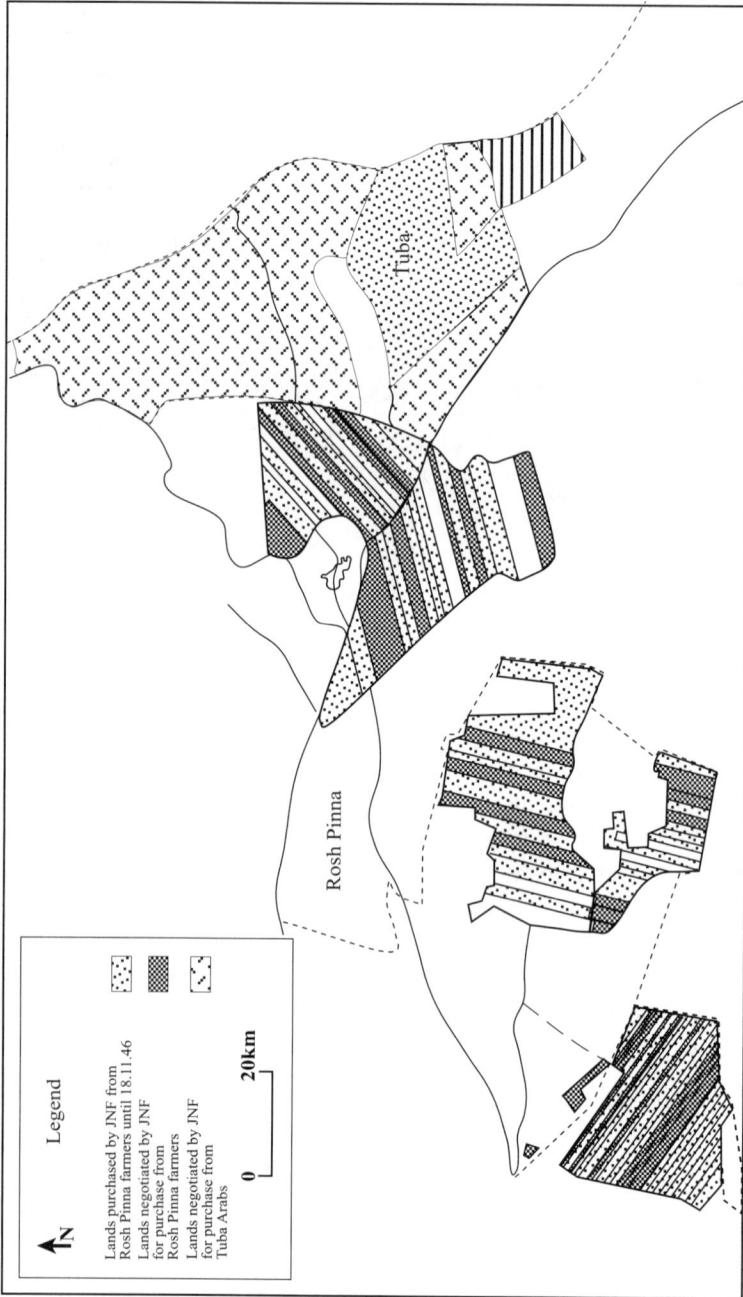

Map 24: JNF lands in Tuba and Rosh Pinna in 1942
Source: JNF map archives, Map 5177

Legend

Lands purchased by JNF from
Rosh Pinna farmers until 18.11.46

Lands negotiated by JNF
for purchase from
Rosh Pinna farmers

Lands negotiated by JNF
for purchase from
Tuba Arabs

0   20km

Tuba

Rosh Pinna

Rosh Pinna, 1927

abandoned, and there are cases where the owners are living in the city or in other Moshavot and Arab tenant farmers are cultivating their plots. The number of inhabitants in the village, farmers and non-farmers alike, totals 350. In practice most of the inhabitants do not earn a living from agriculture.[110]

Neither PICA nor the JCA took any real measures to improve the situation of these Moshavot. Therefore, the Moshavot turned to the JNF and the Jewish Agency, either directly or through the Farmers Cooperative, to ameliorate the situation of the Moshavot. In the first half of the 1940s, the JNF had made purchases of land in a number of Moshavot in order to rehabilitate them. It could not stand aloof at the time that lands suitable for agricultural settlement in the Moshavot were not being utilized for this purpose but were being offered for sale to the highest bidder. This was at a time when the JNF was making prodigious efforts to purchase

---

110   CZA, KKL5/15625, "Veteran Moshavot are being revived," 1947.

land for the establishment of new agricultural settlements. Within this framework, the JNF sought to provide a solution to the problem of army veterans, and it also invested efforts to complete the land quotas of existing farms. Furthermore, the involvement of the JNF in purchase activity in the Moshavot could help enhance its influence on a milieu where it had not established a presence previously.[111]

Thus, the JNF and the Moshavot reached an arrangement whereby the JNF would purchase the land of farmers who had left the Moshavot and would purchase as well part of the land belonging to farmers resident in the Moshavot. With this reservoir of land, as well as additional lands which the JNF would purchase from PICA in the area, the JNF and the Jewish Agency would attempt to revive these Moshavot. The land reservoir that would thus be created by the JNF would be used to establish new settlers in the Moshavot, erect new settlements in the vicinity and complete the land quotas for existing settlements in the area. It should be emphasized that a large portion of the lands purchased by the JNF in the Moshavot was intended to facilitate the settlement of army veterans in the existing Moshavot themselves or in new settlements in the vicinity. In this manner, a solution would be found, albeit only partial, to the problem of settling army veterans, which had sorely vexed the institutions since the close of the Second World War. Thus, for example, at the end of September 1946, the Directorate decided on the purchase of 4,000 dunams in Ekron, in order to increase the number of settlers in this Moshava, to establish a new Moshava of army veterans and to complete the land quota of the adjacent Kibbutz Giv'at Brenner.

The JNF sought to coordinate its purchases in the Moshavot and their immediate vicinity with PICA for a number of reasons. Firstly, historically PICA was considered the patron of the Moshavot, especially as in certain specific areas both the Moshavot and the settlers were still contractually tied to that organization. Secondly, the JNF also sought to amass lands in the Moshavot and their vicinity through purchases from PICA itself.[112]

111 See above, nn. 109–110.
112 See above, nn. 109–110; CZA, KKL5/14042, summary of meeting in Safed on 12.9.1946, discussion with Weitz in JNF Galilee Office on current matters, 2.3.1947; CZA, J15/5856, letter from PICA to JNF 10.3.1947 (also in KKL5/1563), letter from Weitz to PICA 16.3.1947 (also in KKL5/15637); CZA, KKL5/15637, letters from Ariav of the Farmers Cooperative to JNF Executive 20.12.1946, 24.3.1947, letter from Weitz to the Farmers Organization 30.3.1947; CZA, KKL10, minutes of JNF Directorate meetings, 11.6.1946, 20.8.1946, 24.9.1946, 16.12.1947, 18.2.1948.

However, PICA did not always extend its blessing to the JNF plan for purchases in the Moshavot. Thus, the JNF was forced to retreat from its plan to purchase lands from the Metulla farmers (in the wake of the latter's request to expand the Moshava) following a demand from PICA that it desist. PICA claimed that it was already engaged in developing the Moshava.[113]

Transfer to the JNF of Lands Belonging to Persons Missing in the Holocaust and Gathering Information about Abandoned Jewish Properties

From 1944, the JNF was concerned for the future of real estate property that was purchased in Palestine until the beginning of the 1940s, both in urban and rural areas by Jews from abroad (in Eastern and Central Europe) and it was assumed that they and their legal heirs had perished in the Holocaust. According to Granovsky's testimony, this was a "most substantial amount of property belonging to 'missing persons' in plots and houses, totaling many hundreds of thousands Palestine Pounds."[114] The bulk of this real estate property was controlled at that time by the Custodian of Enemy Property. This was by force of the "Trading With the Enemy Act 1939" which was promulgated in England and Palestine in 1939. Under the act, the real estate property and bank deposits in Palestine of Germans (non-Jews and Jews alike), and who resided in Germany was frozen and awarded by decree of the High Commissioner to the Custodian of Enemy Property. The decree also applied to the citizens of those countries conquered by Germany, since these countries and their citizens (non-Jews and Jews alike), were also defined under the ordinance as "the enemy."[115] Part of the property was still registered in the names of companies engaged in

113   CZA, J15/5856, letter from PICA to JNF 10.3.1947 (also in KKL5/15637), letter from Weitz to PICA 16.3.1947 (also in KKL5/15637); CZA, KKL5/15637, letter from Wolfsohn of PICA to JNF 27.3.1947, letter from Weitz to JNF 1.5.1947.

114   CZA, KKL10, minutes of JNF Directorate meeting, 11.6.1946.

115   See in detail, Katz (2000b); see also CZA, KKL5/14338, JNF memorandum "So that Jewish Property will not be Lost Forever,"1946; CZA, KKL5/14340, "Enemy Property," *Palestine Economic News* (Jan. 1946); M. Zilberg, "Why should our property go to aliens," *Haboker*, 6.8.1944; S. Samett, "Who will inherit millions

selling lands because they had not yet managed to transfer rights in the Land Registration Office. An additional portion of the lands was registered in the name of various trustees of the purchasers. The JNF feared that the real estate capital in the end would be lost to the Jewish People, "either because 'redeemers' [quotation marks in the original] would appear in the form of unscrupulous persons; or because the Mandatory Government would attach it, due to arrears on government taxes, or another government would seize the property because it belonged to subjects of that country who were presently located on its territory." A further apprehension was that the Government would invoke the "Mahlul" Laws (sequestration due to non-cultivation of the land) on lands belonging to missing persons and transfer them to its possession. All these constituted the background to the JNF initiative to attempt various measures calculated to ensure the transfer of the property rights to the JNF in order to guarantee the preservation of the aforementioned territorial property: "either for the benefit of the property owner himself, if he were still alive, or for the benefit of his heirs if they were still alive; or if both the property owner and his heirs had perished, would be for the benefit of the Jewish people."[116] In Summer 1945, the JNF reached an agreement with Attorney Gershon Gurevich of Haifa, according to which Gurevich would seek to gather data on real estate property in Palestine, whose Jewish owners had been classed as missing in the Holocaust, and for various reasons, their property had not come under the aegis of the Custodian of Enemy Property. Gurevich proposed that on the basis of the data assembled, he would endeavor to obtain from the

---

in Palestine," *Haaretz*, 31.5.1946; *Guide* (1937) (June 1946), pp. 9–11; *Reshumot*, Proposals for laws 1977, p. 57; The Custodian General Law 1978, section 21;Y. Katz, "The Inheritance of the Custodian of Enemy Property," *Haaretz*, 7.5.1997, p. 3b; JNF Report (1947), pp. 130–132; Zamir & Ben (1993), pp. 116–129, 233–239; Domke (1983). See also CZA, KKL5/14338, survey "Defending the Property of Palestine Jews by the JNF," no date; CZA, KKL5/12676, memorandum sent to Granovsky by S. Singer 30.8.1943 regarding "Jurisdiction in Times of Emergency (1939): On the Basis of the British War Regulations."

116   CZA, KKL10, minutes of JNF Directorate meeting, 11.6.1946 – quotation from there; CZA, KKL5/14338, minutes of a meeting regarding the property of missing Jews in Palestine held on 27.5.1946 with the participation of Y. Ben-Zvi, A. Foeder, and Advocates Doukhan, Horowitz and Eliash (also in KKL5/14340); CZA, KKL5/ 14319, letter from Kimini to JNF Head Office 17.2.1947, letter from Hausner to Jewish Agency Political Department 18.2.1947.

Rabbinate a custodial decree over the missing persons' property which appointed him to manage the properties. The intention was that by virtue of his authority as property manager, these properties would be transferred to the JNF. The properties were to be registered immediately under the name of the JNF, or its subsidiary the Himnuta Company. The JNF undertook the obligation to restore the property, or its equivalent value, to the owners according to the appraised value at the time of the property's transfer to its name (after deducting expenses plus 3.5%) in the event that the owners or their legal heirs would claim the property within a fifteen-year period commencing with the transfer of the property to the JNF or to Himnuta. The meeting of the JNF Directorate that approved this agreement stated that: "Those plots whose purchasers or legal heirs would not arrive in Palestine within fifteen years would become the absolute property of the JNF. The plots would then be registered in the name of the JNF, and it could do with them 'as befitting a rightful owner' [quotation marks in the original] as it totally deemed fit and at its free discretion." However, the obligation of restoring the value of the property persisted even if the owners would arrive after fifteen years.[117] Subsequently in an agreement between Gurevich and the JNF, it was determined that the period in which the JNF would be obligated to restore the property intact to its owners, in the event of their appearance would be fixed at only five years. After this period, the JNF would have the option of either restoring the property intact or its value on the day it was transferred to JNF possession.[118]

Pursuant to the agreement, Gurevich began to amass data regarding the real estate property on the lands of missing persons with a view to obtaining a custodial decree from the Rabbinate. However, not everybody

---

117 CZA, KKL10, minutes of JNF Directorate meeting, 29.1.1946; CZA, KKL5/14340, memorandum regarding "Property in Palestine Belonging to Missing Jews," following upon JNF meeting, 13.5.1946; CZA, KKL5/13847, the following letters: Mohilewer to Department for Special Projects in JNF National Committee 27.6.1945 concerning "Lands in Palestine Belonging to Overseas Jews of whom no Traces had been Found," Gurevich to JNF 23.7.1945, 30.7.1945, 1.8.1945. See also CZA, A402/113, memorandum "JNF Activities Regarding the Property in Palestine of Missing Persons," no date; CZA, KKL5/14328, letter from Weiss to Moller concerning "Land in Kefar Ata Belonging to Missing Persons" 4.12.1946.

118 CZA, KKL5/14328, draft of the agreement between Gurevich, JNF, and Himnuta Company; CZA, KKL5/13847, letter from Gurevich to JNF 23.8.1945; CZA, KKL5/14319, letter from Dunkelblum to Weiss 27.2.1947.

in the JNF was satisfied with the agreement with Gurevich and the modus operandi that it prescribed to "redeem" the real estate property of the missing persons. The legal advisors of the JNF – Aharon Ben-Shemesh and Shmuel Ussishkin – criticized the agreement and expressed grave doubts that the procedure would succeed and that the property transfer to the JNF was secure. They also opposed the very idea of entrusting such a major project to "a private attorney being retained on a fee basis."[119] Instead, Ben-Shemesh proposed reaching an agreement between the JNF and the Custodian General of the Mandatory Government, since he was the person authorized and entitled by virtue of the 1944 Custodian General's Decree to handle the property of missing persons.[120] Pursuantly, and together with Gurevich's activities, and with the full cooperation of the JNF (according to the formula described above), intensive contacts were conducted from the first half of 1946 between Ben-Shemesh and the Custodian General, H. Kanterowitz, who revealed a sympathetic attitude to the JNF's goals.[121]

Pursuant to these contacts, and after an authorization in principle had been received from the JNF Directorate an agreement was signed in August 1946 between the JNF and the Custodian General regarding the property of missing persons. To a large extent, this agreement was meant to remove the property of missing persons from the responsibility of the Custodian of Enemy Property. The agreement contained the following provisions: (1) the Custodian General would assemble with the assistance of the JNF all information regarding the property in Palestine of missing Jews and would

---

119 CZA, KKL5/14340, memorandum regarding "Property in Palestine Belonging to Missing Jews," 13.5.1946.

120 Ibid.

121 Ibid.; CZA, A402/113, memorandum from Weiss on 8.12.1946 regarding "JNF Activities Regarding Property in Palestine of Missing Persons," 8.12.1946; CZA, KKL5/14317, letter from Ben-Shemesh to JNF 26.3.1946; CZA, KKL5/14340, letter from Weiss to Granovsky, Weitz, and Ben-Shemesh 12.4.1946; CZA, A402/113, letter from Weiss to Granovsky, Weitz, S. Ussishkin, Lifschitz, Mohilewer, and Ms. Kessel 25.4.1946 (also in KKL5/14340, KKL5/14318); CZA, KKL5/14317, letter from Ben-Shemesh to JNF 16.5.1946; CZA, KKL5/14340, memorandum written by Weiss regarding "Property of Missing Persons," 21.5.1946, letter from the Attorney General to the Chief Secretary 30.5.1946 (also in KKL5/14317); CZA, KKL5/14318, letter from Bernard Joseph (Dov Yosef) of Jewish Agency to the Chief Secretary 6.6.1946; CZA, KKL5/14340, letter from Weiss to Granovsky, Weitz, Ussishkin, and Ben-Shemesh 17.6.1946; CZA, KKL5/14318, letter from Ben-Shemesh to JNF 18.6.1946.

apply to the courts to be appointed custodian of this property. (2) The Custodian General would request permission from the courts to obtain a loan in order to pay off the tax arrears encumbering the property. After the court had authorized the Custodian General's request, the JNF undertook to provide loans to the Custodian General for 15 years at 5 percent interest for up to 40 percent of the value of the property on condition that the JNF would enjoy first mortgage over the property. The JNF would also be obligated, upon the request of the Custodian General to remove liens on the property. (3) In exchange for the award of a loan, the Custodian General would consult with the JNF in every case involving the use of the property, and would submit a request to the court to appoint the JNF as the agent or the lessee of the property upon its request. (4) If the property owners or their legal heirs would claim the property, the Custodian General would return it to them, after deducting his expenses and the JNF loan. (5) After 15 years, and to the extent that the property would not be claimed by its owners, the Custodian General would foreclose the mortgage by selling the property by private or public sale, and allow the JNF first rights in purchasing the property.[122]

While reaching this agreement, the JNF also came to an agreement with the Jewish Agency regarding the JNF's exclusive handling of the missing persons' real estate property. The Jewish Agency gave its approval to the aforementioned agreement between the JNF and the Mandatory Government. In this manner, the JNF won full recognition both within the institutions of the Jewish community and from the Mandatory Government as the institution designated to represent the affairs of missing persons. It became the prospective beneficiary of these properties as the representative of the Jewish people, in the event that they would not be claimed by their owners. It was also within this context that during the course of

---

122 JNF Report (1947), p. 132; CZA, KKL10, minutes of JNF Directorate meeting, 11.6.1946; CZA, A402/113, memorandum by Weiss concerning "JNF Activities Regarding Property in Palestine of Missing Persons," 8.12.1946 – attached is the agreement between JNF and Custodian General 14.8.1946; CZA, KKL5/14317, letters from Ben-Shemesh to JNF 26.3.1946, 16.5.1946; CZA, KKL5/14329, copy of agreement between JNF (signed on its behalf by Weitz and Granovsky) and Custodian General (Kanterowitz) 14.8.1946; CZA, KKL5/14318, memorandum 15.8.1946 regarding the signing of the agreement between the JNF and the Custodian General, memorandum by Weitz "Dealing with Property of Missing Persons," 3.8.1946.

negotiations with the Custodian General, the JNF had already approached Jewish companies which had sold lands to Jews in Eastern Europe but had not yet registered them in the Lands Registration Office in the names of the owners and requested them to register the lands under the name of the JNF. It addressed similar requests to private individuals and bodies which handled the territorial property of those who had presumably perished in the Holocaust.[123]

However, the JNF did not hasten to implement the agreement with the Custodian General. Soon after the signing, the JNF realized that the very implementation of the clauses of the agreement would result in the immediate transfer of missing persons' property to the supervision of the Mandatory Government, when matters regarding the future were not sufficiently clear. On the other hand, just when the agreement was signed with the Mandatory Government, it became clear that the arrangement with Gurevich was "delivering the goods" while guaranteeing the immediate and full trusteeship of the JNF over the missing persons' lands and final ownership in the future, to the extent that the lands would not be claimed by their owners during a given period. It transpires that during the first half of 1946 – at the time when Ben-Shemesh conducted negotiations with the Custodian General – Gurevich managed not only to draw up lists of missing persons in the Haifa vicinity, but after he had paid the taxes for a number of plots, with JNF funding, he managed to obtain custodial decrees in the Haifa Rabbinate over a number of plots, and with the agreement of the rabbinate made arrangements to transfer the plots to the JNF's benefit.[124] The Chief

---

123   JNF Report (1947), p. 132; *Karnenu* (April 1947), p. 3; CZA, KKL10, minutes of JNF Directorate meeting, 11.6.1946; CZA, A402/113, memorandum by Weiss on 8.12.1946 regarding "JNF Activities Concerning the Property in Palestine of Missing Persons"; CZA, KKL5/14317, letter from Ben-Shemesh to JNF 16.5.1946; CZA, KKL5/14338, minutes of a meeting "Concerning Property in Palestine of Missing Jews," 27.5.1946; CZA, KKL5/14318, letter from Weiss and Mohilewer to Horowitz at Jewish Agency 8.8.1946.

124   CZA, A402/113 in n. 123; CZA, KKL5/13847, letters from Gurevich to JNF 4.9.1945, 6.9.1945; CZA, KKL5/14317, letter from Gurevich to JNF 16.11.1945; CZA, A402/113, letter from Weiss to Granovsky, Weitz, Ussishkin, Ms. Kessel, Mohilewer, and Lifschitz 25.4.1946; CZA, KKL5/14340, memorandum drawn up by Weiss regarding "Property in Haifa of Missing Persons," 12.4.1946; CZA, KKL5/14317, letter from Kamini and Toibman of JNF Department of Special Projects to JNF Head Office 16.5.1946.

Rabbi of Haifa, Rabbi Kaniel who "recognized that if any institution had a right to receive 'ownership' [quotations marks in the original] over the lands of missing persons, it was the JNF."[125] He advised Gurevich and JNF personnel to obtain a fundamental ruling from the Jerusalem Rabbinate, which would obligate every rabbinical court in Palestine to authorize similar custodianships. Indeed, pursuant to an approach by the JNF to the Chief Rabbinical Council, the latter ratified the decisions of the Haifa Rabbinate and reached an agreement in principle with Gurevich and the JNF. Under this agreement, by acting through Gurevich, whom the Haifa Rabbinate would designate custodian over the missing persons' property, the property would be transferred to the JNF or the Himnuta Company as trustee, according to the terms of the agreement concluded in Summer 1945 between the JNF and Gurevich. In this manner, the JNF was to function in practice as the owner of the property and was obligated to return it intact only in the event that it would be claimed by its owners during a period of five years, and return only its equivalent value on the day of the transfer to the JNF, or the Himnuta Company, in the event that it would be claimed by its owners after those additional five years. In this manner, already during the latter half of 1946, the transfer of missing person's property in the Land Registration Office to the name of the Himnuta Company commenced.

> In all those cases where such agreements were conducted [between Gurevich as custodian on behalf of the rabbinical court and the JNF and the Himnuta Company] transfer was authorized in the district deed books and in the Government Land Registration offices in Jerusalem, and thus the legality of this activity establishing a national Jewish Custodian for the missing persons' property was demonstrated officially and unreservedly.[126]

At the end of 1946, the JNF decided conclusively to transfer missing persons' land and property through the method which had been elaborated

---

125 Ibid.
126 CZA, A402/113 in n. 123 – quotation from there; CZA, KKL5/14318, letter from Granovsky to Rabbi Uziel 24.6.1946, letter from Haifa Chief Rabbinate to Jerusalem Chief Rabbinate 26.6.1946; CZA, KKL5/14328, letter from Weiss to Moller 4.12.1946; CZA, KKL5/14336, letter from Gurevich to JNF 28.2.1947; CZA, KKL5/14340, report on "How the Property in Palestine of Missing Persons is Being Dealt with," drawn up by G. Turner, 28.4.1947. See the agreements and formal authorizations between JNF and Gurevich, CZA, KKL5/14333, KKL5/14328.

with Gurevich, and in principle not to implement the agreement with the Custodian General. This line of activity was concealed from the Custodian General.[127] However, the JNF exploited the agreement to its benefit in the following manner: Relying on this agreement and on the directives that were circulated by the Custodian General to various Government authorities "ostensibly with a view toward transferring this property [of missing persons] to joint supervision with him according to the conditions of the agreement with the Government," the JNF received data from various Government authorities, first and foremost the property tax bureau, regarding land and property which could be assumed to belong to missing persons.[128] The information requested pertained to property owners in Europe who had fallen behind on their tax payments for an appreciable period. Furthermore, the JNF intended to activate the agreement with the Custodian General "in cases where we will not succeed in verifying whether the owners are missing and heirless. Those 'questionable' [quotation marks in the original] cases will be turned over to the Custodian General for the purpose of joint management, in accordance with the contract we signed with the Government."[129]

From the end of 1946, the JNF stepped up its handling of the transfer of missing persons' property in accordance with the "Gurevich model." Increased activity was undertaken to amass information from Government bodies and local authorities, and the attorneys the JNF engaged to serve as custodians under rabbinical decrees in order to register lands under the name of the Himnuta Company was expanded. Likewise, the JNF offices

127 There is no mention of this in JNF publications but the arrangement with the Custodian General is stressed. On this see JNF Report 1947, pp. 130–132; *Karnenu* (April 1947), p. 13 (Nov. 1947), p. 12.

128 CZA, A402/113, memorandum from Weiss 8.12.1946 concerning "Activities Relating to the Property in Palestine of Missing Persons" – quotation from there; CZA, KKL5/14340, letter from Weitz to Finance and Economic Department 2.10.1946.

129 CZA, KKL5/14345, memorandum regarding "Property of Missing Persons" drawn up by Turner on 21.11.1946 – quotation from there. See also CZA, A402/113, memorandum by Weiss 8.12.1946 concerning "JNF Activities Relating to Property in Palestine of Missing Persons"; CZA, KKL5/14340, summary of a conversation that took place on 27.12.1946 with the participation of Gurevich, Weiss, and Turner; CZA, KKL5/14320, letter from Landau of the Special Projects Department to JNF Head Office 11.9.1947; CZA, KKL5/14320, letter from Weiss and Mohilewer to Yaeli of JNF Zebulun Valley Office 30.9.1947.

in Haifa and Tiberias were requested to allocate manpower for the benefit of the project, and substantial resources were allotted to the payment of tax arrears of missing persons.

In the course of this activity, numerous difficulties arose. Among them were demands by local authorities for rights to the lands of missing persons – demands which obligated the JNF to reach certain agreements with them. Substantial amounts of real estate property had already come under the control of the Custodian of Enemy Property. For example, regarding the missing persons' lands in the vicinity of Nathanya it emerged that "the Lands Registration Office officials had already provided the Custodian of Enemy Property with complete lists of the property owners resident in Europe and an award decree had been issued against this property. Therefore, we will only have leftover crumbs – thanks to accidental neglect, or in those cases where the location of the property owners could not be ascertained." A number of land purchase companies refused to transfer missing persons' lands to the JNF, and similar refusals were encountered from representatives of missing persons. It was also necessary to contend with those who fraudulently presented claims on missing persons property.[130] It

130   CZA, A402/113, memorandum by Weiss on 8.12.1946 regarding "JNF Activities Relating to Property of Missing Persons"; CZA, KKL5/13847, letter from Gurevich to JNF 6.9.1945; CZA, KKL5/14340, summary of a discussion with the participation of Gurevich, Weiss, and Turner, 27.12.1946; CZA, KKL5/14346, memorandum concerning "Property of Missing Persons" drawn up by Turner on 21.11.1946; CZA, KKL5/14807, letter from Weiss to Granovsky, and Weitz 24.6.1946; CZA, KKL5/ 14328, letter from Moller to Granovsky 26.8.1946; CZA, S12/14992, letter from the Kehilat Tzion Company to Jewish Agency Department for Settlement of Veteran Soldiers 29.9.1946; CZA, KKL5/16036, memorandum regarding "The Visit of G. Turner to Nathanya Concerning Missing Persons' Property," 15.11.1946 – quotation from there; CZA, KKL5/14318, letter from Weiss to Kroglikow 17.11.1946; CZA, KKL5/14328, the following letters: Weiss to Moller 4.12.1946, Kefar Ata local council to JNF 11.12.1946, Gurevich to JNF 31.12.1946; CZA, KKL5/14335, letter from Turner to Nahmani 9.1.1947; CZA, KKL5/14336, letter from Granovsky to Krinitzki, chairman of Ramat Gan local council 24.1.1947; CZA, KKL5/14318, letter from Weiss to Kamini 24.1.1947; CZA, KKL5/14319, letter to Dunkelblum and Bavli, February 1947; CZA, KKL5/14319, letter from Weiss and Mohilewer to Haifa JNF Office 2.2.1947; CZA, KKL5/14328, letter from Weiss and Mohilewer to President of the Kefar Ata local council 2.2.1947; CZA, KKL5/14319, letter from Weiss and Mohilewer to Yavitz 9.2.1947; CZA, KKL5/14340, memorandum drawn up by Turner concerning "Land Property of the Kehilat Tzion Company" 11.2.1947; CZA, KKL5/14328, letter from the Kehilat Tzion Company to Solomon 2.2.1947;

increasingly emerged that a substantial portion of the abandoned lands in Palestine were not necessarily the property of those missing in the wake of the Holocaust, but were the property of Jews residing in the United States and other countries, who for various reasons had ceased making tax payments on their property, or in general no longer evinced an interest in owning property in Palestine.[131]

At the beginning of 1947, the JNF encountered another and unforeseen difficulty when it attempted to obtain through Gurevich a custodial decree from the Tel Aviv Rabbinate, then headed by Rabbi Isser Yehuda Unterman. Although the rabbi in principle supported the JNF project regarding the property of missing persons, and he recognized the fundamental ruling on the issue delivered by the Chief Rabbinate Council in the previous Summer when it upheld the decisions of the Haifa Rabbinate, he raised a number of demands before he was prepared to issue decrees. Rabbi Unterman sought to apply these demands on the national scale as well. First of all, he demanded prolonging to ten years the period in which the JNF was obligated to restore the properties to the owners intact, if they succeeded in proving their ownership. In such an event, the JNF feared that the development of the lands of missing persons transferred to the Himnuta Company would be substantially delayed "and this would retard the development of the entire

---

CZA, KKL5/ 14319, letter from Kamini to JNF 17.2.1947; CZA, KKL5/14336, letter from B. Grinman and Dominas to Turner 28.2.1947; CZA, KKL5/14319, letter to Dunkelblum and Bavli, March 1947; CZA, KKL5/14333, letter from Mohilewer and Weiss to A. Danin 9.3.1947; CZA, KKL5/14336, letter to Dunkelblum 12.3.1947, letter from Dunkelblum to JNF 19.3.1947; CZA, KKL5/14319, letter from Grinman and Dominis to JNF 22.3.1947; CZA, KKL5/14337, letter from Mohilewer to Dunkelman 9.4.1947; CZA, KKL5/14340, memorandum by Turner on 25.4.1947 regarding "Property of Missing Persons in General – Gurewich"; CZA, KKL5/14326, letter from JNF to Yaeli of JNF Zebulun Valley Office 14.5.1947; CZA, KKL5/ 14337, letter from Grinman and Dominis to JNF 30.5.1947; CZA, KKL5/14319, letter from Weiss and Mohilewer to Yaeli of the JNF Zebulun Valley Office 30.5.1947; CZA, KKL5/14340, notes of a discussion with Ashbel 6.6.1947; CZA, KKL5/14337, letter from R. Avraham to Dominis and Grinman 26.6.1947; CZA, KKL5/14320, letter from Weiss and Mohilewer 26.6.1947; CZA, KKL5/14337, letter from Wiesman to JNF 25.7.1947; CZA, KKL5/14321, memorandum concerning "Agreement with the PLDC Regarding Plots of Land in Bat Yam Belonging to Missing Persons," 28.7.1947; CZA, KKL5/14321, letter from Ashbel of the PLDC to JNF 21.9.1947.

131 CZA, KKL5/14340, memorandum drawn up by Turner regarding "Proposal to Make Available Vacant Plots and Their Use," 10.2.1947.

land." Secondly, the rabbi demanded that the value of the property at the end of the ten year period (rather than at the time of the transfer to the Himnuta Company) should constitute the basis for payment to the owners after ten years. A third demand, which the JNF viewed as "in practice an act of extortion on the part of the Rabbinate," spoke of allocating part of the property transferred to the JNF to religious institutions throughout the country. This demand was based on the contention that the majority of the missing Jews were observant, and their names merited commemoration through the establishment of religious institutions. Rabbi Unterman sought to carry his demands to an Expanded Rabbinical Council in Jerusalem, especially since the Chief Rabbi, Rabbi Herzog, explained that he was not familiar with the entire issue because he was not in the country during the summer in which the Rabbinical Council had upheld the decisions of the Haifa Rabbinate. Rabbi Unterman was not prepared to issue custodial decrees of writs, and thus the legal foundation for any possibility to transfer missing persons' properties in the Tel Aviv vicinity to the JNF collapsed.[132]

The JNF could not accept the demands of Rabbi Unterman and was particularly incensed by the third demand. The JNF presented its case to Rabbi Herzog as well as to Rabbi Unterman and his associates, and brought it before a meeting of the Expanded Council of the Chief Rabbinate, which dealt with the issue at the end of May 1947. It explained the necessity for facilitating the development of the lands after a maximum of five years had elapsed from the time that lands were transferred to it. The JNF expressed its resentment over the fact that a rabbinical refusal to deliver custodial decrees could lead to the missing persons' lands being lost to Jewish ownership, or possibly falling into the hands of untrustworthy elements. In those deliberations, Rabbi Unterman finally waived his demands, and all the rabbis shared the opinion that the existing agreement with the JNF, including the period of trusteeship (five years) and the determining date for assessing the property as stipulated in the original agreement should

---

132   CZA, KKL5/14319, letter from Dunkelblum to Weiss 27.2.1947; CZA, KKL5/14336, letter from Gurevich to JNF 28.2.1947; CZA, KKL5/14340, letter from Turner to Weiss 7.5.1947 – quotation from there; CZA, KKL5/14319, letter from Toibman and Landau of JNF Special Projects Department to JNF Head Office 9.5.1947; CZA, KKL5/14340, memorandum regarding "Property in Palestine of Missing Persons: Deliberations with the Rabbinate," 22.5.1947, and memorandum, 25.4.1947 prepared by Turner concerning "Property of Missing Persons in General – Gurevich."

be upheld. Only in exceptional cases was the JNF obligated to return the property intact, until ten years had elapsed from the time the property had been transferred to its name.

There was general consensus in the Rabbinical Council regarding the importance of transferring the lands of missing persons to the JNF. Nonetheless, at the close of the discussion, Rabbi Herzog made a request to the JNF to allocate some plots of missing persons for the purpose of establishing religious institutions and projects, and in this manner commemorate their memory. But this request was not a pre-condition to the rabbinate's fundamental ruling as Rabbi Unterman had demanded at the beginning of the year. JNF representatives clarified in response to Rabbi Herzog's request that "the JNF in any case assented to the extent possible to demands for allocating building plots for religious purposes. There were already quite a few synagogues, study halls and yeshivot on JNF land. It could be assumed that in this case the JNF would give particular consideration to the requests of the Chief Rabbis."[133] Rabbi Unterman had earlier received clarifications from the Mayor of Tel Aviv, to the effect that the city had reached agreements with the JNF on allotting property in Tel Aviv of missing persons for the benefit of various public buildings "synagogues, ritual baths, hospitals," etc., as well as a number of monuments in memory of the missing persons.[134] Following upon the reaffirmed decision by the Chief Rabbinical Council, the Tel Aviv Rabbinate began issuing custodial decrees at the beginning of June 1947.[135]

---

133   CZA, KKL5/14319, letter from Toibman and Landau to JNF 22.5.1947 – quotation from there. See also CZA, KKL5/14340, memorandum prepared by Mohilewer concerning "Property in Palestine of Missing Persons – Deliberations with the Rabbinate," 22.5.1947; CZA, KKL5/14319, letter from Toibman to Rabbi Herzog 27.3.1947; CZA, KKL5/14320, proceedings of Extended Rabbinate Council of Palestine session, May 1947, and letter from Granovsky to Rabbi Herzog 5.6.1947. See also the corrected version of the agreement between JNF and Gurevich as a consequence of the rabbinate ruling, CZA, KKL5/16036 (draft of the agreement 16.11.1947). Cf. the original agreement in CZA, KKL5/14328.

134   CZA, KKL5/14320, excerpts from the statement of Rabbi Unterman at meeting of Extended Rabbinical Council, May 1947. It should be pointed out that Yad Vashem had also requested that property of missing persons be allocated to this institution dedicated to the memory of the victims of the Holocaust during the Second World War. The JNF agreed in principle, see the letter from Weiss to Shenhav of Yad Vashem 31.8.1947.

135   CZA, KKL5/14337, letters from Gurevich to JNF 15.6.1947, 24.8.1947.

Until the establishment of the State of Israel, the transfer of the lands and other real estate property of missing persons to the Himnuta Company through rabbinical custodial decrees, with the JNF covering the taxes of the missing persons, was the method which the property of persons missing in the Holocaust was transferred to the JNF. This method was concealed from the Custodian General, while the JNF's agreement with him from August 1946 was in effect frozen at the initiative of the JNF. There was no little apprehension in the JNF that the method of custodial decrees issued by the rabbinate would be discovered by the Custodian General. The Custodian General was interested in activating the agreement, and he approached the JNF on this matter. The JNF evaded him and intended to consider the future activation of the agreement only in those cases where its investigations had not clearly demonstrated that the property involved was that of a person who had perished.[136] It was clear to the JNF that the activation of the agreement with the Custodian General in all cases would not permit the further transfer of lands to the JNF through rabbinical custodial decrees, because the Custodian General would take the property under his supervision. Furthermore, the argument was put forward as follows:

> We must fully consider the advisability of assisting the Government in obtaining vast amounts of Jewish property which in the end result would be sold in public auction, and we have no guarantee that it would be sold to us at a reasonable price.... It appears to me that any improvements and other factors that would raise the value of the land would be made only to enrich the Government's coffers, since the price at which the property would be sold at public auction would appreciate and would perhaps exceed our feasibility considerations. Hence implementation of the agreement would contravene our interest in improving and developing the land.[137]

---

136 CZA, KKL5/14320, letter from Landau of JNF Department for Special Projects to JNF Head Office 11.9.1947, letter from Weiss and Mohilewer to Yaeli of the JNF Zebulun Valley Office 30.9.1947; CZA, KKL5/14340, Memorandum prepared by Turner concerning "Property of Missing Persons – General," 29.7.1947; Report prepared by Turner concerning "How property in Palestine of missing persons is dealt with," 2.6.1947.

137 CZA, KKL5/14340, report prepared by Turner regarding "Property of Missing Persons – General," 29.7.1947 – quotation is from Turner's comments.

While dealing with the transfer of the missing persons' lands to its ownership through rabbinical custodial decrees, the JNF managed to reach agreements with a number of real estate companies and agents. Under the agreement they transferred to the Himnuta Company or the JNF some of the lands they had sold to those defined as missing persons, and for various reasons these companies had not transferred the lands in the Lands Registration Office to the benefit of those missing persons. Within the framework of these agreements, the JNF paid the companies the balance owed by the purchasers, as well as well as tax arrears and obligated itself to be answerable for any legal process that should be presented against the companies. The companies and real estate agents in question were: Kishon, Cooperative Association for Neighborhood Management in Haifa, Ltd., which transferred to the JNF missing persons' land in Kishon; and the Ma'agal Company, which transferred to the JNF missing persons' land and in Bat Yam.

A detailed report prepared by Attorney Aharon Ben-Shemesh in 1952 regarding "The Property of Missing Persons in Israel Currently Under the Management of the JNF – the Department for the Property of Missing Persons in Israel," and additional data yielded the following totals concerning missing persons' property registered under the name of JNF or the Himnuta Company, in the middle of 1948: In Bat Yam – 176 plots representing a total area of 114 dunams. Of these 104 were building plots in a total area of 68 dunams, obtained in transfers through rabbinical custodial decrees and the balance in the framework of transfers from the Ma'agal and PLDC companies. (From Ma'agal – 27 plots representing an area of 17 dunams and from the PLDC – 45 plots representing an area of 28.5 dunams.) In Afula about 62 plots and parcels representing an area of 293 dunams – all obtained by rabbinical custodial decrees. In the Kishon area, 161 parcels and plots representing an area of 246 dunams, of which 71 parcels and plots representing a total area of 131 dunams, were obtained by rabbinical custodial decrees on the property of the Association of Kishon Land Purchasers, and the balance through transfer from the Kishon Cooperative Association for Neighborhood Management in Haifa, Ltd. (90 parcels and plots representing a total area of 114 dunams). In Kefar Atta – 149 plots in an area of 222 dunams, by rabinnical custodial decrees; in Holon – 17 plots representing an area of 8 dunams, by rabbinical custodial decrees; in Rehovot – one plot representing an area of 0.75 dunam by rabbinical custodial decrees. In Tel Aviv – 9 plots representing an area of 3.7 dunams by rabbinical custodial decrees and in Haifa (the Zebulun Valley, Bat Galim, Mt. Carmel and Ahuza) – 30 plots representing an area of 35.5 dunams, by rabbinical custodial decrees.[138] It transpires that through Gurevich alone, the property ownership of ninety missing persons was transferred to the Himnuta Company.[139]

During the course of 1946–1947 the JNF sought to publicize through its offices throughout the world, lists of all property owners whose property was located in the hands of the Custodian of Enemy Property, with the view of encouraging the owners or their heirs (to the extent that they were still alive) to demand the release of their property with the help of the JNF.[140] In addition, at the beginning of March 1948, the JNF demanded that the Jewish Agency apply to the "Implementation Committee" and the British Government to ensure that the Custodian of Enemy Property would transfer all Jewish property under its control to the JNF as a trustee until the establishment of the states in Palestine. The JNF feared that the Custodian could either sell this property, or accede to the demands of countries whose Jewish residents owned the property to obtain this real estate. As a trustee, the JNF intended to reach a future agreement with the Jewish State and sought permission to sell already Jewish real estate property located within the areas of the future Arab State, "given the danger that if it would remain in the area of that State, it would then prove too late to reach a satisfactory agreement with it."[141] However, the JNF was unable to realize this aspiration.

While gathering data regarding the property in Palestine of missing persons during the period of 1945–1948, it became apparent to the JNF that a large proportion of the abandoned private property did not actually belong to persons missing in the Holocaust. These were generally plots of several hundred square meters, or of a few dunams, that remained uncultivated or

---

138 Israel National Archives, 19/3132c (1203a), survey of the property in Israel of missing persons controlled by the JNF 22.10.1952.
139 CZA, KKL5/16045, letter from Gurevich to JNF 26.3.1948.
140 CZA, KKL5/14340, report drawn up by Turner concerning "How the Property in Palestine of Missing Persons was Dealt with," 2.6.1947; *Karnenu* (Nov. 1947), p. 12.
141 CZA, KKL5/17143, letter from JNF to Adrian of Jewish Agency 7.3.1948. See also CZA, S5/9324, summary by B. Joseph 27.4.1945 that raises the demand that the property of Jews in Palestine held by the Custodian of Enemy Property be transferred to the Zionist institutions.

were not utilized for building, and their owners had ceased to pay taxes on them. It was found that they belonged to Jews living in the United States, Britain or Canada.

The properties of these owners were concentrated in four main locations: In the Moshav of Migdal in Lower Galilee, where lands had been sold in the 1920s by the Migdal Garden Villa Company[142]; in the vicinity of Afula, where lands were sold during the 1920s by the Kehilat Tzion Company; in Gan Yavne, where lands were sold in the early 1930s by the Ahuzat New York Company; and on Mount Carmel, where lands were sold by the Hamanhil Company. In Migdal, some of the plots were cultivated by Arabs. In general, the abandoned private lands could not be developed or utilized for expanding existing farms, establishing new farms or for erecting buildings. Apprehension was also voiced that the owners would sell the properties to Arabs or even to Jews who would use them for speculation, and thus the very sale would result in "a large-scale export of capital from the country." All these considerations induced the JNF to gather data during 1947–1948 regarding the landowners with a view to approaching them with offers to transfer the lands to the JNF as contributions, life bequests, or alternatively under certain conditions, to sell them to the JNF. The overseas offices of the JNF assisted it in tracing the owners, but because of the difficulties involved, little effort was invested in making these contacts, especially as the prospects of concluding such transfers were limited.[143]

---

142   Katz (1994a), pp. 247–276.

143   CZA, KKL5/14340, memorandum drawn up by Turner regarding "Property of Missing Persons – General," 29.7.1947; CZA, KKL5/17134, memorandum drawn up by Turner regarding "Proposal to Make the Vacant Plots Available for Utilization," 10.2.1947 – quotation from there; CZA, KKL5/14320, letter from Weiss and Mohilewer to Mendel Fischer 6.6.1947; CZA, KKL5/16044, letter from Yaeli of JNF Zebulun Office to Granovsky 30.10.1947; CZA, KKL5/14330, letter from the Migdal Agricultural Mutual Aid Society to JNF 18.5.1947, memorandum drawn up by Turner regarding "Lands in Migdal Belonging to American Jews," 24.5.1947; CZA, KKL5/14320, letter from Weiss to Spiegelman 9.9.1947; CZA, KKL5/16037, letter from Weiss to Spiegelman 14.10.1947; CZA, KKL5/14330, letter from Weiss to the Migdal Agricultural Mutual Aid Society 15.6.1947, memorandum regarding "Lands in Migdal and Afula Belonging to American Jews"; CZA, KKL5/16029, letter from JNF to the Custodian General of the Palestine Government regarding "Property in Gan Yavne of Missing Persons – American Citizens," 15.10.1947; CZA, KKL5/16035, letter from Mohilewer to JNF in London 27.10.1947; JNF Conference (1947), pp. 31–33.

In October 1945, the JNF had been approached by the land expert Zalman Lifschitz (who was not a JNF employee) with a proposal to gather information regarding plots owned by Jews that had been abandoned in Jerusalem and its immediate vicinity. Some of these lands had been purchased at the end of the nineteenth century. This was a total of "over 23,000 dunams which were scattered in plots and sub-plots of one to two hundred dunams in 44 Moshavot out of the 91 Moshavot in the Jerusalem district." The JNF agreed to the proposal and asked Lifschitz undertake the project in conjunction with its Lands Department. It considered the work of gathering the data and taking measures to have these lands transferred to the JNF as being essential since the officials of the "Land settlement" were beginning to determine ownership of property in the vicinity of Jerusalem, following upon the bombing by terrorists of the Land Registration Office and the vast damage that had been inflicted on the records. On the basis of the data to be gathered, the JNF intended to approach the owners with the proposal to turn the lands over to the JNF as a donation or in return for covering the expenses they had incurred. The JNF also planned to ascertain from the data gathered whether some of the owners were victims of the Holocaust and to attempt to have these properties transferred to the JNF.[144]

From the end of 1945, Lifschitz gathered information on lands owned by Jews in Jerusalem, for which the JNF allocated a special budget of P£16,000. He also assisted in registering some of the abandoned property – within the "Lands settlement" arrangement – in the names of the owners together with the JNF, which paid the taxes. His detailed findings provided the basis for a map of land ownership in Jerusalem, which he completed in the summer of 1947. It should be noted that very few of the properties in the vicinity of Jerusalem (apart from some in the village of Hizma north of the city) were registered in the name of persons missing in the Holocaust.[145]

144 CZA, KKL10, minutes of JNF Directorate meeting, 28.10.1945 – quotation from there; see also ibid., minutes of JNF Directorate meeting, 2.6.1947; CZA, KKL5/ 15119, the following letters: Lifschitz to JNF 18.10.1945, 7.11.1946, 9.5.1947, 11.6.1947, 17.6.1947, letter from Ben-Gurion to Shertok 27.2.1946, letter from Weitz to Lifschitz 15.6.1947; CZA, KKL5/14340, memorandum prepared by Turner concerning "Property of Missing Persons – General," 29.7.1947. See also Katz (1996b), pp. 76–77; JNF Report (1947), 37–38; Reichman (1989), pp. 303–311; Haboker, 14.12.1945.

145 Reichman (1989), pp. 303–311, which includes the map drawn up by Lifschitz;

Purchase Policy on the Eve of the Establishment
of the State of Israel and Purchase of Lands
from the Germans and the British Army

With the publication in early September 1947 of the UNSCOP Committee
Report, the JNF believed that the recommended partition boundaries
detailed in the map appended to the Report, would not necessarily be fixed
as the final boundaries of the Jewish State. The JNF assumed that changes
could occur both to the benefit and to the detriment of the Jewish State. The
leaders of the JNF were certain that the partition boundary recommended
by the majority of the UNSCOP representatives was in itself influenced
to a large extent by the map of Jewish settlement. Weitz, for example,
found corroboration for this viewpoint, in the Negev's inclusion within
the area of the proposed Jewish State. "It is obvious that they would not
have agreed to offer us the Negev if we hadn't established facts there in the
past year. We have saved it for us by force of settlement and by force of
laying the pipe line." Against this background and amidst the uncertainty
surrounding the date that the partition plan would be implemented, the
JNF believed that purchase efforts should continue as a basis for new
settlements or buttressing existing settlements. This was needed to expand
the boundaries of the future Jewish State to the extent possible over and
beyond the lines recommended by UNSCOP, and reinforce the hold by
Jews in those places "where our status is quite weak." The decision adopted
to make widespread purchases in the South and the Negev, in an area of
65,000 dunams, was also apparently motivated by the goal of guaranteeing
that those regions not included by the UNSCOP recommendations within
the boundaries of the Jewish State, would actually be included within the
State's final boundaries. The JNF's regional offices received directives
from the Lands Department to make every effort to complete purchases

---

CZA, KKL10, minutes of JNF Directorate meetings, 28.10.1945, 2.6.1947; CZA,
KKL5/14340, memorandum prepared by Turner; CZA, KKL5/14327, including the
following documents: memorandum prepared by Weiss regarding "Land in Beit
Zefafa Belonging to Missing Persons," 25.5.1947, memorandum prepared by Weiss
regarding "Land in Jerusalem Belonging to Missing Persons," 13.5.1947, letter from
Lifschitz to JNF 9.5.1947, memorandum regarding "Registration of Lands Owned by
Jews in the Vicinity of Jerusalem," 19.4.1946.

from Arabs, or at least obtain irrevocable powers of attorney from them, and thus the lands would not remain registered in the names of the Arab sellers.[146] The JNF Lands Department undertook a special challenge by designating in its 1947–1948 operational plan to complete the JNF's land capital to a total of a million dunams, since by the end of 1946–1947, the total property reached 928,000 dunams. "This fact imposes upon all of us, the employees of the Lands Department, an obligation that the year 1947–1948 will be the year a million was attained....This is a sacred obligation and it must be met."[147] At the same time, the JNF set out to obtain ownership deeds over Jewish land property, fearing that they would be systematically destroyed by the British, in the event that they would evacuate the country. In the period from the UNSCOP recommendation on 31 August 1947 until the United Nations General Assembly resolution on 29 November 1947 regarding partition and its boundaries, purchases were completed and obligations were signed regarding 7,000 dunams – the majority from Arabs.[148]

The United Nations 29 November 1947 resolution led to a change in JNF policy. Now that the political future in Palestine had been decided by the United Nations, the JNF had to determine its position regarding the implementation of new purchases in areas that were assigned to the Arab State. In general, it was decided to focus on implementing purchases only in the areas assigned to the Jewish State, according to the boundaries set forth under the UN resolution. However, it was also decided that in the areas of the Arab State, purchases would proceed in places adjacent to lands that were already owned by the JNF. This was done in order to strengthen those

---

146 Weitz (1951), p. 540, the first quotation from Weitz's comment; CZA, KKL5/17214, minutes of a meeting with the participation of Stromeza, Wolff, and A. Danin in Haifa, 5.11.1947; CZA, KKL5/17138, summary from JNF Head Office "With the publication of the United Nations Committee's Report in October 1947" (also in KKL5/13995) – second quotation from there; CZA, KKL10, minutes of JNF Directorate meetings, 25.11.1947, 3.2.1948. See also Katz (1992), pp. 34–35, and cf. Granovsky (1951b), pp. 217–218.

147 CZA, KKL5/14040, letter from the JNF to Zuckerman 26.9.1947.

148 CZA, KKL5/17182, letter from Yaeli of JNF Zebulun Valley Office to Granovsky 24.10.1947, letter from S. Ben-Shemesh to JNF Zebulun Valley Office 5.11.1947. See also CZA, KKL5/17143, letter from H. Danin to the Secretariat of the Situation Committee 14.5.1948; CZA, KKL10, minutes of JNF Directorate meeting, 3.2.1948.

settlements that would remain outside the boundaries of the Jewish State
(a total of 31), either through territorial increments to existing settlements,
or by setting up new settlements in their vicinity. Furthermore, purchases
within the boundaries of the Arab State were conditioned on the feasibility
of guaranteeing registration of JNF ownership (regarding those lands
that were registered in the Lands Registration Office) by the end of April
1948.[149] At the same time, the JNF sought to guarantee that the transfer
and registration processes regarding those lands that were in the process
of purchase finalization within the boundaries of the Arab State would be
concluded.[150]

The security situation that developed after the UN resolution in fact
almost totally precluded further purchases from Arabs. Therefore, the JNF
focused its efforts on completing the transfer to its ownership of purchases
that had already been implemented and in purchasing the land owned by
Germans in Palestine and in British army camps, further details of which
are given below.[151] In addition, the JNF and the entire Zionist Organization
attached special importance to implementing purchases in Jerusalem
and its immediate vicinity, in order to strengthen the Jewish hold in the
city, in view of the UN decision to internationalize Jerusalem as part of
its resolution on partition.[152] This was the context of a JNF approach to
the Jewish Agency's delegation to the United Nations requesting that
every effort be made to have the UN's resolution on the boundaries of the
Jerusalem region include three JNF-owned areas located in the periphery
of the city. These JNF lands were Dehaishe, south of Bethlehem, envisaged
as an industrial community; lands near Motza, where the JNF proposed to

---

149   CZA, KKL5/15929, letter from JNF to Zuckerman 4.1.1948; CZA, KKL5/17198,
      memorandum by Weitz "On New Settlements Within the Area of the Arab State,"
      11.12.1947. See also the list of settlements outside the area of the Jewish State, CZA,
      KKL5/17143 (no date).

150   CZA, KKL5/17142, letter from H. Danin to JNF Haifa Office 21.12.1947, letter from
      Yaeli of JNF Zebulun Valley Office to JNF Head Office 22.12.1947; CZA, KKL5/
      17143, letter from Weitz to Zuckerman 4.1.1948.

151   CZA, KKL10, minutes of JNF Directorate meetings, 3.2.1948, 16.3.1948; CZA,
      KKL5/15931, letter from Weitz to Nahmani 18.4.1948; CZA, KKL5/17143,
      memorandum drawn up by Czernowitz regarding "Change of the Scope of JNF's
      Tasks in Light of the Situation," 13.2.1948 (also in KKL5/15911).

152   CZA, KKL10, minutes of JNF Directorate meeting, 16.3.1948; Katz (1996b), pp.
      82–90.

concentrate a few hundred dunams that could be used for establishing an industrial neighborhood, or vacation camps in the vicinity of Jerusalem; and the JNF area on Buregh Hill between Sanhedria and Nebi Samuel, which aside from settlement prospects were of strategic importance.[153] In practice, given the security conditions, the expensive land prices and the small supply available, it was impossible to do anything tangible toward purchasing land in the city and its vicinity during the interim between the UN resolution and the establishment of the State of Israel in May 1948.[154]

Efforts to Purchase the Lands Owned by Germans in Palestine and the Purchase of the Sharona Lands

Upon the outbreak of the Second World War, the German community which had developed in Palestine since the latter half of the nineteenth century totaled 2,000. Two-thirds of them were Templars, and the rest Protestants and German Catholics.[155] In 1947, the Germans owned about 46,000 dunams and by some estimates, they owned more. The majority of the real estate property was concentrated in the German villages of Wilhelma, Waldheim, Bethlehem and Sharona. Germans also owned real estate property in the German colonies of Jerusalem and Haifa, in Bir Salim, in Alkima, in various places throughout the Upper Galilee, etc. About 15,000 dunams of the German–owned properties were located in urban areas where Germans maintained various institutions, such as Augusta Victoria on Mt. Scopus, the Schneller orphanage in West Jerusalem, etc.[156]

At the outbreak of the Second World War, and even prior to it, young Germans left Palestine with a view to serving in the German Army. During the course of the War, the German population resident in Palestine was transferred to local detention camps, and some were exiled to Australia. At the end of the War, an additional part of the German population left Palestine and returned to Germany. In total, the German population in Palestine in 1947 numbered slightly above 400. Under the legislation in

---

153 CZA, KKL5/17143, letter from JNF to Lifschitz in New York 10.12.1947.
154 Katz (1996b), pp. 82–90.
155 CZA, S40/147/1, letter from Arianne to Shertok 5.12.1944.
156 Ibid.; CZA, KKL5/17139, "Memorandum on Property in Palestine Owned by Germans," 28.12.1947, JNF memorandum regarding "Value of Land Owned by Germans in the Agricultural Region," 25.1.1948; *Karnenu* (June–July); ibid. (Dec. 1949).

force until the establishment of the State of Israel, the Germans who were in Palestine or exiled to Australia were defined as "enemy subjects," and their total land capital comprised about a quarter to a third of the total German–owned land capital in Palestine. According to law, the property of "enemy subjects" was not expropriated in favor of the Custodian of Enemy Property. "Enemy subjects" were entitled to trade in their real estate property, but they had to receive the prior approval of the Commissioner of Police. A different legal status applied to German real estate property in Palestine when the owner was already resident in Germany, or in one of the countries conquered by Germany. The extent of real estate property in this category totaled a third to a quarter of German-owned property in Palestine and the Trading with the Enemy Ordinance of 1939 applied to them. Under this ordinance, this property was awarded by virtue of a commissioner's decree to the Custodian of Enemy Property and the option of the German "owners" to trade with them freely was frozen.[157]

Jewish interest in the German real estate property in Palestine arose prior to the end of the Second World War. Two bodies were mainly interested: the Zionist Institutions (through the Jewish Agency) and the Tel Aviv Municipality. The Jewish Agency preferred to view the whole of German–owned property located in Palestine as one of the sources for compensation that would be awarded to the Jewish people and Jewish residents at the end of the War. On this matter, the Jewish Agency had even approached the British Government, and in conjunction with the JNF gathered data regarding German–owned real estate property in Palestine including assets maintained by the Custodian of Enemy Property. The Jewish Agency also approached the British authorities to ensure that the remnants of the German community were evicted from the country, while those who had already left would be prevented from returning. This demand was predicated on the Jewish Agency's contention that the local Germans had openly supported Germany's crimes against the Jewish people during the course of the War (some Germans who had been resident in the German colonies served in the German army and in the extermination camps), and many of them had

---

157   CZA, S40/147/1 as in n. 155; CZA, KKL5/15565, letter from Kaplan to Weiss, no date but obviously from 1947, concerning the lands at Sharona and land owned by Germans in Palestine; CZA, KKL5/15564, memorandum from Fineberg sent to JNF on 26.1.1947.

openly supported Arab terror actions during 1936–1939.[158] However, the British Government was in no hurry to respond to the Jewish Agency's demands. In general, the issue of German–owned property in Palestine as a source for compensation of the Jewish people was complicated, given the general question of compensation which Germany would have to pay within the framework of a peace agreement to the countries which had been damaged. One of the questions that arose was the allocation – as a source of compensation – of German–owned property in the Mandated territories and in the colonies. It would appear that the Zionist Institutions estimated that it would be a long time before British and international recognition would be forthcoming regarding the right of the Jewish community in Palestine to German property there as part of the compensation due to the Jewish people.[159] Action was therefore required to obtain the German property through an alternative route. The Tel Aviv Municipality was the second Jewish body with an interest in purchasing German–owned lands, even prior to the conclusion of the Second World War. The lands of the German Colony, Sharona comprised nearly 7,000 dunams, of which 4,400 were included in the urban building plan of Tel Aviv as well as in the municipal development plans. Most of the land carried the status of property of "enemy citizens" property whose sale was not prohibited. About one-third of the area was awarded to the Custodian of Enemy Property. Already prior to the conclusion of the War, the Municipality requested the Mandatory Government to transfer to it, by expropriation, the areas on the boundaries of the Tel Aviv municipal urban building plans, but the request was rejected.[160] Nonetheless, contacts continued between the Municipality and the Government (i.e., the Custodian of Enemy Property and the other

---

158   CZA, minutes of JNF Directorate meeting, 12.3.1944; proceedings of the meetings of the Smaller Zionist General Council held on 19.6.1945, 30.10.1945; CZA, KKL5/ 15564, letter from Shertok to the High Commissioner 4.6.1945; CZA, S40/147/1 as in n. 155; CZA, S25/9324, memorandum drawn up by B. Joseph 27.4.1945 concerning the work of the sub-committee of the Planning Commission; CZA, S40/114/1, proceedings of the meeting of the Planning Commission of Jewish Agency, 24.1.1944; *Karnenu* (see above, n. 156).

159   CZA, KKL5/15564, as in n. 157.

160   CZA, S40/147/1 (see above, n. 155); CZA, KKL5/15565, summary of a discussion regarding the Sharona lands, 2.1.1947; CZA, KKL5/17139, "Memorandum Concerning German-owned Property in Palestine," 28.12.1947.

authorized bodies regarding the sales of property of "enemy citizens") and with the "enemy citizens" landowners regarding the possibility of purchasing the area. The German–nationals, whether resident in Palestine, or deportees to Australia, were most interested in selling their property and liquidating their capital and affairs in Palestine.[161]

At the beginning of 1947, an agreement in principle was reached – which the British Government in London later approved – between the Tel Aviv Municipality and the German residents of Sharona regarding the sale of 4,400 dunams by Mandatory Government expropriation. The JNF, which had previously begun to display an interest in purchasing all German–owned property in Palestine, joined the Municipality as a partner in the purchase of the Sharona lands.[162] Given the vast activity of the JNF during the 1940s in purchasing urban land in Palestine, and given the vast housing needs in the Tel Aviv vicinity, it viewed the purchase of the Sharona lands:

> As an opportunity to assist the development of Tel Aviv, to implement an orderly urban development plan in the vicinity of the largest Jewish city, and curb speculation and price increases which exerted a negative influence on the development of the city. The fact that the lands of Sharona had not yet been made available for building development in the city, caused many difficulties in the city planning and abetted the appreciation of land prices in other places....[163]

Negotiations between the Germans, the Mandatory Government, the Tel Aviv Municipality and the JNF toward the signing of final accords took place throughout almost the entire year 1947. During this period, the issue arose of German property in Palestine, which was to serve as part of the war indemnity that Germany was required to pay (according to international agreements reached at the time) to England, and the right

---

161 CZA, KKL5/15565, memorandum from Weiss to Kaplan 1947 (no exact date), memorandum following a meeting on 2.1.1947 concerning the Sharona lands.

162 Ibid.; CZA, KKL5/15565, the following documents: draft agreement between JNF and Tel Aviv Municipality, letter from Granovsky to Rokach 21.1.1947, decision of the Directorate regarding the Sharona lands 4.2.1947; CZA, KKL5/15564, letter from Weitz to Weiss (which was meant to have been sent to Y. Levy) 5.5.1947; CZA, KKL5/17139, letter from Weiss to Levy 14.5.1947.

163 CZA, KKL5/17104, memorandum drawn up by Czernowitz and sent to JNF Departments on 21.12.1947 – the quotation from there; *Karnenu* (above, n. 156).

of Jewish institutions to at least part of the said property as part of the compensation to the Jewish people.[164]

In the latter half of 1947, the British Mandatory Government passed a new law according to which the areas of Sharona in its entirety as well as other German–owned lands in Palestine were awarded to the Custodian of Enemy Property. It would appear that this law derived from the resolutions passed at the international conferences in Brussels and Paris at the close of 1945 and during 1946 which credited German property in Palestine to the account of war damages to which Britain would be entitled.[165] In any event, pursuant to the new law, the ownership of Germans residing in Palestine and Australia, who retained two-thirds of the area of Sharona which the JNF and the Tel Aviv Municipality sought to purchase, became void de facto. Thus, the remaining negotiators on the purchase were the Government through the Custodian of Enemy Property, the JNF, and the Tel Aviv Municipality.

At the end of 1947 the Custodian of Enemy Property assented to the Tel Aviv Municipality's request to purchase 4,239 dunams of the Sharona lands at a price of P£2.36 million.[166] Of this total, the JNF undertook to transfer P£1.18 million and in return it received 2,700 dunams within the framework of an agreement with the Municipality. Most of the area (about 1,860 dunams) included in the JNF's share was earmarked for housing,

164   CZA, KKL10, minutes of JNF Directorate meetings, 4.2.1947, 1.4.1947; CZA, KKL5/15564, letter from Landau and Toibman of JNF Special Projects Department to JNF Head Office 10.12.1946; CZA, KKL5/15565, memorandum from Weiss to Kaplan 1947 (no exact date); CZA, KKL5/15564, memorandum from Fineberg sent to JNF 26.1.1947; CZA, S25/6559, memorandum drawn up by Sherf on 24.1.1947 regarding the summary of the meeting with the participation of Kaplan, Granovsky, Gruenbaum, and Meyerson; CZA, KKL5/17139, letter from Weiss to Levy 14.5.1947; CZA, KKL5/15565, letter from Weiss to Rokach 6.8.1947, Borochov memorandum concerning the Sharona lands 18.8.1947.

165   CZA, KKL10, minutes of JNF Directorate meeting, 25.11.1947; CZA, KKL5/15564, letter from Landau and Toibman of JNF Special Projects Department to JNF Head Office 10.12.1946; CZA, KKL5/15565, letter from Weiss to Kaplan 1947 (no exact date); CZA, KKL5/15564, Fineberg memorandum sent to JNF on 26.1.1947.

166   CZA, KKL10, minutes of JNF Directorate meeting, 25.11.1947; CZA, KKL5/17104, letter from the Mayor of Tel Aviv to JNF Head Office 23.10.1947, memorandum regarding the agreement between Tel Aviv Municipality and JNF regarding the Sharona Lands (no date, apparently from the end of 1947 or the beginning of 1948).

and part for industry and institutions. The Municipality obligated itself to the JNF not to sell its portion but to preserve the land under its ownership, and only to assign the area under leasing agreements. In this way, the JNF imposed upon the Municipality the lease principle and the maintenance of ownership by a Jewish public institution. Since the Government placed obstacles on the registration of the JNF's share in the Lands Registration Office and demanded that the Sharona lands be registered exclusively in the name of the Tel Aviv Municipality, the latter obligated itself to transfer the JNF's share for the time being in the form of a 999 year lease, while contracting to do everything necessary to expedite the transfer of the JNF's share in the Lands Registration Office.

In December, the JNF Directorate ratified the complex agreements with the Tel Aviv Municipality and at the end of the discussion the Directorate Members sought to express "their appreciation to the JNF Executive and to the Tel Aviv Municipality for their devoted and faithful activities in realizing such an important matter from a national and settlement standpoint – the redemption of the Sharona lands. Over half will go to the perpetual national ownership of the Jewish people and the balance to the public Jewish ownership of Tel Aviv."[167] A short while before the end of the Mandate, the JNF and the Tel Aviv Municipality succeeded in receiving the agreement of the Custodian of Enemy Property to sell them an additional 1,640 dunams of the Sharona lands. All in all, the total cost of purchasing the lands of Sharona amounted to P£3.035 million. In this manner the JNF's share in the financing totaled P£2.117 million. A few days before the end of the Mandate the purchase was completed and the

---

167   CZA, KKL10, minutes of JNF Directorate meetings, 25.11.1947, 16.12.1947
      – quotation from there, 18.2.1948, 16.3.1948; CZA, KKL5/17104, the following
      documents; memorandum regarding the agreement between Tel Aviv Municipality
      and JNF concerning the Sharona Lands (see above, also n. 166), memorandum
      regarding the agreement with Tel Aviv Municipal concerning the Sharona lands
      21.11.1947, letter from Granovsky to the Mayor of Tel Aviv 5.12.1947, memorandum
      regarding Sharona, 15.12.1947, letter from Granovsky to the Mayor of Tel Aviv (no
      date, but certainly from the end of 1947), memorandum from Czernowitz regarding
      the purchase of the Sharona lands sent to JNF departments on 21.12.1947, letter from
      Aricha, Secretary of JNF Directorate to the members of the Directorate 24.12.1947,
      additional letter from Aricha to members of the Directorate 24.12.1947, letter from
      Weitz to Granovsky 24.12.1947, letter from Konikow to Kroglikow 29.12.1947,
      letter from JNF to APC 5.4.1948.

transfers were registered in the Lands Registration Office.[168] When paying its share to the Government, the JNF and the Anglo-Palestine Bank were to transfer to the Mandatory Government P£1.793 million pounds from the blocked Palestinian accounts in London.[169]

As stated above, following the Second World War, the JNF displayed an interest not only in purchasing the German colony in Sharona, but in purchasing German–owned lands throughout the country in general. Aside from Sharona, the German property totaled 40,000 dunams.[170] Trade was possible on most of the German lands with the authorization of the Commissioner of Police, and only one-quarter to one-third of the German–owned lands were awarded to the Custodian of Enemy Property. The Germans in Palestine were interested in selling their lands (as well as lands belonging to the deportees residing in Australia) because for understandable reasons they sought to leave the country after the War and were even prepared to sell their property in return for property in Germany or for German currency. This property consisted of agricultural land and built-up Moshavot which could be purchased by the JNF without the restrictions of the Lands Law, since such transactions did not involve purchases from Arabs. As urban lands they were suitable for housing while utilizing the institutional structures erected on part of them. Some of the lands were located in the vicinity of existing Jewish settlements which asked the JNF to purchase them also in order to preempt their purchase by Arabs. This was the background to the contacts which the JNF conducted with the Germans and with the Government until mid-1947. The JNF requested the Government not only to remove police restrictions, but also assistance in transferring payments to Australia in order to facilitate the transactions, and by inference lower the price that would be demanded by the German owners.[171] The JNF proposed to the Germans that they transfer

---

168 CZA, KKL5/17139, letter from Granovsky and Weiss, April 1948; CZA, L51/2668, letter from JNF to APC 5.4.1948; CZA, L51/2669, letter from Granovsky to Bart at APC 1.6.1948. On the vast importance of this purchase for the development of Tel Aviv see: *Karnenu* (above, n. 156); Report JNF (1949), p. 9.

169 CZA, L51/2669, letter from Granovsky to Bart at APC 1.6.1948; CZA, KKL5/15924, letter from Weitz to Granovsky 7.6.1948.

170 CZA, KKL5/17139, "Memorandum Concerning German-owned Lands in Palestine," 28.12.1947.

171 CZA, KKL10, minutes of JNF Directorate meeting, 8.10.1945; CZA, KKL5/15564, the following letters: Weiss to Birnbaum 20.10.1946, Weiss and Mohilewer to JNF Lands

a large portion of their property to the JNF as a gift. In recompense, the JNF would intercede with the Government to ensure that the balance of their property would not be expropriated as part of the German reparations within the framework of an international reparations agreement, but would be exchanged for Jewish property in Germany.[172]

Until mid-1947, the JNF did not succeed in implementing purchases from the Germans since they feared to reach agreements with it before the British authorities had finally clarified their stance regarding the sale of Sharona to the Tel Aviv Municipality.[173] In the interim, in the latter half of 1947, the British Government passed the law which awarded all German property in Palestine to the Custodian of Enemy Property. The JNF had no option but to enter into negotiations with the Custodian of Enemy Property at the end of 1947 regarding the possibility of purchasing German–owned land in Palestine (aside from Sharona). All in all, the German–owned property in Palestine (including Sharona) was appraised at P£7 million. The agricultural lands which totaled 13,000 dunams were appraised at P£1 million.[174] Since at that time the boundaries of the Jewish State had already been fixed by the United Nations, the JNF determined "the JNF's preferred order of priorities regarding the purchase of lands as being: (a) Areas of agricultural lands within the boundaries of the Jewish State; (b) Areas of land in the vicinity of Nahariya and Shavei Tziyon in order to strengthen these settlements; (c) The area of the land in Jerusalem's German Colony;

Department 14.11.1946, Landau and Toibman of JNF Special Projects Department to JNF Head Office 10.12.1946, Weiss and Mohilewer to Birnbaum 10.1.1947; CZA, KKL5/15565, memorandum from Weiss to Kaplan (no date, but probably 1947); CZA, KKL5/15564, the following letters: the Be'er Ya'akov local committee to JNF Executive 30.3.1947, Weiss and Mohilewer to Birnbaum 17.4.1947, Birnbaum to JNF 23.4.1947, Weitz to Weiss (copied to Y. Levy) 5.5.1947; CZA, KKL5/15627, summary of deliberations with WZO Settlement Department and Agricultural Center 9.6.1947 which also discussed the German–owned lands.

172 CZA, KKL5/15564, letter from Landau and Toibman to JNF Head Office 10.12.1946.

173 Ibid., letter from Weitz to Weiss (copied to Levy) 5.5.1947.

174 CZA, KKL5/17139, memorandum regarding German–owned land in Palestine 28.12.1947; CZA, KKL5/17139, letter from Levin to Custodian of Enemy Property 18.1.1948, memorandum regarding "The Value of German–owned Property in the Agricultural Area," 25.1.1948.

(d) Areas of land in the German Colony in Haifa."[175] At the same time, the JNF decided on measures to organize a group of capitalists in the United States who would purchase the lands of the German Colony in Haifa.[176] However, since only a few weeks remained until the end of the Mandate, the negotiations with the Custodian of Enemy Property were not concluded and the German–owned lands, save for Sharona, were not purchased by the JNF.[177]

Efforts to purchase the British Army camps

At the end of the Mandate, the British Army put up for sale its army camps in Aqir near Gedera (later Tel Nof), Sarafand (between Ramle and Rishon LeZion), and near Hiam Bay in the Zebulun Valley. All in all, real estate property in the three army camps totaled about 6,400 dunams (in Akir 2,400, in Sarafand 3,200 and Hiam Bay 800). The Akir camp was of vast importance because of the military airfield there which could in the future serve the military needs of the nascent Jewish State. The other camps could also serve future military needs and part of the area could be used for housing purposes. For this reason, at the beginning of 1948, the JNF and the Jewish Agency entered into negotiations with the British Army regarding the purchase of the camps. The JNF was to finance the purchase of the camps, whereas the Jewish Agency was to finance the purchase of the structures and equipment. The completion of negotiations was complex. With regards to Aqir, the Arabs demanded restoring to the site those Arabs from whom the army had expropriated the lands. With regards to the Sarafand Camp, the municipality of Ramle, with the financial backing of the Supreme Arab Council, entered into competition with the JNF. The Zionist institutions

---

175   CZA, KKL10, minutes of JNF Directorate meeting, 3.2.1948 – quotation from there; CZA, KKL5/17139, letter from Levin to Custodian of Enemy Property 18.1.1948; ibid., letter from Levin to Dornan of Palestine Government, 6.2.1948.

176   CZA, S25/6559, memorandum on the decisions taken at a meeting with the participation of Kaplan, Granovsky, Gruenbaum, and Meyerson 24.11.1947, letter from Sherf to Kaplan 24.11.1947.

177   *Karnenu* (June–July 1948). However, already in 1945 the JNF had become a sub-lessee of the German–owned lands at el-Hima near Gadera held by Custodian for Enemy Property. On this see CZA, KKL10, minutes of JNF Directorate meeting, 8.10.1945. On the manner which the German–owned lands were transferred to JNF after the establishment of the State of Israel, see *Karnenu* (ibid.); CZA, KKL10, minutes of JNF Directorate meetings, 24.6.1948, 16.11.1948.

gave priority to finalizing the purchase of the camp in Aqir because of "the importance of this site with its enhanced airfield was clear to us and we could not forego it." Indeed a few weeks before the end of the Mandate, the purchase of the camp was completed and registered under the name of the JNF. The purchase cost to the JNF was P£80,000. Due to the refusal of the British Government to grant its approval, the purchase of the other camps was not completed before the end of the Mandate.[178]

A summary of JNF purchases up to the beginning of the War of Independence and comparisons between the volume of land purchases in the beginning of the period covered by this book and the end of the period can be located in Maps 25, 27–40 and Appendix 3–5.

Preliminary Thoughts on the Role of the JNF as a Land Purchaser in the Jewish State

The imminent establishment of the Jewish State, as it became apparent in Autumn 1947, obligated the JNF to address the question of its place and even existence within the framework of the State. The heads of the JNF deliberated on this issue during the last months preceding the establishment of the State, an issue which was also pertinent to other bodies of the World Zionist Organization as well for the movement in general. It would appear that the JNF was quite apprehensive about facing liquidation in view of the transfer of its functions to the State. Furthermore, there was grave apprehension that the worldwide reservoir of contributors would view the State as the heir to the JNF's roles, and in particular as the successor to the JNF's central role as redeemer of lands in the Land of Israel. Various reports appeared in the Jewish press in Palestine regarding a huge volume of Government lands that would pass to the ownership of the Jewish State, as well as the possibility of expropriating lands from Arabs, only intensified the apprehension within the JNF that in the public's consciousness the establishment of the State would be interpreted as the termination of the JNF's role, and perforce contributions would decline immediately.[179]

---

178   CZA, KKL10, minutes of JNF Directorate meetings, 3.2.1948, 16.3.1948,18.3.1948; *Karnenu* (June–July 1948) – quotation from there.
179   CZA, KKL5/17189, letter from Kamini to Weitz 18.11.1947; CZA, KKL5/17138,

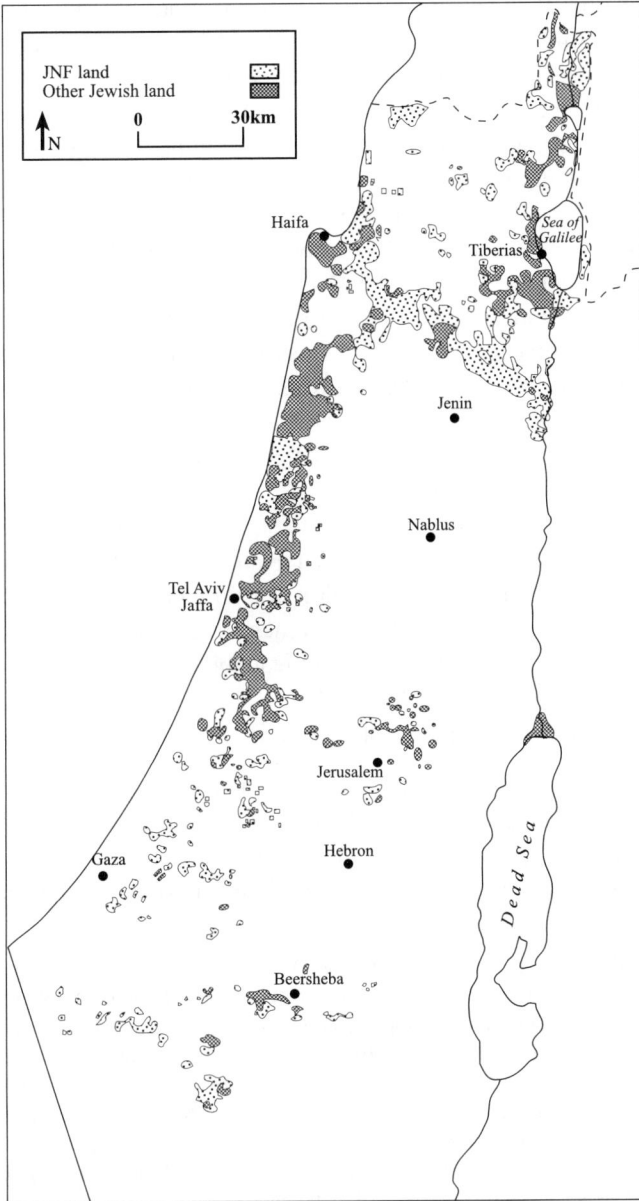

Map 25: Jewish land property and JNF land property in Palestine
at the end of 1947
Source: Weitz, Perot, map appendix

Beyond the JNF leaders' conviction of the need to maintain their institution within the framework of the State, it was but natural that also for personal reasons they did not wish to see its liquidation. In any case, it would appear that the immediate danger posed to the JNF was an immediate decline in contributions in view of the forthcoming establishment of the State, whose institutions, at least in the interpretation of the general public, would succeed the JNF. This was the background to a series of deliberations within the JNF departments, information activities and statements by JNF leaders regarding the issue of the JNF's role and objectives in a Jewish State in the final months preceding the establishment of the State of Israel. Apparently, the preoccupation with the issue of the role and function of the JNF in the Jewish State also derived from preparations for the future. The substantive discussions of the Directorate on the issue however, centering upon the JNF's land policy within the State, took place only after the establishment of the State of Israel.[180]

Immediately after the publication of the UNSCOP Committee Report in September 1947, the Head Office issued a circular letter to the JNF offices worldwide and in Palestine, in which it was emphasized that "the JNF's role would not conclude with the attainment of independence, but it had just begun."[181] Three months later, immediately after the UN resolution at the end of November, an additional circular letter was sent to the same addressees where it was again emphasized:

> In these great days we must remember the work of the Jewish National Fund has not yet reached its final stages. We are on the threshold of Herculean task whose extent cannot be estimated. The establishment of a Jewish State creates a framework. It is for the Jewish people and

---

memorandum from the JNF Head Office "With the Publication of the United Nations Commission's Report," Oct. 1948 (also in KKL5/13995); CZA, KKL5/15991, JNF memorandum "To JNF Supporters in Palestine and the Diaspora," 4.12.1947; *Karnenu* (Nov. 1948); ibid. (Dec. 1948); *Problems* (1948), p. 8.

180   See above, n. 179; CZA, S25/1899, letter from JNF to Meyerson 10.12.1947; CZA, KKL5/15911, the following documents: letter from JNF to Ben-Gurion 9.12.1947, letter from Dayan to JNF 17.12.1947, position paper by Wiesman (no date), memorandum regarding "The Status of the JNF after the Establishment of the Jewish State," drawn up by Czernowitz 14.1.1948, memorandum "General Lines Regarding the Issue of the Future of the JNF," 16.2.1948.

181   CZA, KKL5/17138, memorandum from JNF Head Office "With the Publication of the UNSCOP Committee Report," Oct. 1948 (also in KKL5/13995).

the Zionist Movement to endow it with content. As before, but ever more so, the JNF will be entrusted with creating the basis for the existence and development of the Jewish State: **land**.[182]

The two circulars conveyed a clear message to the effect that the State would be incapable of implementing the task of the JNF centering upon the purchase of lands. This was the case because the country's resources would have to satisfy first and foremost the current needs of the State and its citizens – Jews and Arabs alike. These resources would not suffice for purchasing land in the immense quantity necessary for absorbing mass immigration and settling it in urban and rural areas, as well as the realization of the development plans for that very same purpose, in whose framework agricultural settlement would have to occupy a prominent place. Some of those development plans which the JNF would also undertake would be the establishment of extensive irrigation projects, land preparation, reviving deserts and urban development. It was emphasized that "within the boundaries of the partitioned Palestine in which the Jews constitute a majority, there is a minority of land owned by Jews. The area represented by government lands within the boundaries of the State is also minute."[183]

It was hinted that only through the JNF could land redeemed in Palestine remain as the perpetual property of the Jewish people. Furthermore, it would appear that the leaders of the JNF stated fairly clearly that their institution, as well as those of the Zionist Organization, could carry out tasks for the State which discriminated in favor of its Jewish population and which the State therefore could not openly carry out.[184] In any case, the JNF did not

---

182 CZA, KKL5/15991, JNF memorandum "To Supporters of the JNF in Palestine and the Diaspora," 4.12.1947.

183 Ibid.

184 See above, nn. 181–182. See also CZA, KKL5/15911, the following documents: letter from Dayan to JNF 17.12.1947, position paper by Wiesman (no date), memorandum regarding "The Status of the JNF after the Establishment of the Jewish State," 14.1.1948, memorandum "General Lines for the Future of the JNF," 16.2.1948. See also Granot (1951b), pp. 234–235, 242–243; *Karnenu* (Dec. 1948), the article "Dr. A. Granovsky on the Activities of the JNF in the Jewish State." The area of state lands within the Jewish State was estimated at 420,000 dunams only. The majority consisted of lands that were already in public use and lands that were not suitable for cultivation. On this see *Karnenu* (ibid.); Granot (1951b) p. 227; *Problems* (1948), pp. 8–9. Regarding the division of tasks between the Zionist Organization, including the JNF, and the State after its establishment, Granovsky stated (Granot 1951b, pp. 234–

await the establishment of the State to prepare for the purchase of land. Already in the final months preceding the establishment of the State, the plan was to purchase land to the extent of 2.5–3 million dunams during the following decade[185] and the Lands Department even began to prepare more detailed plans. Thus, the regional offices were instructed to prepare multi-year plans for the purchase of lands in the areas under their responsibility "within the partition boundaries and under normal conditions which make possible orderly purchase." Such plans were drafted by the JNF regional offices.[186]

According to the concept of its leaders, the JNF was therefore to serve on behalf of the Jewish State as a tool for land purchases. Most of the lands in the Jewish State within the partition boundaries belonged to the Arab minority and the state lands were not extensive. The question now was whether a change should ensue in the JNF's method of purchasing lands following upon the establishment of the Jewish State, beyond the implications of the repeal of the White Paper and the Lands Law. On this

---

235) immediately after the passing of the United Nations resolution on partition: "In a schematic manner it can be said that the concern for the absorption of the masses of Jewish immigrants that will flow into the Jewish State will be the concern of the Zionist Movement and its institutions. There are thus three tasks: The organization of the immigration, including the training of the new immigrants in the Diaspora and their transport to Palestine; the purchase of lands for urban and rural settlement; agricultural settlement and to a certain extent the construction of housing. The State and its institutions will have all the other tasks involved in the building of a State; organizing the administration and the establishment of government institutions and services; security and defense of the integrity of the State; providing the needs of both the Jewish and Arab population, such as education and culture, medical and social services; in sum – providing for the State and its population. Furthermore, seeing to the needs of the new citizens who will come with the wave of immigration...it is the obligation of the Jewish State to provide for the population consisting of two peoples; on the other hand the World Zionist Organization – its concern will be the Jews in the Diaspora, whom it will have to bring to the land, to provide for their absorption in productive occupations for their own and the State's benefit." See also *Problems* (1948), pp. 41–42 on discrimination on the part of the Jewish population of the Jewish State regarding the purchase of water through the JNF.

185 CZA, KKL5/15911, memorandum "Points Regarding the Problem of the JNF's Future," 16.2.1948.

186 CZA, KKL5/15927, letter from Wolf of JNF Haifa Office to Weitz 29.12.1947 – quotation from there; CZA, KKL9/31, letter from Nahmani to JNF Lands Department 5.1.1948; CZA, KKL5/15927, letter from Weitz to JNF Haifa Office 7.1.1948.

issue Granovsky and Weitz expressed their almost identical position in the months preceding the establishment of the State. Both of them emphasized the "idea of development" as the main basis for purchasing lands from Arabs after the establishment of the State. In accordance with this idea, development and irrigation projects which the JNF and the institutions of the Zionist Movement would implement in coordination and cooperation with the State, would enable the Arab population to continue to live on an area whose size would be determined by the operators of the development plan and which would be much smaller than the land retained by this population at present. The surplus land would be purchased by the JNF and turned over to Jewish settlements. From the return the Arab landowner would receive, he would have to deduct his share in the development and financing of the project because he was to be one of the major beneficiaries of the project. It should be stressed that both Granovsky and Weitz spoke of a development project that would legally obligate the landowners to join it where the sale of land to the JNF would be carried out within the framework of some sort of expropriation where the price would be economically reasonable, but to a certain extent lower than that determined "through negotiations with the landowner. Granovsky defined such expropriations as paying a price which would be determined in advance, according to a certain method.[187]

Not everybody within the JNF agreed with Granovsky and Weitz that the development method could serve as the primary basis for land purchases by the JNF after the establishment of the Sate. Yosef Nahmani, who managed the JNF Tiberias Office, believed that the Jewish State could not be involved in any measure with expropriations and discrimination in favor of the Jewish sector. He stated:

> The Jewish Government in Israel will not be able and will not want to use discriminatory laws to expropriate land exclusively for Jewish settlement. Its status will obligate it to exercise equal concern for the entire agricultural class without religious distinctions, and it will

---

187 Granot 1951b, pp. 64–66, 218–243; Katz (1998a); *Problems* (1948), 10–12, 18, 46–47; CZA, A246/699, letter from Weitz to Ben-Shemesh 26.1.1948; CZA, KKL5/ 15991, JNF memorandum "To JNF Supporters in Palestine and the Diaspora," 4.12.1947 (also in S8/92, S25/1889); CZA, KKL9/31, memorandum "Principles for the Planning of Surplus Lands for the Purpose of Dense Settlement Relating to the Security of the State" (no date, but apparently from 1948); *Karnenu* (above, n. 184).

not be able to ignore within the boundaries of the Jewish State the needs of Arab farmers who are bereft or short of land; any incautious and inconsiderate agricultural reform can freeze the expansion of agricultural settlement.

Nahmani believed, therefore, that the JNF would have to continue purchasing lands in the manner in which it had operated until then and it would have to carry out its operations at a more intensified pace and in adjustment to the new conditions that would be created with the establishment of the State. His plan to implement purchases in the Tiberias and Safad districts was based on the assistance of the JNF for the voluntary transfer from within the boundaries of the State of a large number of the land-holders, whether they owned the land themselves or were tenant farmers.[188] It should be added that the JNF Haifa Office proposed predicating a large part of the land purchase in the areas within its responsibility, on the encouragement of landowners to transfer voluntarily.[189]

The War of Independence, and the freeing of a vast reservoir of Arab-owned lands both within the areas of the Jewish State, according to the partition boundaries and outside of it, posed a new challenge that had not been foreseen, either by the State which had just arisen, or by the JNF. This new reality is what dictated the functioning of the JNF in the first years of the State.[190]

---

188   CZA, KKL9/31, letter from Nahmani to JNF Lands Department 5.1.1948.
189   CZA, KKL5/15927, letter from Wolf of the JNF Haifa Office to Weitz 29.12.1947.
190   See in detail Katz (2002).

Epilogue

From the time that the Jewish National Fund was established by the World
Zionist Organization at the beginning of the twentieth century, it was one
of the many bodies engaged in purchasing land in Palestine. What largely
distinguished it from other Jewish land purchasing bodies was that its capital
derived almost entirely from contributions from the Jewish people and the
lands it had purchased, passed into national ownership. During 1936–1948,
the JNF became the principal Jewish body involved in purchasing land
throughout Palestine on a significant basis, paralleling its progressive
assumption of a central role in the national settlement project in general. As
the years progressed from 1936 until the declaration of the State of Israel
in 1948, the JNF's almost total dominance in purchasing lands in Palestine
became still more apparent. During these years the JNF purchased 596,500
dunams and its territorial property on the day the State was declared was
about 955,000 dunams, which constituted 51% of the total Jewish–owned
land area in Palestine. However, the total area purchased by the JNF during
1936–1947 constituted about 91% of the area purchased in Palestine by
Jews during this period. On the other hand, up to and including 1935, the
JNF's total land purchases constituted only 30% of the total land purchases
made by Jewish bodies since the inception of renewed Jewish settlement
activity in Palestine at the close of the nineteenth century.[1] In addition, it
should be emphasized, that the volume of purchases the JNF decided to
make during 1936–1948 was greater than the volume of purchases actually
completed, given the various attendant difficulties described in detail in the
course of the preceding chapters. The JNF's central role in land purchases
during this period can be understood first and foremost as a function of the
core concept maintained by the supreme institutions of the World Zionist
Organization – the Zionist Congress and the Zionist General Council on
the one hand, and the implementing institutions of the movement – the

---

1   See Appendix 3.

Jewish Agency and the JNF, on the other. These bodies all believed in the supreme importance of settlement praxis in promoting the Zionist Movement's interests in Palestine, and primarily the political interests of obtaining a Jewish State in Palestine within ample borders. It is clear that without the creation of tangible land property the promotion of settlement activity would have been impossible.

More than in any other period in the JNF's history, the last twelve years of the Mandate were characterized by expectations for immediate political decisions on the Palestine Question, on the one hand, and by a British policy that constrained the development of the Jewish national home including the options for purchasing lands and settlement, on the other. Furthermore, the JNF had to make purchases to meet the needs of existing farms, and in response to the demands of settlement bodies and movements. This, however was also the period when other bodies that had previously engaged in land purchases on a significant basis, including private capital, the PLDC and PICA severely retrenched their land purchases, or abandoned the area. This was due to current events such as the Arab disturbances, the Lands Law, the White Paper and Arab hindrances, or to unique causes, which were detailed below with respect to the PLDC.

During 1936–1948 the JNF became the leading Jewish factor in the field of land purchases, with all that this signified in terms of the status of lands purchased and their intended use. These facts constituted the realization of a central portion of the JNF's goals formulated upon its establishment in 1901, and at the London Conference in 1920, and constituted a vindication of the thesis the JNF had sustained for many years regarding the robustness of national capital in land purchases as compared with the long-term frailty of private capital.

However, in the years covered by this book, the JNF also assumed extraordinary purchase tasks, such as the issue of the lands belonging to persons missing in the Holocaust, the amassing of information regarding private Jewish lands that were not being maintained by their owners, or the purchase of the Sharona lands. These undertakings reinforced the JNF's primacy, its hegemony and its almost quasi-monopoly in the sphere of agricultural land purchases still further. Concomitant to this process, the organization sought to concentrate in its hands all matters connected with purchases, beginning with delineating policy and goals and concluding with the implementation and conclusion of the purchases. The JNF began detaching itself from the PLDC, and created independent purchase apparatuses that were under its control, with the JNF's Lands Department filling the staff functions.[2]

It is clear that the JNF could not have fulfilled the special lands purchase missions which confronted it during the critical period discussed by this work (and perforce accomplished the transformation into the central and leading factor in purchases at that time), had it remained true to its traditional path until the year 1936 and by adhering to the strict letter of its by-laws. This was the substantial change that occurred in JNF policy since the end of the 1930s, regarding significant purchases from Jews (including even purchases from farmers in the Moshavot), the implementation of joint purchases with private capital, and the establishment and activation of the Himnuta Company. The needs of the hour left the JNF with no option but to abandon the principle of generally avoiding purchases from Jews (although the JNF's by-laws made no reference to this),[3] of involving private capital in land purchases, and of engaging de facto in the sale of land. The flexibility the JNF instituted in the aforementioned issues carried a moral price and constituted a form of "ideological adjustment," which had to be paid for the sake of fulfilling the JNF's goals in land purchases and settlement needs in general.

JNF land purchase policy in the period covered by this work was determined by the Directorate, but there is no doubt that the attitude of the Lands Department, i.e., the position of Weitz, exerted an influence on the decisions of the Directorate. Nonetheless, it cannot be said that the Directorate was a sort of rubber stamp to Weitz's policy – an impression that could ostensibly be created both from a perusal of the diaries and works of Weitz on the period as well as from Weitz's central role in the purchase process. But this was not the case. Members of the Directorate had broad discretionary powers and fundamental positions (in general sectorial partisanship in the positions of the Directorate members was not apparent), which found expression in their statements and positions taken during discussions, and the decisions reflected the position of the majority.

---

2   It would be worthwhile to carry out research which would examine the question as to whether the JNF's detachment from the PLDC and the creation of its own apparatuses was in the long run more efficient than continued cooperation with the PLDC.

3   It should be pointed out that the purchases from Jews resulted in the transfer of lands from private ownership to national ownership, which was essential for attaining the JNF's goals.

The Directorate never waived its position as arbiter of policy and as the body that decided and authorized the implementation of purchases. This ran counter to requests raised on more than one occasion, by the Executive and the Lands Department, for freedom of action.

While differences of opinion between the Jewish Agency Executive and personages in the JNF existed, these disputes derived mainly from the JNF's basic and natural tendency to minimize the risk involved in its land purchases (since it had to display responsibility toward the public capital in its hands and pursuantly not to invest beyond its means). However, in the end the Directorate's policy in the sphere of purchases and determining priorities, corresponded to the goals of the Jewish Agency in the political and settlement sphere, and was coordinated with it. Thus, for example, despite Ussishkin's hesitancy at the close of 1938 concerning implementing the purchase of Hirbat Samach in the Western Galilee, since this area could fall within the areas prohibited to Jewish settlement according to the anticipated recommendation of the Partition Commission, he decided in the end "that in these matters the [Jewish Agency] Political Department decides and its opinion has to be taken into account."[4] Indeed, not only did the Political Department sanction the purchase, but the Jewish Agency Executive felt the same.

Thus, the JNF's land purchase policies during the period of the White Paper and the Lands Law found expression in keeping with the Zionist institutions in their struggle against the decrees. [It would appear that the membership of Jewish Agency Chairman, David Ben-Gurion, in the JNF Directorate, although he did not participate in many meetings, contributed greatly to a coordination of goals in land purchases between the Jewish Agency and the JNF.] Likewise, the membership of Ussishkin and Rabbi Berlin in the supreme bodies of the Jewish Agency and the World Zionist Organization made its contribution.

The goal of JNF land purchases in the period covered by this book was primarily politico–strategic: To expand the control by Jews over most of the country's regions "and not restrict ourselves due to inherently sound economic or settlement considerations to certain areas." Within the framework of this goal, the JNF had to assign orders of priorities for

---

4   See above, p. 104.

purchases, which reflected a gamut of variables such as the existing and anticipated political–juridical situation, the JNF's financial state, and other variables which were detailed in the course of the book's chapters.

Through the purchase of lands and settlement on them (the JNF indeed pressed the Jewish Agency to immediately settle the lands it purchased), the JNF sought to thwart British and international decisions, and intentions calculated to confine Jewish land purchases and settlement to specific regions, thus demarcating the boundaries of the Jewish State to include only very limited regions in Palestine.

The tendency toward expanding the JNF's hold in various regions of the country where it had been insignificant prior to 1936 (amidst a prodigious effort to overcome legal and economic obstacles, including the tremendous rise in land prices, problems with tenant farmers, a drop in supply, Arab terror and activity under conditions of political uncertainty), are exemplified by the following statistics: In the Negev and the South, during 1939–1947, the JNF purchased 166,000 dunams, as opposed to 42,000 dunams which it had held in the entire Judean Plain (to the north and south) until 1939. In the Negev alone, the JNF purchased 91,000 dunams during this period, whereas prior to that no JNF purchases had been made there. In the Galilee, and primarily the Upper Galilee in all its sectors, during 1936–1947 the JNF purchased about 133,000 dunams (about 22% of the total area purchased by the JNF during those years), as opposed to 3,750 in JNF hands prior to 1935. "The volume of activity expanded primarily in the Upper Galilee, where extensive areas were purchased in the mountains as well, and its western part, also in the Hula Valley, in the area whose development potential is immense." In the Judean Hills, 25,000 dunams were purchased during 1940–1947, as opposed to 8,000 dunams purchased there till 1939. In Samaria, the JNF's real estate property during 1940–1947 increased by 2.6 as opposed to the JNF's real estate property there prior to 1939 (42,000 dunams in 1947 as opposed to 16,000 in 1939), with a large portion of the purchase targeted to meet the need of linking the coastal plain and the Galilee. In contradistinction, in the valleys where the JNF had concentrated purchase activities until 1936, the JNF's territorial property during 1940–1947 grew by only 1.2 (the land areas in 1939, totaled 292,000 dunams, whereas by 1947 the total rose to 359,000 dunams). In the Sharon, JNF land property during 1940–1947 doubled (62,000 dunams until 1939 as compared with 112,000 dunams in 1947). But this growth was almost entirely related to supplementing existing farms and settlements.

The breakthrough, therefore, which occurred in the Negev and in the South on the one hand, and in the Galilee on the other, is particularly striking in the period covered by this book, but the breakthrough to the Judean Hills, the reinforcement of the foothold in Samaria and buttressing the foothold in the Beisan Valley (JNF–owned land property in the period covered by this book doubled from 23,000 dunams to 46,000) are also most impressive.[5] Beyond that, 75% of JNF land purchases that were carried out from the promulgation of the Lands Law until the end of 1946 (and it is likely that this proportion did not change in 1947 as well as in the first half of 1948) were located in Zone A and Zone B, whereas "in the Free Zone the lands purchased represented in particular settlement areas which antedated the Lands Law's entry into force, lands that were needed for supplementing blocs of territory or existing settlements as well as for housing purposes in the vicinity of the towns and the villages."[6]

There is no doubt that land purchases which the JNF implemented during 1936–1947, as well as the numerous settlements that were established on them (see Appendices 7–8), exerted an important influence on the international decisions concerning the Palestine Question, which found expression in the United Nations' partition map. Hence the boundaries of the Jewish State included the Eastern Upper Galilee, the Beisan Valley, the Hills of Ephraim connecting between the Coast and the Galilee, and most of the South and the Negev (see Map 26). Nonetheless, despite land purchases and settlement activity carried out in the Western Galilee, as well as in the Jerusalem region and the corridor, these areas were not incorporated within the boundaries of the Jewish State, and this applies also to parts of the south. Thus a number of settlements found themselves outside the designated area.[7] JNF leaders ascribed this reality to the paucity of Jewish settlement in these locations, both from the standpoint of land property and

5   Activities (1947), pp. 9–10 – quotation from there; Activities (1938), p. 9; Weitz
     (1947), pp. 77, 85; Appendix 3.
6   JNF Report (1947), p. 31.
7   The settlements were as follows: the Jerusalem region – Neve Ya'aqov, Atarot, Beit
     Ha'arava, Kefar Etziyon, Messuot Yitzhaq, Ein Tsurim, Revadim; the Jerusalem
     Corridor – Ma'aleh Hahamisha, Neve Ilan, Kiryat Anavim, Hartuv, Kefar Uriah, Ben
     Shemen; Western Galilee – Eilon, Hanita, Matzuba, Yechiam, Regba, Nahariya, Shavei
     Tziyon, Evron; Samaria – Kefar Hahoresh; the South – Nitzanim, Yad Mordechai,
     Kefar Darom, Nirim, Kefar Menachem, Gat, Galon. On this see CZA, KKL5/17143.

from the limited quantity of settlements that had been established on them, as was contended for example regarding the Western Galilee:

> In contradistinction, the Western Galilee was not incorporated because we didn't act during the initial period and the little we were able to accomplish in the latter period was insufficient to drive home real stakes. Only eight Jewish settlements exist in this region, almost all of them, save for one, on JNF lands.... And the number of their inhabitants does not exceed 2,000. If we had managed over these years to create 20 agricultural settlements, just as we did in the Eastern Galilee, there is no doubt that we would not be confronting the fact that this vital and valuable region is to be severed from our area of settlement.[8]

Based on the UN partition map, it can be seen then that the JNF, as well as the Zionist institutions in general, contributed only slightly to expanding the boundary lines of the Jewish State, during 1936–1948. However, it would appear that the very existence of the settlements even beyond these boundaries were of importance in the context of the War of Independence and in setting the boundaries of the State of Israel after this war. Except for the six agricultural settlements south of Jerusalem and to its north, as well as Kefar Darom, the other settlements beyond the boundaries at the time were in the event included within the boundaries of the State of Israel.

Furthermore, from the standpoint of agricultural land purchases, the JNF's marked contribution during 1936–1948 was primarily the transfer of nearly 600,000 dunams to national ownership, and creating the infrastructure for many new settlements (in total about 130 agricultural settlements were established on JNF lands during 1936–1948, constituting nearly all new agricultural Jewish settlements established in Palestine during that period).[9] The lands and settlements were vitally important for realizing Zionism's social and economic goals, and served as a destination for agricultural absorption. The JNF's contribution toward redeeming many Jewish–

---

8 CZA, KKL5/17138, JNF memorandum at the time of the publication of the UN report – quotation from there; Granot (1951b), pp. 218–220.

9 Activities (1947), p. 14; Activities (1948), p. 10; from these sources it becomes apparent that on the eve of the establishment of the State the agricultural settlements in Palestine numbered approximately 330, 70% of which were on land that had been purchased by the JNF.

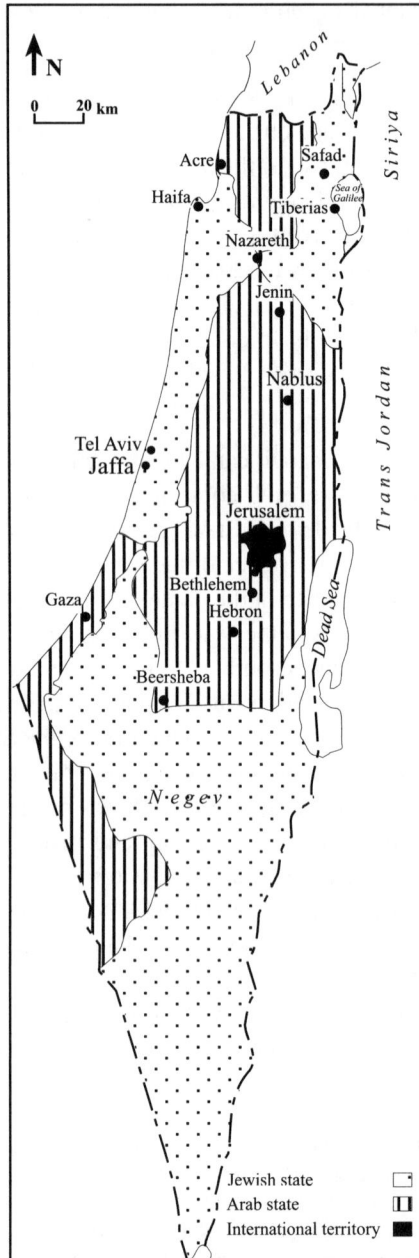

Map 26: UN map for the partition of Palestine, November 1947

owned lands that otherwise would have been lost to Jewish ownership, is also prominent (their purchase was tantamount to their redemption). Additional achievements can be credited to the JNF. It created Jewish–owned territorial contiguities, expanded existing settlements, reestablished abandoned settlements, rescued and reinforced the Moshavot, strengthened the Jewish hold in the vicinity of Safad; purchased Sharona and drew up lists of Jewish–owned land in the Jerusalem vicinity.

The economic reality which transformed the JNF during the course of the 1940s into a financial body with a significant income, enabled the organization to implement a major portion of its land purchase objectives. However, this reality also invited pressures upon the JNF from the Jewish Agency to progressively increase the resources the JNF allocated toward developing and promoting settlements – objectives which were not connected to land purchases. Hence, the JNF increasingly became the leading body in promoting settlement. Nonetheless, we observed how precisely, because it had accumulated capital, the JNF came under Jewish Agency pressure and had to allocate on the eve of the State of Israel's establishment (and immediately subsequent to its establishment) appreciable sums for settlement purposes and for non-settlement purposes (such as security) which were tied to the establishment of the State. There is no doubt that these demands were prejudicial to the JNF's independence, and to a certain extent diminished its land purchase options. But it is clear that if the JNF had refused to assume these tasks, it would have confronted a real threat to its very existence. On the other hand, it was precisely the JNF's significant participation in the vital needs related to the establishment of the State, even when these were not directly related to the JNF's customary role in land purchase or settlement activities, that helps us to situate in historical perspective the JNF's contribution during the decisive period of 1936–1948 to building the country and establishing the State of Israel.

Members of the JNF Directorate During the Years 1936–1948

Auster, Daniel (1893–1963)
Born in Eastern Galicia, Auster studied law at the University of Vienna, where he was a leader of the Zionist Youth Movement. He received a law degree and immigrated to Palestine in 1914. During 1919–1920, he served as the secretary of the Delegates Committee Legal Department. He was a founder of the Rehavia neighborhood in Jerusalem, and for 10 years headed the neighborhood committee. Auster served on the board of directors of various companies. In 1934 he was elected to the Jerusalem City Council and in 1935 he was appointed Deputy Mayor to the Arab Mayor Haladi. When the Mayor died Auster was appointed Acting Mayor, a position which he held until July 1945. Auster took part in various public and social activities and was elected as a delegate to the Zionist Congress that convened in Geneva in 1939. At the end of 1947 he was elected a member of the JNF Directorate, and was the first Mayor of Jerusalem after the establishment of the State of Israel.

Ben-Gurion, David (1886–1973)
Born in Plonsk, Ben-Gurion was a leader of the Labor Movement in Palestine and the first Prime Minister of the State of Israel. He participated in 1903, in the foundation of the Po'alei Zion Party in Poland, immigrated to Palestine in 1906, worked in Moshavot in Judea and the Galilee, and was an active leader of Po'alei Zion. He was one of the initiators of Jewish volunteering to the British army in the First World War and among the first to join the Jewish Legion. Ben-Gurion pioneered in the establishment of Ahdut Ha'avoda faction of the Labor Party, and the Histadrut, and was a leader of the Mapai Party when it was established in 1930. Until 1935, he served as the Secretary General of the Histadrut. He organized and

consolidated the Histadrut and transformed it into the power base of the Labor Movement in its quest for hegemony within the Jewish Community and within the Zionist Movement. He was the moving spirit, the man of initiative and execution in every Histadrut project and activity. In 1920, Ben-Gurion participated in the London Conference and was elected to the Zionist General Council. In 1933 he was elected to the Va'ad Leumi and became a member of the Jewish Agency Executive. From that time onward, he shifted his public activity from the Labor Party and Histadrut leadership to devote himself to activities in the Jewish Agency. In 1935, he was appointed Chairman of the Jewish Agency Executive, and at the end of the year he was appointed Director-Governor in the JNF Directorate. He supported the partition plan, and in 1941 initiated the Biltmore Conference. Ben-Gurion represented Jewish interests before the Palestine investigations commissions, was chosen in 1948 to head the Provisional Government, and it was he who proclaimed the establishment of the State of Israel in May 1948. He published many books and articles.

Berlin (Bar-Ilan), Rabbi Meyer (1880–1949)
Born in Volozhin, Berlin was the son of the "Netziv," Rabbi Yehuda Berlin. He studied in yeshivas and as a youth joined the Zionist Movement and the Mizrachi Movement, acquiring a reputation as a publicist. Berlin was a Mizrachi delegate to the Zionist Congress in 1903 at which the plan for a temporary refuge in Uganda was put forward, and spoke against the Uganda Plan. After the Congress he moved to Vilna, and worked energetically to cultivate the Mizrachi Movement in Russia, and later was elected chief secretary of World Mizrachi Organization whose headquarters were in Berlin. In 1913, he participated at the organization and foundation of Mizrachi in the United States and returned to Berlin. During the First World War he remained in the United States, where he took part in the activities of the Committee for Aiding and Rescuing the Jewish Community in Palestine. Meyer Berlin served as President of the Rabbi Yitzchak Elhanan Theological Seminary in New York, was one of the founders of the Histadruth Ivrit of America and also was the founder of the Mizrachi Teachers Training College in New York. In 1920, at the London Conference, Berlin was elected to the Zionist General Council and from then was a member of the Presidium at the Zionist Congresses and sessions of the Zionist General Council. He was a leading member of the Mizrachi World Movement and in 1927 he was officially chosen President

of the Movement. In 1924 Berlin immigrated to Palestine, and at the Zionist Congress of 1925 was elected a member of the JNF's Directorate. In 1929, he was elected to the Jewish Agency Executive, but resigned due to disputes with Chaim Weizmann on political issues. In 1936, he was one of the founders of the daily newspaper *Hazofeh*, and served as its editor.

Granovsky (Granot), Avraham (1890–1962)
Born in Bessarabia, Granovsky frequented Ussishkin's home and assisted him when he resided in Odessa. Granovsky immigrated to Palestine in 1907, and studied at the Herzliya Gymnasium. In 1911, he traveled abroad to pursue his studies. He was about to complete medical studies, but switched to study law and political economy in Lausanne and Paris. In 1917, he received the degree of Doctor of Jurisprudence with honors. In 1919, Granovsky accepted the invitation of Nechemiah De Lieme to come to The Hague and join the JNF's Head Office. Upon the transfer of the Head Office to Jerusalem in 1922, Granovsky returned to Palestine, and was one of the senior workers in the head office and director of the JNF's Finance and Economic Department. In 1934, Granovsky was elected to membership on the JNF's Directorate while continuing his work as Director of the Economic and Finance Department and in 1945 was elected Chairman of the JNF Directorate. Granovsky published many books and articles on the topics of land, land redemption, Jewish settlement, real estate taxes and agrarian economy.

Hartzfeld, Avraham (1888–1973)
Born in the Ukraine, Hartzfeld immigrated to Palestine in 1914, and initially worked as a laborer in Petah Tiqva. He organized the first workers' loan funds in Palestine and after the War was active among the worker population and in the institutions of the Jewish community. Hartzfeld was a member of Po'alei Zion and Ahdut Ha'avoda central committee. He served as a delegate to the Zionist Congresses from the 12th Congress onwards, and was active in the Histadrut and various Jewish communal institutions. However, his main activity was Chairman of the Histadrut Agricultural Center from its inception – a task which ranked him among the leaders of the Zionist settlement project. Hartzfeld was the Histadrut and JNF emissary to Europe, the United States and South Africa and founder of the Nir and Yahin Companies. In 1945, he was elected to membership on the JNF's Directorate.

Hazan, Ya'akov (1899–1992)

Born in Lithuania, Hazan was one of the founders of Hashomer Hatza'ir and the Hehalutz Movements. He immigrated to Palestine in 1923, and was a founding member of Kibbutz Mishmar Ha'emek. From the 15th Congress, he participated in all the Zionist Congresses, was a member of the Zionist General Council, a delegate to Histadrut Conferences, member of its central institutions, and fulfilled many missions abroad. In 1945, Hazan was elected a member of the JNF Directorate.

Katznelson, Berl (1877–1944)

Born in Boibrisk, Katznelson was one of the founders of the Jewish Labor Movement, a philosopher and arbiter, a moral authority for his generation., and a founder of the Labor Movement institutions. He immigrated to Palestine in 1908, and joined Po'alei Zion. He worked in the Moshavot and exchanged views with A. D. Gordon and Y. H. Brenner. He assisted in the establishment of the Agricultural Workers Confederation in Judea and the Galilee and in the independent economic institutions of the workers, such as Hamashbir and the Kupat Holim Sick Fund. In 1917, Katznelson was one of the leading proponents of volunteering in the Palestine unit of the Jewish Legion, in which he enlisted. In this manner he drew close to the leaders of Po'alei Zion who served in the Legion, primarily Ben-Gurion and Yizhak Ben-Zvi. Katznelson and Ben-Gurion were the moving spirits in the formation of the Ahdut Ha'avoda party. It was Katznelson who drafted its platform and he won general recognition as the shaper of the new party's ideological path. He participated in the foundation of the Histadrut in 1920 and was regularly elected to its Executive Committee. He served as a member of the Histadrut's Agricultural Center. In 1921, Katznelson assisted in the establishment of Bank Hapoalim. In 1925, he established the daily newspaper Davar, becoming its first editor. He participated in most of the Zionist Congresses where he was elected to the Zionist General Council. In 1925, Katznelson was elected a member of the JNF Directorate, even though he held no official executive status in the Zionist Movement or Jewish community institutions. His opinions had a decisive influence thanks to his moral stature and his sagacity. He advocated the unification of the workers movement and the Kibbutz streams. He sought to unify Ahdut Ha'avoda and Hapo'el Hatza'ir into Mapai, and was a member of the Party's central committee. Katznelson edited compendia, published many articles in the workers' publications, and in 1942 established the Am Oved Publishing House.

Kestenbaum, Avraham (1896–1956)
Born in Galicia, Kestenbaum studied in yeshivot and served in the Polish
army during the First World War. He was active in "Young Mizrachi"
and in 1922 immigrated to Palestine. He participated in the Second
Conference of the Hapo'el Hamizrachi Confederation in 1923 where he
was elected a member of the Zionist General Council – a post in which
he served for many years. It was Kestenbaum who proposed the name
"Bnei Akiva" for the youth organization of Hapo'el Hamizrachi which was
established in 1929. Kestenbaum was a leader of the settlement, economic
and educational projects of Hapo'el Hamizrachi, including the Hapo'el
Hamizrachi Agricultural Center the Mishkenot Company, Mizrachi Bank,
Torah U'Melaha Yeshiva, the Agriculture Yeshiva and Kerem B'Yavne
Yeshiva. In 1945, he was elected a member of the JNF Directorate.

Schocken, Shlomo Zalman (1877–1959)
Born in Germany, Schocken received a traditional Jewish and German
education. In 1901, he founded a department store in Saxony, which he
turned into a chain of similar stores in the main German cities. This chain
achieved great success and Schocken had an important place in Germany's
trade and economy. Schocken also took an interest in treasures of Jewish
and general culture, collected the finest works of art and painstakingly
created vast collections of rare books in Hebrew and other languages. Prior
to the First World War, he joined the Zionist Movement, and attempted to
institute the efficiency that he had instilled in his private business. In the
First World War he headed the Jewish cultural committee of the German
Zionist Confederation. After the War, Schocken found his niche in the
economic activity of World Zionist Organization as well. He was elected
a delegate to Zionist Conferences and Congresses, served as a member of
the Zionist General Council, and as a member of the WZO Executive's
Economic and Financial Committee. At the end of 1929, he was chosen by
the WZO Executive to serve as Director-Governor on the JNF Directorate.
He supported Hebrew literature and its publication and founded the Institute
for the Study of Hebrew Poetry. Schocken continued collecting materials
of antiquarian rare Judaica as well as building a collection of manuscripts.
He visited Palestine in 1922, 1925, and 1926. In 1933, he immigrated to
Palestine and settled in Jerusalem to where he transferred his large private
library and the Institute for the Study of Poetry. Upon his immigration
he founded the Schocken Publishing House. In 1935–1945 he served as a

member of The Hebrew University's Board of Trustees and the Chairman of its Executive Committee. In 1936 he purchased the daily newspaper *Ha'aretz*.

Stroock, Herman (1876–1944)

Born in Berlin, Stroock received a religious and secular education and from his youth revealed a talent for drawing. Stroock studied at the Academy of Art in Berlin and distinguished himself especially in illuminating books and painting portraits. He joined the Zionist Movement from its inception, took part in Zionist Congresses and was one of the founders of Mizrachi in Germany. During the First World War he was a staff officer in the German command for the occupied area in Lithuania and White Russia, in charge of liaison between headquarters and the Jewish residents. Stroock visited Palestine in 1903 and in 1922 settled in Haifa. He served as a member of the Mizrachi World Central Committee, and at the end of 1923 was elected as a Mizrachi representative to the Directorate of the JNF. He was also the honorary president of Hapo'el Hamizrachi, participated in 1926 in the founding of the Mizrachi Girls School in Haifa, and assisted in its consolidation. Stroock was a member of cultural and artistic institutions and was the main initiator in the establishment of the Tel Aviv Museum.

Ussishkin, Menachem (1863–1941)

Born in Mohilev, Ussishkin graduated in engineering at a Moscow technical school. He was one of the original members of Hovevei Zion and a leader of the Zionist Movement in Russia. In 1884, he initiated together with Yehiel Chlenov the formation of the student association B'nai Zion, which was considered one of the most veteran Zionist associations. He was a member of B'nai Moshe and a leader of Zionei Zion. He vigorously opposed the Uganda Plan, energetically advocated practical activity by the World Zionist Organization in Palestine, and was considered one of the leaders of practical Zionism. From 1906, Ussishkin headed the Odessa Committee of Hovevei Zion, from 1898 he was a member of the Zionist General Council and during 1905–1907 he served as a member of the Smaller Zionist General Council. He was a proponent of the plan to establish a Hebrew University, and did a great deal to ameliorate the situation of the Jewish community in Jerusalem. Ussishkin was among the heads of Geulah – a private Zionist company for purchasing land established at the beginning of the twentieth century. In 1903 he established the Histadrut

Hayishuv (Jewish community organization) in Zikhron Ya'aqov. Until his immigration to Palestine in 1919, he visited the country on a number of occasions and in 1905 published his views and plans for the development of the Jewish community in Palestine in a pamphlet entitled "Our Zionist Program." In 1919, Ussishkin immigrated to Palestine and headed the Delegates Committee, and in 1921–1923 served as Chairman of the Executive of the WZO. At the end of 1921, he joined the JNF Directorate as a Director-Governor and at the end of 1922 was chosen to head the JNF Head Office. He served as Chairman of the JNF Directorate and president of the JNF. He continued to lead the JNF until his death. Ussishkin was a member of the executive of central institutions in the Jewish community in Palestine and in 1935 he was elected President of the Zionist General Council and a member of Jewish Agency Executive. In the period of the polemic on the partition plan during the years 1937–1938, he vigorously opposed the plan.

Ussishkin, Shmuel (1899–1978)
Shmuel, the son of Menachem Ussishkin was born in Yekaterinoslav. He graduated from Cambridge University in the field of law. In 1920 he immigrated to Palestine, worked as a lawyer, was active in the General Zionists Confederation and was chosen on its behalf as a delegate to the 18th–20th Zionist Congresses. He served as a member of the General Zionists Central Committee, a member of the Supreme Court of the World Zionist Organization, published many articles in Palestine's daily newspapers and published books on legal matters. At the end of 1941, he was elected to membership in the JNF Directorate.

Vilkansky, Professor Yizhak (1880–1955)
Born in the Vilna District, Vilkansky studied natural sciences, philosophy, and political economy at Bern University in Switzerland, and then studied at the Superior Agricultural School in Berlin and in the Agricultural Institute at Königsberg University. In 1908, Vilkansky immigrated to Palestine, and was a member of Hapo'el Hatza'ir's leadership. He was one of the early proponents of establishing a mixed agricultural economy, founded a mixed farming economy at the Ben Shemen and Hulda farms, and managed them during 1909–1918. Vilkansky was chief advisor to the Palestine Bureau, published many articles on agricultural matters through which he educated and trained generations of farmers. He participated in

almost all the Zionist Congresses where he lectured on settlement affairs. During the First World War he tried to conserve the existing achievements of Jewish agriculture in the country. Vilkansky was a member of Delegates Committee and of the Zionist delegation to London and Paris in 1919 when negotiations on the Mandate were taking place. Subsequently, he fulfilled various functions in his Party's leadership and in the Histadrut and especially in the development of agricultural training and the economy. In 1929, Vilkansky was appointed as a member of the JNF Directorate. He was one of the founders of the Institute for Agricultural Studies in Rehovot which he managed, and headed the Agricultural Faculty of the Hebrew University. Vilkansky made prolonged study trips to the United States, Canada, and Europe and was on the editorial board of the British monthly for experimental agriculture.

Weitz, Yosef (1890–1972)
Weitz was born in the Wohlin district of Poland, and from his youth was active in Zionist groups. He immigrated to Palestine in 1908, was a laborer in the Rishon Leziyon vineyards and joined Hapoʻel Hatzaʻir. In 1909, he moved to the Galilee and worked in Moshavot there and was one of the first to go to Um Juni that became Kibbutz Degania. In 1910 he relocated to work in Hadera, and was elected Chairman of the Association of Agricultural Workers. In 1912, he began working as the director of the Netaʻim Association in Rehovot. In 1915, he managed the Sejera farm which at that time was owned by the Netaʻim Association. In 1919, he began working in the Delegates Committee as a supervisor for plantations in the settlements of the World Zionist Organization and for the JNF orchards under the management of Akiva Ettinger. In 1921, Weitz moved to Jerusalem, and in 1929 was appointed Ettinger's deputy in the management of the JNF's Lands Department while continuing his duties as supervisor of plantations. In 1932, when Ettinger left the JNF, Weitz was appointed director of the JNF's Lands and Forestry Department. In 1950, Weitz was elected a member of the JNF's Directorate.

Yanover, Yosef (1883–1952)
Yanover was a founding member of the Zionist Organization of South Africa and one of its prominent activists. He immigrated to Palestine in 1934, but maintained his close ties with South African Zionism and managed various economic projects in Palestine connected to investments

by South African Zionists. In 1945 he was elected as a member of the JNF Directorate. During the War of Independence he assisted Jewish youth from South Africa who volunteered to serve in the Israel Defense Forces.

Zuchovitzky, Shmuel (1884–1968)
Born in Minsk, Zuchovitzky studied in a heder and received rabbinical ordination in 1902. He turned to forestry, thus continuing in his father's footsteps, while continuing to devote time to Torah study and toward completing his general education. In 1902 he moved to Slonim, where he engaged in public activity as a member of the clandestine committee for the protection of Jewish rights. He was one of the representatives to the First Russian Duma, and operated openly as a member of the Jewish community committee as well as in other public bodies in Slonim. He was particularly active in national Zionist activities. During 1914–1917 he served as Mayor of Baranowicz and at the end of the War he moved to Warsaw. Zuchovitzky was a member of the Mizrachi Executive Committee in Poland and a member of the JNF's national committee. Beginning with the 12th Congress, he was elected to Zionist Congresses, where he served as a member of the Presidium. He headed the national committee of Keren Hayesod in Poland from its formation in 1920. In 1924, Zuchovitzky immigrated to Palestine and moved from the Mizrachi Party to the General Zionists Party. He helped initiate the establishment of the village Magdiel, chaired its committee and was president of the local council. In 1929 he was elected a director of the JNF. Zuchovitzky also served as a member of the Farmers' Union Executive, Chairman of the Jewish Farmers Organization, Chairman of the Sharon Moshavot Committee, as a member of the Zionist General Council, Chairman of the Ammamit Sick Fund and as a member of the General Zionists' Executive Committee.

Sum Total of JNF Lands in 1946

Agricultural land	Dunams
Negev	35,681
Southern Judea	92,212
Judean Hills	24,890
Sharon	55,176
Samaria	39,671
Hefer Valley	40,558
Zebulun Valley	44,120
Acre Valley	4,031
Jezreel Valley	194,767
Beisan and Jordan Valleys	77,511
Lower Galilee	60,484
Upper Galilee	65,132
Ussishkin stronghold	9,273
Galilee Mountains	16,929

760,433

Urban lands	
Beersheba	1,020
Jerusalem	1,922
Tel Aviv	4,990
Haifa	21,496
Jezreel Valley – Afula	190
Tiberias	1,104
Safed	135

30,860

791,293

Source: JNF map archives, document no. 390

APPENDIX 3

Increase by Year of JNF Land up to the Establishment of the State of Israel

Year	Purchases during the year in dunams	Total JNF land at end of year in dunams	Total of Jewish-owned land in selected years	Percentage of JNF land %
1914	–	16,000	421,000	4
1920	–	22,363		
1921	43,021	65,384		
1922	6,977	72,361		
1923	18,459	90,820		
1924	40,225	131,045		
1925	33,090	164,135		
1926	13,744	177,879		
1927	18,779	196,658	903,000	22
1928	5,433	202,091		
1929	59,549	261,640		
1930	16,987	278,627		
1931	9,978	288,605	1,007,000	29
1932	8,305	296,910		
1933	32,371	329,281		
1934	12,575	341,856		
1935	16,524	358,380		
1936	13,161	371,541	1,232,000	30
1937	13,507	385,048		
1938	34,223	419,271		
1939	53,499	472,770		
1940	43,180	515,590		
1941	45,460	561,410	1,439,500	39
1942	48,981	610,391		
1943	67,265	677,656		

Year	Purchases during the year in dunams	Total JNF land at end of year in dunams	Total of Jewish-owned land in selected years	Percentage of JNF land %
1944	67,357	745,013	1,505,000	49
1945	65,644	810,657		
1946	52,090	862,747	1,795,504	48
1947	63,002	925,749	1,850,000	50
1948	29,094	954,843		

Sources: Achievements 1932, p. 9; Activities 1947, p. 10; Activities 1944, p. 7; Activities 1941, p. 5; Activities 1948, p. 36; JNF Report (1947), p. 44; CZA, A246/397, memorandum by Zalman Lifschitz, "Jewish-owned land property in Palestine up to 1.4.1936," Tel Aviv, 25.9.1936; CZA, A402/403, summary of Jewish-owned land in Palestine by districts up to 31.12.1946.

APPENDIX 4

Extent of JNF Activities in Land Purchase in Selected Periods by Region

Region	Purchases up to the end of 1939 (in dunams)	Purchases during 1940–1946 (in dunams)
Judea	50,000	152,000
Jezreel Valley	169,000	24,000
Upper Galilee	38,000	66,000
Sharon	55,000	43,000
Jordan and Beisan Valleys	64,000	11,000
Zebulun Valley	59,000	6,000
Lower Galilee	15,000	46,000
Samaria	23,000	14,000

Source: JNF Report (1947), p. 32.

JNF Lands by Region in Selected Years
(in thousands of dunams)

Year \ Region	1914	1927	1939	1947
The Valleys	9	164	292	359
Judean Plains	5	19	42	117
Sharon	–	6	62	112
Samaria	–	–	16	42
Galilee	2	4	53	174
Judean Hills	–	4	8	33
Negev	–	–	–	91

Source: Activities (1947), p. 9.

APPENDIX 6

JNF Land Purchases (By Dunams) During 1940–1947 by Regions Set by the Lands Law

%	1946	%	1945	%	1944	%	1943	%	1942	%	1941	%	1940	
40	19,500	30	8,900	57	31,600	82	124,100	30	14,900	23	10,300	39	16,991	A
49	23,900	11	3,300	31	17,100	10	15,100	52	25,300	53	24,100	29	12,582	B
11	5,600	59	17,400	12	7,100	8	12,400	18	8,800	24	11,100	32	13,571	C

1947 1st half	%	Total	%
11,000	49	137,300	40
7,200	32	128,600	37
4,300	19	80,300	23

Sources: CZA, KKL5/15635, statistics by Y. Ziman 27.4.1947; Activities (1940), p. 7.

APPENDIX 7

Total Number of Settlements on JNF Land
in Selected Years

Year	Total Jewish settlements	Number of Jewish settlements on JNF land	Settlements on JNF land (%)
1914	53	7	13
1927	111	43	39
1936	199	104	52
1947	330	235	71

Source: Activities (1947), p. 14.

Total Settlements on JNF Land in 1947 by Region

Region	No. of settlements	No. of settlements on JNF land	Settlements on JNF land (%)
South and Negev	28	28	100
Judean plains	55	34	62
Judean hills	14	10	71
Sharon	82	56	68
Samaria	13	8	62
Zebulun Valley	24	15	63
Jezreel Valley	32	30	94
Beisan Valley	12	12	100
Jordan Valley	19	8	42
Lower Galilee	18	9	50
Upper Galilee	33	25	76

| Total | 330 | 235 | 71 |

Source: Activities (1947), p. 15.

JNF Income from Its Establishment to 1948
(in Palestine Pounds)

Year	Annual income
Up to 1920	560,600
1921	101,200
1922	88,000
1923	98,300
1924	136,100
1925	190,900
1926	201,100
1927	218,700
1928	204,000
1929	197,500
1930	203,800
1931	146,500
1932	129,600
1933	151,500
1934	209,500
1935	256,900
1936	309,000
1937	381,100
1938	403,100
1939	560,000
1940	617,300
1941	620,100
1942	680,700
1943	1,146,100
1944	1,766,400
1945	2,285,000

Appendix 9

Year	Annual income
1946	3,317,600
1947	4,599,400
1948	10,951,000

Source: Activities (1948), p. 35.

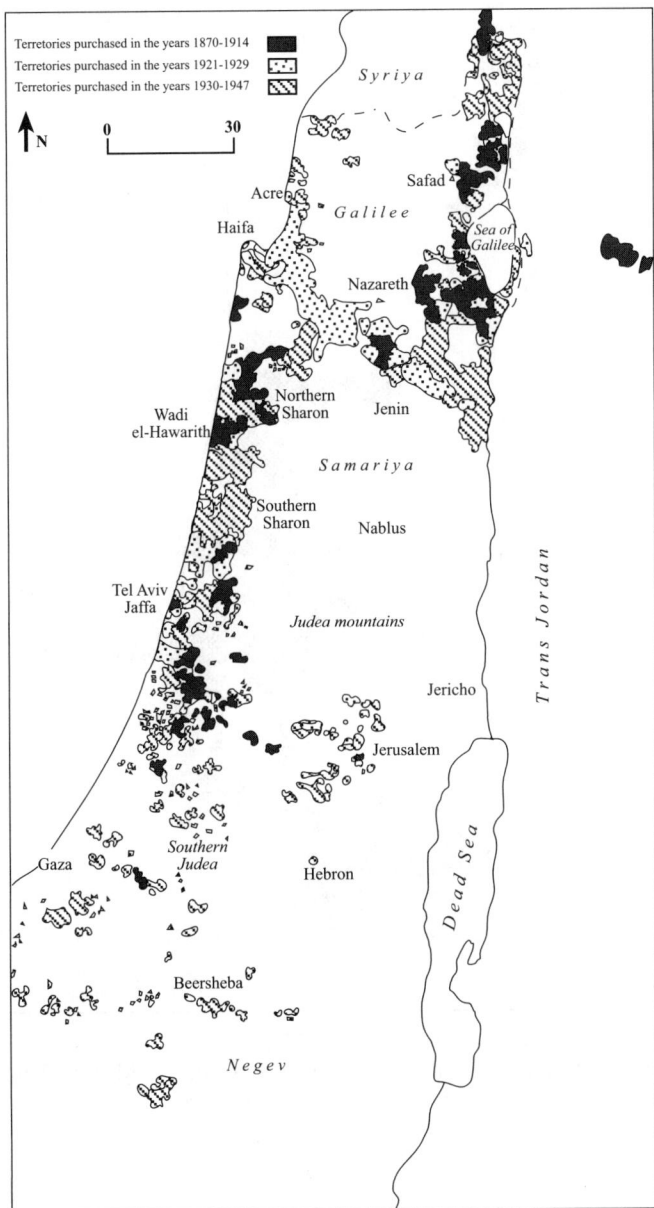

Appendix 10 (Map 27)
The development of Jewish-owned land property in the years 1870-1947
Source: JNF map archives, Map 4088

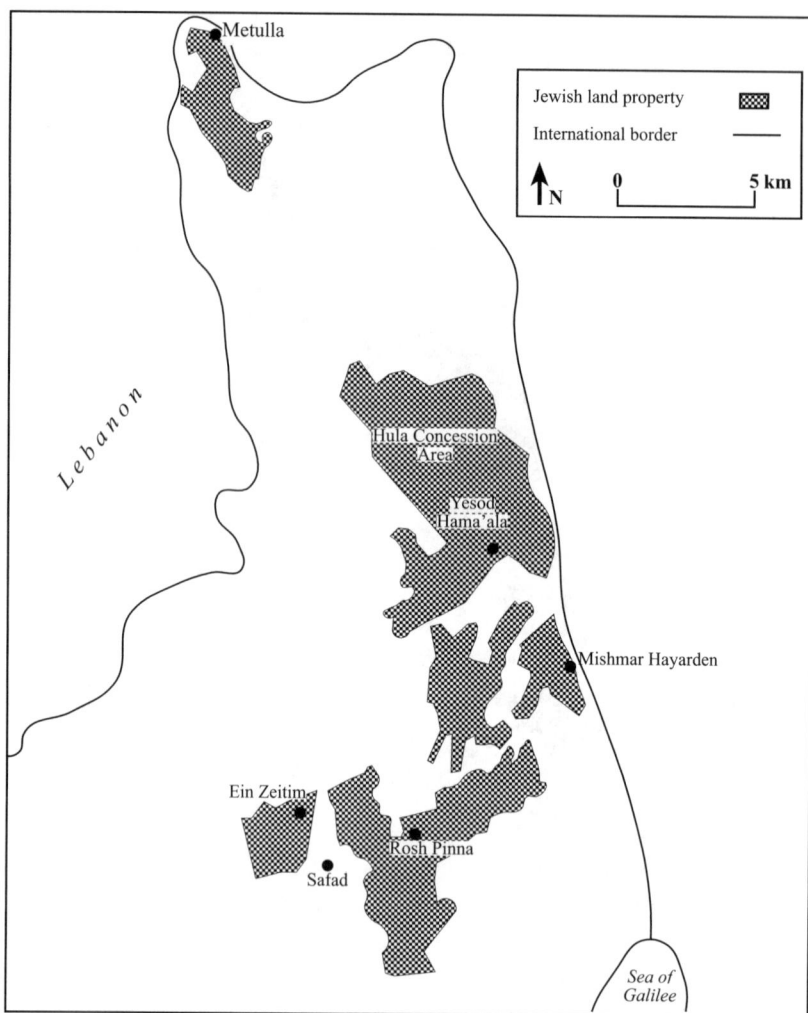

Appendix 11 (Map 28)
Jewish land property in the eastern Upper Galilee in March 1936
Source: JNF maps archive, Map 2796

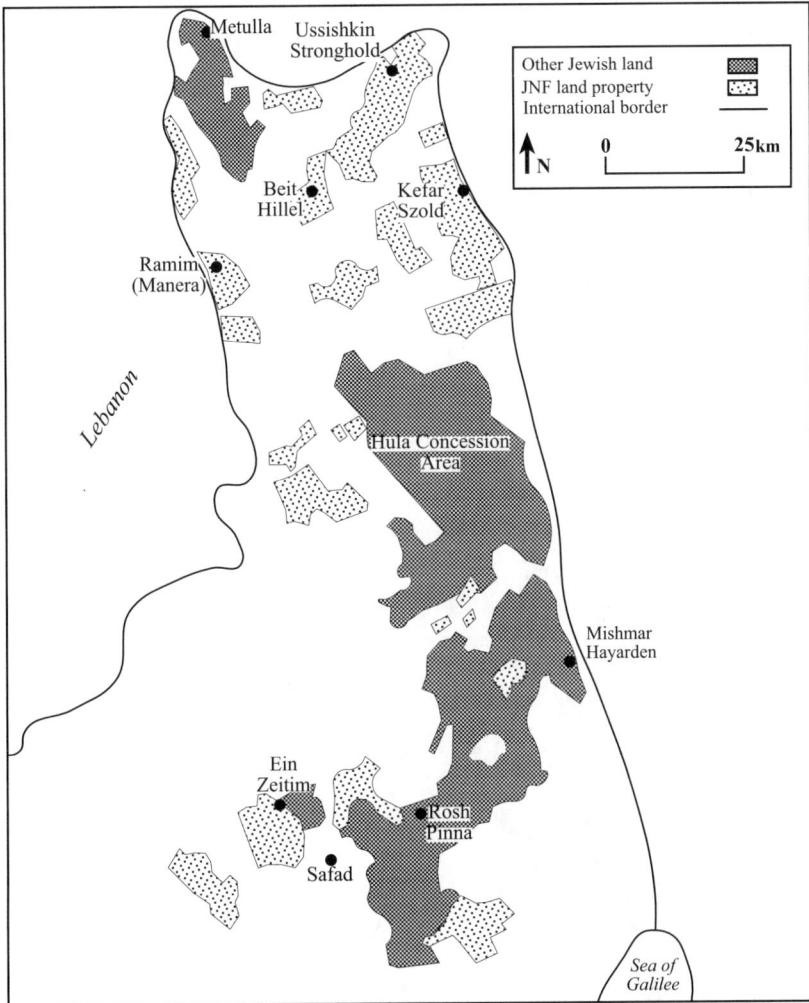

Appendix 12 (Map 29)
Jewish land property and JNF land property in the eastern Upper Galilee
in March 1947
Source: JNF map archives, Map 2800

Appendix 13 (Map 30)
Jewish land property and JNF land property in western Galilee
in March 1936
Source: JNF map archives, Maps 2797, 2799

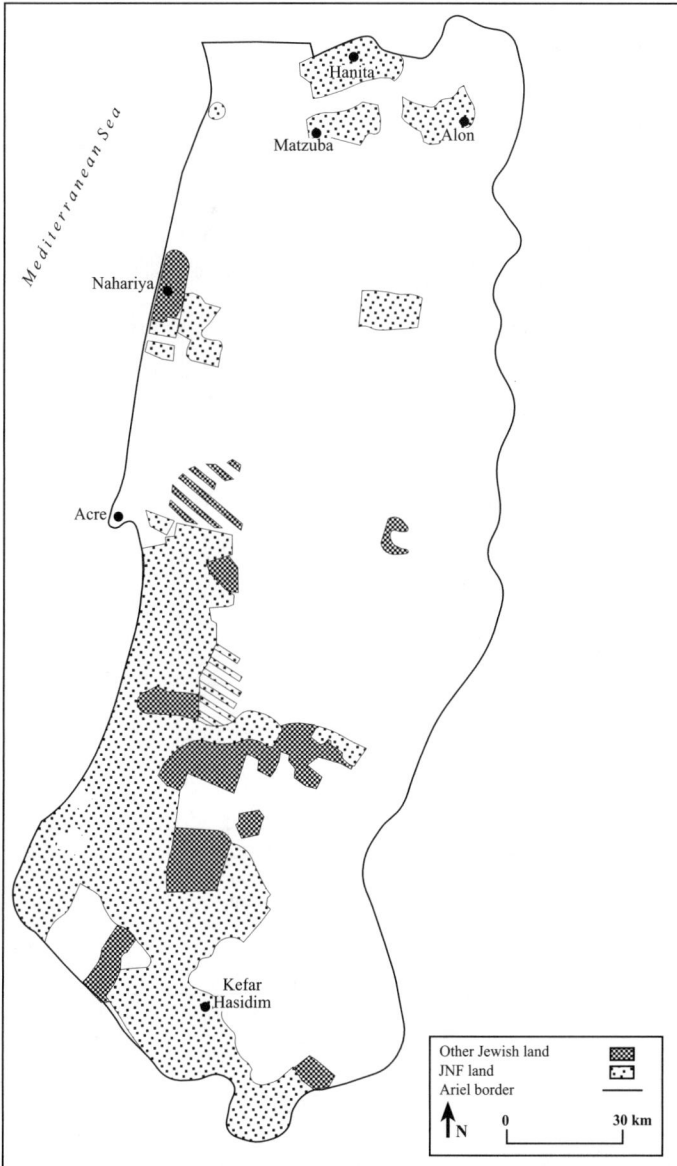

Appendix 14 (Map 31)
Jewish land property and JNF land property in western Galilee
in March 1947
Source: JNF map archives, Maps 2795, 2803

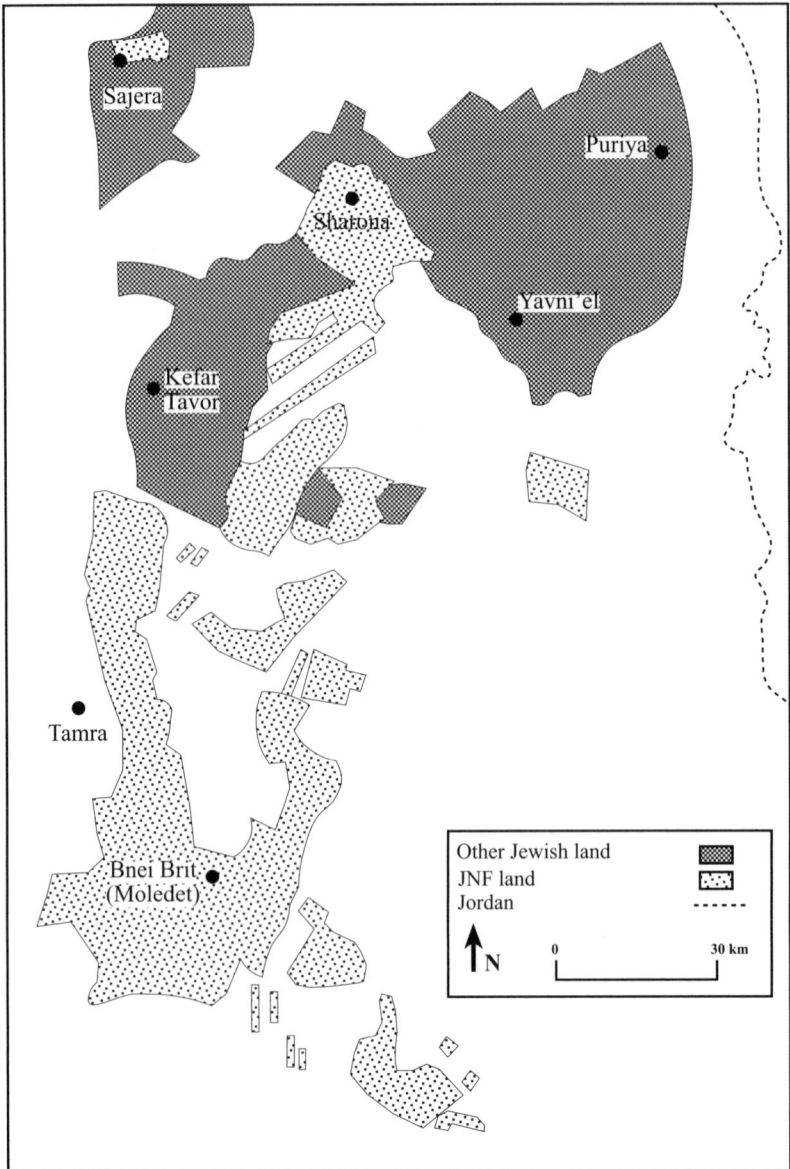

Appendix 15 (Map 32)
Jewish land property and JNF land property in the lower Galilee
in March 1947
Source: JNF maps archive, Map 27803A

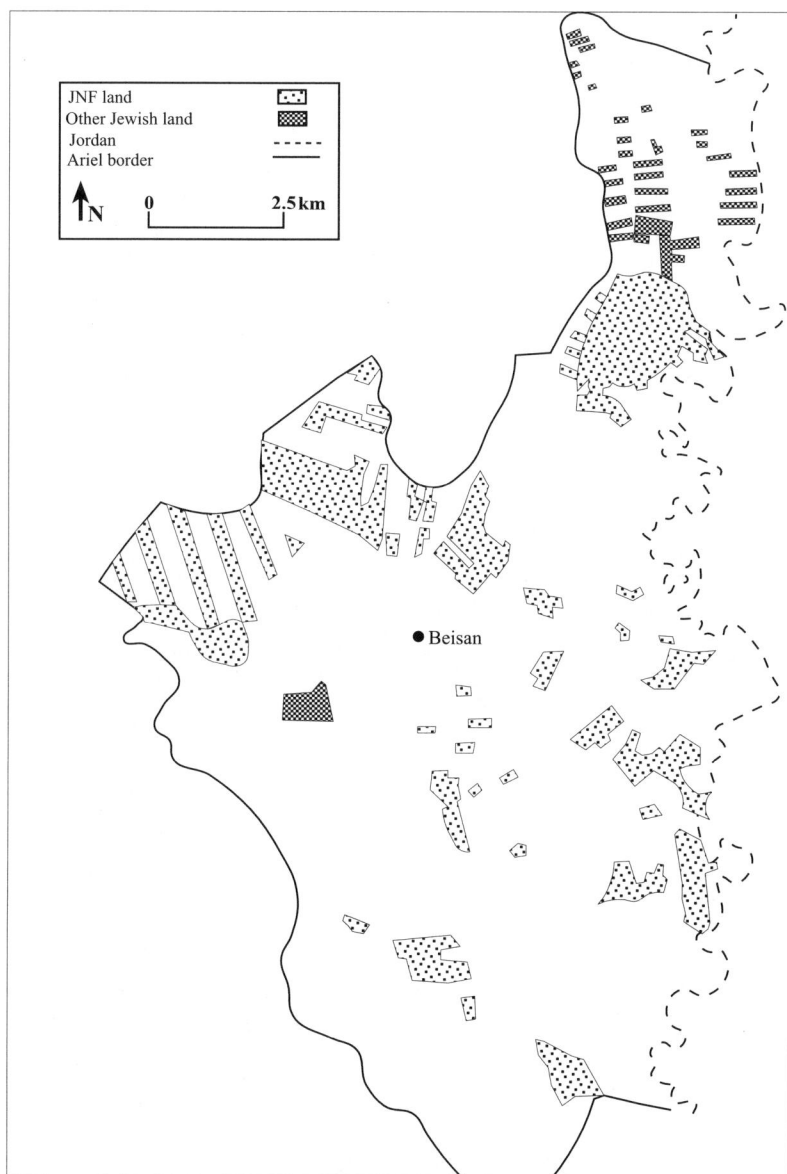

Legend:
- JNF land
- Other Jewish land
- Jordan
- Ariel border

N   0   2.5 km

● Beisan

Appendix 16 (Map 33)
Jewish land property and JNF land property in the Beisan Valley
in March 1936
Source: JNF map archives, Map 2801

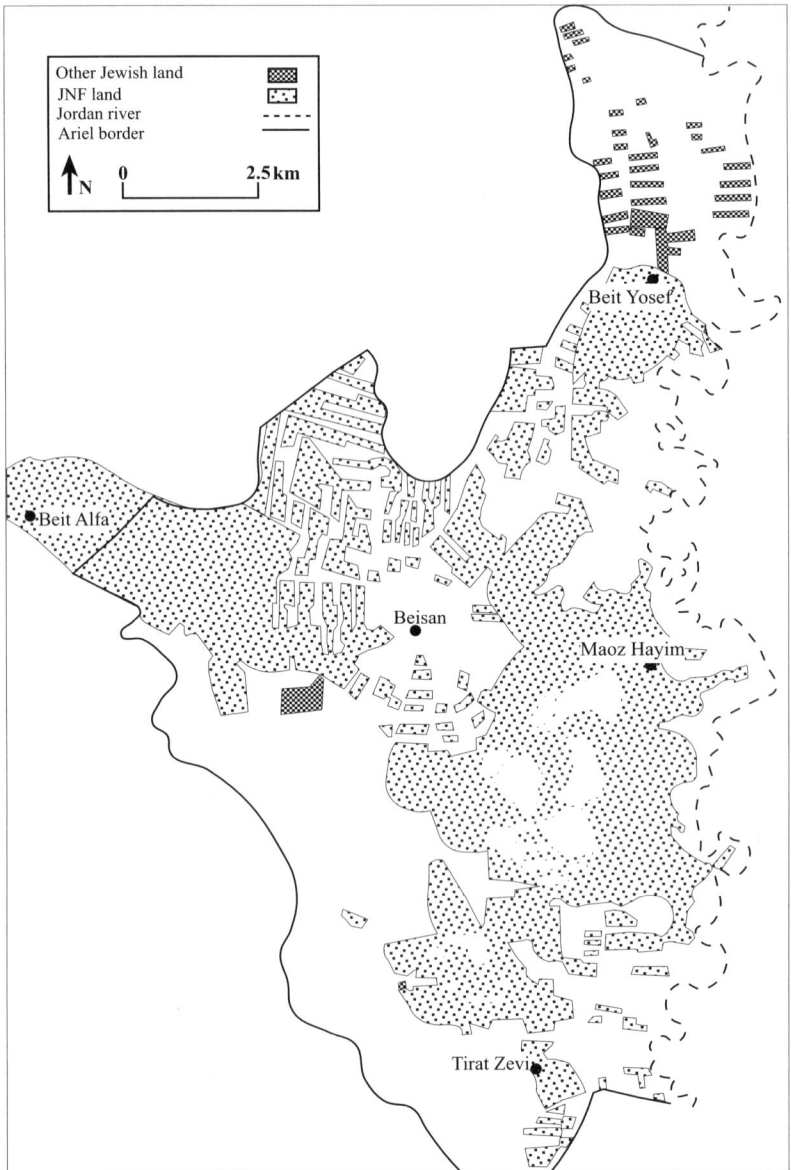

Appendix 17 (Map 34)
Jewish land property and JNF land property in the Beisan Valley
in March 1947
Source: JNF maps archive, Map 2804

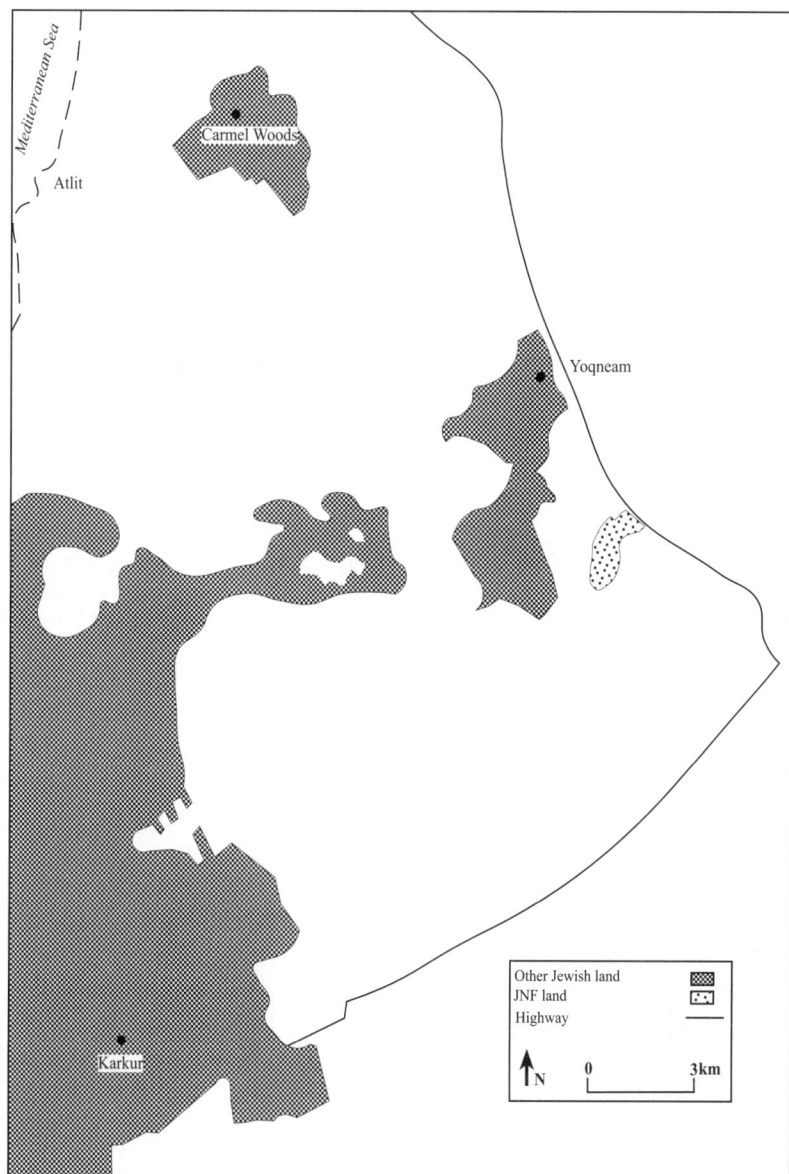

Appendix 18 (Map 35)
Jewish land property and JNF land property in the Samaria lowland
in March 1936
Source: JNF map archives, Map 2798A

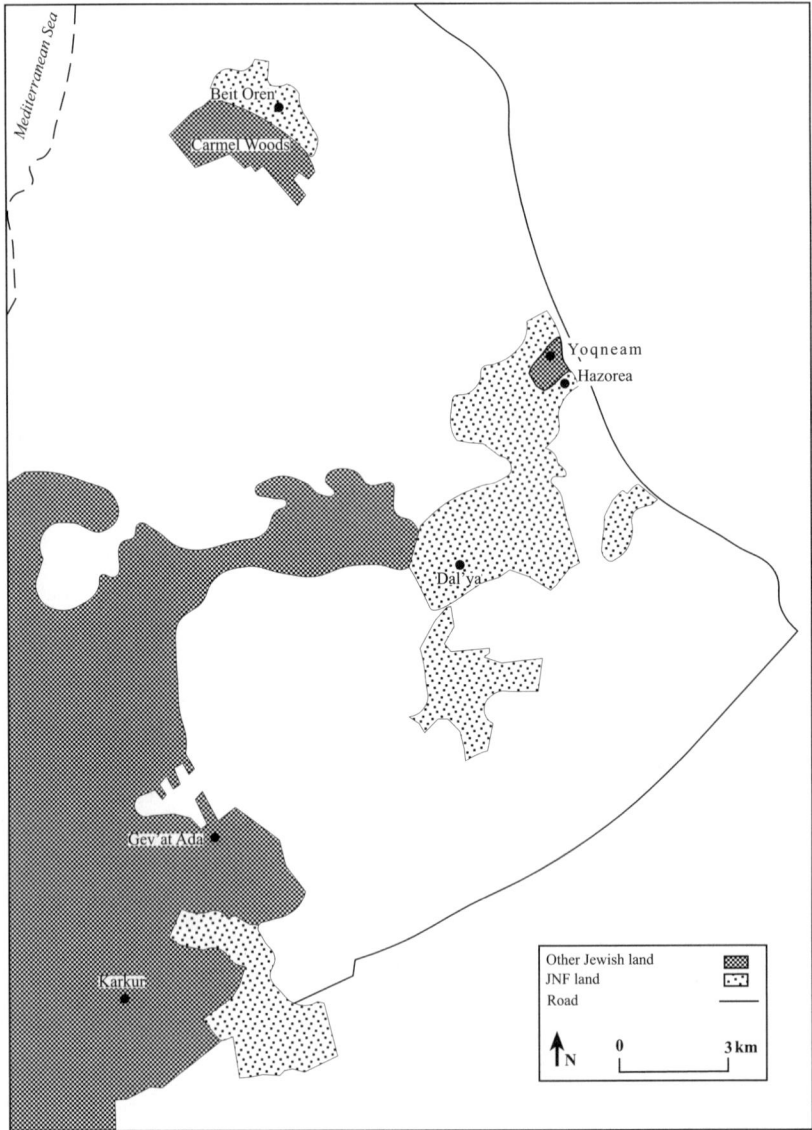

Appendix 19 (Map 36)
Jewish land property and JNF land property in the Samaria lowland
in March 1946
Source: JNF map archives, Map 2798

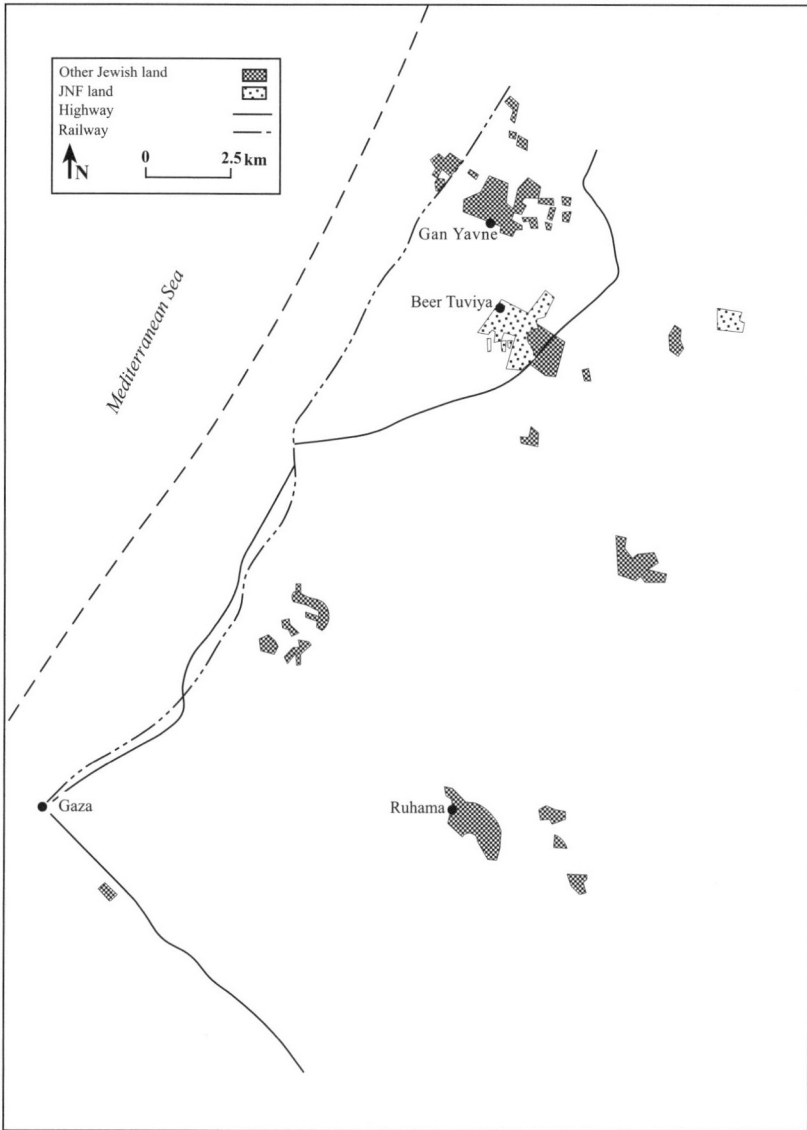

Appendix 20 (Map 37)
Jewish land property and JNF land property in South Palestine
in March 1936
Source: JNF map archives, Map 2792

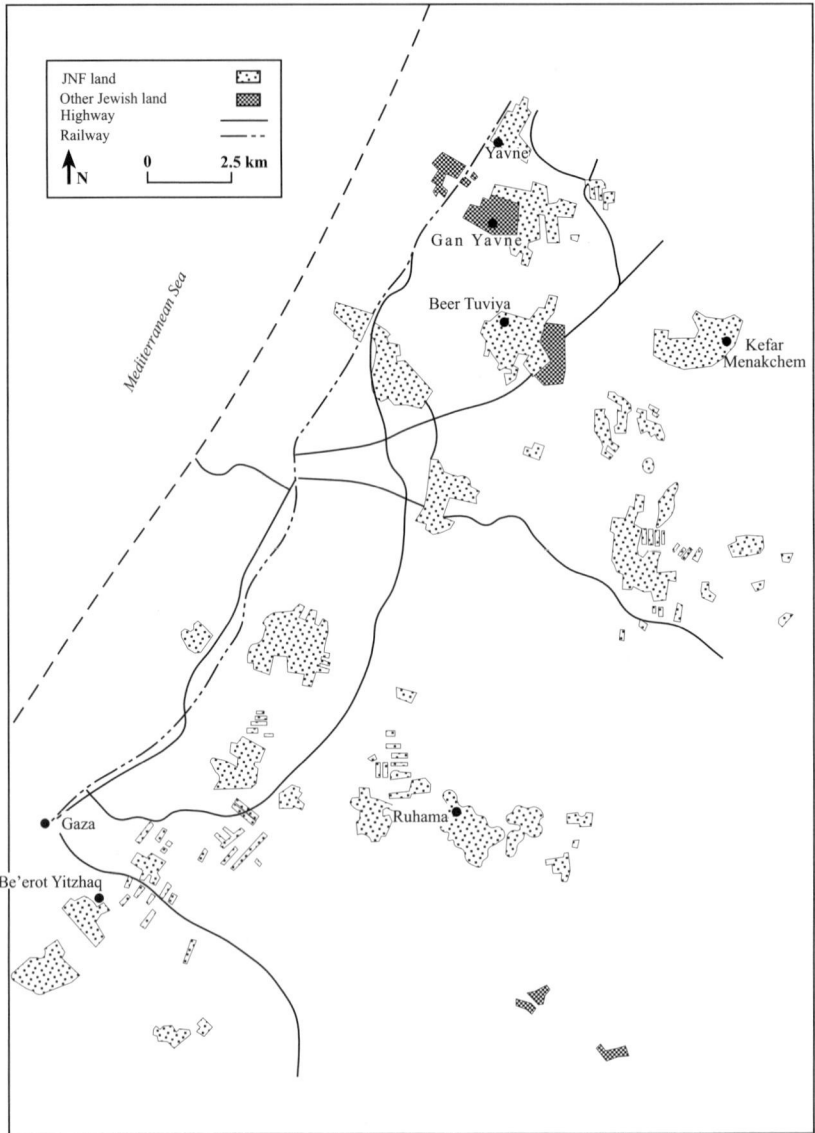

Appendix 21 (Map 38)
Jewish land property and JNF land property in South Palestine
in March 1947
Source: JNF map archives, Map 2793

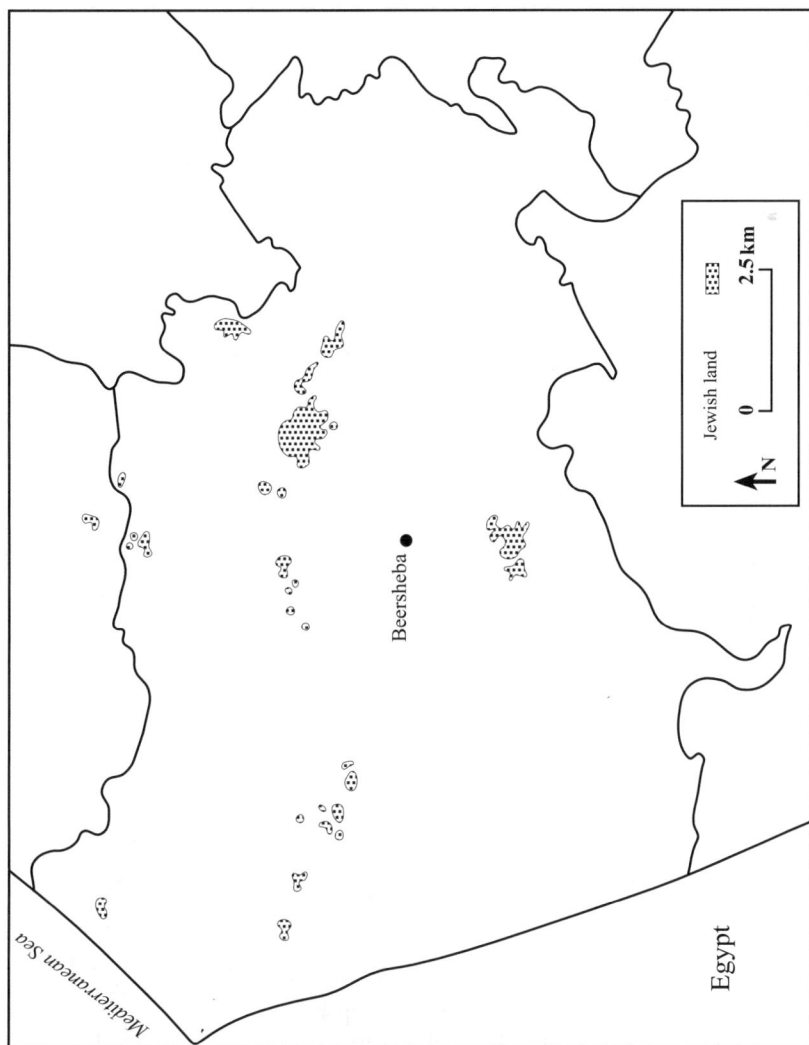

Appendix 22 (Map 39)
Jewish land property in the Negev in 1936
Source: JNF map archives, Map 6085

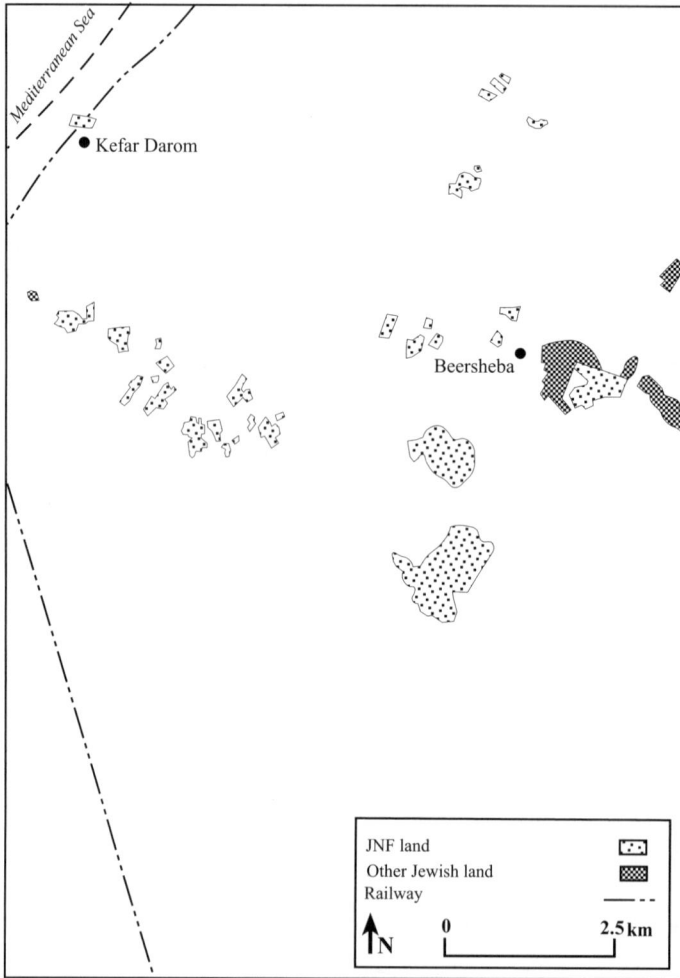

Appendix 23 (Map 40)
Jewish land property and JNF land property in the Negev in March 1947
Source: JNF map archives, Map 2794

SOURCES

ARCHIVES

Archives of Tirat Zevi
Central Archives of the World Mizrachi
Israel Government Archives, Jersalem
Mossad Harav Kook Archives, Jerusalem
The Central Zionist Archives, Jerusalem (CZA)
The Jewish National Fund Maps Archives

NEWSPAPERS

Haboker
Ha'aretz
Hazofeh
Hadashot

PERIODICALS

Daily Bulletins
Eretz Israel Information Bulletin
JNF Internal Information Bulletin, Jerusalem
Agricultural Center Bulletin
Eretz Israel Press Bulletin
JNF: National Committee for Eretz Israel Bulletin

Weekly Press Service
Karnenu
Eretz Israel Economic News
Telalim
Reshumot

BOOKS AND ARTICLES IN HEBREW (titles in English appear in parenthesis)

Achievements (1935)
Achievements of the Jewish National Fund, Jerusalem 1935.

Activities (1933)
Activities of the Jewish National Fund 1932, Jerusalem 1933.

Activities (1934)
Activities of the Jewish National Fund, 1933, Jerusalem 1934.

Activities (1935)
Activities of the Jewish National Fund, 1934, Jerusalem 1935.

Activities (1936)
Activities of the Jewish National Fund, 1935, Jerusalem 1936.

Activities (1937)
Activities of the Jewish National Fund, 1936, Jerusalem 1937.

Activities (1938)
Activities of the Jewish National Fund, 1937, Jerusalem 1938.

Activities (1939)
Activities of the Jewish National Fund, 1938, Jerusalem 1939.

Activities (1940)
Activities of the Jewish National Fund, 1939, Jerusalem 1940.

Activities (1941)
Activities of the Jewish National Fund, 1940, Jerusalem 1941.

Activities (1942)
Activities of the Jewish National Fund, 1941, Jerusalem 1942.

Activities (1943)
Activities of the Jewish National Fund, 1942, Jerusalem 1943.

Activities (1944)
Activities of the Jewish National Fund, 1943, Jerusalem 1944.

Activities (1945)
Activities of the Jewish National Fund, 1944, Jerusalem 1945.

Activities (1946)
Activities of the Jewish National Fund, 1945, Jerusalem 1946.

Activities (1947)
Activities of the Jewish National Fund, 1946, Jerusalem 1947.

Activities (1948)
Activities of the Jewish National Fund, 1947, Jerusalem 1948.

Activities (1949)
Activities of the Jewish National Fund, 1948, Jerusalem 1949.

Agmon (1951a)
Agmon, N. (Bistritzky), *In the Paths of the Pioneers: In Memory of M. Bodenheimer*, Jerusalem 1951.

Agmon (1951b)
Agmon, N., *Personalities*, Jerusalem 1951.

Alexander (1988)
Alexander, G., "Land Transactions in Haifa between Germans and the Jewish National Fund 1936–1937," *Cathedra* 48 (June1988), pp. 164–184.

Alexander (1993)
Alexander, G., "The Establishment of the Himnuta Company," *Cathedra* 68 (July 1993), pp. 80–97.

Amikam (1990)
Amikam, B., "Arab Riots and Jewish Settlement Policy during 1936–1939," in Kark (1990a), pp. 290–297.

Amikam (1980)
Amikam, B., *First Tillings: The Jewish Agricultural Settlements in the 1930s,* Jerusalem 1980.

Amit (1998)
Amit, I., "Policy of Land Purchase in Palestine during the Period of the Mandate," *Studies in the Geography of Palestine* 15 (1998), pp. 151–178.

Arab Villages (1941)
Arab Villages in Palestine up to the End of 1940, Jerusalem 1941.

Arbel (1981)
Arbel, N. (ed.), *Major Periods in the History of Palestine*, VI, Tel Aviv 1981.

Ashbel (1969)
Ashbel., A. (ed.), *Sixty Years of the Israel Land Development Company*, Jerusalem 1969.

Avneri (1980)
Avneri, A. L., *The Jewish Land Settlement and Arab Claim of Dispossession 1878–1948,* Tel Aviv 1980.

Banker (1977)
Banker to a Nation Being Rebuilt: The History of Bank Leumi, Jerusalem 1977.

Bein (1976)
Bein, A., *History of Jewish Settlement in Palestine*, Ramat Gan 1976.

Bein & Perlmann (1982)
Bein, A., and R. Perlmann, *Immigration and Settlement in the State of Israel*, Jerusalem 1982.

Beginning (1942)
From the Beginning of Activities in Palestine up to the Purchase of the Jezreel Valley (1907–1922), Jerusalem 1942.

Ben-Artzi & Biger (1983)
Ben-Artzi, Y., and G. Biger, "Changes in the Settlement Scene in Upper Galilee during the Mandate," *Artzot Hagalil* 1 (1983), pp. 443–460.

Ben-Gurion (1951)
Ben-Gurion, D., *The Campaign*, III, Tel Aviv 1951.

Ben-Gurion (1982)
Ben-Gurion, D., *Memoirs*, III–V, Tel Aviv 1973–1982.

Ben-Shemesh (1953)
Ben-Shemesh, A., *Land Laws in the State of Israel*, Tel Aviv 1953.

Bistritsky (1948)
Bistritsky, N. (ed.), *Kama: Jewish National Fund Yearbook of Problems of the People and the Land*, Jerusalem 1948.

Bistritsky (1949)
Bistritsky, N. (ed.), *Kama: Jewish National Fund Yearbook of Problems of the People and the Land*, Jerusalem 1949.

Bistritsky (1950a)
Bistritsky, N. (ed.), *In the Path of Fulfillment: A Festschrift in Honor of Yosef Weitz on his 60th Birthday*, Jerusalem 1950.

Bistritsky (1950b)
Bistritsky, N., *In the Footsteps of an Individual*: *Memorial Volume for Nechemia De Lieme*, Jerusalem 1950.

Bistritsky (1950c)
Bistritsky, N. (ed.), *Kama: Jewish National Fund Yearbook of Problems of the People and the Land*, Jerusalem 1950.

Bistritsky (1952)
Bistritsky, N. (ed.), *Kama: Jewish National Fund Yearbook of Problems of the People and the Land*, Jerusalem 1952.

Blass (1973)
Blass, S., *Water in Strife and Action*, Ramat Gan 1973.

Buying Land (1939)
We are Buying Land: The Year 1938, on the Redemption of the Soil, Lectures by Dr. A. Granovsky, Jerusalem 1939.

Cohen, A. (1978)
Cohen, A., *The Economy of the Arab Sector in Palestine during the Mandate*, Giv'at Haviva 1978.

Cohen, M. (1978)
Cohen, M., *Palestine Retreat from the Mandate: The Making of British Policy, 1936–1945*, London 1978 (English).

Conference (1944)
From Conference to Conference: Summaries of Activities, the General Federation of Hebrew Workers in Palestine, the Federation of Agricultural Workers, 1939–1944, Tel Aviv 1944.

Congress (1925)
The 14th Zionist Congress, Summary, Resolutions, Explanations, London 1925.

Congress (1937)
The 20th Zionist Congress, Stenographic Report, Jerusalem 1937.

Congress (1939)
The 21st Zionist Congress, Stenographic Report, Jerusalem 1939.

Congress (1947)
The 22nd Zionist Congress, Stenographic Report, Jerusalem 1947.

Conquest (1937)
Conquest of the Land in Palestine, based on an article by Avraham Hartzfeld, Jerusalem 1937.

Cytrin (1987)
Cytrin, I., "The Hula Concession: A Chapter in the Jewish Settlement of Upper Galilee," Ph.D. dissertation, Bar-Ilan University 1987.

Domke (1983)
Domke, M., *Trading with the Enemy in World War II*, New York 1943 (English).

Dothan (1983)
Dothan, S., *The Struggle for Eretz Israel, 1918–1948*, Tel Aviv 1983.

Doukhan (1925)
Doukhan., M. J., *Land Laws in Eretz Israel*, Jerusalem 1925.

Doukhan-Landau (1979)
Doukhan-Landau, L., *The Zionist Companies for Land Purchase in Eretz Israel, 1897–1914*, Jerusalem 1979.

Eliav (1976)
Eliav, B. (ed.), *The Jewish National Home*, Jerusalem 1976.

Eretz Israel (1923)
Eretz Israel, Year Book of the Jewish National Fund: Report to the Directors of the Jewish National Fund, 1921–1923, Jerusalem 1923.

Ettinger (1947)
Ettinger, M. (ed.), *The Settlement Economy Book for 1947*, Tel Aviv 1947.

Galilee (1938)
Galilee, *The 1938 Project*, Jerusalem 1938.

Gavish (1990)
Gavish, D., "Land Settlement during the British Mandate Period," Kark (1990a), pp. 185–198.

Gavish (1991)
Gavish, D., *Land and Map: The Survey of Palestine, 1920–1948*, Jerusalem 1991.

Gavish (1992)
Gavish, D., "The Ghar Mudawara (Beisan State Land Agreements): The Beisan Valley," *Studies in the Geography of Eretz Israel* 13 (1992), pp. 13–22.

Gelber (1995)
Gelber, Y., "The First World War and Its Aftereffects," M. Lissak et al. (eds.), *The History of The Jewish Community in Palestine since 1882: The British Mandate*, II, Jerusalem 1995, pp. 303–463.

Gerts (1940)
Gerts, A., *The New Settlement*, Jerusalem 1940.

Giladi (1973)
Giladi, D., *Jewish Palestine during the Fourth Aliya Period 1924–1929: Economic and Social Aspects*, Tel Aviv 1973.

Goldenberg (1956)
Goldenberg, M., *The Fund Still Exists: Selected Memories*, Merhavia 1956.

Goldstein (1999)
Goldstein, Y., *Ussishkin's Biography, I: The Russian Period 1863–1919*, Jerusalem 1999.

Goldstein (2001)
Goldstein, Y., *Ussishkin's Biography, II: Eretz Israel 1919–1941*, Jerusalem 2001.

Granot (1951a)
Granot, A. [Granovsky], *The Settlement of a People*, Jerusalem 1951.

Granot (1951b)
Granot, A., *In the Fields Rebuilt*, Jerusalem 1951.

Granot (1952)
Granot, A., *Paths and Pioneers*, Jerusalem and Tel Aviv 1952.

Granovsky (1929)
Granovsky, A., *Land and Settlement*, Jerusalem 1929.

Granovsky (1938)
Granovsky, A., *Land Policy in Palestine*, Jerusalem 1938.

Granovsky (1939)
Granovsky, A., *The Year 1938 on the Front of Redemption of the Land: Lectures by A. Granovsky*, Jerusalem 1939.

Granovsky (1940)
Granovsky [Granot], A., *In the Land System*, Jerusalem 1940.

Granovsky (1943)
Granovsky, [Granot] A., *The Land Issue in Palestine*, Jerusalem 1943.

Granovsky (1944)
Granovsky, A., *Land Policy for the Future*, Jerusalem 1944.

Granovsky (1949)
Granovsky, A., *Land Regime in Palestine*, Tel Aviv 1949.

Granovsky [n.d. (a)]
Granovsky, A., *The Land Front during the Arab Attacks*, Jerusalem [n.d.]

Granovsky [n.d. (b)]
Granovsky, A., *National Land Policy in Practice*, Jerusalem [n.d.]

Greizer (1983)
Greizer, I., "The Jewish National Fund's Urban Land Policy and Its Influence on Development Planning in Palestine During the Mandate," Reichman (1983).

Gross & Greenberg (1994)
Gross, N., and I. Greenberg, *Bank Hapoalim: The First 50 Years, 1921–1971*, Tel Aviv 1994.

Gross & Metzer (1993)
Gross, N. T., and J. Metzer, "Palestine in World War II: Some Economic Aspects," *Research Paper*, 207, The Falk Institute for Economic Research in Israel, Jerusalem 1993 (English).

Grossman & Degani (1990)
Grossman, D., and A. Degani (eds.), *Hasharon: Between Yarkon and the Carmel*, Tel Aviv 1990.

Gurevich & Gertz (1939a)
Gurevich, D., and A. Gertz, *Statistical Handbook of Jewish Agricultural Settlement in Palestine*, Jerusalem 1939.

Gurevich & Gertz (1939b)
Gurevich, D., and A. Gertz, *Agricultural Settlement Activities of the Zionist Organization and the Jewish Agency*, Jerusalem 1939.

Gurevich & Gertz (1947)
Gurevich, D., and A. Gertz, *Jewish Agriculture and Agricultural Settlement in Palestine*, Jerusalem 1947.

Guide (1937)
Guide for Jewish National Fund Activists, Jerusalem 1937.

Gvati (1981)
Gvati, C., *A Century of Settlement: The History of Jewish Agricultural Settlement in Palestine*, Tel Aviv 1981.

Halevi (1979)
Halevi, N., *The Economic Development of the Jewish Community in Palestine, 1917–1947*, Jerusalem 1979.

Halili (1983)
Halili, A., "Land Rights: A Historical Review of the Development of Land Purchase in Palestine," *Artzot Hagalil* 2 (1983), pp. 575–610.

Halperin (1944)
Halperin, C., *Agrarian Laws in Palestine*, Tel Aviv 1944.

Hartzfeld (1955)
Hartzfeld, A., *Conquest of the Land in Palestine*, Jerusalem 1937.

Herskovits (1955)
Herskovits, A., "The Goals of the Jewish Agency for Palestine: A Reappraisal," *Zion* 40 (1995), pp. 425–448.

Historical (1937)
Historical Material about the Jewish National Fund, Jerusalem 1937.

Horowitz (1944)
Horowitz, D., *The Development of the Economy of Palestine*, Jerusalem 1944.

Horowitz (1948)
Horowitz, D., *The Development of the Economy of Palestine*, new edition, Jerusalem 1948.

Horowitz (1954)
Horowitz, D., *The Economy of Israel*, Tel Aviv 1954.

Hour (1940)
At this Hour, Jerusalem 1940

Howard (1970)
Howard, E., *Garden City of Tomorrow*, London 1970 (English).

Ilan (1984)
Ilan, Z., *Attempts at Jewish Settlement in Transjordan, 1871–1947*, Jerusalem 1984.

JNF Conference (1947)
The 15th National Conference of the Jewish National Fund in Palestine, Tel Aviv 1947.

JNF Report (1929)
Jewish National Fund, Report of the Head Office for 1927–1929, submitted to the 16th Zionist Congress, Jerusalem 1929.

JNF Report (1937)
Jewish National Fund Report for the Years 1936–1937, submitted to the 20th Zionist Congress, Jerusalem 1937.

JNF Report (1939)
Jewish National Fund, Report for the Years 1938–1939, submitted to the 21st Zionist Congress, Jerusalem 1939.

JNF Report (1947)
Jewish National Fund, Activities and Achievements, 1940–1946: Report submitted to the 22nd Zionist Congress, Jerusalem 1947.

Kano (1980)
Kano, J., *The Land Conflict between Jews and Arabs in Palestine during the British Mandate and After*, Giv'at Haviva 1980.

Kano (1992)
Kano, J., *The Problem of Land in the Jewish–Arab Conflict 1917–1990*, Tel Aviv 1992.

Karilinsky (2000)
Karilinsky, N., *Citrus Blossoms: Jewish Entrepreneurship in Palestine, 1890–1939*, Jerusalem 2000.

Kark (1974)
Kark, R., *Pioneering Jewish Settlement in the Negev*, Ramat Gan 1974.

Kark (1990a)
Kark, R. (ed.), *Redemption of the Land of Palestine: Ideology and Practice*, Jerusalem 1990.

Kark (1990b)
Kark, R., "Land Acquisition in the Hefer Valley," Grossman & Degani (1990), pp. 345–362.

Katz (1982)
Katz, Y., "Stages in the Purchase of the Jezreel Valley," *Karka* 21–22 (1982), pp. 47–51.

Katz (1983)
Katz, Y., "The Colonization Activity in Palestine of the Zionist Private Companies and Associations between 1900–1914," Ph.D. dissertation, The Hebrew University of Jerusalem, 1983.

Katz (1986a)
Katz, Y., "Ideology and Urban Development: Zionism and the Origins of Tel Aviv," *Journal of Historical Geography* 12 (1986), pp. 402–424 (English).

Katz (1986b)
Katz, Y., "The Jewish National Fund Assists in the Establishment of Tel Aviv: The Attitude of the Zionist Organization to Urban Neighborhoods prior to the First World War," *Studies in the Geography of Israel* 12 (1986), pp. 99–108.

Katz (1987)
Katz, Y., *Redemption of the Land: The Company for the Redemption of the Land*, Jerusalem 1987.

Katz (1990a)
Katz,Y., "Abandoned Settlements in the Sharon: The Case of Heftziba 1906–1930," Grossman & Degani (1990), pp. 385–396.

Katz (1990b)
Katz, Y., "Purchase of Jewish National Fund Land in Gush Etzion and South of Bethlehem 1940–1947," *Cathedra* 56 (July 1990), pp. 109–135.

Katz (1991)
Katz, Y., "The Formulation of the Jewish Agency's Proposal for the Boundaries of Partition 1937–1938," *Zion* 56 (1991), pp. 401–439.

Katz (1992)
Katz, Y., *Jewish Settlement in the Hebron Mountains and the Etzion Bloc, 1940–1947*, Ramat Gan 1992. (Second edition, 2003).

Katz (1994a)
Katz, Y., *The "Business" of Settlement: Private Entrepreneurship in the Jewish Settlement of Palestine, 1900–1914*, Jerusalem and Ramat Gan 1994 (English).

Katz (1994b)
Katz, Y., "Zionist Political and Settlement Activity in the Latter Thirties Aimed at Influencing the Partition Borders Proposed by the Peel Commission," *Land and Settlement* 15 (1994), pp. 5–28.

Katz (1994c)
Katz, Y., "The Partition Plan of Palestine and Zionist Proposals for the Beisan Valley," *Jewish Journal of Sociology* 36 (1994), pp. 81–98 (English).

Katz (1994d)
Katz, Y., "The Palestinian Mountain Region and Zionist Settlement Policy, 1882–1948," *Middle Eastern Studies* 30 (1994), pp. 304–329 (English).

Katz (1996a)
Katz, Y., "The Establishment of the Southern Settlement Bloc of the Religious Kibbutz Movement," 1943–1947," *Iyunim Bitkumat Israel* 6 (1996), pp. 202–225.

Katz (1996b)
Katz, Y., "The Place of Jerusalem in Zionist Activities Toward the End of the British Mandate in Palestine," *Zion* 61 (1996), pp. 67–90.

Katz (1997)
Katz, Y., " 'Garden City' in Practice," Y. Friedman and Z. Safari (eds.), *Studies in the History of the Land of Israel,* Ramat Gan 1997, pp. 343–354.

Katz (1998a)
Katz, Y., "The Burden of Proof Still Remains," *Yahadut Ze'manenu* 11–12 (1998), pp. 39–50.

Katz (1998b)
Katz,Y., *Partner to Partition: The Jewish Agency's Partition Plan in the Mandate Era*, London 1998 (English).

Katz (1999)
Katz, Y., *The Religious Kibbutz Movement in the Land of Israel 1930–1948*, Jerusalem and Ramat Gan 1999 (English). (Second edition, 2003).

Katz (2000a)
Katz, Y., *A State in the Making: Zionist Plans for the Partition of Palestine and Establishment of the Jewish State*, Jerusalem 2000.

Katz (2000b)
Katz, Y., *Forgotten Property: What Became of Assets in Israel of Holocaust Victims*, Jerusalem 2000.

Katz (2002)
Katz, Y., *"The Land shall not be Sold in Perpetuity": Legacy and Principles of National Land in Israeli Legislation*, Jerusalem 2002.

Katz (in press)
Katz, Y., *The Creation of a Zionist Land Basis in Palestine: Policy and Implementation in the Purchase of Land by the Zionist Institutions in 1897–1948* (in press).

Katz & Sandler (1995)
Katz,Y., and S. Sandler, "The Origins of the Conception of Israel's State Borders and Its Impact on the Strategy of War in 1948–1949," *Journal of Strategic Studies* 18 (1995), pp. 149–171 (English).

Katzburg (1974)
Katzburg, N., *From Partition to the White Paper: British Policy in Palestine 1936–1940*, Jerusalem 1974.

Katzburg (1993)
Katzburg, N., "The Second Decade of Mandatory Rule in Palestine," M. Lissak (ed.), *The History of the Jewish Community in Palestine Since 1882*, Jerusalem 1993, pp. 329–432.

Kimmerling (1973)
Kimmerling, B., *The Struggle for Land: A Chapter in the Sociology of the Jewish–Arab Conflict*, Jerusalem 1973.

Kimmerling (1983)
Kimmerling, B., *Zionism and Territory: The Socio-territorial Dimensions of Zionist Politics*, Berkeley 1983 (English).

Klein (1937)
Klein, S., *The Land: Historical Survey of the Land Problem in Palestine*, Jerusalem 1937.

Klieman (1983)
Klieman, A., *Divide or Rule: Britain's Policy and the Partition of Palestine – A Missed Opportunity? 1936–1939*, Jerusalem 1983.

Kressel (1951)
Kressel, G., *Events*, Jerusalem 1951.

Lador (1952)
Lador, Y., *Settlement in Palestine, 1870–1952: History and Forms*, Tel Aviv 1952.

Land (1937)
Land and Settlement at the Zionist General Council Session, Jerusalem 1937.

Lavsky (1994)
Lavsky, H., "The Jewish National Fund: Theory and Practice during the British Mandate," *Research Institute for the History of the Jewish National Fund and Jewish Settlement in Palestine* 8 (1994), pp. 2–27.

Liberman
Liberman, Z., *Settlement of Soldiers and Watchmen*, Tel Aviv [n.d.].

Meerovitch (1975)
Meerovitch, M., *Hartzfeld Speaks*, I–II, Tel Aviv 1969–1975.

Merhavia
Merhavia, H. (ed.), *The People and the Homeland: Collection of Documents Concerning Hebrew Zionist Citizenship and the Jewish Community in Palestine*, Jerusalem [n.d.].

Metzer (1979)
Metzer, J., *National Capital for a National Home, 1919–1921*, Jerusalem 1979.

Metzer (1998)
Metzer, J., *The Divided Economy of Mandatory Palestine*, Cambridge: Cambridge University Press 1998 (English).

Ofer (1976)
Ofer, P., "Galilee in the Peel Partition Plan," *Artzot Hagalil* 1 (1983), pp. 461–468.

Oren (1976)
Oren, E., "The Settlement Strategy in the Negev during the Struggle for Independence, 1946–1947," *Shalem* 2 (1976), pp. 327–348.

Oren (1983)
Oren, E., "Settlement Policy in Galilee Prior to the State," *Artzot Hagalil* 2 (1983), pp. 787–818.

Oren (1992)
Oren, E., "Settlement in Northern Galilee 1936–1947," *Idan* 17 (1992), pp. 125–143.

Orni (1983)
Orni, E., "Purchase of Land in Galilee from World War I up to the Establishment of the State of Israel," *Artzot Hagalil* (1983), pp. 469–477.

Orni (1990)
Orni, E., "Settlement Crystallization and Land Acquisition in the Sharon 1890–1947," Grossman & Degani (1990), pp. 363–372.

Orren (1978)
Orren, E., *Settlement Amid Struggle: The Prestate Strategy of Settlement*, Jerusalem 1978.

Palestine Partition (1938)
Palestine Partition Commission Report, Presented by the Secretary of State for the Colonies to Parliament by Command of His Majesty, London 1938 (English).

Palestine Policy (1939)
Palestine (Palestine), Manifest of the Policy of His Majesty's Government, Official Proclamation No. 2/39, 1939.

Palestine Royal (1937)
Palestine Royal Commission Report, Presented by the Secretary of State for the Colonies to Parliament by Command of His Majesty, London 1937 (English).

PLDC (1939)
PLDC, Palestine Land Development Company, Ltd., *Report for 1938*, Jerusalem 1939.

PLDC (1940)
PLDC, *Report for 1939*, Jerusalem 1940.

PLDC (1941)
PLDC, *Report for 1940*, Jerusalem 1941.

PLDC (1942)
PLDC, *Report for 1941*, Jerusalem 1942.

PLDC (1943)
PLDC, *Report for 1942*, Jerusalem 1943.

PLDC (1944)
PLDC, *Report for 1943*, Jerusalem 1944.

PLDC (1945)
PLDC, *Report for 1944*, Jerusalem 1945.

PLDC (1946)
PLDC, *Report for 1945*, Jerusalem 1946.

Pogravinsky (1956)
Pogravinsky, Y. (ed.), *The Book of the Geulah Company*, Tel Aviv 1956.

Polak (1939)
Polak, A., *The Activities and Achievements of the Jewish National Fund*, Jerusalem 1939.

Political Report (1937)
Political Report of the Jewish Agency Executive submitted to the 20th Zionist Congress and the 5th Session of the Jewish Agency Council, Jerusalem 1937.

Political Struggle (1939)
The Political Struggle Around the New Settlements, Jerusalem 1939.

Porat (1990)
Porat, C., "Methods of Purchasing Land in the Negev in the 1930s and early 1940s," Kark (1990a).

Porat (1992)
Porat, C., "Zionist Policy on Land Settlement in the Negev 1947," *Cathedra* 62 (Dec. 1992), pp. 123–154.

Porat (1994)
Porat, C., "The Negev Committees and the Negev Project: Settling and Developing the Negev after the War," *Land and Settlement* 13 (1994), pp. 5–25.

Porat (1996)
Porat, C., *From Wasteland to Inhabited Land: Land Purchase and Settlement in the Negev 1930–1957*, Jerusalem 1996.

Problems (1948)
Problems of Settlement and Investment in the State, Internal Report of the Israel Labor Party, Tel Aviv 1948.

Redemption (1942)
Redemption of the Land in the History of the Yishuv, Jerusalem 1942.

Redemption Report (1950)
Redemption and Development, Report of the Jewish National Fund Activities submitted to the Session of the Zionist General Council, Jerusalem 1950.

Reichman (1979)
Reichman, S., *From Foothold to Settled Territory: The Jewish Settlement 1918–1948*, Jerusalem 1979.

Reichman & Ben-Shemesh (1983)
Reichman S., and A. Ben-Shemesh (eds.), *Karka*, Collection of Essays on the Occasion of the Jewish National Fund's 80th Anniversary, Jerusalem 1983.

Reichman (1989)
Reichman, S., "A Map of Land Ownership in Jerusalem in 1947," H. Lavsky, *Jerusalem in Zionist Vision and Realization*, Jerusalem 1989, pp. 303–312.

Reichman *et al.* (1991)
Reichman, S., Y. Katz, and Y. Paz, "The Absorptive Capacity of Palestine 1882–1948: A Geographical Appraisal," *Eretz Israel* 22 (1991), pp. 206–226.

Reichman *et al.* (1997)
Reichman, S., Y. Katz, and Y. Paz, "The Absorptive Capacity of Palestine 1882–1948," *Middle Eastern Studies* 33, no. 2 (1997), pp. 338–361.

Report Exec. (1921)
Report of the Executive of the Zionist Organization submitted to the 12th Zionist Congress, London 1921.

Report Exec. (1923)
Report of the Executive of the Zionist Organization submitted to the 13th Zionist Congress, London 1923.

Report Exec. (1925)
Report of the Executive of the Zionist Organization submitted to the 14th Zionist Congress, London 1925.

Report Exec. (1927)
Report of the Executive of the Zionist Organization submitted to the 15th Zionist Congress, Report of the Jewish National Fund, London 1927.

Report Exec. (1929)
Report of the Executive of the Zionist Organization submitted to the 16th Zionist Congress, London 1929.

Report Exec. (1931)
Report of the Executive of the Zionist Organization submitted to the 17th Zionist Congress, London 1931.

Report Exec. (1933)
Report of the Executive of the Zionist Organization and the Jewish Agency submitted to the 18th Zionist Congress and to the Jewish Agency Assembly, London 1933.

Report Exec. (1935)
Report of the Executive of the Zionist Organization and the Jewish Agency Council submitted to the 19th Zionist Congress and 4th Session of the Jewish Agency Council, London 1935.

Report Exec. (1937)
Report of the Executive of the Zionist Organization and of the Jewish Agency submitted to the 20th Zionist Congress and the 5th Session of the Jewish Agency Council, Jerusalem 1937.

Report Exec. (1939)
Report of the Executive of the Zionist Organization and of the Jewish Agency submitted to the 21st Zionist Congress and the 6th Session of the Jewish Agency Council, Jerusalem 1939.

Report Exec. (1951)
Reports of the Executives of the Zionist Organization and the Jewish Agency for the years 1947–1948 Submitted to the 23rd Zionist Congress, Jerusalem 1951.

Report JNF (1949)
Report to the Zionist General Council Session, May 1949, presented by the Jewish National Fund, Jerusalem 1949.

Report PLDC (1946)
Report of the Palestine Land Development Company (PLDC) submitted to the 22nd Zionist Congress, London 1946.

Report WZO (1921)
Report of the Zionist Organization submitted to the 12th Zionist Congress, the Palestine Report, London 1921.

Report WZO (1946)
Report of Activities 1940–1946, submitted to the 22nd Zionist Congress, Jerusalem 1946.

Report WZO (1951)
Report of the Zionist Organization and the Jewish Agency for the Years 1947–1951 submitted to the 23rd Zionist Congress, Jerusalem 1951.

Resolutions (1936)
Resolutions of the 19th Zionist Congress, Jerusalem 1936.

Resolutions (1937)
Resolutions of the 20th Zionist Congress and the 5th Session of the Jewish Agency Council, Jerusalem 1937.

Resolutions (1939)
Resolutions of the 21st Zionist Congress, Jerusalem 1939.

Resolutions (1947)
Resolutions of the 22nd Zionist Congress, Jerusalem 1947.

Rozenman (1992)
Rozenman, A., *The History of Service: Ruppin and Eshkol*, Jerusalem 1992.

Rozenman (1997)
Rozenman, A., *Settling the Country: The Story of the WZO Settlement Department prior to the Establishment of the State of Israel*, Jerusalem 1997.

Ruppin (1937)
Ruppin, A., *Thirty Years of Building Palestine*, Jerusalem 1937.

Shapiro (1944)
Shapiro, Y., *History of the Jewish National Fund*, Jerusalem 1944.

Schama (1978)
Schama, S., *Two Rothschilds and the Land of Israel*, London 1978 (English).

Schenkolewski (1996)
Schenkolewski-Kroll, S., *The Zionist Movement and Zionist Parties in Argentina, 1935–1948*, Jerusalem 1996.

Shafir (1989)
Shafir, G., *Land, Labour and the Origin of the Israeli–Palestinian Conflict*, Cambridge 1989 (English).

Sharett (1971)
Sharett, M., *Political Diary*, I–IV, Tel Aviv 1971–1976.

Shilo (1985)
Shilo, M. "The Settlement Policy of the Palestine Office 1908–1914," Ph.D. dissertation, The Hebrew University of Jerusalem, 1985.

Shilony (1990a)
Shilony Z., "The First Land Purchases by the Jewish National Fund 1904–1908," Kark (1990a), pp. 118–150.

Shilony (1991)
Shilony, Z., "Academic Discussion on the Jewish National Fund and Settlement in Palestine 1903–1914," *Land and Settlement* (1991), pp. 2–50.

Shilony (1998)
Shilony, Z., *Jewish National Fund and Settlement in Palestine 1903–1914*, Jerusalem 1998.

Smilansky
Smilansky, M., *The Path of Redemption*, Jerusalem [n.d.].

Smilansky (1942)
Smilansky, M., *The Blessing of the Land*, Jerusalem 1942.

Smilansky (1945)
Smilansky, M., *An Eyewitness Account of the Redemption of the Land*, Jerusalem 1945.

Smilansky (1948)
Smilansky, M., "PICA and its Projects in Palestine," Bistritsky (1948), pp. 151–170.

Stein (1980)
Stein, K., "Laws Defending Tenant Rights and their Implementation in Mandatory Palestine," *Hamizrach Hehadash* 29 (1980), pp. 66–88.

Stein (1984)
Stein, K., *The Land Question in Palestine 1917–1935*, Chapel Hill and London 1984 (English).

Stern (1986)
Stern, S., "Sale of German Owned Lands to German Jews in Palestine in the 1930s," *Cathedra 41* (Oct. 1986), pp. 200–205.

Testimonies (1946)
The Country, the Land and Development, Extracts from Testimonies before the Anglo–American Commission, Jerusalem 1946.

Tsur (1980)
Tsur, Z., *Settlement and Borders of the State*, Tel Aviv 1980.

Tzahor (1997)
Tzahor, Z., *Ya'akov Hazan: A Biography*, Jerusalem 1997.

Ulitzur (1939)
Ulitzur, A., *The National Resources and Building up the Land, Facts and Figures, 1918–1937*, Jerusalem 1939.

Ussishkin (1934)
The Ussishkin Book, Jerusalem 1934.

Villages (1949)
Jewish Villages in Israel, Jerusalem 1949 (English).

Weitz (1934)
Weitz, Y., *The Middle Classes and the Jewish National Fund*, Jerusalem 1934.

Weitz (1937a)
Weitz, Y., *Our New Project: The Redemption of the Land in the Hula Valley and Upper Galilee*, Jerusalem 1937.

Weitz (1937b)
Weitz, Y., *The Galilee*, Jerusalem 1937.

Weitz (1939)
Weitz, Y., *The Calumny of the Land*, Jerusalem 1939.

Weitz (1940)
Weitz, Y., "Land of the Jewish State," Bistritsky (1948), pp. 44–60.

Weitz (1941)
Weitz, Y., *The Story of Land Acquisition in 1940*, a Lecture Delivered at the Session of the National Committee of the Jewish National Fund, Jerusalem 1941.

Weitz (1944)
Weitz, Y., *Recent Ways of Settlement*, Lectures at a Seminar for Coordinators of the Work of the Jewish National Fund for Youth, Jerusalem 1944.

Weitz (1947)
Weitz, Y., *Our Settlement Activities in a Period of Storm and Stress 1936–1947*, Merhavia 1947.

Weitz (1950a)
Weitz, Y., "The History of our Struggle for the Negev," Bistritsky (1950c), pp. 439–458.

Weitz (1950b)
Weitz, Y., *The Struggle for the Land*, Tel Aviv 1950.

Weitz (1951)
Weitz, Y., *Birth Pangs of Settlement: Chapters of a Diary*, Tel Aviv 1951.

Weitz (1952)
Weitz, Y., *Fruits*, Jerusalem 1952.

Weitz (1964)
Weitz, Y., *Beginnings: The History of the Settlement of the Hills in Western and Upper Galilee*, Jerusalem 1964.

Weitz (1965)
Weitz,Y., *My Diary and Letters to the Children* I–III, Ramat Gan 1965.

Weitz (1967)
Weitz, Y., *Profiles*, Tel Aviv 1967.

Weitz (1969)
Weitz,Y. (ed.), *Yosef Nahmani: Man of Galilee*, Ramat Gan 1969.

Weitz (1995)
Weitz, Y. "The Vision of Joseph Weitz," *Eretz Israel* 16 (1995), pp. 5–20.

Zamir & Benvenisti (1993)
Zamir, E., and E. Benvenisti, *The Legal Status of Lands Acquired by Jews before 1948 in the West Bank, Gaza Strip and East Jerusalem*, Jerusalem 1993.

Zionist Activity (1922)
Zionist Activity during 1921–1922, Report of the Zionist Executive, 1922.

Ziman (1951)
Ziman, Y., *The 50th Anniversary of the Jewish National Fund: Facts and Activities*, Jerusalem 1951.

ORAL TESTIMONY
Interviews the author carried out with Shimon Ben-Shemesh and Hiram Danin
Interviews: Shimon Ben-Shemesh and Dr. Gabriel Alexander carried out with Adiya Konikow
Interview with Yosef Weitz carried out by the Oral History Institute, the Institute of Contemporary Jewry, The Hebrew University of Jerusalem

Index of Subjects and Places

* Note: A bold page number stands for a page with a picture

Index of Names

---

* Note: A bold page number stands for a page with a picture